5—

Ravi Boppana

# Fundamentals of the Average Case Analysis of Particular Algorithms

# Wiley-Teubner Series in Computer Science

# Fundamentals of the Average Case Analysis of Particular Algorithms

**Rainer Kemp**
*Fachbereich Informatik*
*Universität Frankfurt*
*Germany*

B. G. TEUBNER
Stuttgart

JOHN WILEY & SONS
Chichester · New York · Brisbane · Toronto · Singapore

**Library of Congress Cataloging in Publication Data:**

Kemp, Rainer.
  Fundamentals of the average case analysis of
particular algorithms.
  (Wiley-Teubner series in computer science)
  Includes bibliographical references and index.
  1. Electronic digital computers—Programming.
2. Algorithms.  I. Title.  II. Series.
QA76.6.K53  1984        519.4        83–16663

ISBN 0 471 90322 1  (Wiley)


**British Library Cataloguing in Publication Data:**

Kemp, Rainer.
  Fundamentals of the average case analysis of
  particular algorithms.–(Wiley-Teubner series
  in computer science)
  1. Algorithms.
  I. Title.
  511'.6        QA9.58

ISBN 0 471 90322 1


**CIP-Kurztitelaufnahme der Deutschen Bibliothek:**

Kemp, Rainer.
Fundamentals of the average case analysis of
particular algorithms / Rainer Kemp.–Stuttgart:
Teubner; Chichester; New York; Brisbane;
Toronto; Singapore: Wiley, 1984.
  (Wiley-Teubner series in computer science)

  ISBN 3–519–02100–5 (Teubner)
  ISBN 0–471–90322–1 (Wiley)


Typeset by Mid-County Press, London, SW15.
Printed by St Edmundsbury Press, Bury St Edmunds, Suffolk

# Preface _____

This book provides an introduction to the analysis of particular algorithms. It has its origin in lecture courses given at the Universität des Saarlandes, Saarbrücken in 1980 and at the Johann Wolfgang Goethe-Universität, Frankfurt a.M. in 1982. The material can be covered in a one-semester course.

In preparing the notes for publication as a book, I have added a considerable amount of material additional to the lecture notes, with the intention of making the book more useful. My prime consideration has been to produce a textbook whose scope is selective; some of the omitted material is outlined in various exercises and should be useful in indicating possible approaches to certain problems. Moreover, problems are provided to furnish examples, to expand on the material or to indicate related results, and occasionally to guide the reader through the steps of lengthy proofs and derivations. I have referred, in various places, to those books and original papers which have been of particular assistance to me.

I wish to take this opportunity to thank all those who have had a part in this work, and who have made this book possible. I am particularly indebted to Professor Dr. Günter Hotz for his encouragement in the writing of this textbook. Special thanks are due to Ute Schürfeld for careful reading of the text. Dr. P. Spuhler from Teubner-Verlag provided co-operative and competent support in all editorial problems. Finally, I wish to thank Teubner-Verlag and John Wiley & Sons for very good and timely editorial work.

Frankfurt a.M., West Germany                                                    R. Kemp
December 1982

# Contents _____

viii

# 1

# *Introduction*

'Analysis of algorithms' is quite important in computer programming, because there are generally several algorithms available for a particular application and we would like to measure and compare the *time* and *storage* requirements. Time may be measured by counting steps, statements, or the number of times some given operation is performed; space may be measured by bits, words, or the number of registers and cells required during execution of the algorithm.

The analysis usually consists of determining the behaviour of an algorithm in the *best case*, in the *worst case* and in the *average case*. The best (worst) case is characterized by the minimum (maximum) total amount of time or space requirements taken over all inputs of some fixed size. To characterize the average case, it is necessary to define what we mean by the average; in general, we must make some assumptions about the expected characteristics of the inputs of some fixed size. If an input $x$ of size $n$ has the probability $p_x$ and requires the total amount of time or space $k_x$, then the average case is characterized by the behaviour of the *expected value* (Appendix A) of the random variable which has the value $k_x$ with probability $p_x$. In most problems we will make the reasonable assumption that each of the inputs of size $n$ is equally likely, but the analysis can also be carried out under other assumptions. To obtain a quantitative indication of how close to the average we may expect the amount of time or storage requirements to be, we will compute further characteristics of the given distribution such as the *variance*, the *standard deviation*, the *moments about the origin*, or the *(cumulative) distribution function* (Appendix A).

Now an important problem is to compare the time and space requirements of algorithms available for a particular application. Sometimes we want to decide which is best. But this is easier said than done. In many cases we may only compare the time requirements or the storage requirements of two algorithms, because the one algorithm requires less time but more space than the other. Similarly, comparing two algorithms in the best, worst, or average case, the same situation can occur. For example, the sorting algorithm 'Heapsort' is faster than the algorithm 'Quicksort' in the worst case, but not in the average case. Summing up, a comparison of two algorithms should be made only for the time or storage requirements in the best or worst or average case. (Nevertheless, there are other criteria of goodness of algorithms such as the product of time and space requirements or the adaptability to computers.)

The classical complexity theory deals with the time and storage requirements of algorithms in the worst case. In practice, there are some objections to the measuring of the goodness of an algorithm by these quantities, although their computation can be an extremely difficult task. If an algorithm requires time or space of order $O(f(n))$ in the worst case, then the constant in the $O$-term can be fantastically large and the result is only of theoretical interest. Furthermore, if the inputs corresponding to the worst case have a probability which tends to zero for large input sizes, then it is hard to see why the goodness of the algorithm is measured by its worst case. Therefore, the importance of the worst case can be reduced by the knowledge of its probability. But the computation of this probability can be rather difficult, unless impossible. In practice, an algorithm requiring time $n$ on the average in 99 per cent of all possible inputs of size $n$ should be preferred to an algorithm for the same problem which needs time $n^2$ in the worst and average case, even though the former algorithm needs time $n^3$ in the worst case.

Study of the behaviour of an algorithm on the average is accompanied by many mathematical calculations; we need to use the results of complex variable theory, number theory, probability theory, discrete mathematics and combinatorics. The principal techniques involved in the analysis of algorithms consist of counting of certain objects, solving of recurrences, working with finite summations, handling of generating functions and asymptotic evaluating of expressions. The last part of this introductory section is devoted to some simple examples elucidating the above ideas and concepts.

EXAMPLE 1.1  We consider the following one-tape Turing machine $T$ which adds one to a binary number $a_{n-1}a_{n-2} \ldots a_1 a_0$ of length $n$.

*Initial configuration:*

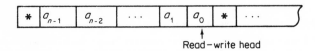

*Final configuration:*

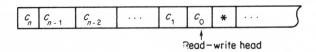

where

$$\sum_{0 \leqslant i \leqslant n} c_i 2^i = 1 + \sum_{0 \leqslant i \leqslant n-1} a_i 2^i.$$

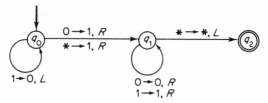

*State-transition diagram:* Here, $q_0$ is the initial state and $q_2$ is the final state. The label '$x \to u, v$' on an arc means: take this transition if the input symbol is $x$; replace $x$ by $u$ and move the read–write head one square in direction $v$, where $v$ is $L$ for left, $R$ for right, and $S$ for 'don't move'. The Turing machine $T$ moves the head to the left and replaces all ones by zeros until it has found the rightmost zero (or $*$) in $*a_{n-1}a_{n-2}\ldots a_1a_0*$; after replacing this symbol by one, it starts back and enters the final state.

We will measure the time requirements of the described Turing machine by the number of moves $T(n)$ necessary to transfer the initial configuration to the final configuration.

*Best case:* Obviously, the minimum number of moves is two; this happens if $a_0 = 0$. Assuming that all binary numbers of length $n$ are equally likely, the probability that $T$ visits exactly two squares is $2^{-1}$, because there are $2^{n-1}$ numbers with $a_0 = 0$.

*Worst case:* The maximum number of moves is $2n + 2$; this happens if $a_{n-1} = a_{n-2} = \cdots = a_1 = a_0 = 1$. The probability that this case occurs is $2^{-n}$.

*Average case:* We will assume that each of the $2^n$ numbers is equally likely. An input $*a_{n-1}a_{n-2}..a_1a_0*$ requires exactly $2m$, $1 \leqslant m \leqslant n + 1$, moves if and only if $a_{m-1} = 0 \wedge a_{m-2} = a_{m-3} = \cdots = a_1 = a_0 = 1 \wedge m \neq n + 1$ or $a_{m-2} = a_{m-3} = \cdots = a_1 = a_0 = 1 \wedge m = n + 1$. Therefore, the probability that an input of length $n$ requires time $2m$ is equal to $2^{-m+\delta_{n+1,m}}$, $1 \leqslant m \leqslant n + 1$. Since

$$\sum_{1 \leqslant m \leqslant n} mx^m = \frac{nx^{n+2} - (n+1)x^{n+1} + x}{(x-1)^2},$$

if $x \neq 1$, we find that the average time $T(n)$ is given by the expected value

$$T(n) = \sum_{1 \leqslant m \leqslant n+1} (2m)2^{-m+\delta_{n+1,m}} = 4 - 2^{-n+1}.$$

The $s$-th moment about the origin is (Appendix A)

$$\mu_s'(n) = \sum_{1 \leqslant m \leqslant n+1} (2m)^s 2^{-m+\delta_{n+1,m}}$$

$$= 2^s \sum_{m \geqslant 1} m^s 2^{-m} + (n+1)^s 2^{s-n-1} - 2^s \sum_{m \geqslant n+2} m^s 2^{-m}$$

$$= 2^{2s+1} A_s(\tfrac{1}{2}) + O(n^s 2^{-n}),$$

where $A_s(u)$ is the $s$-th Eulerian polynomial (see Appendix B, 2.3). As special cases, we have $\mu_1'(n) = T(n) \sim 4$, $\mu_2' \sim 24$, $\mu_3' \sim 208$.

For the variance, we have therefore $\sigma^2(n) \sim 8$. To complete our analysis, we compute the cumulative distribution function. Using the geometric series, we obtain for $x \in [1:n-1]$

$$V_n(2x) = \sum_{1 \leqslant k \leqslant x} 2^{-k+\delta_{n+1,k}} = 1 - (1 - \delta_{n+1,x})2^{-x}.$$

Thus the probability that an input of length $n$ needs less than or equal to $2m$ moves is $V_n(2m)$. For example, 93.75 per cent of all inputs of length $n$ require less than or equal to eight moves. Chebyshev's inequality (Appendix A) tells us that the probability that $T(n)$ fails to lie within $2\sqrt{2} \times 10 \approx 28.28$ of its average is less than or equal to $10^{-2}$. This example shows that the worst case behaviour is two pessimistic, in order to measure the goodness of the given algorithm. Considering the storage requirements of our algorithm, that is, the number of squares $S(n)$ required by a computation with input of length $n$, it is easy to see that $S(n) = n$ in the best case, $S(n) = n+1$ in the worst case, and $S(n) = n + 2^{-n}$ in the average case. The best case has the probability $1 - 2^{-n}$ and the worst case $2^{-n}$.

EXAMPLE 1.2   We consider the following one-tape Turing machine $T$ which copies the ones appearing in the binary number $*a_{n-1}a_{n-2} \ldots a_1a_0*$ of length $n$ behind the right-hand end of the input.

*Initial configuration:*

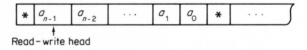

*Final configuration:*

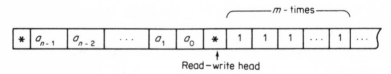

where $\sum_{0 \leqslant i \leqslant n-1} a_i = m$.

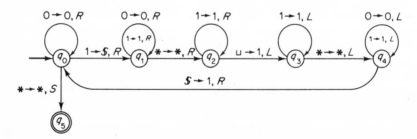

*State-transition diagram:* Here, $q_0$ is the initial state and $q_5$ is the final state. The label '$x \to u, v$' on an arc has the same meaning as in Example 1.1; the input symbol $\sqcup$ stands for the blank tape symbol. Each square of the tape behind the rightmost * contains a blank symbol in the initial configuration. The Turing machine $T$ moves the head to the right and searches successively the ones appearing in $*a_{n-1}a_{n-2}\ldots a_1a_0*$; when it finds a one, $T$ replaces this one by \$ and starts right along the tape until the first $\sqcup$. After replacing this $\sqcup$ by one, the head moves back to \$. \$ is replaced by one, and $T$ searches the next one in $*a_{n-1}a_{n-2}\ldots a_1a_0*$. $T$ enters the final state if it finds * behind $a_0$.

We will measure the time requirements of $T$ by the number of moves $T(n)$ necessary to transfer the initial configuration to the final configuration. First, we shall compute the number of moves required to transform the configuration

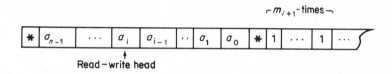

into

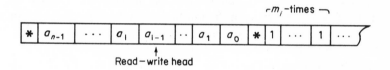

Obviously, $m_{i+1} = \sum_{i+1 \leqslant j < n} a_j$ and $m_i = \sum_{i \leqslant j < n} a_j$. If $a_i = 0$, then there is exactly one move. If $a_i = 1$, then we have to copy $a_i$ behind the right-hand end. $T$ replaces $a_i$ by \$, starts right along the tape and finds the first $\sqcup$ after $(i + m_{i+1} + 2)$ moves. The Turing machine now writes one, and the head moves back to \$ again giving the contribution $(i + m_{i+1} + 2)$ to the total amount of moves. After replacing \$ by one, the head moves one square right and finds $a_{i-1}$. Thus our task requires $1 + 2a_i(i + m_{i+1} + 2)$ moves for any $i \in [0:n-1]$. To obtain the total time requirements $T(n)$ for a given input $*a_{n-1}a_{n-2}\ldots a_1a_0*$, we have to sum over all $i$ such that $0 \leqslant i \leqslant n - 1$. We obtain

$$T(n) = \sum_{0 \leqslant i \leqslant n-1} [1 + 2a_i(i + m_{i+1} + 2)]$$

$$= n + 2 \sum_{0 \leqslant i \leqslant n-1} ia_i + 4 \sum_{0 \leqslant i \leqslant n-1} a_i + 2 \sum_{0 \leqslant i \leqslant n-1} \sum_{i+1 \leqslant j \leqslant n-1} a_i a_j$$

$$= n + 2 \sum_{0 \leqslant i \leqslant n-1} ia_i + 3 \sum_{0 \leqslant i \leqslant n-1} a_i + \left[ \sum_{0 \leqslant i \leqslant n-1} a_i \right]^2$$

*Best case:* Evidently, the best case is characterized by the condition $a_{n-1} =$

$a_{n-2} = \cdots = a_1 = a_0 = 0$. It follows that the minimum number of moves is $n$. Assuming that all binary numbers of length $n$ are equally likely, the probability that $T$ visits exactly $n$ squares is $2^{-n}$.

*Worst case:* Since all terms on the right-hand side of the general formula given above for $T(n)$ are non-negative, the worst case happens if $a_{n-1} = a_{n-2} = \cdots = a_1 = a_0 = 1$. Hence the maximum number of moves is $n(2n + 3)$, because $\sum_{0 \leqslant i \leqslant n-1} i = n(n-1)/2$. The probability that this case occurs is $2^{-n}$.

*Average case:* We will assume that each of the $2^n$ inputs is equally likely. There is no simple condition of two binary numbers of length $n$, so that both have the same time requirements. Therefore, we do not know the probability that an input of length $n$ requires time $m$. Fortunately, we can compute the total number of moves $\tau_n$ necessary for all inputs of length $n$. We obtain (see Exercise 1.1) $\tau_n = 3n(n + 3)2^{n-2}$. Since the average time $T(n)$ is given by $2^{-n}\tau_n$, we find $T(n) = \frac{3}{4}n(n + 3)$. In contrast with Example 1.1, the time requirements of our algorithm in the worst and average case have the same order, namely $O(n^2)$. Here, the worst case is really appropriate to measure the goodness of the algorithm, although its probability is exponentially small. Furthermore, our example shows that it is sometimes possible to compute the average case behaviour of an algorithm, even though the probability that an input of size $n$ requires time (or space) $m$ is unknown; in this case, we have no exact information about the moments, distribution function, etc.

Finally, let us consider the storage requirements of our algorithm. We will measure the space by the number of squares $S(n)$ which are scanned by the read–write head in any computation starting in the initial configuration with input $*a_{n-1}a_{n-2} \ldots a_1 a_0*$ and leading to the final configuration. Obviously, we have

$$S(n) = n + 1 + \sum_{0 \leqslant i \leqslant n-1} a_i$$

*Best case:* This case is characterized by the condition $a_{n-1} = a_{n-2} = \cdots = a_1 = a_0 = 0$. Hence the minimum number of scanned squares is $n + 1$. The probability that this case occurs is $2^{-n}$, provided that all binary numbers of length $n$ are equally likely.

*Worst case:* The maximum number of scanned squares is $2n + 1$; this happens if $a_{n-1} = a_{n-2} = \cdots = a_1 = a_0 = 1$. The probability that this case occurs is $2^{-n}$.

*Average case:* We will assume that each of the $2^{-n}$ numbers is equally likely. An input $*a_{n-1}a_{n-2} \ldots a_1 a_0*$ requires exactly $n + 1 + m, 0 \leqslant m \leqslant n$, squares if and only if it contains $m$ ones. Since there are $\binom{n}{m}$ inputs with $m$ ones, the probability that an input of length $n$ requires $n + 1 + m$ squares is $\binom{n}{m}2^{-n}$.

Therefore, the average space $S(n)$ is given by the expected value

$$S(n) = \sum_{0 \leqslant m \leqslant n} (n + 1 + m)\binom{n}{m}2^{-n} = \tfrac{3}{2}n + 1,$$

because

$$\sum_{0 \leqslant m \leqslant n} (n + 1 + m)\binom{n}{m} = 3n2^{n-1} + 2^n \quad \text{(see Exercise 1.2)}.$$

The $s$-th moment about the origin is (see Exercise 1.2)

$$\mu'_s(n) = \sum_{0 \leqslant m \leqslant n} (n + 1 + m)^s\binom{n}{m}2^{-n} = 3^s2^{-s}n^s + O(n^{s-1}).$$

As special cases, we obtain the exact values $\mu'_1(n) = S(n) = \tfrac{3}{2}n + 1$, $\mu'_2(n) = \tfrac{9}{4}n^2 + \tfrac{13}{4}n + 1$. For the variance, we have therefore $\sigma^2(n) = n/4$. Finally, let us consider the cumulative distribution function $V_n(x)$ which gives the probability that an input requires less than or equal to $(n + 1 + x)$ squares. For $0 \leqslant x \leqslant n - 1$ we obtain (see Exercise 1.4)

$$V_n(x) = \sum_{0 \leqslant m \leqslant x} \binom{n}{m}2^{-n}$$

$$= (n - x)\binom{n}{x} \int_{1/2}^{1} t^x(1 - t)^{n-x-1} \, dt.$$

This is a binomial distribution with point probability $p = \tfrac{1}{2}$.

EXAMPLE 1.3  This example is devoted to a generalization of Example 1.1. We consider the following two-tape Turing machine $T$ which transforms a positive integer $n$ given in the unary number system into the binary number system.

*Initial configuration:*

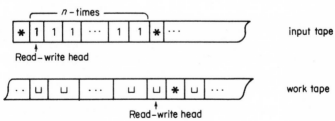

*Final configuration:*

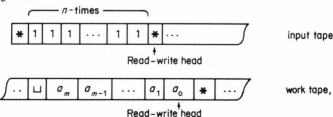

where $\sum_{0 \leqslant i \leqslant m} a_i 2^i = n$.

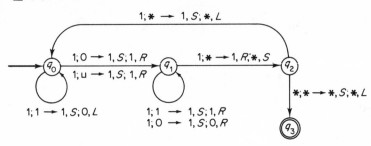

*State-transition diagram:* Here, $q_0$ is the initial state and $q_3$ is the final state. The label '$x; y \rightarrow u, v; p, q$' on an arc means: take this transition if the read–write head on the input tape scans $x$ and the head on the work tape scans $y$; replace $x$ by $u$, $y$ by $p$, and move the head on the input tape (on the work tape) one square in direction $v$ (in direction $q$), where $L$, $R$, and $S$ have the same meaning as in Example 1.1. The Turing machine $T$ moves the head on the input tape to the right; when it finds a one, $T$ adds one to the binary number on the work tape. The addition of one is performed according to the procedure given in Example 1.1.

Since there is exactly one input of length $n$ for each integer $n$, the worst and best case of our algorithm coincide with the average case. The Turing machine $T$ visits $(n + 1)$ squares on the input tape and $(\lfloor \mathrm{ld}(2n) \rfloor + 1)$ squares on the work tape, because a number $n$ has $\lfloor \mathrm{ld}(2n) \rfloor$ bits in its binary representation. Thus the space requirements $S(n)$ of our Turing machine are

$$S(n) = n + \lfloor \mathrm{ld}(2n) \rfloor + 2.$$

Let us now consider the time requirements of $T$ given by the sum of moves on the input and the work tape. Evidently the number of moves on the input tape is $n$. In order to transform the configuration on the work tape

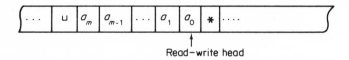

into

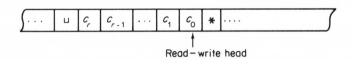

with

$$\sum_{0 \leqslant i \leqslant r} c_i 2^i = \sum_{0 \leqslant i \leqslant m} a_i 2^i + 1,$$

the Turing machine $T$ has to perform $(2t + 2)$ moves, where $t$ is the maximum number of zeros appearing as suffix in $c_r c_{r-1} \ldots c_1 c_0$. Obviously, $t$ is the unique integer such that

$$\sum_{0 \leqslant i \leqslant r} c_i 2^i = 2^t(2k + 1)$$

for $k \geqslant 0$ or in other words, $t$ is the number of all positive divisors of the form $2^s$, $s \in \mathbb{N}$, of the integer $\sum_{0 \leqslant i \leqslant r} c_i 2^i$. Therefore, an input consisting of $n$ ones requires $\sum_{1 \leqslant i \leqslant n} (2\partial(i) + 2)$ moves on the work tape, where $\partial(x)$ is the number of all positive divisors of the form $2^s$, $s \in \mathbb{N}$, of the integer $x$. Hence the time requirements $T(n)$ are given by

$$T(n) = 3n + 2 \sum_{1 \leqslant i \leqslant n} \partial(i).$$

If we let $S_2(n)$ denote the number of ones appearing in the binary representation of $n$, we have further (see Exercise 1.5(d))

$$T(n) = 5n - 2S_2(n).$$

This equation implies

$$5n - 2\lfloor \operatorname{ld}(n) \rfloor \leqslant T(n) \leqslant 5n - 2$$

for $n \geqslant 1$, because $1 \leqslant S_2(n) \leqslant \lfloor \operatorname{ld}(2n) \rfloor$. Evidently, the function $S_2(n)$ has a very erratic behaviour which is clarified by the following result given in [22]: there exists a continuous function $F: \mathbb{R} \to \mathbb{R}$, periodic with period 1, such that

$$\sum_{1 \leqslant i \leqslant n-1} S_2(i) = \tfrac{1}{2} n \operatorname{ld}(n) + n F(\operatorname{ld}(n))$$

for $n \geqslant 1$. Furthermore, the function $F$ is nowhere differentiable and has the Fourier series

$$F(x) = \sum_{-\infty \leqslant k \leqslant \infty} f_k \exp(2\pi i k x)$$

which converges absolutely and has the coefficients $f_k$ given by

$$f_0 = \tfrac{1}{2} \operatorname{ld}(\pi) - \tfrac{1}{2} \ln^{-1}(2) - \tfrac{1}{4} = -0.1456$$

$$f_k = -\zeta(\chi_k)\chi_k^{-1}(1 + \chi_k)^{-1} \ln^{-1}(2) \quad \text{with } \chi_k = 2\pi i k \ln^{-1}(2), \; k \neq 0.$$

(For similar problems concerning digital sums see [33], [84].) Using this result, we immediately obtain

$$T(n) = 5n - [(n + 1) \operatorname{ld}(n + 1) - n \operatorname{ld}(n)]$$

$$+ 2[(n + 1)F(\operatorname{ld}(n + 1)) - n F(\operatorname{ld}(n)]$$

$$= 5n - \operatorname{ld}(n) - \ln^{-1}(2)$$

$$+ 2[(n + 1)F(\operatorname{ld}(n + 1)) - n F(\operatorname{ld}(n))] + O(n^{-1}).$$

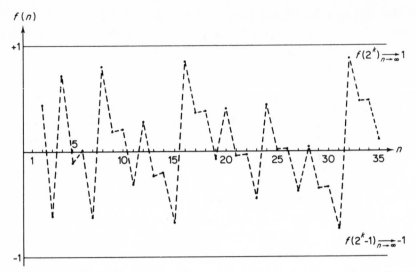

FIGURE 1. Graph of the function $f(n) = 2\,\mathrm{ld}^{-1}(n)[(n+1)F(\mathrm{ld}(n+1)) - nF(\mathrm{ld}(n))]$.

The erratic behaviour of the function

$$f(n) = \mathrm{ld}^{-1}(n)[T(n) - 5n + \mathrm{ld}(n) + \ln^{-1}(2)]$$

is illustrated in Figure 1. An elementary computation shows that $|f(n)| \leqslant 1$ (see Exercise 1.6). This example shows that the functions appearing in a detailed analysis of algorithms are sometimes very mysterious (compare also Chapter 5). They necessarily involve a knowledge of calculus or higher mathematics.

### Exercises

**1.1** Show that

(a) $\displaystyle\sum_{0 \leqslant a_0 \leqslant 1} \cdots \sum_{0 \leqslant a_n \leqslant 1} \sum_{0 \leqslant i \leqslant n} a_i = (n+1)2^n.$

(b) $\displaystyle\sum_{0 \leqslant a_0 \leqslant 1} \cdots \sum_{0 \leqslant a_n \leqslant 1} \sum_{0 \leqslant i \leqslant n} ia_i = n(n+1)2^{n-1}.$

(c) $\displaystyle\sum_{0 \leqslant a_0 \leqslant 1} \cdots \sum_{0 \leqslant a_n \leqslant 1} \left[\sum_{0 \leqslant i \leqslant n} a_i\right]^2 = (n+1)(n+2)2^{n-1}.$

**1.2** Let

$$s \in \mathbb{N}_0 \quad \text{and} \quad \tilde{\mu}_s(n) = \sum_{0 \leqslant m \leqslant n} (n+1+m)^s \binom{n}{m}.$$

Show that $\tilde{\mu}_0(n) = 2^n$, $\tilde{\mu}_1(n) = (3n+2)2^{n-1}$, $\tilde{\mu}_2(n) = (n+1)(9n+4)2^{n-2}$ and generally $\tilde{\mu}_s(n) = n^s 3^s 2^{n-s} + O(n^{s-1}2^n)$. (*Hint*: Take the derivatives of

$$f_n(x) = \sum_{0 \leqslant m \leqslant n} \binom{n}{m} x^{n+m+1} = x^{n+1}(1+x)^n$$

and use formulae (B8) and (B25).)

**1.3** Show that for $u \geqslant s \geqslant 0$, $w \geqslant 0$, $r \geqslant 0$:

$$\sum_{0 \leqslant k \leqslant r} \binom{r-k}{w}\binom{s+k}{u} = \binom{r+s+1}{w+u+1}.$$

**1.4** (a) Show that for $0 \leqslant k < n$:

$$\sum_{0 \leqslant i \leqslant k} \binom{n}{i} x^{n-i} y^i = (n-k)\binom{n}{k} \int_y^{x+y} u^k (x+y-u)^{n-k-1}\, du.$$

(b) Show that for $0 \leqslant k \leqslant n$:

$$\binom{n}{k} = 2^{n+1}\pi^{-1} \int_0^{\pi/2} \cos^n(\alpha) \cos((n-2k)\alpha)\, d\alpha.$$

**1.5** Let $\partial(n)$ be the unique integer such that $n = 2^{\partial(n)}(2k+1)$ for $n \geqslant 1$, $k \geqslant 0$, and let $S_2(n)$ be the number of ones appearing in the binary representation of $n$.

(a) Show that $\partial(2i+1) = 0$ for $i \geqslant 0$ and $\partial(2i) = \partial(i) + 1$ for $i > 0$.
(b) Show that $\partial(n)$ is multiplicative, i.e. $\partial(r) + \partial(s) = \partial(rs)$.
(c) Show that $\partial(n!) = n - S_2(n)$.
(d) Show that $\sum_{1 \leqslant j \leqslant n} \partial(j) = n - S_2(n)$.

**1.6** Prove that the function $f(n)$ given at the end of Example 1.3 is an oscillating function with $|f(n)| \leqslant 1$.

# 2

# *A Simple Class of Algorithms*

## 2.1 Definition of a Random Algorithm

The purpose of this section is to present a well-known class of algorithms, the so-called *random algorithms*. In practice, many algorithms do not satisfy the strong assumptions of a random algorithm, but analysis of the computation time for algorithms of this kind affords a welcome occasion for introducing some basic definitions.

DEFINITION 2.1    Let $S$ be a set and $r_M\colon S \to \mathbb{N}_0$ be a mapping. The tuple $\tilde{M} = (S, r_M)$ is called a *multiset over* $S$. If $r_M(a) = n$, then the element $a \in S$ occurs exactly $n$ times in $\tilde{M}$. The *union*, *intersection* and *inclusion* of two multisets $\tilde{M}$ and $\tilde{N}$ over $S$ are defined in the following way:

$$\tilde{M} \subseteq \tilde{N} :\Leftrightarrow (\forall a \in S)(r_M(a) \leqslant r_N(a));$$

$$\tilde{M} \cap \tilde{N} := (S, r_{M \cap N}) \quad \text{where } (\forall a \in S)(r_{M \cap N}(a) = \mathrm{MIN}(r_M(a), r_N(a)));$$

$$\tilde{M} \cup \tilde{N} := (S, r_{M \cup N}) \quad \text{where } (\forall a \in S)(r_{M \cup N}(a) = \mathrm{MAX}(r_M(a), r_N(a))).$$

(Note that these definitions are simple generalizations of the corresponding concepts for sets in the usual sense.)

DEFINITION 2.2    Let $V$ be a finite set, $k \in \mathbb{N}$ and $\mathfrak{P}_k(V)$ be the set of all subsets of $V$ containing $k$ elements. A *graph* is a tuple $G = (V, \tilde{A})$, where

(a)  $V$ is a finite set of *nodes* (or *vertices*);
(b)  $\tilde{A}$ is a finite multiset over $\mathfrak{P}_2(V)$, the so-called *arcs* (or *edges*).

Two nodes $v_1, v_2 \in V$ are called *adjacent* if $\{v_1, v_2\} \in \tilde{A}$. The graph $G$ is *simple* if $r_A(\{v_1, v_2\}) \leqslant 1$ for all $\{v_1, v_2\} \in \mathfrak{P}_2(V)$. The $n$-tuple $(v_1, v_2, \ldots, v_n) \in V^n$, $n \in \mathbb{N}$, is called a *path* of length $n$ from $v$ to $v'$ if $v = v_1$ and $v' = v_n$ and $\{v_k, v_{k+1}\} \in \tilde{A}$ for $1 \leqslant k < n$. The path $(v_1, v_2, \ldots, v_n)$ is *simple* if $v_1, \ldots, v_{n-1}$ are distinct and $v_2, \ldots, v_n$ are distinct; it is *closed*, if $v_1 = v_n$. The graph $G$ is *connected* if every two nodes are connected by at least one path. $G$ is called *acyclic* if all paths appearing in $G$ are not closed.

FIGURE 2. Plane representation of the graph $G$.

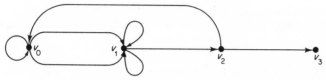

FIGURE 3. Plane representation of the digraph $G$.

EXAMPLE 2.1   Let $V = \{v_0, v_1, v_2, v_3\}$ and $\tilde{A} = \{\{v_0, v_1\}, \{v_1, v_2\}, \{v_0, v_2\},$ $\{v_2, v_3\}\}$. $G = (V, \tilde{A})$ is a graph with four nodes and four arcs. For example, the nodes $v_0$ and $v_1$ or $v_0$ and $v_2$ are adjacent. The 7-tuple $(v_0, v_1, v_2, v_0, v_1, v_2, v_3)$ is a path of length seven from $v_0$ to $v_3$; this path is not simple. Moreover, the graph $G$ is connected and simple.

A convenient plane representation of a graph $G$ consists in drawing the nodes as points and the edges as segments. Figure 2 represents the graph $G$.

DEFINITION 2.3   A *directed graph* (or *digraph*) is a tuple $G = (V, \tilde{A})$, where:

(a) $V$ is a finite set of *nodes* (or *vertices*);
(b) $\tilde{A}$ is a finite multiset over $V \times V$, the so-called *arcs* (or *edges*).

The graph $G$ is *simple* if $r_A((v_1, v_2)) \leqslant 1$ for all $(v_1, v_2) \in V \times V$. If

$$a = (v_1, v_2) \in \tilde{A},$$

we say $v_1$ is the *initial node* and $v_2$ is the *final node* of the arc $a$; we write $v_1 = \text{init}(a)$ and $v_2 = \text{fin}(a)$. The *out-degree out*$(v)$ (*in-degree in*$(v)$) of a vertex $v \in V$ is defined by

$$\text{out}(v) := \text{card}(\{a \in \tilde{A} | \text{init}(a) = v\}) \ (\text{in}(v) := \text{card}(\{a \in \tilde{A} | \text{fin}(a) = v\})).$$

EXAMPLE 2.2   Let $V = \{v_0, v_1, v_2, v_3\}$ and $\tilde{A} = \{(v_0, v_0), (v_0, v_1), (v_0, v_1), (v_2, v_0),$ $(v_1, v_1), (v_1, v_1), (v_1, v_2), (v_2, v_3)\}$. $G = (V, \tilde{A})$ is a directed graph with four nodes and eight arcs. For example, $\text{in}(v_1) = 4$, $\text{out}(v_0) = \text{out}(v_1) = 3$, $\text{in}(v_0) = \text{out}(v_2) = 2$, $\text{in}(v_2) = \text{in}(v_3) = 1$ and $\text{out}(v_3) = 0$. For $a = (v_2, v_0) \in \tilde{A}$, $\text{init}(a) = v_2$ and $\text{fin}(a) = v_0$. Moreover, $G$ is not a simple digraph. There is again a plane representation of a digraph $G$, analogous to that introduced in Example 2.1. The nodes correspond to points and the arcs to oriented segments. Figure 3 represents the given digraph $G$.

DEFINITION 2.4   Let $G = (V, \tilde{A})$ be a directed graph and $n \in \mathbb{N}$. The $n$-tuple $(v_1, \ldots, v_n) \in V^n$, is called an *oriented path* of length $(n - 1)$ from $v$ to $v'$ if $v = v_1$

and $v' = v_n$ and $(v_k, v_{k+1}) \in \tilde{A}$ for $1 \leqslant k < n$. We say the oriented path $(v_1, \ldots, v_n)$ is *simple* if the nodes $v_1, \ldots, v_{n-1}$ are distinct and the nodes $v_2, \ldots, v_n$ are distinct. A simple oriented path from a vertex to itself is an *oriented cycle*.

As an example of these definitions, we may refer to our Example 2.2. The 6-tuple $(v_0, v_1, v_1, v_1, v_2, v_0)$ is an oriented path of length five from $v_0$ to $v_0$; this path is not simple. The path $(v_1, v_1)$ is an oriented cycle of length one and $(v_1, v_2, v_0, v_1)$ is an oriented cycle of length three.

DEFINITION 2.5 Let $G = (V, \tilde{A})$ be a directed graph. The *associated graph* $G' = (V', \tilde{A}')$ is the simple graph defined by

(a) $V' := V$;
(b) $\tilde{A}' := \{\{v_1, v_2\} \in \mathfrak{P}_2(V) \,|\, (v_1, v_2) \in \tilde{A} \vee (v_2, v_1) \in \tilde{A}\}$.

$G$ is said to be *strongly connected* if there is an oriented path from $v$ to $v'$ for any two nodes $v, v' \in V$ with $v \neq v'$. $G$ is *connected* if the associated graph $G'$ is connected. $G$ is called *rooted* if there is at least one vertex $v_r$ such that there is an oriented path from $v$ to $v_r$ for all $v \in V$ with $v \neq v_r$.

Evidently, the associated graph $G'$ of the digraph $G$ given in Example 2.2 is the graph of Example 2.1. The graph $G$ is not strongly connected because there is no oriented path from $v_3$ to one of the nodes $v_0, v_1$, or $v_2$. On the other hand, $G$ is connected and rooted with root $v_3$.

DEFINITION 2.6 Let $G = (V, \tilde{A})$ be a digraph with one root $v_r$ of out-degree 0 and let $\tilde{A}_v$, $v \in V$, be the multiset of all arcs $a \in \tilde{A}$ with $\mathrm{init}(a) = v$. A (total) mapping $p: \tilde{A} \to \langle 0, 1]$ satisfying the condition

$$(\forall v \in V)\left( \sum_{a \in \tilde{A}_v} p(a) = 1 - \delta_{0, |\tilde{A}_v|} \right)$$

is called a *probability distribution on $G$*. A *random algorithm* $(G, p)$ is a digraph $G$ with one root of out-degree 0 together with a probability distribution on $G$. The random algorithm $(G, p)$ is said to be *simple*, if the digraph $G$ is simple, i.e. $\tilde{A}$ is a set in the usual sense.

A random algorithm serves as a model for certain algorithms. The graph $G = (V, \tilde{A})$ represents the control relations. For example, a flow chart resembles the kinds of control constructs usually encountered in programming, and a state diagram of any mathematical machine can be interpreted as a description of the control relations of the algorithm performed on this machine. In the former case, $G$ is in the main a directed graph with unlabelled arcs, and in the case of state diagrams, $G$ is a digraph with labelled edges. The nodes of $G$ represent steps in the computation and the arcs represent the possible sequence of these steps.

Given a simple random algorithm $(G, p)$, a computation corresponds in an obvious manner to an oriented path from the vertex $v_s$ to the root $v_r$ of $G$, where $v_s$ $(v_r)$ represents the 'start' step ('stop' step) of the algorithm. The given probability distribution $p$ assigns a probability $p(a)$ to each arc $a \in \tilde{A}$. Therefore, each computation corresponds to a *random path* which starts at $v_s$ and which subsequently chooses edge $a \in \tilde{A}$ with probability $p(a)$, until $v_r$ is reached; the choice of edge taken at each branch is to be independent of all previous choices. This assumption is very strong and is not satisfied by many realistic algorithms.

Evidently, if $G$ is not a simple graph, then the one-to-one correspondence between computations and random paths can no longer be stated. (We have defined an oriented path by a sequence of nodes and not by a sequence of arcs!) But in this case, we can modify the graph $G$ of the random algorithm $(G, p)$ in the following way: if there are two or more edges $a_i = (v_1, v_2)$ joining the same two vertices $v_1, v_2$, then add an extra node $v_{1,i}$ for each arc $a_i$ which divides this arc into two parts. If $p(a_i) = w_i$ holds in $G$, then define $p((v_1, v_{1i})) := w_i$ and $p((v_{1i}, v_2)) := 1$ in the modified graph. For example, the graph

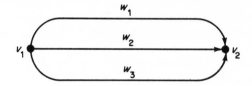

becomes

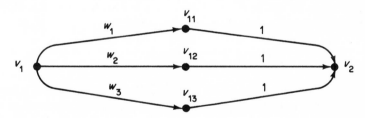

Obviously, if we carry out this modification, the new graph is simple and henceforth, we can restrict our considerations to simple random algorithms.

## 2.2 Analysis of Random Algorithms

In this section we shall give a detailed analysis of the computation time for simple random algorithms.

DEFINITION 2.7 Let $(G, p)$ be a simple random algorithm with $G = (V, \tilde{A})$ and $\text{card}(V) = s$. The $s \times s$-matrix $\pi = (p_{ij})$ with

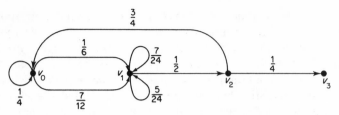

FIGURE 4. A random algorithm with a probability distribution.

$$p_{ij} = \begin{cases} p((v_i, v_j)) & \text{if } (v_i, v_j) \in \tilde{A} \\ 0 & \text{if } (v_i, v_j) \notin \tilde{A} \end{cases}$$

is called the *fundamental matrix* of the random algorithm $(G, p)$.

EXAMPLE 2.3 Consider the digraph $G$ of Example 2.2 (Figure 3) which represents the control relations of the Turing machine given in Example 1.3. The probabilities associated with the arcs are defined in Figure 4. The node $v_0$ represents the 'start' step and $v_3$ the 'stop' step. The corresponding simple random algorithm is illustrated in Figure 5. For example, the computation corresponding to the oriented path $(v_0, v_0, v_{01}, v_1, v_{11}, v_1, v_{12}, v_1, v_2, v_0, v_{02}, v_1, v_2, v_3)$ is chosen with the probability

$$\tfrac{1}{4} \cdot \tfrac{1}{6} \cdot 1 \cdot \tfrac{7}{24} \cdot 1 \cdot \tfrac{5}{24} \cdot 1 \cdot \tfrac{1}{2} \cdot \tfrac{3}{4} \cdot \tfrac{7}{12} \cdot 1 \cdot \tfrac{1}{2} \cdot \tfrac{1}{4} = \frac{245}{3\,538\,944}.$$

The fundamental matrix of the simple algorithm is given by

|   | $v_0$ | $v_{01}$ | $v_{02}$ | $v_1$ | $v_{11}$ | $v_{12}$ | $v_2$ | $v_3$ |   |
|---|---|---|---|---|---|---|---|---|---|
| | $\frac{1}{4}$ | $\frac{1}{6}$ | $\frac{7}{12}$ | 0 | 0 | 0 | 0 | 0 | $v_0$ |
| | 0 | 0 | 0 | 1 | 0 | 0 | 0 | 0 | $v_{01}$ |
| | 0 | 0 | 0 | 1 | 0 | 0 | 0 | 0 | $v_{02}$ |
| $\pi =$ | 0 | 0 | 0 | 0 | $\frac{7}{24}$ | $\frac{5}{24}$ | $\frac{1}{2}$ | 0 | $v_1$ |
| | 0 | 0 | 0 | 1 | 0 | 0 | 0 | 0 | $v_{11}$ |
| | 0 | 0 | 0 | 1 | 0 | 0 | 0 | 0 | $v_{12}$ |
| | $\frac{3}{4}$ | 0 | 0 | 0 | 0 | 0 | 0 | $\frac{1}{4}$ | $v_2$ |
| | 0 | 0 | 0 | 0 | 0 | 0 | 0 | 0 | $v_3$ |

Let us now consider a simple random algorithm $(G, p)$ with the nodes $V = \{v_1, \ldots, v_n\}$ and the fundamental matrix $\pi = (p_{ij})$. It is easily seen that $(\pi^n)_{ij}$ is the probability that a computation starting at node $v_i$ will be at node $v_j$ after $n$ steps. We prove the following basic result.

THEOREM 2.1 If $(G, p)$ is a simple random algorithm with the fundamental

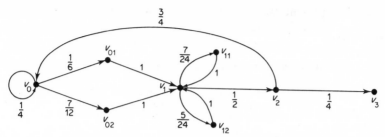

FIGURE 5. The corresponding simple algorithm.

matrix $\pi$, then the matrix $(I - \pi)$ is non-singular. Moreover, $(I - \pi)^{-1} = \sum_{k \geqslant 0} \pi^k$.

*Proof* First we prove that the powers $\pi^k$ of the matrix $\pi$ tend to the matrix $\mathbf{0}$ with all entries 0 as $k$ increases. Note that there is an integer $n$ such that an oriented path from any node $v \in V$ to the root $v_r$ has a length less than or equal to $n$. Since there are only a finite number of nodes, $n$ is simply the maximum of the lengths of the paths required from each node. Hence there is a positive number $w \in \langle 0, 1]$ such that the probability of reaching the root $v_r$ by an oriented path of length less than or equal to $n$ is at least $w$, from any node $v \in V$. Thus the probability of not reaching the root $v_r$ by a path of length less than or equal to $n$ is at most $(1 - w)$. Since the probability of not reaching $v_r$ by a path of length less than or equal to $kn$ is less than or equal to $(1 - w)^k$ (which tends to zero as $k$ increases), the sequence $\pi^k$ converges to the zero matrix.

Next we shall show that the matrix $I - \pi$ has an inverse. For this purpose, consider the identity

$$(I - \pi)(I + \pi + \pi^2 + \pi^3 + \cdots + \pi^{n-1}) = I - \pi^n$$

which is easily verified by multiplying out the left-hand side. By the first part of our proof we know that the right-hand side tends to $I$ as $n$ increases. Since $\det(I) = 1$, $\det(I - \pi^n) \neq 0$ for sufficiently large $n$. Hence $\det(I - \pi) \neq 0$, because the determinant of a product of two matrices is the product of the determinants. Therefore, the matrix $(I - \pi)$ is non-singular and has an inverse. Multiplying both sides of the above identity by $(I - \pi)^{-1}$, we obtain

$$I + \pi + \pi^2 + \cdots + \pi^{n-1} = (I - \pi)^{-1}(I - \pi^n).$$

Now the right-hand side of this new identity tends to $(I - \pi)^{-1}$ as $n$ increases. This completes the proof of our theorem. ∎

We will now give a probabilistic interpretation to $(I - \pi)^{-1}$.

THEOREM 2.2 Let $(G, p)$ be a simple random algorithm with the fundamental matrix $\pi$. The average number $R_{ij}$ of times node $v_j$ appears in a random path from node $v_i$ to node $v_j$ is given by $((I - \pi)^{-1})_{ij}$.

*Proof* We will present two different proofs of this fact.

(a) Obviously,

$$R_{ij} = \sum_{k \geq 0} \left[ \underbrace{(1 - (\pi^k)_{ij}) \cdot 0}_{} + \underbrace{(\pi^k)_{ij} \cdot 1}_{} \right]$$

probability that the    probability that the
node $v_j$ is not reached   node $v_j$ is reached
from $v_i$ after $k$ steps    from $v_i$ after $k$ steps

Hence, by Theorem 1.1,

$$R_{ij} = \sum_{k \geq 0} (\pi^k)_{ij} = \left( \sum_{k \geq 0} \pi^k \right)_{ij} = ((I - \pi)^{-1})_{ij}.$$

(b) Consider a random path $(v_i, v_k, \ldots, v_j)$. We may add up the contributions to $R_{ij}$ in the initial node $v_i$, plus each contribution to $R_{ij}$ in the following nodes. Therefore,

$$R_{ij} = \underbrace{\delta_{ij}}_{} + \underbrace{\sum_{1 \leq k \leq s} p_{ik}}_{} \cdot \underbrace{R_{kj}}_{}$$

contribution 1,    probability that   average number
if $v_i = v_j$, and    the arc $(v_i, v_k)$   of times node
contribution 0,    is chosen    $v_j$ appears in
if $v_i \neq v_j$                     $(v_k, \ldots, v_j)$

Hence, with matrix $R := (R_{ij})$, $R = I + \pi R$ which is equivalent to $R = (I - \pi)^{-1}$. ∎

This theorem establishes the fact that the mean of the total number of times the random algorithm is in a given step $v_j$ is always finite, and that these means are simply given by $(I - \pi)^{-1}$. The variance $\sigma_{ij}^2$ can also be expressed by the matrix $(I - \pi)^{-1}$ (see Exercise 2.4).

EXAMPLE 2.4   We will apply this result to the random algorithm given in the previous Example 2.3. We have

$$(I - \pi)^{-1} = \begin{array}{c} \\ \\ \end{array}
\begin{array}{cccccccc}
v_0 & v_{01} & v_{02} & v_1 & v_{11} & v_{12} & v_2 & v_3 \\
\end{array}$$

| | $v_0$ | $v_{01}$ | $v_{02}$ | $v_1$ | $v_{11}$ | $v_{12}$ | $v_2$ | $v_3$ | |
|---|---|---|---|---|---|---|---|---|---|
| | $\frac{16}{3}$ | $\frac{8}{9}$ | $\frac{28}{9}$ | $8$ | $\frac{7}{3}$ | $\frac{5}{3}$ | $4$ | $1$ | $v_0$ |
| | $4$ | $\frac{5}{3}$ | $\frac{7}{3}$ | $8$ | $\frac{7}{3}$ | $\frac{5}{3}$ | $4$ | $1$ | $v_{01}$ |
| | $4$ | $\frac{2}{3}$ | $\frac{10}{3}$ | $8$ | $\frac{7}{3}$ | $\frac{5}{3}$ | $4$ | $1$ | $v_{02}$ |
| | $4$ | $\frac{2}{3}$ | $\frac{7}{3}$ | $8$ | $\frac{7}{3}$ | $\frac{5}{3}$ | $4$ | $1$ | $v_1$ |
| | $4$ | $\frac{2}{3}$ | $\frac{7}{3}$ | $8$ | $\frac{10}{3}$ | $\frac{5}{3}$ | $4$ | $1$ | $v_{11}$ |
| | $4$ | $\frac{2}{3}$ | $\frac{7}{3}$ | $8$ | $\frac{7}{3}$ | $\frac{8}{3}$ | $4$ | $1$ | $v_{12}$ |
| | $4$ | $\frac{2}{3}$ | $\frac{7}{3}$ | $6$ | $\frac{7}{4}$ | $\frac{5}{4}$ | $4$ | $1$ | $v_2$ |
| | $0$ | $0$ | $0$ | $0$ | $0$ | $0$ | $0$ | $1$ | $v_3$ |

Considering all computations starting at node $v_0$ and stopping in $v_3$, the vertices $v_0, v_{01}, v_{02}, v_1, v_{11}, v_{12}, v_2, v_3$ are traversed $\frac{16}{3}, \frac{8}{9}, \frac{28}{9}, 8, \frac{7}{3}, \frac{5}{3}, 4, 1$ times on the average, respectively. A computation of the matrix $\sigma^{(2)} := (\sigma_{ij}^2)$ giving the variance yields (see Exercise 2.4)

$$
\sigma^{(2)} = 
\begin{array}{cccccccc}
v_0 & v_{01} & v_{02} & v_1 & v_{11} & v_{12} & v_2 & v_3
\end{array}
\left[
\begin{array}{cccccccc}
\frac{208}{9} & \frac{104}{81} & \frac{644}{81} & 56 & \frac{70}{9} & \frac{40}{9} & 12 & 0 \\
\frac{68}{3} & \frac{10}{9} & \frac{70}{9} & 56 & \frac{70}{9} & \frac{40}{9} & 12 & 0 \\
\frac{68}{3} & \frac{10}{9} & \frac{70}{9} & 56 & \frac{70}{9} & \frac{40}{9} & 12 & 0 \\
\frac{68}{3} & \frac{10}{9} & \frac{70}{9} & 56 & \frac{70}{9} & \frac{40}{9} & 12 & 0 \\
\frac{68}{3} & \frac{10}{9} & \frac{70}{9} & 56 & \frac{70}{9} & \frac{40}{9} & 12 & 0 \\
\frac{68}{3} & \frac{10}{9} & \frac{70}{9} & 56 & \frac{70}{9} & \frac{40}{9} & 12 & 0 \\
\frac{68}{3} & \frac{10}{9} & \frac{70}{9} & 54 & \frac{329}{48} & \frac{185}{48} & 12 & 0 \\
0 & 0 & 0 & 0 & 0 & 0 & 0 & 0
\end{array}
\right]
\begin{array}{l}
v_0 \\ v_{01} \\ v_{02} \\ v_1 \\ v_{11} \\ v_{12} \\ v_2 \\ v_3
\end{array}
$$

We will conclude this section by presenting some further basic results of random algorithms. The simple proofs are left to the reader.

THEOREM 2.3  Let $(G, p)$ be a simple random algorithm with the fundamental matrix $\pi$. The probability $w_{ij}$ that the node $v_j$ occurs in a random path from node $v_i$ to node $v_j$ is given by $w_{ij} = ((I - \pi)^{-1})_{ij}/((I - \pi)^{-1})_{jj}$. The probability $q_j$ that a random path starting at $v_j$ will never return to node $v_j$ is $q_j = 1/((I - \pi)^{-1})_{jj}$. ∎

Applying this result to our running example, we find that the nodes $v_0, v_{01}, v_{02}, v_1, v_{11}, v_{12}, v_2, v_3$ occur in a computation starting at $v_0$ and stopping in $v_3$ with probability $1, \frac{8}{15}, \frac{14}{15}, 1, \frac{7}{10}, \frac{5}{8}, 1, 1$, respectively.

In this section we have given some fundamental definitions concerning directed and undirected graphs; moreover, we have presented a simple class of algorithms and their analysis of the computation time. Readers familiar with stochastic processes may recognize that random algorithms are essentially a special case of finite Markov chains, the so-called absorbing Markov chains. There are many papers and textbooks dealing with extensive studies of stochastic processes of this kind (e.g. [57], [112]).

## Exercises

**2.1** Show that a strongly connected digraph is rooted and that a rooted digraph is connected. Is the converse of these implications also true?

**2.2** Consider the state diagram of the Turing machine defined in Example 1.1. Can this algorithm be interpreted as a random algorithm? Assume that the probabilities for the transitions are given by

| Transition | $1 \to 0, L$ | $0 \to 1, R$ | $* \to 1, R$ | $0 \to 0, R$ | $1 \to 1, R$ | $* \to *, L$ |
|---|---|---|---|---|---|---|
| Probability | $p$ | $r$ | $1 - p - r$ | $q$ | $w$ | $1 - q - w$ |

Set up the fundamental matrix $\pi$ of the corresponding random algorithm and compute the average number of times a node appears in a computation. Compute also the variance and the probabilities that a node occurs in a computation.

**2.3** Prove Theorem 2.3.

**2.4** Let $(G, p)$ be a simple random algorithm with the fundamental matrix $\pi$.

(a) Compute the probability that a node $v$ occurs exactly $k$ times in a random path from node $v'$ to the root $v_r$.

(b) Show that the variance concerning the average number $R_{ij}$ of times node $v_j$ appears in a random path from node $v_i$ to node $v_j$ is given by $((I - \pi)^{-1}(2(I - \pi)_d - I) - (I - \pi)_s)_{ij}$, where the matrix $A_s$ is formed from $A$ by squaring each entry and the matrix $A_d$ by setting off-diagonal entries equal to zero.

# 3

# *Permutations and Their Applications*

## 3.1 Motivation

In this section we shall investigate the average behaviour of some characteristic quantities of permutations which appear in the analysis of many algorithms. We shall rediscover some well-known numbers such as Stirling numbers, Euler numbers, Eulerian numbers, etc.

For example, consider the following obvious procedure for the computation of the maximum of $n$ distinct numbers.

ALGORITHM MAX
Input: $n, A[1], \ldots, A[n]$, where $A[i] \neq A[j]$ for $i \neq j$, $1 \leqslant i, j \leqslant n$.
Output: $MAX(A[i])$.

Method: The algorithm is described by Figure 6. Starting with $k = 1$, the algorithm MAX examines successively the values $A[k]$, $1 \leqslant k \leqslant n$. If it scans $A[k]$, then $m = MAX_{1 \leqslant r < k}(A[r])$. The value $A[k]$ is now compared with $m$ (step ⑨); if $A[k]$ is greater than $m$, then the value of the current maximum $m$ is changed (step ⑩); otherwise, the next value $A[k + 1]$ is examined.

Evidently, algorithm MAX requires a fixed amount of storage in the best, worst, and average case, because it uses only the four variables $a$, $k$, $m$, and $n$.

Let us now consider the time requirements $T(n)$ of the algorithm MAX. For this purpose, we will count the number of times each step is executed. We have:

| Step | Number of times |
|------|-----------------|
| ① | 1 |
| ② | 1 |
| ③ | 1 |
| ④ | 1 |
| ⑤ | 1 |
| ⑥ | $n$ |
| ⑦ | $n$ |
| ⑧ | $n - 1$ |
| ⑨ | $n - 1$ |
| ⑩ | $A_n$ |
| ⑪ | 1 |
| ⑫ | 1 |

21

22

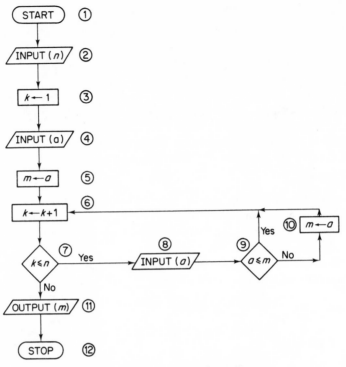

FIGURE 6. Flowchart of algorithm MAX.

Here, $A_n$ is the number of times the value of the current maximum $m$ must be changed. Knowing the costs of each step and the number of times each step is executed gives us the information necessary to determine the time requirements of the algorithm MAX on a particular computer. It remains to study the quantity $A_n$.

*Best case:* Evidently, the best case is characterized by the condition $A[1] > A[i + 1]$, $1 \leqslant i < n$. It follows that the minimum number of times the value $m$ must be changed is zero. Assuming that all inputs $A[1], \ldots, A[n]$ are equally likely, the probability that $A_n = 0$ is $n^{-1}$ (cf. the average case).

*Worst case:* The maximum number of times the value $m$ must be changed is $n - 1$; this happens if $A[i] < A[i + 1]$, $1 \leqslant i < n$. The probability that this case occurs is $n!^{-1}$ (cf. the average case).

*Average case:* We will assume that each of the $n!$ inputs $A[1], \ldots, A[n]$ is equally likely. Let $M_{n,k}$ be the number of inputs $A[1], \ldots, A[n]$ with $A_n = k$, $k \in [0:n - 1]$. If $A[n] = \text{MAX}_{1 \leqslant i \leqslant n}(A[i])$, the value of $A_n$ is one higher than the value $A_{n-1}$ obtained on $A[1], \ldots, A[n - 1]$; if $A[n] \neq \text{MAX}_{1 \leqslant i \leqslant n}(A[i])$, the value of $A_n$ is the same as $A_{n-1}$ on $A[1], \ldots, A[n - 1]$. Therefore,

$$M_{n,k} = M_{n-1,k-1} + (n-1)M_{n-1,k}.$$

Obviously, the initial conditions are $M_{1,k} = \delta_{0,k}$ and $M_{n,k} = 0$ for $k < 0$. Since $p_{n,k} = n!^{-1}M_{n,k}$ is the probability that an input $A[1],\ldots,A[n]$ requires $k$ changes of the value $m$ in step ⑩, we find immediately

$$p_{n,k} = n^{-1}p_{n-1,k-1} + (1-n^{-1})p_{n-1,k}$$

with

$$p_{1,k} = \delta_{0,k} \quad \text{and} \quad p_{n,k} = 0 \quad \text{for } k < 0.$$

Now we have to solve this recurrence. To do this, we consider the generating function $P_n(x)$ of the numbers $p_{n,k}$, $k \geq 0$, defined by (Appendix A)

$$P_n(x) = \sum_{k \geq 0} p_{n,k}x^k.$$

Using the above recurrence for $p_{n,k}$, we obtain

$$P_n(x) = n^{-1}\sum_{k \geq 0} p_{n-1,k-1}x^k + (1-n^{-1})\sum_{k \geq 0} p_{n-1,k}x^k$$

$$= n^{-1}\sum_{k \geq 0} p_{n-1,k}x^{k+1} + (1-n^{-1})\sum_{k \geq 0} p_{n-1,k}x^k$$

$$= n^{-1}xP_{n-1}(x) + (1-n^{-1})P_{n-1}(x)$$

$$= \frac{x+n-1}{n}P_{n-1}(x).$$

The last equation implies further

$$P_n(x) = \frac{1}{x+n}\binom{x+n}{n}.$$

In order to obtain an explicit expression for the probabilities $p_{n,k}$, we have now to compute the coefficient of $x^k$ in the expansion of $P_n(x)$. An application of formula (B8) leads directly to ($n \geq 1$)

$$P_n(x) = (-1)^{n-1}\frac{1}{n!}\sum_{k \geq 0} S_n^{(k+1)}(-1)^k x^k,$$

where $S_n^{(k)}$ are the *Stirling numbers of the first kind*. Hence

$$p_{n,k} = (-1)^{n+k-1}S_n^{(k+1)}/n!$$

An inspection of (B15) shows that $p_{n,k} \sim [\gamma + \ln(n)]^k/(nk!)$ for $k = o(\ln(n))$, where $\gamma$ is *Euler's constant*. As special cases, we obtain further by (B10)

$$p_{n,0} = (-1)^{n-1}S_n^{(1)}/n! = n^{-1}$$

and

$$p_{n,n-1} = S_n^{(n)}/n! = n!^{-1},$$

which are the probabilities of the best and worst case. To compute the $s$-th moments about the origin given by

$$\mu'_s(n) = \sum_{k \geqslant 0} k^s p_{n,k},$$

we consider the generating function $f_s(z)$ defined by

$$f_s(z) = \sum_{n \geqslant 0} \mu'_s(n) z^n$$

$$= \sum_{k \geqslant 0} k^s (-1)^{k-1} \sum_{n \geqslant 0} z^n (-1)^n \frac{1}{n!} S_n^{(k+1)}.$$

Using (B12), $f_s(z)$ can be transformed into

$$f_s(z) = \sum_{k \geqslant 0} k^s (-1)^{k-1} \frac{1}{(k+1)!} [\ln(1-z)]^{k+1}.$$

Thus, by the binomial theorem,

$$f_s(z) = \sum_{k \geqslant 2} (-1)^k \frac{(k-1)^s}{k!} [\ln(1-z)]^k$$

$$= \sum_{j \geqslant 0} \binom{s}{j} (-1)^{s-j} \sum_{k \geqslant 2} (-1)^k \frac{k^j}{k!} [\ln(1-z)]^k$$

$$= (-1)^s \sum_{k \geqslant 2} (-1)^k \frac{1}{k!} [\ln(1-z)]^k$$

$$+ \sum_{j \geqslant 1} \binom{s}{j} (-1)^{s-j} \sum_{k \geqslant 2} (-1)^k \frac{k^j}{k!} [\ln(1-z)]^k.$$

Obviously, the first sum is equal to

$$(-1)^s [\exp(-\ln(1-z)) - 1 + \ln(1-z)].$$

Applying (B21) to the second sum, we further obtain

$$f_s(z) = (-1)^s [\ln(1-z) - 1 + (1-z)^{-1}]$$

$$+ \frac{1}{1-z} \sum_{j \geqslant 1} \binom{s}{j} (-1)^{s-j} \sum_{k \geqslant 1} (-1)^k \mathscr{S}_j^{(k)} [\ln(1-z)]^k$$

$$+ \ln(1-z) \sum_{j \geqslant 1} \binom{s}{j} (-1)^{s-j},$$

where $\mathscr{S}_j^{(k)}$ are the *Stirling numbers of the second kind.* Therefore,

$$f_s(z) = (-1)^s \frac{z}{1-z} + (-1)^s \sum_{j \geqslant 1} \binom{s}{j} (-1)^j \sum_{k \geqslant 1} \mathscr{S}_j^{(k)} \frac{[\ln(1-z)]^k}{1-z} (-1)^k.$$

Henceforth, let $\langle z^n \rangle f(z)$ be the coefficient of $z^n$ in the expansion of a function $f$. By definition, $\mu'_s(n) = \langle z^n \rangle f_s(z)$. Since

$$f_1(z) = -\frac{z}{1-z} + \frac{1}{1-z}\ln\left(\frac{1}{1-z}\right)$$

$$= \sum_{n\geqslant 1} z^n \left[\sum_{1\leqslant i\leqslant n} \frac{1}{i} - 1\right]$$

and

$$f_2(z) = \frac{z}{1-z} + \frac{1}{1-z}\left[\ln\left(\frac{1}{1-z}\right)\right]^2 - \frac{1}{1-z}\ln\left(\frac{1}{1-z}\right).$$

$$= \sum_{n\geqslant 2} z^n \left[2\sum_{2\leqslant j\leqslant n}\frac{1}{j}\sum_{1\leqslant i<j}\frac{1}{i} - \sum_{1\leqslant i\leqslant n}\frac{1}{i} + 1\right]$$

$$= \sum_{n\geqslant 2} z^n \left[\left(\sum_{1\leqslant i\leqslant n}\frac{1}{i}\right)^2 - \sum_{1\leqslant i\leqslant n}\frac{1}{i^2} - \sum_{1\leqslant i\leqslant n}\frac{1}{i} + 1\right],$$

we obtain

$$\mu_1'(n) = H_n^{(1)} - 1 \quad \text{and} \quad \mu_2'(n) = [H_n^{(1)}]^2 - H_n^{(2)} - H_n^{(1)} + 1,$$

where $H_n^{(r)}$ is the *generalized Harmonic number* (Appendix B, 1.4). Therefore, the average number $\mathbf{A}_n$ of times the value of the current maximum $m$ must be changed is $H_n^{(1)} - 1 = \ln(n) + \gamma - 1 + O(n^{-1})$ (see (B29)). For the variance, we obtain (see (B30))

$$\sigma^2(n) = \mu_2'(n) - [\mu_1'(n)]^2$$

$$= H_n^{(1)} - H_n^{(2)}$$

$$= \ln(n) + \gamma - \tfrac{1}{6}\pi^2 + O(n^{-1}),$$

where $\gamma$ is Euler's constant.

It remains to study the $s$-th moment $\mu_s'(n)$ for large $n$ and fixed $s \geqslant 3$. For this purpose, we return to the above function $f_s(z)$. Fortunately, the expansion of the function $(1-z)^{-1}[\ln(1-z)^{-1}]^k$ is known (see [91]). We have

$$(1-z)^{-1}[\ln(1-z)^{-1}]^k = \sum_{n\geqslant k} b_{k,n} z^n,$$

where

$$b_{k,n} = [\ln(n)]^k \left(1 + \frac{\gamma k}{\ln(n)} + O([\ln(n)]^{-2})\right)$$

for fixed $k$ and large $n$. Therefore,

$$f_s(z) = (-1)^s \frac{z}{1-z} + (-1)^s \sum_{j\geqslant 1}\binom{s}{j}(-1)^j \sum_{k\geqslant 1}\mathscr{S}_j^{(k)}\sum_{n\geqslant k} z^n b_{k,n}$$

which implies

$$\mu_s'(n) = \langle z^n\rangle f_s(z)$$

$$= (-1)^s + (-1)^s \sum_{j\geqslant 1}\binom{s}{j}(-1)^j \sum_{1\leqslant i\leqslant n}\mathscr{S}_j^{(i)} b_{i,n}.$$

Using (B50) and (B51), we further obtain

$$\sum_{1 \leqslant i \leqslant n} \mathcal{S}_j^{(i)} b_{i,n} = \mathcal{B}_j(\ln(n)) + \gamma \mathcal{B}_j'(\ln(n)) + O([\ln(n)]^{-2} \mathcal{B}_j(\ln(n)))$$

$$= \mathcal{B}_j(\ln(n)) + \frac{\gamma}{\ln(n)} \mathcal{B}_{j+1}(\ln(n))$$

$$- \gamma \mathcal{B}_j(\ln(n)) + O([\ln(n)]^{-2} \mathcal{B}_j(\ln(n)))$$

$$= [\ln(n)]^j + O([\ln(n)]^{j-1}),$$

where $\mathcal{B}_n(x)$ is the $n$-th *Bell polynomial*. Since

$$\sum_{j \geqslant 1} \binom{s}{j} (-1)^j x^j = (1-x)^s - 1,$$

we immediately obtain

$$\mu_s'(n) = (-1)^s[(1 - \ln(n))^s + O((1 - \ln(n))^s/\ln(n))]$$

$$= [\ln(n)]^s + O([\ln(n)]^{s-1}).$$

Thus the $s$-th moment about the origin is asymptotically given by $\ln^s(n)$ for all fixed $s \geqslant 1$.

This example shows that the time requirements of the algorithm depend on the quantity $A_n$ associated with the input; we shall see in section 3.2.1 that $A_n$ can be interpreted as a characteristic quantity of a permutation of $n$ objects.

## 3.2 Average Values of Characteristic Quantities of Permutations

DEFINITION 3.1   A *permutation* of a set $M$ is a bijective map of $M$ on to itself. The set of all permutations of $M$ is denoted by $\mathfrak{S}(M)$. The permutation $\sigma_0 \in \mathfrak{S}(M)$ with $\sigma_0(x) = x$ for all $x \in M$ is called the *identity permutation*.

It is well known that $\mathfrak{S}(M)$ is a group (*symmetric group*) with the unit element $\sigma_0 \in \mathfrak{S}(M)$ and with the composition 'o' of maps as operation. Generally, a subgroup $G$ of $\mathfrak{S}(M)$ is called *permutation group of* $M$; we write $G \leqslant \mathfrak{S}(M)$. Without loss of generality, we restrict our further considerations to the case that $M$ is a finite subset of $\mathbb{N}$. There are many ways of representing a permutation $\sigma \in \mathfrak{S}(M)$:

(a) *Standard notation*
The permutation $\sigma \in \mathfrak{S}(M)$ is written in a two-line notation; the elements of $M$ appear in a top row, and underneath each element under the mapping $\sigma$. Thus

$$\begin{pmatrix} 1 & 2 & 3 & 4 & 5 & 6 & 7 & 8 & 9 \\ 2 & 5 & 6 & 4 & 8 & 7 & 3 & 1 & 9 \end{pmatrix}$$

represents a $\sigma \in \mathfrak{S}(\mathbb{N}_9)$, where $\sigma(1) = 2$, $\sigma(2) = 5$, $\sigma(3) = 6$, $\sigma(4) = 4$, $\sigma(5) = 8$, $\sigma(6) = 7$, $\sigma(7) = 3$, $\sigma(8) = 1$, and $\sigma(9) = 9$.

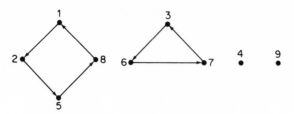

FIGURE 7. Graph notation of $\sigma$.

(b) *Linear notation*

The linear notation of a permutation $\sigma \in \mathfrak{S}(M)$, $M = \mathbb{N}_n$, is the sequence $\sigma(1)$, $\sigma(2), \ldots, \sigma(n)$. Thus, $\boldsymbol{\sigma}$ has the linear notation 2, 5, 6, 4, 8, 7, 3, 1, 9. (Generally, the linear notation of a permutation requires a fixed ordering on $M$.)

(c) *Graph notation*

The permutation $\sigma \in \mathfrak{S}(M)$ is represented by a simple digraph $G_\sigma = (M, \tilde{A})$, where $\tilde{A} := \{(x, y) \mid y = \sigma(x) \wedge x \neq y\}$. Thus Figure 7 corresponds in this way to the above permutation $\boldsymbol{\sigma}$.

(d) *Matrix notation*

The permutation $\sigma \in \mathfrak{S}(M)$ is represented by a $m \times m$-matrix $T_\sigma$, where $m = \text{card}(M)$. $T_\sigma = (t_{ij})$ is defined by $t_{ij} := \delta_{j,\sigma(i)}$. Thus the matrix

$$T_\sigma = \begin{bmatrix} 0 & 1 & 0 & 0 & 0 & 0 & 0 & 0 & 0 \\ 0 & 0 & 0 & 0 & 1 & 0 & 0 & 0 & 0 \\ 0 & 0 & 0 & 0 & 0 & 1 & 0 & 0 & 0 \\ 0 & 0 & 0 & 1 & 0 & 0 & 0 & 0 & 0 \\ 0 & 0 & 0 & 0 & 0 & 0 & 0 & 1 & 0 \\ 0 & 0 & 0 & 0 & 0 & 0 & 1 & 0 & 0 \\ 0 & 0 & 1 & 0 & 0 & 0 & 0 & 0 & 0 \\ 1 & 0 & 0 & 0 & 0 & 0 & 0 & 0 & 0 \\ 0 & 0 & 0 & 0 & 0 & 0 & 0 & 0 & 1 \end{bmatrix}$$

represents our permutation $\sigma \in \mathfrak{S}(\mathbb{N}_9)$. Clearly, a $m \times m$-matrix represents a permutation if and only if all rows and columns have exactly one entry 1 and $(m - 1)$ entries 0. Such a matrix is called a *permutation matrix*.

(e) *Cycle notation*

Let $\sigma \in \mathfrak{S}(M)$ and $i_1 \in M$. The sequence $i_1, i_2, i_3, \ldots$ with $i_j = \sigma(i_{j-1})$, $j = 2, 3, 4 \ldots$, has the property that there is an element $i_n$ which has already appeared among $i_1, i_2, \ldots, i_{n-1}$, because $M$ is a finite set. Let $i_n$ be the first element with this property; $i_n$ must be $i_1$, because, in the contrary case, we have for some $j \in M$: $j = \sigma(i_k) = \sigma(i_t)$ with $i_k \neq i_t$. The sequence $i_1, i_2, \ldots, i_l$ of minimal length $l$ with $\sigma(i_l) = i_1$ is called a *cycle of $\sigma$ generated by $i_1$*. Obviously, a cycle of $\sigma$ generated by some element $i_1 \in M$ is uniquely determined by each of its elements. The set of cycles of a permutation $\sigma \in \mathfrak{S}(M)$ forms a partition on $M$. A permutation $\sigma$ is written in cycle notation, if

$$\sigma = i_{11}, i_{12}, \ldots, i_{1r_1} | i_{21}, i_{22}, \ldots, i_{2r_2} | \ldots | i_{p1}, i_{p2}, \ldots, i_{pr_p},$$

where $i_{j1}, i_{j2}, \ldots, i_{jr_j}$, $1 \leqslant j \leqslant p$, are the cycles of $\sigma$. Thus the cycle notation of the above permutation $\sigma$ is 4|5, 8, 1, 2|7, 3, 6|9. It is not unique; for example, 9|4|1, 2, 5, 8|3, 6, 7 or 7, 3, 6|9|2, 5, 8, 1|4 are both equivalent to 4|5, 8, 1, 2|7, 3, 6|9. Note that there is a one-to-one correspondence between the cycles appearing in the graph notation and the cycles in the cycle notation of a permutation $\sigma$.

### 3.2.1 Average Number of Cycles of a Permutation

DEFINITION 3.2   Let $\sigma \in \mathfrak{S}(M)$ be a permutation. The cycle notation

$$\sigma = i_{11}, \ldots, i_{1r_1} | i_{21}, \ldots, i_{2r_2} | \ldots | i_{p1}, \ldots, i_{pr_p}$$

is called *canonical*, if

(1) $(\forall j \in [1:p])\left(i_{j1} > \underset{2 \leqslant \lambda \leqslant r_j}{\text{MAX}} (i_{j\lambda})\right)$

and

(2) $(\forall j \in [1:p-1])(i_{j1} < i_{(j+1)1})$.

The canonical cycle notation of a permutation is unique. The above permutation $\sigma = 4|5, 8, 1, 2|7, 3, 6|9$ has the canonical cycle notation 4|7, 3, 6|8, 1, 2, 5|9.

There is a nice one-to-one correspondence between the permutations in canonical cycle notation and in linear notation. Obviously, replacing the symbol '|' in the canonical cycle notation by ',', we get a permutation in linear notation. For example, our permutation $\sigma$ is changed into the permutation 4, 7, 3, 6, 8, 1, 2, 5, 9. On the other hand, there is only one way to insert the symbol '|' in the linear notation of a permutation to obtain a canonical cycle form; one must find the *left-to-right maxima*, where $i_r$ is a left-to-right maximum of the permutation $\sigma = i_1, i_2, \ldots, i_n$ given in linear notation, if $i_r > \text{MAX}_{1 \leqslant j < r}(i_j)$. To obtain the canonical cycle form, we have to replace the symbol ',' before each left-to-right maximum by '|'. For example, the permutation in linear notation 4, 7, 3, 6, 8, 1, 2, 5, 9 has the left-to-right maxima 4, 7, 8, 9; therefore, we can uniquely reconstruct the canonical notation of our permutation $\sigma$ and obtain 4|7, 3, 6|8, 1, 2, 5|9.

This one-to-one correspondence shows that the number of cycles in the cycle notation of a permutation $\sigma \in \mathfrak{S}(\mathbb{N}_n)$ is equal to the number of left-to-right maxima in the linear notation of the permutation $\sigma'$ which arises from $\sigma$ by eliminating '|'. We have already computed this number in section 3.1: the number of left-to-right maxima in a permutation $\sigma \in \mathfrak{S}(\mathbb{N}_n)$ is one higher than the number of times the value of the current maximum $m$ must be changed in step ⑩ during the execution of algorithm MAX with input $\sigma$. Using the results of section 3.1, we immediately obtain the following theorem.

THEOREM 3.1    Assuming that all $n$! permutations $\sigma \in \mathfrak{S}(\mathbb{N}_n)$ are equally likely, the probability that a permutation has $k$ cycles is

$$p_{n,k} = (-1)^{k+n} S_n^{(k)}/n! \sim [\gamma + \ln(n)]^{k-1}/(n(k-1)!)$$

for $k = 1 + o(\ln(n))$. The average number of cycles appearing in a permutation $\sigma \in \mathfrak{S}(\mathbb{N}_n)$ is

$$\mu_1'(n) = H_n^{(1)} = \ln(n) + \gamma + O(n^{-1}).$$

The variance is given by

$$\sigma^2(n) = H_n^{(1)} - H_n^{(2)} = \ln(n) + \gamma - \tfrac{1}{6}\pi^2 + O(n^{-1}). \quad \blacksquare$$

A similar computation as in section 3.1 shows that an asymptotic equivalent of the $s$-th moment about the origin is $\mu_s'(n) = [\ln(n)]^s + O([\ln(n)]^{s-1})$ (see Exercise 3.1).

### 3.2.2 Average Length of a Cycle

We shall now compute the average length of a cycle; this is equivalent to asking about the average distance between left-to-right maxima in a permutation $\sigma$. An inspection of Theorem 3.1 shows that the total number of cycles appearing in all permutations $\sigma \in \mathfrak{S}(\mathbb{N}_n)$ is equal to $n! H_n^{(1)}$. First, we shall compute the number of all cycles of length $l$ among all $n$! permutations. Let $i_1, i_2, \ldots, i_l$ be such a cycle. This cycle occurs in $(n-l)$! permutations, because there are $(n-l)$! possibilities to permute the remaining elements in $\mathbb{N}_n \backslash \{i_1, \ldots, i_l\}$. Next, we shall determine the number of different cycles of length $l$. This number is $(n)_l/l$, because there are $(n-j)$ choices for $i_{j+1}, 0 \leqslant j < l$, and the same cycle appears in the $l$ different forms $i_r, i_{r+1}, \ldots, i_{l-1}, i_l, i_1, \ldots, i_{r-1}$, $1 \leqslant r \leqslant l$. Thus the total number of cycles of length $l$ appearing in all permutations $\sigma \in \mathfrak{S}(\mathbb{N}_n)$ is $(n-l)! (n)_l/l = n!/l$. Note that $\sum_{1 \leqslant l \leqslant n} n!/l = n! H_n^{(1)}$, which is an alternative proof of the fact that the total number of cycles appearing in all permutations $\sigma \in \mathfrak{S}(\mathbb{N}_n)$ is equal to $n! H_n^{(1)}$. Assuming that all these cycles are equally likely, the probability that a cycle has the length $l$ is $l^{-1} n!/(n! H_n^{(1)}) = 1/(l H_n^{(1)})$. The computation of the $s$-th moment about the origin leads to (see (B72))

$$\mu'_s(n) = \sum_{1 \leqslant l \leqslant n} l^s \frac{1}{lH_n^{(1)}}$$

$$= [H_n^{(1)}]^{-1} \sum_{1 \leqslant l \leqslant n} l^{s-1}$$

$$= [sH_n^{(1)}]^{-1}[B_s(n+1) - B_s - \delta_{s-1,0}],$$

where $B_s(x)$ is the $s$-th *Bernoulli polynomial* and $B_s$ the $s$-th *Bernoulli number*. As special cases, we obtain the exact values

$$\mu'_1(n) = [H_n^{(1)}]^{-1}[n + 1 - \tfrac{1}{2} + \tfrac{1}{2} - 1] = n/H_n^{(1)}$$

and

$$\mu'_2(n) = [2H_n^{(1)}]^{-1}[(n+1)^2 - (n+1) + \tfrac{1}{6} - \tfrac{1}{6}] = \tfrac{1}{2}n(n+1)/H_n^{(1)}.$$

Thus the computation of the variance yields

$$\sigma^2(n) = \mu'_2(n) - [\mu'_1(n)]^2 = \tfrac{1}{2}n[n(H_n^{(1)} - 2) + H_n^{(1)}]/[H_n^{(1)}]^2.$$

Since $B_s(x) = x^s + O(x^{s-1})$ for $x \geqslant 1$, an asymptotic equivalent of $\mu'_s(n)$ is given by

$$\mu'_s(n) = [sH_n^{(1)}]^{-1}(n+1)^s + O((n+1)^{s-1}/H_n^{(1)})$$

$$= s^{-1}n^s/\ln(n) + O(n^{s-1}/\ln(n)).$$

Combining the above results, we have proved the following theorem.

THEOREM 3.2  Assuming that all cycles appearing in all permutations $\sigma \in \mathfrak{S}(\mathbb{N}_n)$ are equally likely, the probability $p_{n,l}$ that a cycle has a length $l$, $1 \leqslant l \leqslant n$, is

$$p_{n,l} = [lH_n^{(1)}]^{-1}$$

$$= [l(\ln(n) + \gamma)]^{-1} + O([nl(\ln(n))^2]^{-1})$$

The average length of a cycle appearing in a permutation $\sigma \in \mathfrak{S}(\mathbb{N}_n)$ is

$$\mu'_1(n) = n/H_n^{(1)}$$

$$= n/(\ln(n) + \gamma) + O([\ln(n)]^{-2}).$$

The variance is given by

$$\sigma^2(n) = n[n(H_n^{(1)} - 2) + H_n^{(1)}]/(2[H_n^{(1)}]^2)$$

$$= \frac{n(n+1)}{2(\ln(n) + \gamma)} - \frac{n(4n+1)}{4(\ln(n) + \gamma)^2} - \frac{n}{(\ln(n) + \gamma)^3} + O([\ln(n)]^{-2}). \quad \blacksquare$$

### 3.2.3 *A General Approach*

In the previous section we have computed some statistical results concerning the cycles in a permutation. This section is devoted to the presentation of a general approach to the solution of similar problems.

DEFINITION 3.3  Let $G \leqslant \mathfrak{S}(\mathbb{N}_n)$ be a permutation group. A permutation $\sigma \in G$ is said to be of *type* $\langle c_1(\sigma), c_2(\sigma), \ldots, c_n(\sigma) \rangle$ if its cycle notation contains exactly $c_l(\sigma)$ cycles of length $l$, $1 \leqslant l \leqslant n$. The *cycle indicator* $Z(G; t_1, \ldots, t_n)$ of $G$ is a polynomial in the variables $t_i$, $1 \leqslant i \leqslant n$, defined by

$$Z(G; t_1, \ldots, t_n) = \frac{1}{\text{card}(G)} \sum_{\sigma \in G} \prod_{1 \leqslant i \leqslant n} t_i^{c_i(\sigma)}.$$

For example, the symmetric group $\mathfrak{S}(\mathbb{N}_3)$ consisting of the permutations $1|2|3$; $1|2, 3$; $1, 2, 3$; $1, 2|3$; $1, 3|2$; $1, 3, 2$ of types $\langle 3, 0, 0 \rangle$, $\langle 1, 1, 0 \rangle$, $\langle 0, 0, 1 \rangle$, $\langle 1, 1, 0 \rangle$, $\langle 1, 1, 0 \rangle$, $\langle 0, 0, 1 \rangle$ respectively, has the cycle indicator

$$Z(\mathfrak{S}(\mathbb{N}_3); t_1, t_2, t_3) = \tfrac{1}{6}[t_1^3 + 3t_1 t_2 + 2t_3].$$

Note that $\sum_{1 \leqslant j \leqslant n} j c_j(\sigma) = n$, if $\sigma \in G$ has the type $\langle c_1(\sigma), \ldots, c_n(\sigma) \rangle$. Obviously, $Z(G; t_1, \ldots, t_n)$ can also be written in the form

$$Z(G; t_1, \ldots, t_n) = \frac{1}{\text{card}(G)} \sum_{\substack{c_1, \ldots, c_n \geqslant 0 \\ \sum_{1 \leqslant i \leqslant n} i c_i = n}} G_{c_1, \ldots, c_n} \prod_{1 \leqslant i \leqslant n} t_i^{c_i},$$

where $G_{c_1, c_2, \ldots, c_n} = \text{card}(\{\sigma \in G \mid \sigma \text{ is of type } \langle c_1, \ldots, c_n \rangle\})$. Generally, the cycle indicator plays an important part in many enumeration problems concerning graphs and their colouring ([18], [19], [93]). We shall now prove the following lemma.

LEMMA 3.1  Let $G \leqslant \mathfrak{S}(\mathbb{N}_n)$ be a permutation group.

(a) The total number of cycles appearing in all permutations $\sigma \in G$ is given by

$$\text{card}(G) \times \frac{\partial}{\partial t} Z(G; t, t, \ldots, t)|_{t=1}.$$

(b) The number of all cycles of length $l$ appearing in all permutations $\sigma \in G$ is given by

$$\text{card}(G) \times \frac{\partial}{\partial t} Z(G; 1, 1, \ldots, 1, t, 1, \ldots, 1)|_{t=1}.$$

$$\nearrow$$
$(l + 1)$-th argument

(c) The number of all permutations $\sigma \in G$ with $k$ cycles is given by

$$\text{card}(G) \times \langle t^k \rangle Z(G; t, t, \ldots, t).$$

(d) The number of all permutations $\sigma \in G$ with $k$ cycles of length $l$ is given by

$$\text{card}(G) \times \langle t^k \rangle Z(G; 1, 1, \ldots, 1, t, 1, \ldots, 1)$$

$$\nearrow$$
$(l + 1)$-th argument

*Proof*  Let $\sigma \in G$ be of type $\langle c_1(\sigma), \ldots, c_n(\sigma) \rangle$.

(a) Evidently, $\sigma$ has $\sum_{1 \leqslant i \leqslant n} c_i(\sigma)$ cycles. Thus the total number of cycles appearing in all permutations $\sigma \in G$ is given by $\sum_{\sigma \in G} \sum_{1 \leqslant i \leqslant n} c_i(\sigma)$. On the other hand, we have

$$\text{card}(G) \times \frac{\partial}{\partial t} Z(G; t, \ldots, t)|_{t=1} = \frac{\partial}{\partial t} \sum_{\sigma \in G} t^{\sum_{1 \leqslant i \leqslant n} c_i(\sigma)}|_{t=1}$$

$$= \sum_{\sigma \in G} \sum_{1 \leqslant i \leqslant n} c_i(\sigma).$$

This proves part (a).

(b) Obviously, the number of all cycles of length $l$ appearing in all permutations $\sigma \in G$ is given by $\sum_{\sigma \in G} c_l(\sigma)$. Since

$$\text{card}(G) \times \frac{\partial}{\partial t} Z(G; 1, \ldots, 1, t, 1, \ldots, 1)|_{t=1} = \frac{\partial}{\partial t} \sum_{\sigma \in G} t^{c_l(\sigma)}|_{t=1}$$

$(l+1)$-th argument $\qquad = \sum_{\sigma \in G} c_l(\sigma)$

we have proved part (b).

Similar arguments yield the results given in parts (c) and (d) of Lemma 3.1. ∎

We will apply Lemma 3.1 to the special case $G = \mathfrak{S}(\mathbb{N}_n)$. It is not hard to see that the number $\mathfrak{S}(\mathbb{N}_n)_{c_1,\ldots,c_n}$ of all permutations of type $\langle c_1, \ldots, c_n \rangle$ is equal to $n! \prod_{1 \leqslant i \leqslant n} (i^{c_i} c_i!)^{-1}$ (see Exercise 3.2). Therefore,

$$Z(\mathfrak{S}(\mathbb{N}_n); t_1, \ldots, t_n) = \sum_{\substack{c_1,\ldots,c_n \geqslant 0 \\ \sum_{1 \leqslant j \leqslant n} j c_j = n}} \prod_{1 \leqslant i \leqslant n} \frac{1}{c_i!} \left( \frac{t_i}{i} \right)^{c_i}.$$

The formal ordinary generating function $f_{\mathfrak{S}(\mathbb{N}_n)}(u, t_1, t_2, \ldots)$ of $Z(\mathfrak{S}(\mathbb{N}_n); t_1, \ldots, t_n)$ can be computed as follows:

$$f_{\mathfrak{S}(\mathbb{N}_n)}(u, t_1, t_2, \ldots) := \sum_{n \geqslant 0} u^n Z(\mathfrak{S}(\mathbb{N}_n); t_1, \ldots, t_n)$$

$$= \sum_{n \geqslant 0} u^n \sum_{\substack{c_1,\ldots,c_n \geqslant 0 \\ \sum_{1 \leqslant j \leqslant n} j c_j = n}} \prod_{1 \leqslant i \leqslant n} \frac{1}{c_i!} \left( \frac{t_i}{i} \right)^{c_i}$$

$$= \prod_{i \geqslant 1} \sum_{c_i \geqslant 0} \frac{1}{c_i!} \left( \frac{u^i t_i}{i} \right)^{c_i}$$

$$= \exp\left( \sum_{i \geqslant 1} \frac{1}{i} u^i t_i \right).$$

Using (B11), we have

$$f_{\mathfrak{S}(\mathbb{N}_n)}(u, t, t, \ldots) = \exp\left( t \sum_{i \geqslant 1} \frac{1}{i} u^i \right)$$

$$= \exp(-t \ln(1 - u))$$

$$= (1 - u)^{-t}$$

$$= 1 + \sum_{n \geqslant 1} \sum_{1 \leqslant k \leqslant n} u^n t^k \frac{1}{n!} (-1)^{n+k} S_n^{(k)}.$$

An application of Lemma 3.1(c) leads immediately to

$$\mathrm{card}(\mathfrak{S}(\mathbb{N}_n)) \times \langle u^n t^k \rangle f_{\mathfrak{S}(\mathbb{N}_n)}(u, t, t, \ldots) = (-1)^{n+k} S_n^{(k)}.$$

This result was proved in the first part of Theorem 3.1. Since

$$\frac{\partial}{\partial t} f_{\mathfrak{S}(\mathbb{N}_n)}(u, t, t, \ldots)|_{t=1} = \frac{\partial}{\partial t}(1 - u)^{-t}|_{t=1} = \frac{1}{1 - u} \ln\left(\frac{1}{1 - u}\right)$$

$$= \sum_{n \geqslant 1} u^n H_n^{(1)}$$

we obtain with part (a) of Lemma 3.1:

$$\mathrm{card}(\mathfrak{S}(\mathbb{N}_n)) \times \langle u^n \rangle \frac{\partial}{\partial t} f_{\mathfrak{S}(\mathbb{N}_n)}(u, t, t, \ldots)|_{t=1} = n! \, H_n^{(1)}.$$

This proves the second part of Theorem 3.1.
    Considering

$$f_{\mathfrak{S}(\mathbb{N}_n)}(u, 1, \ldots, 1, t, 1, \ldots),$$
$$\nearrow$$
$$(l + 1)\text{-th argument}$$

we find

$$f_{\mathfrak{S}(\mathbb{N}_n)}(u, 1, \ldots, 1, t, 1, \ldots) = \exp\left(\sum_{i \geqslant 1} \frac{1}{i} u^i + \frac{1}{l}(t - 1)u^l\right)$$

$$= \exp\left(-\ln(1 - u) + \frac{1}{l}(t - 1)u^l\right)$$

$$= \frac{1}{1 - u} \sum_{i \geqslant 0} \frac{1}{l^i i!} u^{li}(t - 1)^i$$

$$= \sum_{\kappa \geqslant 0} \sum_{0 \leqslant i \leqslant \kappa} \frac{1}{l^i i!}(t - 1)^i u^{li + \kappa - i}$$

$$= \sum_{n \geqslant 0} u^n \sum_{0 \leqslant i \leqslant \lfloor n/l \rfloor} \frac{1}{l^i i!}(t - 1)^i$$

$$= \sum_{n \geqslant 0} \sum_{k \geqslant 0} u^n t^k \sum_{0 \leqslant i \leqslant \lfloor n/l \rfloor} \frac{1}{l^i i!} \binom{i}{k}(-1)^{i-k}.$$

Hence, by part (d) of Lemma 3.1,

$$\text{card}(\mathfrak{S}(\mathbb{N}_n)) \times \langle u^n t^k \rangle f_{\mathfrak{S}(\mathbb{N}_n)}(u, 1, \ldots, 1, \underset{\nearrow}{t}, 1, \ldots)$$

$(l+1)$-th argument

$$= n! \sum_{0 \leqslant i \leqslant \lfloor n/l \rfloor} \frac{1}{l^i i!} \binom{i}{k}(-1)^{i-k}$$

$$= \frac{n!}{l^k k!} \sum_{0 \leqslant i \leqslant \lfloor n/l \rfloor - k} (-1)^i \frac{1}{l^i i!}.$$

The last expression gives the number of all permutations $\sigma \in \mathfrak{S}(\mathbb{N}_n)$ with $k$ cycles of length $l$. As a special case, the number of all permutations with no cycle of length one is given by $n! \sum_{0 \leqslant i \leqslant n} (-1)^i i!^{-1}$. Permutations of this kind are called *derangements*. Furthermore, the number of all permutations with exactly $k$ cycles of length one is $n! k!^{-1} \sum_{0 \leqslant i \leqslant n-k} (-1)^i i!^{-1}$.

Finally, let us compute the number of all cycles of length $l$ appearing in all permutations $\sigma \in \mathfrak{S}(\mathbb{N}_n)$. Since

$$\frac{\partial}{\partial t} f_{\mathfrak{S}(\mathbb{N}_n)}(u, 1, \ldots, 1, \underset{\nearrow}{t}, 1, \ldots)\Big|_{t=1} = \frac{\partial}{\partial t} \frac{1}{1-u} \exp\left(\frac{1}{l}(t-1)u^l\right)\Big|_{t=1}$$

$(l+1)$-th argument

$$= \frac{1}{l} \frac{u^l}{1-u}$$

$$= \frac{1}{l} \sum_{j \geqslant 0} u^{l+j},$$

we obtain with part (b) of Lemma 3.1,

$$\text{card}(\mathfrak{S}(\mathbb{N}_n)) \times \langle u^n \rangle \frac{\partial}{\partial t} f_{\mathfrak{S}(\mathbb{N}_n)}(u, 1, \ldots, 1, t, 1, \ldots)\Big|_{t=1} = \frac{n!}{l}$$

for $1 \leqslant l \leqslant n$. This again proves our result given in the previous section.

### 3.2.4 Average Number of Falls and Rises of a Permutation

DEFINITION 3.4 Let $\sigma = i_1, i_2, \ldots, i_n \in \mathfrak{S}(\mathbb{N}_n)$ be a permutation in linear notation. The pair $(i_r, i_{r+1})$, $r \in [1:n-1]$, is called a *fall* (*rise*), if $i_r > i_{r+1}$ ($i_r < i_{r+1}$).

For example, the permutation $\sigma = 2, 5, 6, 4, 8, 7, 3, 1, 9$ has the four falls $(6, 4)$, $(8, 7)$, $(7, 3)$, $(3, 1)$ and the four rises $(2, 5)$, $(5, 6)$, $(4, 8)$, $(1, 9)$. It is not hard to see that the sum of the falls and the rises appearing in a permutation $\sigma \in \mathfrak{S}(\mathbb{N}_n)$ is always equal to $n - 1$. Falls and rises are important in the analysis of sorting algorithms because they divide a given sequence of data into sorted segments.

Let us compute the number $a_{n,k}$ of all permutations $\sigma \in \mathfrak{S}(\mathbb{N}_n)$ with $k$ falls. For this purpose, consider a permutation $i_1, i_2, \ldots, i_{n-1} \in \mathfrak{S}(\mathbb{N}_{n-1})$ with the $k$

falls $(i_{r_j}, i_{r_j+1})$, $1 \leqslant j \leqslant k$. Inserting the new element $n$ in all possible places, such a permutation generates exactly $n$ permutations in $\mathfrak{S}(\mathbb{N}_n)$, namely $\sigma_j = i_1, \ldots, i_j, n, i_{j+1}, \ldots, i_{n-1}, 0 \leqslant j \leqslant n-1$, where $\sigma_0 = n, i_1, \ldots, i_{n-1}$ and $\sigma_{n-1} = i_1, \ldots, i_{n-1}, n$. Now we can make the following observations:

—$(k+1)$ of the generated permutations have $k$ falls. This case happens if $n$ is inserted between $i_{r_j}$ and $i_{r_j+1}$, $1 \leqslant j \leqslant k$, or after $i_{n-1}$.

—The remaining $(n-k-1)$ permutations have $(k+1)$ falls because a new fall is generated if $n$ is inserted between $i_\lambda$ and $i_{\lambda+1}$, where $\lambda \neq r_j$, $1 \leqslant j \leqslant k$, or before $i_1$.

Thus we find the recurrence

$$a_{n,k} = (k+1)a_{n-1,k} + (n-k)a_{n-1,k-1}$$

for $n, k \geqslant 1$. The initial conditions are $a_{n,0} = 1$ for $n \geqslant 0$ and $a_{0,k} = 0$ for $k \geqslant 1$, because only the identity permutation has zero falls and $\mathfrak{S}(\mathbb{N}_0) = \varnothing$. If we put $a_{n,k} := A(n, k+1)$, then the above recurrence becomes exactly the formula (B34) which defines the *Eulerian numbers* $A(n, k)$. Hence, assuming that each of the $n!$ permutations $\sigma \in \mathfrak{S}(\mathbb{N}_n)$ is equally likely, the probability that a permutation has $k$ falls is given by $p_{n,k} = A(n, k+1)/n!$.

We now consider the $s$-th moment about the origin. We obtain

$$\mu_s'(n) = \sum_{k \geqslant 0} k^s p_{n,k}$$

$$= \frac{1}{n!} \sum_{k \geqslant 1} (k-1)^s A(n, k)$$

$$= \frac{1}{n!} \sum_{0 \leqslant \lambda \leqslant s} \binom{s}{\lambda} (-1)^{s-\lambda} \sum_{k \geqslant 1} k^\lambda A(n, k).$$

Generally, we have the identity (see Exercise 3.8)

$$1 + \sum_{n \geqslant 1} \sum_{k \geqslant 1} A(n, k) \frac{t^n}{n!} x^k = \sum_{n \geqslant 0} A_n(x) \frac{t^n}{n!}$$

$$= (1-x)/[1 - x \exp(t(1-x))],$$

where $A_n(x)$ is the $n$-th Eulerian polynomial introduced in Example 1.1 (see Appendix B, 2.2). Replacing $t$ by $t/(x-1)$, we further obtain

$$1 + \sum_{n \geqslant 1} A_n(x) x^{-1} (x-1)^{-n} \frac{t^n}{n!} = \frac{1}{1 - \dfrac{\exp(t) - 1}{x - 1}}$$

$$= \sum_{k \geqslant 0} [\exp(t) - 1]^k/(x-1)^k.$$

Hence for $n \geqslant 1$

$$A_n(x) = x \sum_{1 \leqslant k \leqslant n} (x-1)^{n-k} c_{n,k},$$

where $c_{n,k}$ is the coefficient of $t^n/n!$ in the expansion of $(\exp(t)-1)^k$. Applying (B20), we immediately obtain $c_{n,k} = k! \, \mathscr{S}_n^{(k)}$, where $\mathscr{S}_n^{(k)}$ is the Stirling number of the second kind. Replacing $x(x-1)^{n-k}$ by $(x-1)^{n+1-k} + (x-1)^{n-k}$ and using (B18), we finally obtain

$$A_n(x) = \sum_{0 \leqslant k \leqslant n} k! \, \mathscr{S}_{n+1}^{(k+1)} (x-1)^{n-k},$$

a relation which was first proved in [46]. Now we differentiate this equation with respect to $x$:

$$\frac{1}{\lambda!} A_n^{(\lambda)}(x) = \sum_{0 \leqslant k \leqslant n} k! \binom{n-k}{\lambda} \mathscr{S}_{n+1}^{(k+1)} (x-1)^{n-k-\lambda}.$$

Taking $x = 1$, we have

$$A_n^{(\lambda)}(1) = \lambda! \, (n-\lambda)! \, \mathscr{S}_{n+1}^{(n-\lambda+1)},$$

because only the term for $k = n - \lambda$ in the sum appearing on the right-hand side of the above equation is unequal to zero. Since by (B17)

$$k^\lambda = \sum_{0 \leqslant m \leqslant \lambda} m! \binom{k}{m} \mathscr{S}_\lambda^{(m)},$$

we further obtain

$$\sum_{k \geqslant 1} k^\lambda A(n,k) = \sum_{0 \leqslant m \leqslant \lambda} m! \, \mathscr{S}_\lambda^{(m)} \sum_{k \geqslant 1} \binom{k}{m} A(n,k)$$

$$= \sum_{0 \leqslant m \leqslant \lambda} \mathscr{S}_\lambda^{(m)} A_n^{(m)}(1)$$

$$= \sum_{0 \leqslant m \leqslant \lambda} m! \, (n-m)! \, \mathscr{S}_{n+1}^{(n-m+1)} \mathscr{S}_\lambda^{(m)}$$

Returning to the above expression for $\mu_s'(n)$, we have shown that

$$\mu_s'(n) = \sum_{0 \leqslant \lambda \leqslant s} \binom{s}{\lambda} (-1)^{s-\lambda} \sum_{0 \leqslant m \leqslant \lambda} \binom{n}{m}^{-1} \mathscr{S}_{n+1}^{(n-m+1)} \mathscr{S}_\lambda^{(m)}.$$

As special cases, we obtain by (B19)

$$\mu_1'(n) = (n-1)/2 \quad \text{and} \quad \mu_2'(n) = (3n^2 - 5n + 4)/12.$$

Therefore, the variance is given by $\sigma^2(n) = \mu_2'(n) - \mu_1'^2(n) = (n+1)/12$.

Summarizing the above results, we have proved the following theorem.

THEOREM 3.3   Assuming that all permutations $\sigma \in \mathfrak{S}(\mathbb{N}_n)$ are equally likely, the probability $p_{n,k}$ that a permutation has $k$ falls, $0 \leqslant k \leqslant n-1$, is

$$p_{n,k} = A(n, k+1)/n!,$$

where $A(n, k)$ is a Eulerian number. The average number of falls appearing in a permutation $\sigma \in \mathfrak{S}(\mathbb{N}_n)$ is

$$\mu_1'(n) = \tfrac{1}{2}(n-1).$$

The variance is given by $\sigma^2(n) = \tfrac{1}{12}(n+1)$.   ■

### 3.2.5   Average Length of a Run

Let $\sigma = i_1, i_2, \ldots, i_n \in \mathfrak{S}(\mathbb{N}_n)$ be a permutation in linear notation. The falls appearing in $\sigma$ divide the sequence $i_1, i_2, \ldots, i_n$ into segments or *runs*. For example, the permutation $\sigma = 2, 5, 6, 4, 8, 7, 3, 1, 9$ has the five runs $2, 5, 6; 4, 8; 7; 3; 1, 9$. The number of elements in a run is its *length*.

Let us now compute the number $r_{n,p}$ of all runs of length $p$ appearing in all permutations $\sigma \in \mathfrak{S}(\mathbb{N}_n)$. For this purpose, we consider the number $\tilde{r}_{n,p,q}$ of all permutations $\sigma = i_1, i_2, \ldots, i_n \in \mathfrak{S}(\mathbb{N}_n)$ having the property that the element $i_q$ at position $q$ is the beginning of a run of length greater than or equal to $p$.

LEMMA 3.2

$$\tilde{r}_{n,p,q} = \begin{cases} n!\,(p + \delta_{q,1})/(p+1)! & \text{iff } q \leqslant n - p + 1 \\ 0 & \text{otherwise} \end{cases}$$

*Proof*

(a)  First we shall consider the case $q = 1$. We have to compute the number of all permutations $\sigma = i_1, i_2, \ldots, i_n \in \mathfrak{S}(\mathbb{N}_n)$ with

$$i_1 < i_2 < \cdots < i_p \gtrless i_{p+1} \gtrless i_{p+2} \gtrless \cdots \gtrless i_n.$$

The number of such permutations may be enumerated as follows:

—We have $i_\lambda \in \{i_1 + 1, \ldots, n\}$, $2 \leqslant \lambda \leqslant p$, for fixed $i_1 \in [1:n]$. Therefore, there are $\binom{n - i_1}{p - 1}$ ways to choose the elements $i_2, \ldots, i_p$ for fixed $i_1$. Thus there exist $\sum_{1 \leqslant i_1 \leqslant n} \binom{n - i_1}{p - 1}$ ways to arrange the elements $i_1, i_2, \ldots, i_p$.

—The number of ways to choose the remaining elements $i_{p+1}, \ldots, i_n$ is equal to the number of permutations in $\mathfrak{S}(\{1, \ldots, n\} \backslash \{i_1, \ldots, i_p\})$, namely $(n - p)!$.

Thus there are $(n - p)! \sum_{1 \leqslant i_1 \leqslant n} \binom{n - i_1}{p - 1}$ permutations in $\mathfrak{S}(\mathbb{N}_n)$ of the above form. Using the identity given in Exercise 1.3 with $R := n$, $w := p - 1$, $u := 0$ and $s := 0$, we obtain our result for $q = 1$.

(b) Let us now consider the case $q \geqslant 2$. We have to compute the number of all permutations $\sigma = i_1, i_2, \ldots, i_n \in \mathfrak{S}(\mathbb{N}_n)$ with

$$i_1 \gtreqless i_2 \gtreqless \cdots \gtreqless i_{q-1} > i_q < i_{q+1} < \cdots < i_{q+p-1} \gtreqless i_{q+p} \gtreqless \cdots \gtreqless i_n.$$

To obtain the number of such permutations, we compute the following contributions:

—We have $i_q \in \{1, \ldots, i_{q-1} - 1\}$ for fixed $i_{q-1} \in [1:n]$. Therefore,

$$i_\lambda \in \{i_q + 1, \ldots, n\} \backslash \{i_{q-1}\} \qquad q + 1 \leqslant \lambda \leqslant q + p - 1,$$

for fixed $i_{q-1}$ and $i_q$. Thus there are $\binom{n - i_q - 1}{p - 1}$ ways to choose the elements $i_{q+1}, \ldots, i_{q+p-1}$ for fixed $i_{q-1}$ and $i_q$. Hence we have

$$\sum_{1 \leqslant i_{q-1} \leqslant n} \sum_{1 \leqslant i_q \leqslant i_{q-1} - 1} \binom{n - i_q - 1}{p - 1}$$

ways to arrange $i_{q-1}, i_q, \ldots, i_{q+p-1}$.

—The number of ways to choose the remaining elements $i_1, i_2, \ldots, i_{q-2}$, $i_{q+p}, \ldots, i_n$ is equal to the number of permutations in $\mathfrak{S}(\{1, \ldots, n\} \backslash \{i_{q-1}, i_q, \ldots, i_{q+p-1}\})$, namely $(n - p - 1)!$.

Thus there are

$$(n - p - 1)! \sum_{1 \leqslant i_{q-1} \leqslant n} \sum_{1 \leqslant i_q \leqslant i_{q-1} - 1} \binom{n - i_q - 1}{p - 1}$$

permutations in $\mathfrak{S}(\mathbb{N}_n)$ of the above form. It is easy to see that the double sum appearing in this expression is equal to the sum $\sum_{0 \leqslant k \leqslant n-2} (k + 1) \binom{k}{p - 1}$. Using Exercise 1.3, we obtain our result for $q \geqslant 2$. This completes the proof. ∎

We are now ready to show the following theorem.

THEOREM 3.4  The number $r_{n,p}$ of all runs of length $p$ appearing in all permutations $\sigma \in \mathfrak{S}(\mathbb{N}_n)$ is given by

$$r_{n,n} = 1$$

$$r_{n,p} = n! \left[ (n + 1) \frac{p^2 + p - 1}{(p + 2)!} - \frac{p^2 - p - 1}{(p + 1)!} \right] \qquad 1 \leqslant p \leqslant n - 1.$$

*Proof* Obviously, $\tilde{r}_{n,p,q} - \tilde{r}_{n,p+1,q}$ is the number of all permutations $\sigma = i_1, i_2, \ldots, i_n \in \mathfrak{S}(\mathbb{N}_n)$ such that the element $i_q$ at position $q$ is the beginning of a run of length $p$. Therefore, by Lemma 3.2,

$$r_{n,p} = \sum_{1 \leqslant q \leqslant n} \left[ \tilde{r}_{n,p,q} - \tilde{r}_{n,p+1,q} \right]$$

$$= \sum_{1 \leqslant q \leqslant n-p+1} \frac{n!\,(p + \delta_{q,1})}{(p+1)!} - \sum_{1 \leqslant q \leqslant n-p} \frac{n!\,(p + 1 + \delta_{q,1})}{(p+2)!}.$$

An elementary computation shows that this expression is identical to our desired result. ∎

Since the number of runs appearing in a permutation $\sigma \in \mathfrak{S}(\mathbb{N}_n)$ is one greater than the number of falls in $\sigma$, we obtain with Theorem 3.3 and Theorem 3.4 the following corollary.

COROLLARY   Assuming that all permutations $\sigma \in \mathfrak{S}(\mathbb{N}_n)$ are equally likely, the probability $p_{n,k}$ that a permutation has $k$ runs, $0 \leqslant k \leqslant n$, is $p_{n,k} = A(n,k)/n!$, where $A(n,k)$ is a Eulerian number. The average number of runs appearing in a permutation is $\mu_1'(n) = (n+1)/2$. The variance is given by $\sigma^2(n) = (n+1)/12$. The average number of runs of length $p$ in a permutation is

$$(n+1)\frac{p^2 + p - 1}{(p+2)!} - \frac{p^2 - p - 1}{(p+1)!}$$

for $1 \leqslant p \leqslant n-1$ and $n!^{-1}$ for $p = n$. ∎

Next we shall determine the average length of a run.

THEOREM 3.5   Assuming that all runs appearing in all permutations $\sigma \in \mathfrak{S}(\mathbb{N}_n)$ are equally likely, the probability $p_{n,k}$ that a run has the length $p$ is

$$p_{n,k} = \begin{cases} 2\dfrac{p^2 + p - 1}{(p+2)!} - \dfrac{2}{n+1}\dfrac{p^2 - p - 1}{(p+1)!} & \text{if } p \in [1:n-1] \\[3mm] \dfrac{2}{(n+1)!} & \text{if } p = n. \end{cases}$$

The average length of a run is $\mu_1'(n) = 2 + O(n^{-1})$. The variance is given by $\sigma^2(n) = 4e - 10 + O(n^{-1})$.

*Proof*   First we compute the number $R_n$ of all runs appearing in all permutations $\sigma \in \mathfrak{S}(\mathbb{N}_n)$. Using Lemma 3.2 and Theorem 3.4, this number is given by

$$R_n = \sum_{1 \leqslant p \leqslant n} r_{n,p} = \sum_{1 \leqslant p \leqslant n} \sum_{1 \leqslant q \leqslant n} \left[ \tilde{r}_{n,p,q} - \tilde{r}_{n,p+1,q} \right]$$

$$= \sum_{1 \leqslant q \leqslant n} \left[ \tilde{r}_{n,1,q} - \tilde{r}_{n,n+1,q} \right] = \tfrac{1}{2}(n+1)!.$$

Hence the desired probability $p_{n,k}$ is equal to $R_n^{-1} r_{n,p}$ which is equivalent to our proposition.

The $s$-th moment about the origin is

$$\mu'_s(n) = R_n^{-1} \sum_{1 \le p \le n} p^s r_{n,p}.$$

Using Lemma 3.2 and Theorem 3.4, this expression can be easily transformed into

$$\mu'_s(n) = \frac{2}{n+1} \sum_{1 \le p \le n} [p^s - (p-1)^s] \left[ \frac{p(n+1)}{(p+1)!} - \frac{p-1}{p!} \right].$$

We can now apply the identity given in (B21); we find

$$\sum_{1 \le p \le n} [p^s - (p-1)^s] \frac{p-1}{p!} \le \sum_{p \ge 1} \frac{p^{s+1}}{p!} = e \sum_{1 \le p \le s+1} \mathcal{S}_{s+1}^{(p)},$$

where the $\mathcal{S}_{s+1}^{(p)}$ are the Stirling numbers of the second kind. Therefore, we further obtain

$$\mu'_s(n) = 2 \sum_{1 \le p \le n} [p^s - (p-1)^s] \frac{p}{(p+1)!} + O(n^{-1}).$$

Since by (B56)

$$\begin{aligned}
\sum_{p \ge n+1} [p^s - (p-1)^s] \frac{p}{(p+1)!} &\le \sum_{p \ge n+1} \frac{p^s}{p!} \\
&= \frac{(n+1)^s}{(n+1)!} \sum_{p \ge 1} \frac{(n+p)^s(n+1)!}{(n+1)^s(n+p)!} \\
&\le \frac{(n+1)^s}{(n+1)!} \sum_{p \ge 1} \frac{p^s(n+1)!}{(n+p)!} \\
&\le \frac{(n+1)^s}{(n+1)!} \sum_{p \ge 1} \frac{p^s}{(n+2)^{p-1}} \\
&= \frac{(n+2)^{s+2}}{(n+1)(n+1)!} A_s\left(\frac{1}{n+2}\right) \\
&= O\left(\frac{(n+2)^s}{(n+1)!}\right) = O(e^n/n^{n-s+3/2}),
\end{aligned}$$

we immediately obtain

$$\mu'_s(n) = 2 \sum_{p \ge 1} [p^s - (p-1)^s] \frac{p}{(p+1)!} + O(n^{-1}).$$

Thus the value of $\mu'_s(n)$ tends to a constant for large $n$. Using (B21), we find finally

$$\mu'_s(n) = 2(-1)^s[1 - 2^s] + 2e \sum_{1 \le i \le s-1} \sum_{1 \le p \le i+1} \binom{s}{i}$$
$$\times (-1)^{s-i}[1 - 2^{s-i}][\mathcal{S}_{i+1}^{(p)} - \mathcal{S}_i^{(p)}] + O(n^{-1}).$$

As special cases, we have by (B19) $\mu'_1(n) = 2 + O(n^{-1})$ and $\mu'_2(n) = 4e - 6 + O(n^{-1})$.

This establishes Theorem 3.5. ∎

### 3.2.6 Average Length of the k-th Run

In this section we shall study the average length $l_k$ of the $k$-th run in a permutation $\sigma \in \mathfrak{S}(\mathbb{N}_n)$. These numbers play an important part in the theory of replacement-selection sorting. We restrict our considerations to the study of the length of the $k$-th run in a random infinite sequence of distinct numbers $i_1, i_2, i_3, \ldots$; in other words, we assume that each of the $n!$ possible relative orderings of the first $n$ elements $i_1, i_2, \ldots, i_n$ is equally likely. Therefore, our results are valid for permutations $\sigma \in \mathfrak{S}(\mathbb{N}_n)$, where $n$ tends to infinity.

Let $w_{k,p}$ be the probability that the first $k$ runs have a total length greater than or equal to $p$. Obviously, $w_{k,p}$ is the number of all permutations $\sigma \in \mathfrak{S}(\mathbb{N}_p)$ with less than or equal to $k$ runs divided by $p!$ Hence by the corollary following Theorem 3.4

$$w_{k,p} = \frac{1}{p!} \sum_{1 \leqslant i \leqslant k} A(p, i),$$

where the $A(p, k)$ are the Eulerian numbers. Since $w_{k,p} - w_{k,p+1}$ is the probability that the first $k$ runs have a total length $p$, we obtain for the average total length of the first $k$ runs

$$\sum_{1 \leqslant i \leqslant k} l_i = \sum_{p \geqslant 1} p[w_{k,p} - w_{k,p+1}] = \sum_{p \geqslant 1} w_{k,p}.$$

Hence

$$l_k = \sum_{1 \leqslant i \leqslant k} l_i - \sum_{1 \leqslant i \leqslant k-1} l_i$$

$$= \sum_{p \geqslant 1} [w_{k,p} - w_{k-1,p}]$$

$$= \sum_{p \geqslant 1} \frac{1}{p!} A(p, k).$$

Using (B33), we immediately find

$$l_k = \langle x^k \rangle \left( \frac{(1-x)x}{\exp(x-1) - x} - x \right).$$

An explicit expression of $l_k$ can be derived by (B35) as follows:

$$l_k = \sum_{p \geqslant 1} \frac{1}{p!} A(p, k)$$

$$= \sum_{p \geqslant 1} \frac{1}{p!} \sum_{0 \leqslant j \leqslant k} (-1)^j (k-j)^p \binom{p+1}{j}$$

$$= \sum_{p \geqslant 1} \sum_{0 \leqslant j \leqslant k} (-1)^{k-j} j^p \binom{p+1}{k-j} \frac{1}{p!}$$

$$= \sum_{0 \leqslant j \leqslant k} (-1)^{k-j} \sum_{p \geqslant 1} \left[ \binom{p}{k-j} \frac{j^p}{p!} + \binom{p}{k-j-1} \frac{j^p}{p!} \right]$$

$$= \sum_{0 \leqslant j \leqslant k} (-1)^{k-j} \left[ \frac{1}{(k-j)!} \sum_{p \geqslant k-j} \frac{j^p}{(p-k+j)!} \right.$$

$$\left. + \frac{1}{(k-j-1)!} \sum_{p \geqslant k-j-1} \frac{j^p}{(p-k+j+1)!} \right]$$

$$= \sum_{0 \leqslant j \leqslant k} (-1)^{k-j} \left[ \frac{j^{k-j}}{(k-j)!} \sum_{p \geqslant 0} \frac{j^p}{p!} \right.$$

$$\left. + \frac{j^{k-j-1}}{(k-j-1)!} \sum_{p \geqslant 0} \frac{j^p}{p!} \right]$$

$$= k \sum_{0 \leqslant j \leqslant k} e^j (-1)^{k-j} \frac{j^{k-j-1}}{(k-j)!}.$$

We have proved the following theorem.

THEOREM 3.6   Assuming that all $n!$ permutations in $\mathfrak{S}(\mathbb{N}_n)$ are equally likely, the average length $l_k$ of the $k$-th run in $\sigma \in \mathfrak{S}(\mathbb{N}_n)$ is for large $n$ given by

$$l_k = k \sum_{0 \leqslant j \leqslant k} e^j (-1)^{k-j} \frac{j^{k-j-1}}{(k-j)!}.$$

As special values, we obtain $l_1 = e - 1 = 1.7183$, $l_2 = e^2 - 2e = 1.9525$, and $l_3 = e^3 - 3e^2 + \frac{3}{2}e = 1.9958$. ∎

Using techniques given in section 4.4.1, we can show that $l_k$ tends to the limiting value of two for $k \to \infty$ (see Exercise 4.5). The sequence $l_k$ is not monotone; for example, $l_4 > 2$, $l_7 < 2$, $l_{10} > 2$, $l_{12} < 2$. For further analysis see [47], [55].

### 3.2.7 Average Number of Inversions of a Permutation

DEFINITION 3.5   Let $\sigma = i_1, i_2, \ldots, i_n \in \mathfrak{S}(\mathbb{N}_n)$ be a permutation in linear notation. The pair $(i_r, i_s)$, $r, s \in [1:n]$, is called an *inversion*, if $r < s$ and $i_r > i_s$.

For example, the permutation $\sigma = 2, 5, 6, 4, 8, 7, 3, 1, 9$ has 15 inversions $(2, 1)$, $(5, 4)$, $(5, 3)$, $(5, 1)$, $(6, 4)$, $(6, 3)$, $(6, 1)$, $(4, 3)$, $(4, 1)$, $(8, 7)$, $(8, 3)$, $(8, 1)$, $(7, 3)$, $(7, 1)$, $(3, 1)$. Inversions are important in the analysis of sorting algorithms, because each inversion is a pair of elements that is 'out of sort'. Obviously, only the identity permutation $\sigma_0$ has no inversions. The maximum number of inversions appearing in any permutation $\sigma \in \mathfrak{S}(\mathbb{N}_n)$ is $\binom{n}{2}$; this is the case if $\sigma = n, n-1, \ldots, 2, 1$.

DEFINITION 3.6   Let $\sigma = i_1, i_2, \ldots, i_n \in \mathfrak{S}(\mathbb{N}_n)$ be a permutation in linear notation and let $I(\sigma)$ be the set of inversions in $\sigma$. The sequence $j_1, j_2, \ldots, j_n$ with $j_\lambda = \text{card}(\{(i_s, \lambda) \mid (i_s, \lambda) \in I(\sigma) \wedge s \in [1:n]\})$, $1 \leqslant \lambda \leqslant n$, is called the *inversion table* of $\sigma$.

Thus the above permutation $\sigma \in \mathfrak{S}(\mathbb{N}_9)$ has the inversion table 7, 0, 5, 2, 0, 0, 1, 0, 0. By definition, we have always $0 \leqslant j_\lambda \leqslant n - \lambda$, $1 \leqslant \lambda \leqslant n$, and $\text{card}(I(\sigma)) = \sum_{1 \leqslant \lambda \leqslant n} j_\lambda$.

Generally, an inversion table uniquely describes the corresponding permutation; successively, we have to find the relative placement of the elements $n, n-1, \ldots, 2, 1$ in this order. This can be done as follows:

(a) Write down the number $n$.
(b) Consider successively the numbers $j_{n-1}, j_{n-2}, \ldots, j_1$ appearing in the inversion table. The number $\lambda$ follows $j_\lambda$ of the numbers already written down.

For example, consider the above inversion table 7, 0, 5, 2, 0, 0, 1, 0, 0. The algorithm produces the following sequences: 9 then 8, 9 (since $j_8 = 0$), then 8, 7, 9 (since $j_7 = 1$), then 6, 8, 7, 9 (since $j_6 = 0$), then 5, 6, 8, 7, 9 (since $j_5 = 0$), then 5, 6, 4, 8, 7, 9 (since $j_4 = 2$), etc. Inserting 3, 2 and 1 in an analogous way, we get our original permutation. It is often easier to solve a problem stated in terms of inversion tables than the equivalent problem stated in terms of permutations, because the elements of the inversion table are completely independent while the elements of the permutation must be mutually disjoint.

Next, we shall compute the generating function of the numbers $I_{n,k}$ of all permutations $\sigma \in \mathfrak{S}(\mathbb{N}_n)$ with $k$ inversions.

THEOREM 3.7   Let $I_n(z) = \sum_{k \geqslant 0} I_{n,k} z^k$ be the generating function of the numbers $I_{n,k}$ of all permutations $\sigma \in \mathfrak{S}(\mathbb{N}_n)$ with $k$ inversions. We have

$$I_n(z) = (1 - z)^{-n} \prod_{1 \leqslant j \leqslant n} (1 - z^j)$$

*Proof*   Let $\sigma = i_1, i_2, \ldots, i_n$ be a permutation in $\mathfrak{S}(\mathbb{N}_n)$ with $k$ inversions and let $j_1, j_2, \ldots, j_n$ be the corresponding inversion table. Since $\sum_{1 \leqslant \lambda \leqslant n} j_\lambda = k$ and $0 \leqslant j_\lambda \leqslant n - \lambda$, $1 \leqslant \lambda \leqslant n$, we immediately obtain

$$I_{n,k} = \sum_{\substack{0 \leqslant j_1 \leqslant n-1 \\ j_1 + j_2 + \cdots + j_n = k}} \sum_{0 \leqslant j_2 \leqslant n-2} \cdots \sum_{0 \leqslant j_{n-1} \leqslant 1} \sum_{0 \leqslant j_n \leqslant 0} 1$$

$$= \sum_{0 \leqslant j_1 \leqslant n-1} \left[ \sum_{\substack{0 \leqslant j_2 \leqslant n-2 \\ j_2 + \cdots + j_n = k - j_1}} \cdots \sum_{0 \leqslant j_n \leqslant 0} 1 \right] = \sum_{0 \leqslant j_1 \leqslant n-1} I_{n-1, k-j_1}.$$

Hence

$$I_n(z) = \sum_{k \geqslant 0} z^k \sum_{0 \leqslant j_1 \leqslant n-1} I_{n-1,k-j_1}$$

$$= \sum_{0 \leqslant j_1 \leqslant n-1} \sum_{k \geqslant 0} z^{k+j_1} I_{n-1,k}$$

$$= \sum_{0 \leqslant j_1 \leqslant n-1} z^{j_1} \sum_{k \geqslant 0} I_{n-1,k} z^k = \frac{1 - z^n}{1 - z} I_{n-1}(z).$$

Solving this recurrence, we obtain our result with $I_1(z) = 1$. ■

COROLLARY  The numbers $I_{n,k}$ satisfy the following relations:

(a) $I_{n,k} = I_{n,k-1} + I_{n-1,k}$  for $k < n$.

(b) $\displaystyle\sum_{k \geqslant 0} I_{n,k} = n!$.

(c) $\displaystyle\sum_{k \geqslant 0} (-1)^k I_{n,k} = 0$  for $n > 1$.

(d) $I_{n,k} = I_{n,\binom{n}{2} - k}$.

*Proof*  Using the above recurrence $I_n(z) = (1 - z)^{-1}(1 - z^n)I_{n-1}(z)$, (a), (b), (c), and (d) can be easily proved: (a) is implied by the recurrence itself, (b) and (c) corresponds to $I_n(1)$ and $I_n(-1)$, and (c) follows from $I_n(z) = z^{\binom{n}{2}} I_n(z^{-1})$. ■

An explicit expression for $I_{n,k}$ can be easily derived by an application of Euler's pentagonal theorem ([3]) to the function $I_n(z)$ given in Theorem 3.7.

Let us now consider the average number of inversions appearing in a permutation $\sigma \in \mathfrak{S}(\mathbb{N}_n)$.

THEOREM 3.8  Assuming that all $n!$ permutations $\sigma \in \mathfrak{S}(\mathbb{N}_n)$ are equally likely, the average number of inversions appearing in a permutation is $n(n-1)/4$. The variance is given by $\sigma^2(n) = n(n-1)(2n+5)/72$.

*Proof*  Let $p_{n,k}$ be the probability that a permutation has $k$ inversions and let $f_n(z) = \sum_{k \geqslant 0} p_{n,k} z^k$ be the generating function of the numbers $p_{n,k}$. Obviously, $f_n(z) = n!^{-1} I_n(z)$. Since $I_n(z) = z^{\binom{n}{2}} I_n(z^{-1})$, we obtain

$$\frac{d}{dz} I_n(z) = \binom{n}{2} z^{\binom{n}{2}-1} I_n(z^{-1}) - z^{\binom{n}{2}-2} \frac{d}{dz} I_n(z^{-1}).$$

Choosing $z = 1$, this equation implies

$$I_n'(z) = \frac{1}{2}\binom{n}{2} I_n(1) = \frac{1}{2}\binom{n}{2} n!.$$

Hence

$$f'_n(1) = \frac{1}{2}\binom{n}{2}.$$

An inspection of Theorem 3.7 shows that $f_n(z) = \prod_{1 \leqslant i \leqslant n} g_i(z)$, where $g_i(z) = \sum_{0 \leqslant j < i} z^j/i$. Now an elementary computation leads to

$$\frac{d^2}{dz^2} f_n(z) = \left(\frac{d}{dz} f_n(z)\right) \sum_{1 \leqslant \lambda \leqslant n} g_\lambda^{-1}(z) \frac{d}{dz} g_\lambda(z)$$

$$+ f_n(z) \sum_{1 \leqslant \lambda \leqslant n} g_\lambda^{-2}(z) \left[ g_\lambda(z) \frac{d^2}{dz^2} g_\lambda(z) - \left(\frac{d}{dz} g_\lambda(z)\right)^2 \right].$$

Choosing $z = 1$, we obtain further with $g_\lambda(1) = 1$, $1 \leqslant \lambda \leqslant n$,

$$f''_n(1) = f'_n(1) \sum_{1 \leqslant \lambda \leqslant n} g'_\lambda(1) + f_n(1) \sum_{1 \leqslant \lambda \leqslant n} [g''_\lambda(1) - (g'_\lambda(1))^2].$$

Since

$$g'_\lambda(1) = \lambda^{-1} \sum_{1 \leqslant j < \lambda} j = (\lambda - 1)/2$$

and

$$g''_\lambda(1) = \lambda^{-1} \sum_{1 \leqslant j < \lambda} j(j-1) = (\lambda - 1)(\lambda - 2)/3,$$

we find finally

$$f''_n(1) = \frac{1}{4}\binom{n}{2} \sum_{1 \leqslant \lambda \leqslant n} (\lambda - 1) + \frac{1}{12} \sum_{1 \leqslant \lambda \leqslant n} (\lambda - 1)(\lambda - 5)$$

$$= \tfrac{1}{144} n(n-1)(n-2)(9n+13).$$

Now an application of (A5) and (A7) yields

$$\mu'_1(n) = f'_n(1) = \tfrac{1}{4} n(n-1)$$

$$\sigma^2(n) = f''_n(1) + f'_n(1) - [f'_n(1)]^2 = \tfrac{1}{72} n(n-1)(2n+5).$$

This completes the proof of Theorem 3.8. ∎

In this section we have investigated the average behaviour of some important characteristic quantities of permutations which appear in the analysis of sorting and searching algorithms. Some further parameters and classes of permutations are considered in the Exercises.

## Exercises

**3.1** Show that the $s$-th moment about the origin of the real random variable $x$ which describes the distribution of all permutations $\sigma \in \mathfrak{S}(\mathbb{N}_n)$ with $k$ cycles (Theorem 3.1) is asymptotically given by $\ln^s(n) + O(\ln^{s-1}(n))$.

**3.2** Show that the number $\mathfrak{S}(\mathbb{N}_n)_{c_1,c_2,\ldots,c_n}$ of permutations of type $\langle c_1, c_2, \ldots, c_n \rangle$ is equal to

$$n! \prod_{1 \leqslant i \leqslant n} (i^{c_i} c_i!)^{-1}.$$

**3.3** In section 3.2.3 it is shown that the number of all permutations $\sigma \in \mathfrak{S}(\mathbb{N}_n)$ with $k$ cycles of length $l$ is given by

$$n! \, l^{-k} (k!)^{-1} \sum_{0 \leqslant i \leqslant \lfloor n/l \rfloor - k} (-1)^i l^{-i}/i!.$$

Assume that each of the $n!$ permutations in $\mathfrak{S}(\mathbb{N}_n)$ is equally likely. Show that the average number of cycles of length $l$ appearing in a permutation $\sigma \in \mathfrak{S}(\mathbb{N}_n)$ is $l^{-1}$; the variance is given by $l^{-1}$.

**3.4** Show that the number of derangements is equal to $e^{-1}n!$ rounded to the nearest integer ($n \geqslant 1$).

**3.5** Let $G \leqslant \mathfrak{S}(\mathbb{N}_n)$ be a permutation group with the cycle indicator $Z(G; t_1, \ldots, t_n)$.

(a) Show that the number of permutations $\sigma \in G$ with a shortest cycle of length $l$ is given by

$$\text{card}(G) \times \langle u^n \rangle (f_G(u, 0, \ldots, 1, 1, \ldots) - f_G(u, 0, \ldots, 0, 0, 1, \ldots)),$$

$$\underset{(l+1)\text{-th argument}}{\underbrace{\qquad\qquad\qquad\qquad}}$$

where $f_G(u, t_1, t_2, \ldots)$ is the formal ordinary generating function of $Z(G; t_1, \ldots, t_n)$.

(b) Assume that all permutations in $G$ are equally likely. Show that the average length of the shortest cycle is

$$\langle u^n \rangle \sum_{1 \leqslant l \leqslant n} f_G(u, 0, \ldots, 0, 1, 1, \ldots)$$

$$\underset{(l+1)\text{-argument}}{\uparrow}$$

(c) Consider the symmetric group $G = \mathfrak{S}(\mathbb{N}_n)$. Show that the average length of the shortest cycle is asymptotically given by $e^{-\gamma} \ln(n) + O(1)$, where $\gamma$ is Euler's constant. (Use the methods described in section 4.4.1.)

**3.6** This exercise gives a generalization of the concept of permutations suggested by the matrix notation given in 3.2. The $n \times n$-matrix $T$ is called a $k$-*permutation* when all rows and all columns have exactly $k$ entries 1 and $(n - k)$ entries 0. Choosing $k = 1$, $T$ is a permutation matrix in the sense of 3.2.

(a) Show that the number of all $k$-permutations of $\mathbb{N}_n$ is given by

$$P(n, k) = \langle x_1^k x_2^k \ldots x_n^k y_1^k y_2^k \ldots y_n^k \rangle \prod_{1 \leqslant i,j \leqslant n} (1 + x_i y_j).$$

(b) Deduce from (a)

(b1) $P(n, 1) = n!$.

(b2) $P(n, 2) = \sum_{\lambda \geqslant 0} (-1)^\lambda (2n - 2\lambda)! \, \lambda! \binom{n}{\lambda}^2 2^{\lambda - 2n}$.

(c) Show that

$$\sum_{n \geqslant 0} P(n, 2) z^n n!^{-2} = (1 - z)^{-1/2} \exp(-z/2).$$

(For further information see [26].)

**3.7** Show that the exponential generating function of the numbers $a_n(S)$ of all permutations $\sigma \in \mathfrak{S}(\mathbb{N}_n)$ such that all cycle lengths belong to a set $S \subseteq \mathbb{N}$ is given by

$$\sum_{n \geq 0} a_n(S) \frac{z^n}{n!} = \exp\left(\sum_{k \in S} \frac{z^k}{k}\right).$$

**3.8** (a) Start with the recurrence $A(n, k) = kA(n - 1, k) + (n - k + 1)A(n - 1, k - 1)$, where $A(0, k) = \delta_{0,k}$ and $A(n, 0) = \delta_{0,n}$ and show that the Eulerian numbers $A(n, k)$ have the following double generating function:

$$1 + \sum_{n \geq 1} \sum_{k \geq 1} A(n, k) \frac{t^n}{n!} x^k = (1 - x)[1 - x \exp(t(1 - x))]^{-1}.$$

(b) Use (a) to derive the explicit expression (convention: $0^0 = 1$)

$$A(n, k) = \sum_{0 \leq j \leq k} (-1)^j \binom{n + 1}{j}(k - j)^n.$$

(c) Show that $\sum_{1 \leq k \leq n} kA(n, k) = (n + 1)!/2$.

**3.9** Consider the set of all sequences $b_1, b_2, \ldots, b_n$ with $b_i \in \{0, 1\}$, $1 \leq i \leq n$. The pair $(b_r, b_{r+1})$, $r \in [1 : n - 1]$ is a fall, if $b_r > b_{r+1}$. Assume that all sequences of length $n$ are equally likely. Compute the probability that a sequence has $k$ falls. Show that the average number of falls appearing in a sequence of length $n$ is $(n - 1)/4$. The variance is $(n + 1)/16$.

**3.10** Let $\sigma \in \mathfrak{S}(\mathbb{N}_n)$ be a permutation and $I(\sigma) \subseteq \mathfrak{P}(\mathbb{N}_n)$ be defined by

$$I(\sigma) = \{I \subseteq \mathbb{N}_n | \ (\exists i, j \in I) \ (i \leq j \wedge \sigma(i) \leq \sigma(j))\}.$$

The elements of $I \in I(\sigma)$ are called an *increasing subsequence* of $\sigma$. For example, if $\sigma = 2, 4, 3, 1, 5 \in \mathfrak{S}(\mathbb{N}_5)$, then $I(\sigma) = \{\varnothing, \{1\}, \{2\}, \{3\}, \{4\}, \{5\}, \{1,2\}, \{1,3\}, \{1,5\}, \{2,5\}, \{3,5\}, \{1,2,5\}, \{1,3,5\}\}$. (Increasing subsequences play a part in the analysis of the computation time of a special knapsack algorithm ([81]).)

(a) Show that $\text{MIN}_{\sigma \in \mathfrak{S}(\mathbb{N}_n)}(\text{card}(I(\sigma))) = n + 1$.

(b) Show that $\text{MAX}_{\sigma \in \mathfrak{S}(\mathbb{N}_n)}(\text{card}(I(\sigma))) = 2^n$.

(c) Assume that each of the $n!$ permutations in $\mathfrak{S}(\mathbb{N}_n)$ is equally likely. Show that the average number $\mathbf{I}(n)$ of increasing subsequences appearing in a permutation $\sigma \in \mathfrak{S}(\mathbb{N}_n)$ is given by

$$\mathbf{I}(n) = \sum_{0 \leq k \leq n} \binom{n}{k} \frac{1}{k!}.$$

(d) Show that $\mathbf{I}(n) = L_n^{(0)}(-1)$, where $L_n^{(\alpha)}(x)$ is the *n-th generalized Laguerre polynomial*. (*Hint*: Use (B87) with $\alpha = 0$ and $x = -1$.)
(For further information about the asymptotic behaviour of $\mathbf{I}(n)$ and the computation of the second moment about the origin see [82].)

**3.11** Let $\sigma = i_1, i_2, \ldots, i_n \in \mathfrak{S}(\mathbb{N}_n)$ be a permutation in linear notation. The pair $(i_r, i_{r+1})$ is a *succession* of $\sigma$, if $i_{r+1} = i_r + 1$, $0 \leq r \leq n - 1$.

(a) Show that the number of permutations in $\mathfrak{S}(\mathbb{N}_n)$ with exactly $k$ successions is given by

$$R(n, k) = \binom{n - 1}{k}[D_{n-k} + D_{n-k-1}],$$

where $D_n$ is the number of derangements in $\mathfrak{S}(\mathbb{N}_n)$ computed at the end of section 3.2.3.

(b) Assume that all permutations in $\mathfrak{S}(\mathbb{N}_n)$ are equally likely. Prove that a permutation $\sigma \in \mathfrak{S}(\mathbb{N}_n)$ has exactly one succession on the average for large $n$. (See also [105], [113].)

**3.12** Let $\sigma = i_1, i_2, \ldots, i_n$ be a permutation in $\mathfrak{S}(\mathbb{N}_n)$ and let $i_0 := 0$ and $i_{n+1} := 0$. The element $i_\lambda \in [1:n]$ is called a *positive peak* (*negative peak*), if $i_{\lambda-1} < i_\lambda > i_{\lambda+1}$ ($i_{\lambda-1} > i_\lambda < i_{\lambda+1}$), $1 \leqslant \lambda \leqslant n$. The element $i_\lambda$ is said to be a *double rise* (*double fall*), if $i_{\lambda-1} < i_\lambda < i_{\lambda+1}$ ($i_{\lambda-1} > i_\lambda > i_{\lambda+1}$), $1 \leqslant \lambda \leqslant n$. Let $P_+(\sigma)$ ($P_-(\sigma)$, $DR(\sigma)$, $DF(\sigma)$) be the set of all positive peaks (negative peaks, double rises, double falls) appearing in $\sigma$. The quadruple $(P_+(\sigma), P_-(\sigma), DR(\sigma), DF(\sigma))$ is the *pattern* of the permutation $\sigma$. Thus $\sigma = 2, 5, 6, 4, 8, 7, 3, 1, 9$ has the pattern $(\{6, 8, 9\}, \{1, 4\}, \{2, 5\}, \{3, 7\})$.

(a) Show that the quadruple $(A, B, C, D)$ is the pattern of a permutation $\sigma \in \mathfrak{S}(\mathbb{N}_n)$ if and only if the following conditions are satisfied:
  (1) The sets $A, B, C, D$ form a partition of $\mathbb{N}_n$.
  (2) $n \in A$.
  (3) $\mathrm{Card}(A) = 1 + \mathrm{card}(B)$.
  (4) If $b_1, \ldots, b_k$ ($a_1, \ldots, a_k, n$) are the elements of $B \neq \varnothing$ ($A$) in ascending order, then
   $b_i < a_i$, $1 \leqslant i \leqslant k$.

(b) Let $(A, B, C, D)$ be a quadruple of sets satisfying the conditions (1)–(4) of part (a). Show that the number of permutations with pattern $(A, B, C, D)$ is given by the product $\prod_{1 \leqslant i \leqslant n} \gamma(i)$, where $\gamma: \mathbb{N}_n \to \mathbb{N}$ is recursively defined by $\gamma(1) = 1$ and

$$\gamma(i+1) = \begin{cases} \gamma(i) - 1 & \text{if } i \in A \\ \gamma(i) + 1 & \text{if } i \in B \\ \gamma(i) & \text{if } i \in C \cup D. \end{cases}$$

(Thus there are $1 \cdot 2 \cdot 2 \cdot 2 \cdot 3 \cdot 3 \cdot 2 \cdot 2 \cdot 1 = 288$ permutations in $\mathfrak{S}(\mathbb{N}_9)$ with the above pattern $(\{6, 8, 9\}, \{1, 4\}, \{2, 5\}, \{3, 7\})$.)

(c) Show that the number of possible patterns associated with the permutations $\sigma \in \mathfrak{S}(\mathbb{N}_n)$ is the *Catalan number*

$$C_n = \frac{1}{n+1}\binom{2n}{n}.$$

(d) Show that the number of possible patterns associated with the permutations $\sigma \in \mathfrak{S}(\mathbb{N}_n)$ having exactly $k$ negative peaks is

$$\binom{n-1}{k} C_k 2^{n-2k-1}.$$

(Parts (c) and (d) lead to the well-known identity

$$C_n = \sum_{k \geqslant 0} \binom{n-1}{k} C_k 2^{n-2k-1},$$

which was found in [114]. For further information about the enumeration of permutations by a given pattern see [11], [38], [40], [44], [83].)

**3.13** Let $\sigma = i_1, i_2, \ldots, i_n \in \mathfrak{S}(\mathbb{N}_n)$ be a permutation in linear notation. Here, $\sigma$ is called *alternating* if the $(n-1)$ differences $(i_{\lambda+1} - i_\lambda)$, $1 \leqslant \lambda \leqslant n - 1$, have alternating signs. Thus the permutation $\sigma = 2, 5, 6, 4, 8, 7, 3, 1, 9$ is not alternating, but $5, 2, 6, 4, 8, 7, 9, 1, 3$ is alternating. Let $a_n$ be the number of all alternating permutations in $\mathfrak{S}(\mathbb{N}_n)$ and set $a_0 = a_1 = a_2 = 2$.

(a) Prove the recurrence

$$4a_{n+1} = \sum_{0 \leqslant k \leqslant n} \binom{n}{k} a_k a_{n-k}, \qquad n \geqslant 2.$$

(b) Deduce from (a) that the exponential generating function $f(z) = \sum_{n \geqslant 0} a_n z^n / n!$ satisfies the differential equation $4f'(z) = 4 + f^2(z)$. Use this to obtain $f(z) = 2 \tan(\pi/4 + z/2)$.

(c) Show that

$$a_{2n} = 2|E_{2n}| \quad \text{and} \quad a_{2n+1} = (-1)^n B_{2n+2} 4^{n+1}(4^{n+1} - 1)/(n + 1),$$

where $E_{2n}$ are the *Euler numbers* and $B_{2n}$ the Bernoulli numbers introduced in section 3.2.2. (*Hint*: Use (B38) and (B42).)

(The numbers $a_{2n}/2$ ($a_{2n+1}/2$) are often called *tangent* (*secant*) *numbers*. Alternating permutations were extensively studied in [2]; see also [25].)

**3.14** A permutation $\sigma \in \mathfrak{S}(\mathbb{N}_n)$ is called an *involution* if the composition $\sigma \circ \sigma = \sigma_0$, the identity permutation.

(a) Show that $\sigma \in \mathfrak{S}(\mathbb{N}_n)$ is an involution if and only if the cycle notation of $\sigma$ consists solely of cycles of lengths one or two.

(b) Derive from (a) that the exponential generating function of the numbers $i(n)$ of involutions in $\mathfrak{S}(\mathbb{N}_n)$ is given by

$$\sum_{i \geqslant 0} i(n) z^n/n! = \exp(z + z^2/2).$$

(c) Prove that

$$i(n) = \sum_{0 \leqslant k \leqslant \lfloor n/2 \rfloor} 2^{-k} \frac{n!}{k! (n - 2k)!}.$$

(An asymptotic expression for $i(n)$ is given by $i(n) \sim (4e)^{-1/4}(n/e)^{n/2} \exp(\sqrt{n})$ and was first derived as a special case in [89].)

# 4

# *Random Walks, Trees, Lists*

## 4.1 Random Walks

DEFINITION 4.1 Let $f: \mathbb{N}_n \cup \{0\} \to \mathbb{Z}$ be a (total) mapping with $|f(t) - f(t-1)| \leqslant 1$, $0 \leqslant t \leqslant n$. The $(n+1)$-tuple $\rho_f = (f(0), f(1), \ldots, f(n))$ is called a *random walk of length n from $f(0)$ to $f(n)$*. Here, $\rho_f$ is said to be *simple*, if $|f(t) - f(t-1)| = 1$, $0 \leqslant t \leqslant n$. The tuple $(f(t-1), f(t))$, $t \in \mathbb{N}_n$, is called the *t-th segment* of $\rho_f$ and is denoted by $\rho_f^t$. A segment $\rho_f^t$ is of *type* ↑ (*type* ↓, *type* ↕), if $f(t) > f(t-1)$ ($f(t) < f(t-1)$, $f(t) = f(t-1)$). The *level of the t-th segment* $\rho_f^t$ is the value $f(t-1)$, $t \in \mathbb{N}_n$.

For example, let $n = 10$ and $f$ be defined by $f(4) = f(6) = f(9) = 0$, $f(2) = f(3) = f(5) = 1$, $f(7) = f(8) = f(10) = -1$, and $f(0) = f(1) = 2$. Obviously, $\rho_f$ is a random walk of length 10 from 2 to $-1$; $\rho_f$ is not simple. The third segment $\rho_f^3$ is of type ↕ and has the level one. Similarly, the segment $\rho_f^7$ is of type ↓ and has the level zero.

One can represent a random walk $\rho_f$ by an oriented path in the plane which starts in the point $(0, f(0))$ and is straight between the points with coordinates $(t, f(t))$, $0 \leqslant t \leqslant n$. Obviously, the straight lines correspond to the segments of $\rho_f$. Thus the path in Figure 8 represents the above random walk $\rho_f$. Obviously, a random walk is simple if its corresponding path has no horizontal lines.

DEFINITION 4.2 Let $\rho_f$ be a random walk of length $n$; $\rho_f$ is called *non-negative*, if $f(t) \geqslant 0$ for all $t \in \mathbb{N}_n \cup \{0\}$. The *maximal deviation $d(\rho_f)$* of $\rho_f$ is defined by $d(\rho_f) = \text{MAX}_{0 \leqslant t \leqslant n} (|f(t)|)$. The value $s(\rho_f) = \text{MAX}_{0 \leqslant t, p \leqslant n} (f(t) - f(p))$ is called the *maximal span* of $\rho_f$; $\rho_f$ is said to be *$(k, h)$-bounded*, if $\text{MAX}_{0 \leqslant t \leqslant n} (f(t)) \leqslant k$ and $\text{MIN}_{0 \leqslant t \leqslant n} (f(t)) \geqslant h$.

Thus the random walk of our running example has the maximal deviation $d(\rho_f) = 2$ and the maximal span $s(\rho_f) = 3$. If $\rho_f$ is a non-negative random walk, then the maximal deviation $d(\rho_f)$ is also called the *height* of $\rho_f$ and is denoted by $h(\rho_f)$.

We can generalize the concept of random walks by attaching additional labels to the segments appearing in $\rho_f$. This leads to the following definition.

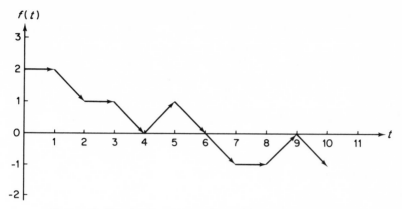

FIGURE 8. Graphical representation of the random walk $\rho_f$.

DEFINITION 4.3　Let $L$ be a set, $\rho_f$ a random walk of length $n$ with segments $\rho_f^1, \rho_f^2, \ldots, \rho_f^n$, and $\pi: \{\rho_f^t \mid 1 \leqslant t \leqslant n\} \to L$ a (total) mapping. The $(2n + 1)$-tuple $\rho_{f,\pi} = (f(0), f(1), \ldots, f(n); \; \pi(\rho_f^1), \pi(\rho_f^2), \ldots, \pi(\rho_f^n))$ is an $L$-weighted random walk of length $n$ from $f(0)$ to $f(n)$ with labels in $L$.

In the same way as in the case of random walks, one can represent an $L$-weighted random walk $\rho_{f,\pi}$ by an oriented marked path in the plane, where the label $\pi(\rho_f^t)$ is attached to the straight line which corresponds to the $t$-th segment.

　　Random walks and $\mathbb{N}_0$-weighted (non-negative) random walks play an important part in the analysis of algorithms dealing with dynamic data structures, trees, or expressions (see section 4.3 and Chapter 5). Furthermore, several other mathematical objects correspond to certain sets of (weighted) random walks.

　　For example, let $\tilde{M} = (\mathbb{N}_n, r_M)$ be a multiset over $\mathbb{N}_n$ with $r_M(x) \geqslant 1$ for all $x \in \mathbb{N}_n$, $\tilde{P} \subseteq \tilde{M}$ and $g: \mathbb{N}_n \cup \{0\} \to \mathbb{Z}$ be a function recursively defined by $g(0) = 0$, and

$$g(t + 1) = \begin{cases} g(t) + 1 & \text{if } r_P(t + 1) \geqslant 1 \\ g(t) - 1 & \text{if } r_P(t + 1) = 0 \end{cases}$$

for $t = 0, 1, \ldots, n - 1$. Obviously, $\rho_g$ is a simple random walk of length $n$ from 0 to $g(n) = n - 2 \sum_{1 \leqslant t \leqslant n} \delta_{0, r_P(t)}$. Choosing $L = \{r_P(t) \mid 1 \leqslant t \leqslant n\}$, we can define $\pi(\rho_g^t) := r_P(t)$, $1 \leqslant t \leqslant n$. Hence $\rho_{g,\pi} = (g(0), g(1), \ldots, g(n); \; r_P(1), \ldots, r_P(n))$ is a simple $\mathbb{N}_0$-weighted random walk of length $n$. Obviously, $\rho_{g,\pi}$ satisfies the conditions $|g(t)| \leqslant t$ for $0 \leqslant t \leqslant n$, $\pi(\rho_g^t) = 0$, if $\rho_g^t$ is of type $\downarrow$, and $\pi(\rho_g^t) \in [1 : r_M(t)]$, if $\rho_g^t$ is of type $\uparrow$. Conversely, some reflection shows that each simple $\mathbb{N}_0$-weighted random walk of length $n$ satisfying the above three conditions corresponds to a subset of $\tilde{M}$. Thus we have a one-to-one correspondence between the set of all simple $\mathbb{N}_0$-weighted random walks of length $n$ defined above and the set of all subsets of the multiset $\tilde{M} = (\mathbb{N}_n, r_M)$, where

$r_M(x) \geq 1$ for all $x \in \mathbb{N}_n$. In the case $r_M(x) = 1$ for all $x \in \mathbb{N}_n$, all segments of type ↑ (type ↓) are labelled by one (zero). In other words, we can omit the labels and obtain a one-to-one correspondence between the power set of $\mathbb{N}_n$ and the set of simple random walks $\rho_f$ of length $n$ with $|f(t)| \leq t$, $0 \leq t \leq n$.

Another well-known mathematical interpretation of $\{0,1\}$-weighted random walks consists of the game of heads or tails, played with $n$ throws of a coin, or generally, of stochastic processes. In this case, the labels can be interpreted as probabilities.

DEFINITION 4.4 Let $\rho_f = (f(0), f(1), \ldots, f(n); \pi(\rho_f^1), \ldots, \pi(\rho_f^n))$ be a $\mathbb{R}$-weighted random walk of length $n$. The *weight* $w(\rho_f)$ is defined by

$$w(\rho_f) = \prod_{1 \leq t \leq n} \pi(\rho_f^t).$$

If $\mathbb{P}$ is a set of $\mathbb{R}$-weighted random walks, then the number $\sum_{\rho_f \in \mathbb{P}} w(\rho_f)$ is called the *total weight of* $\mathbb{P}$ and is denoted by $w(\mathbb{P})$.

When the elements of a set $\mathbb{P}$ are only $[0{:}1]$-weighted random walks, then $w(\mathbb{P}) = \text{card}(\mathbb{P}) - \text{card}(\mathbb{P}_0)$, where $\mathbb{P}_0$ is the subset of $\mathbb{P}$ consisting of all $[0{:}1]$-weighted random walks with a segment labelled by zero.

## 4.2 Enumeration of Random Walks

### 4.2.1 Uniform Random Walks

In this section we shall enumerate certain classes $\mathbb{P}$ of random walks. First we introduce the notion of a uniform set of random walks.

DEFINITION 4.5 Let $\mathbb{P}$ be a set of $L$-weighted random walks and let $S$ be the set of all segments appearing in the random walks of $\mathbb{P}$. Here, $\mathbb{P}$ is called a *uniform set* (with respect to $L$) if there is a mapping $\varphi \colon S \to L$ such that for all $\rho_{f,\pi} \in \mathbb{P}$ and all segments $\rho_f^t$ appearing in $\rho_{f,\pi}$ the equation $\pi(\rho_f^t) = \varphi(\rho_f^t)$ is valid.

For example, let $L = \{3, 4, 5, 6, 7\}$. Consider the set $\mathbb{P} = \{0, 1, 2; 3, 7), (0, 1, 0, 1, 2; 3, 5, 3, 7), (0, 1, 0, -1, -1; 3, 5, 4, 3), (0, -1, -1, -1; 4, 3, 3), (0, -1, 0, 1, 2, 1; 4, 6, 3, 7, 6)\}$. We obtain $S = \{(0,1), (1,2), (-1,0), (1,0), (0,-1), (2,1), (-1,-1)\}$. For each random walk in $\mathbb{P}$, we have the following labels of the segments:

| Segment $s$ | $(0,1)$ | $(1,2)$ | $(-1,0)$ | $(1,0)$ | $(0,-1)$ | $(2,1)$ | $(-1,-1)$ |
|---|---|---|---|---|---|---|---|
| Label $l_s$ | 3 | 7 | 6 | 5 | 4 | 6 | 3 |

Defining $\varphi$ by $\varphi(s) := l_s$, we see that $\mathbb{P}$ is a uniform set of random walks. The set $\mathbb{P} = \{(0,1,1,0; 3,4,5), (0,1,0; 3,3)\}$ is not uniform. Here, we have $S = \{(0,1),$

$(1,1)$, $(1,0)\}$. The existence of a mapping $\varphi$ would imply $\varphi((1,0)) = 5$ (from $(0,1,1,0; 3,4,5))$ and $\varphi((1,0)) = 3$ (from $(0,1,0; 3,3))$, which is a contradiction.

Next we will compute the total weight $w(\mathbb{P}_{k,h}^\varphi(n,p))$ of the uniform set $\mathbb{P}_{k,h}^\varphi(n,p)$ consisting of all $(k,h)$-bounded $\mathbb{R}$-weighted random walks of length $n$ from 0 to $p$. For this purpose, we specify the mapping $\varphi$ by

$$\varphi((i, i+1)) = \begin{cases} u_i & \text{if } (i, i+1) \text{ is of type } \uparrow \\ d_i & \text{if } (i, i+1) \text{ is of type } \downarrow \\ e_i & \text{if } (i, i+1) \text{ is of type } \updownarrow \end{cases}$$

Some reflection shows that the elements of $\mathbb{P}_{k,h}^\varphi(n,p)$, $p \in [-h\!:\!k]$, $k, h \geqslant 0$, can be represented by labelled oriented paths in a diagram. Figure 9 presents such a diagram for the set $\mathbb{P}_{2,3}^\varphi(7, -1)$; for example, the random walk $(0, 1, 2, 1, 1, 0, 0, -1; u_0, u_1, d_2, e_1, d_1, e_0, d_0) \in \mathbb{P}_{2,3}^\varphi(7, -1)$ corresponds to the marked path. In the subsequent sections (especially section 4.3) we shall see that certain subsets of $\mathbb{P}_{k,h}^\varphi(n,p)$ play an important part in the analysis of certain algorithms.

Let us now turn to the computation of the total weight of $\mathbb{P}_{k,h}^\varphi(n,p)$. For this purpose, let

$$E_{p,k,h}(z) = \sum_{n \geqslant 0} w(\mathbb{P}_{k,h}^\varphi(n,p))z^n$$

be the ordinary generating function of the total weights $w(\mathbb{P}_{k,h}^\varphi(n,p))$. Our first goal is to derive an explicit expression for $E_{p,k,h}(z)$. One way to do this is to compute recurrences for the total weights $w(\mathbb{P}_{k,h}^\varphi(n,p))$; for example, if $n \geqslant p + 2$, $1 \leqslant p \leqslant k - 1$, $w(\mathbb{P}_{k,h}^\varphi(n,p))$ is given by the sum of the following three products:

(1) $d_{p+1}$ times the total weight $w(\mathbb{P}_{k,h}^\varphi(n-1, p+1))$;
(2) $e_p$ times the total weight $w(\mathbb{P}_{k,h}^\varphi(n-1, p))$;
(3) $u_{p-1}$ times the total weight $w(\mathbb{P}_{k,h}^\varphi(n-1, p-1))$.

Hence

$$w(\mathbb{P}_{k,h}^\varphi(n,p)) = d_{p+1}w(\mathbb{P}_{k,h}^\varphi(n-1, p-1)) + e_p w(\mathbb{P}_{k,h}^\varphi(n-1, p))$$
$$+ u_{p-1}w(\mathbb{P}_{k,h}^\varphi(n-1, p-1)).$$

for $n \geqslant p + 2$ and $1 \leqslant p \leqslant k - 1$. Similar recurrences for the other cases can be derived. The next step consists of translating these recurrences into terms of the generating functions $E_{p,k,h}(z)$; for example, taking the above recurrence together with the valid conditions $w(\mathbb{P}_{k,h}^\varphi(n,p)) = 0$ for $n < p$, we obtain

$$E_{p,k,h}(z) = \sum_{n \geqslant 0} w(\mathbb{P}_{k,h}^\varphi(n,p))z^n$$

$$= \sum_{n \geqslant p} w(\mathbb{P}_{k,h}^\varphi(n,p))z^n$$

54

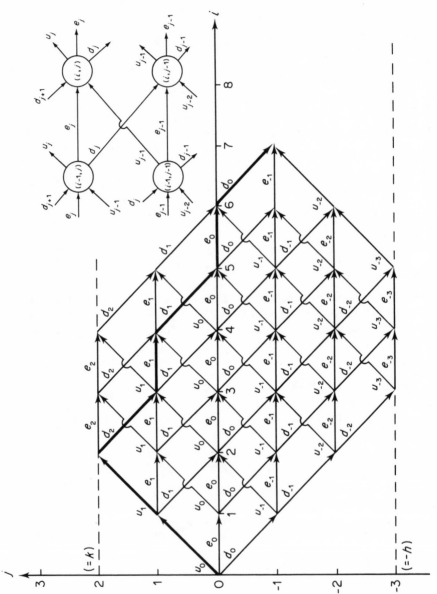

FIGURE 9. Representation of all (2, 3)-bounded, weighted random walks of length 7 from 0 to (−1) in $\mathbb{P}^{\varphi}_{2,3}(7, -1)$.

$$= w(\mathbb{P}^{\varphi}_{k,h}(p, p))z^p + w(\mathbb{P}^{\varphi}_{k,h}(p + 1, p))z^{p+1}$$

$$+ \sum_{n \geqslant p+2} w(\mathbb{P}^{\varphi}_{k,h}(n, p))z^n$$

$$= u_{p-1}w(\mathbb{P}^{\varphi}_{k,h}(p - 1, p - 1))z^p$$

$$+ [e_p w(\mathbb{P}^{\varphi}_{k,h}(p, p)) + u_{p-1}w(\mathbb{P}^{\varphi}_{k,h}(p, p - 1))]z^{p+1}$$

$$+ \sum_{n \geqslant p+2} [d_{p+1}w(\mathbb{P}^{\varphi}_{k,h}(n - 1, p + 1)) + e_p w(\mathbb{P}^{\varphi}_{k,h}(n - 1, p))$$

$$+ u_{p-1}w(\mathbb{P}^{\varphi}_{k,h}(n - 1, p - 1))]z^n$$

$$= u_{p-1}zE_{p-1,k,h}(z) + e_p z E_{p,k,h}(z) + d_{p+1}E_{p+1,k,h}(z).$$

Doing this for all recurrences, we obtain a set of equations for the functions $E_{p,k,h}(z)$.

An alternative, more elegant method consists of an application of formal languages and formal power series with non-commuting variables (see [108]). It is assumed that the reader is familiar with the basic definitions concerning context-free grammars and languages as stated in [53] and formal power series as stated in [107]. (A short summary is given in Appendix A, 2.) The basic ideas are as follows:

(1) Each object to be counted is represented as a word in a free monoid $X^*$ generated by the countable set $X$. The set of the objects corresponds to the set of words $\mathscr{L} \subseteq X^*$.
(2) A context-free, unambiguous substitution scheme $G$ (context-free, unambiguous grammar, if $X$ is finite) is found that generates $\mathscr{L}$.
(3) The scheme $G$ defines a system of formal equations, one of whose solutions in the ring of formal power series over the monoid $X^*$ is the formal power series $f = \sum_{w \in \mathscr{L}} w$.
(4) We have to choose the property by which we wish to enumerate the objects. A homomorphism is then constructed which maps the monoid into a commutative semigroup such that the induced map on the ring of formal power series maps $f$ on to a generating function $F$ in commuting variables which is the desired enumerator. Here, $F$ will satisfy the system of formal equations and this enables us to find a solution for $F$.

Let us apply this method to the computation of $E_{p,k,h}(z)$. We choose

$$X = \{\mathbf{u}_i \,|\, -h \leqslant i \leqslant k - 1\} \cup \{\mathbf{d}_i \,|\, -h + 1 \leqslant i \leqslant k\}$$

$$\cup \{\mathbf{e}_i \,|\, -h \leqslant i \leqslant k\} \cup \{\mathbf{p}\}.$$

Considering the path diagram given in Figure 9, each random walk $\rho_f = (0, \ldots, p; \ a_1, \ldots, a_n) \in \mathbb{P}^{\varphi}_{k,h}(n, p)$ can be described by the word $a_1 a_2 \ldots a_n \mathbf{p} \in X^*$; for example, the marked path in Figure 9 corresponds to the word $\mathbf{u}_0 \mathbf{u}_1 \mathbf{d}_2 \mathbf{e}_1 \mathbf{d}_1 \mathbf{e}_0 \mathbf{d}_0(-1)$. Thus the objects to be counted are represented by

$$\mathcal{L} = \{w \in X^* \mid w = \mathbf{a}_1\mathbf{a}_2 \dots \mathbf{a}_n\mathbf{p} \wedge a_i = \varphi((f(i-1), f(i)), 1 \leq i \leq n\}.$$

We now consider the context-free grammar $G$ with the following productions:

$$S_i \to \mathbf{e}_i S_i, \qquad -h \leq i \leq k \qquad \text{(rule } f_i)$$

$$S_i \to \mathbf{d}_i S_{i-1}, \qquad -h+1 \leq i \leq k \quad \text{(rule } g_i)$$

$$S_i \to \mathbf{u}_i S_{i+1}, \qquad -h \leq i \leq k-1 \quad \text{(rule } h_i)$$

$$S_p \to \mathbf{p} \qquad\qquad\qquad\qquad\qquad \text{(rule } p)$$

Some reflection shows that each word $w \in \mathcal{L}$ can be derived from $S_0$ in $(n+1)$ steps. For example, let $k = 2$, $h = 3$, $n = 7$, and $p = -1$. The word corresponding to the random walk $(0, 1, 2, 1, 1, 0, 0, -1; u_0, u_1, d_2, e_1, d_1, e_0, d_0) \in \mathbb{P}^\varphi_{2,3}(7, -1)$ has the following derivation in $G$:

$$
\begin{aligned}
S_0 &\to \mathbf{u}_0 S_1 & \text{(rule } h_0) \\
&\to \mathbf{u}_0\mathbf{u}_1 S_2 & \text{(rule } h_1) \\
&\to \mathbf{u}_0\mathbf{u}_1\mathbf{d}_2 S_1 & \text{(rule } g_2) \\
&\to \mathbf{u}_0\mathbf{u}_1\mathbf{d}_2\mathbf{e}_1 S_1 & \text{(rule } f_1) \\
&\to \mathbf{u}_0\mathbf{u}_1\mathbf{d}_2\mathbf{e}_1\mathbf{d}_1 S_0 & \text{(rule } g_1) \\
&\to \mathbf{u}_0\mathbf{u}_1\mathbf{d}_2\mathbf{e}_1\mathbf{d}_1\mathbf{e}_0 S_0 & \text{(rule } f_0) \\
&\to \mathbf{u}_0\mathbf{u}_1\mathbf{d}_2\mathbf{e}_1\mathbf{d}_1\mathbf{e}_0\mathbf{d}_0 S_{-1} & \text{(rule } g_0) \\
&\to \mathbf{u}_0\mathbf{u}_1\mathbf{d}_2\mathbf{e}_1\mathbf{d}_1\mathbf{e}_0\mathbf{d}_0(-1) & \text{(rule } -1)
\end{aligned}
$$

Thus $\mathcal{L} = \mathcal{L}_0 \cap X^{n+1}$, where $\mathcal{L}_i$ denotes the set of words which can be derived from $S_i$, $i \in [-h:k]$, using the productions of $G$. Obviously, the grammar $G$ is unambiguous. The system of formal equations induced by $G$ is

$$S_k = \mathbf{e}_k S_k + \mathbf{d}_k S_{k-1}$$

$$S_i = \mathbf{e}_i S_i + \mathbf{d}_i S_{i-1} + \mathbf{u}_i S_{i+1}, \qquad -h+1 \leq i \leq k-1$$

$$S_{-h} = \mathbf{e}_{-h} S_{-h} + \mathbf{u}_{-h} S_{-h+1},$$

where the additional item $\mathbf{p}$ appears on the right-hand side of the equation for $S_p$. Let now $S_i = \sum_{w \in \mathcal{L}_i} w$ be the solution for the variable $S_i$, $i \in [-h:k]$. To derive the generating function $E_{p,k,h}(z)$, we introduce the homomorphism $\theta$ defined by $\theta(\mathbf{a}) = az$, $\mathbf{a} \in X \backslash \{\mathbf{p}\}$, and $\theta(\mathbf{p}) = 1$. $\theta$ induces a homomorphism $\boldsymbol{\theta}$ of formal power series over the monoids: let $\rho \in \mathbb{P}^\varphi_{k,h}(n, p)$ and $u_\rho = \mathbf{a}_1\mathbf{a}_2 \dots \mathbf{a}_n\mathbf{p}$ be the corresponding word in $\mathcal{L}$. We have

$$\theta(u_\rho) = \theta(\mathbf{a}_1)\theta(\mathbf{a}_2) \dots \theta(\mathbf{a}_n)\theta(\mathbf{p})$$

$$= a_1 a_2 \dots a_n z^n$$

$$= w(\rho)z^n$$

and therefore,

$$\theta(S_0) = \theta\left(\sum_{u_\rho \in \mathscr{L}} u_\rho\right) = \sum_{n \geqslant 0} \sum_{u_\rho \in \mathscr{L}_0 \cap X^{n+1}} \theta(u_\rho)$$

$$= \sum_{n \geqslant 0} \sum_{\rho \in \mathbb{P}^\varphi_{k,h}(n,p)} w(\rho)z^n$$

$$= E_{p,k,h}(z).$$

Since the context-free grammar $G$ is unambiguous, the generating function $E_{p,k,h}(z)$ is equal to $F_0(z)$, where the functions $F_i(z)$, $-h \leqslant i \leqslant k$, satisfy the above system of formal equations. We obtain

$$F_k(z) = e_k z F_k(z) + d_k z F_{k-1}(z)$$

$$F_i(z) = e_i z F_i(z) + d_i z F_{i-1}(z) + u_i z F_{i+1}(z), \qquad -h+1 \leqslant i \leqslant k-1$$

$$F_{-h}(z) = e_{-h} z F_{-h}(z) + u_{-h} z F_{-h+1}(z),$$

where an additional 1 appears on the right-hand side of the equation for $F_p(z)$. (It should be obvious that the method described can also be applied to enumerate other objects, e.g. the total number of occurrences of a label in all random walks $\rho \in \mathbb{P}^\varphi_{k,h}(n, p)$. We have only to change the homomorphism $\theta$!)

Combining the above results, we have proved the following theorem.

THEOREM 4.1    Let $\mathbb{P}^\varphi_{k,h}(n, p)$ be the uniform set consisting of all $(k, h)$-bounded, $\mathbb{R}$-weighted random walks of length $n$ from 0 to $p$ and let

$$E_{p,k,h}(z) = \sum_{n \geqslant 0} w(\mathbb{P}^\varphi_{k,h}(n, p))z^n$$

be the ordinary generating function of the total weights $w(\mathbb{P}^\varphi_{k,h}(n, p))$. The function $E_{p,k,h}(z)$, $p \in [-h:k]$, is equal to $F_0(z)$, where the functions $F_i(z)$, $-h \leqslant i \leqslant k$, are defined by the system of linear equations

$$A \cdot \overrightarrow{F(z)} = \overrightarrow{\varepsilon_p},$$

where

$$\overrightarrow{F(z)} = \begin{bmatrix} F_k(z) \\ F_{k-1}(z) \\ \vdots \\ F_0(z) \\ \vdots \\ F_{-h+1}(z) \\ F_{-h}(z) \end{bmatrix}, \qquad \overrightarrow{\varepsilon_p} = \begin{bmatrix} 0 \\ 0 \\ \vdots \\ 1 \\ \vdots \\ 0 \\ 0 \end{bmatrix} \leftarrow (k - p + 1)\text{-th component}$$

and

$$
A = \begin{bmatrix}
[1-e_k z] & -d_k z \\
-u_{k-1}z & [1-e_{k-1}z] & -d_{k-1}z & & & & 0 \\
& -u_{k-2}z & [1-e_{k-2}z] & -d_{k-2}z \\
& & \ddots\, u_i z \, \ddots & [1-e_i z] & \ddots\, -d_i z \, \ddots \\
& & & & \ddots & \ddots\, -d_{-h+1}z \\
0 & & & & -u_{-h+1}z & [1-e_{-h+1}z] & \ddots\, d_{-h+1}z \\
& & & & & -u_{-h}z & [1-e_{-h}z]
\end{bmatrix}. \quad \blacksquare
$$

Hence the computation of the generating function $E_{p,k,h}(z)$ leads to a system of linear equations which has a special form. An application of Cramer's rule yields the following lemma.

LEMMA 4.1 Let $M_{r,N}$ be the non-singular $(N - r + 1) \times (N - r + 1)$-matrix given by

$$
\begin{bmatrix}
b_r & c_r \\
a_{r+1} & b_{r+1} & c_{r+1} & & 0 \\
& a_{r+2} & b_{r+2} & c_{r+2} \\
& & \ddots & \ddots & \ddots \\
0 & & a_{N-1} & b_{N-1} & c_{N-1} \\
& & & a_N & b_N
\end{bmatrix}.
$$

The system of the $N$ linear equations $M_{1,N} \cdot \vec{x} = \vec{\varepsilon}_i$, where

$$
\vec{x} = \begin{bmatrix} x_1 \\ x_2 \\ \vdots \\ x_N \end{bmatrix} \quad \text{and} \quad \vec{\varepsilon}_i = \begin{bmatrix} 0 \\ 0 \\ \vdots \\ 1 \\ \vdots \\ 0 \end{bmatrix} \leftarrow i\text{-th component}
$$

has the solution (convention: $\det(M_{r,n}) = \delta_{r-1,n}$ for $n \leqslant r - 1$)

$$
x_j = \begin{cases}
(-1)^{i+j} c_j c_{j+1} \cdots c_{i-1} \det(M_{1,j-1}) \det(M_{i+1,N})/\det(M_{1,N}) \\
\qquad\qquad\qquad\qquad\qquad\qquad\qquad \text{if } j \in [1:i-1] \\
\det(M_{1,i-1}) \det(M_{i+1,N})/\det(M_{1,N}) \qquad\quad \text{if } j = i \\
(-1)^{i+j} a_{i+1} a_{i+2} \cdots a_j \det(M_{1,i-1}) \det(M_{j+1,N})/\det(M_{1,N}) \\
\qquad\qquad\qquad\qquad\qquad\qquad\qquad \text{if } j \in [i+1:N]
\end{cases} \quad \blacksquare
$$

Expanding $\det(M_{r,N})$ by the elements of the last row, we obtain the recurrence

$$
\det(M_{r,N}) = \delta_{r-1,N} \quad \text{for } N \leqslant r - 1
$$

$$
\det(M_{r,N}) = b_N \det(M_{r,N-1}) - a_N c_{N-1} \det(M_{r,N-2}) \quad \text{for } N \geqslant r.
$$

We will now apply our results to the equations induced by the functions $F_i(z)$ given in Theorem 4.1. We have to choose: $N := k + h + 1$, $i := k - p + 1$, $b_j :=$ $1 - e_{k-j+1}z$, $x_j := F_{k-j+1}(z)$, $c_\lambda := -d_{k-\lambda+1}z$ and $a_m := -u_{k-m+1}z$, where $1 \leqslant j \leqslant N$, $1 \leqslant \lambda \leqslant N - 1$ and $2 \leqslant m \leqslant N$. We obtain

$$
F_i(z) = \begin{cases}
z^{i-p} d_i d_{i-1} \cdots d_{p+1} \dfrac{P^{(k)}_{1,k-i}(z) P^{(k)}_{k-p+2,k+h+1}(z)}{P^{(k)}_{1,k+h+1}(z)} & \text{if } i \in [p+1:k] \\[4mm]
\dfrac{P^{(k)}_{1,k-p}(z) P^{(k)}_{k-p+2,k+h+2}(z)}{P^{(k)}_{1,k+h+1}(z)} & \text{if } i = p \\[4mm]
z^{p-i} u_{p-1} u_{p-2} \cdots u_i \dfrac{P^{(k)}_{1,k-p}(z) P^{(k)}_{k-i+2,k+h+1}(z)}{P^{(k)}_{1,k+h+1}(z)} & \text{if } i \in [-h:p+1],
\end{cases}
$$

where the $P^{(k)}_{r,s}(z)$ are polynomials in $z$ recursively defined by

$$P^{(k)}_{r,s}(z) = \delta_{r-1,s} \quad \text{for } s \leqslant r - 1$$

$$P^{(k)}_{r,s}(z) = [1 - e_{k-s+1}z] P^{(k)}_{r,s-1} - u_{k-s+1} d_{k-s+2} z^2 P^{(k)}_{r,s-2}(z) \quad \text{for } s \geqslant r.$$

Since $F_0(z) = E_{p,k,h}(z)$, we have proved the following theorem.

THEOREM 4.2   The generating function $E_{p,k,h}(z)$ of the total weight $w(\mathbb{P}^{\varphi}_{k,h}(n, p))$ of the uniform set $\mathbb{P}^{\varphi}_{k,h}(n, p)$ consisting of all $(k, h)$-bounded, $\mathbb{R}$-weighted random walks of length $n$ from 0 to $p$ is given by

$$E_{p,k,h}(z) = z^p u_{p-1} u_{p-2} \cdots u_0 \frac{P^{(k)}_{1,k-p}(z) P^{(k)}_{k+2,k+h+1}(z)}{P^{(k)}_{1,k+h+1}(z)} \quad \text{if } p \in [1:k]$$

$$E_{0,k,h}(z) = \frac{P^{(k)}_{1,k}(z) P^{(k)}_{k+2,k+h+1}(z)}{P^{(k)}_{1,k+h+1}(z)}$$

$$E_{-p,k,h}(z) = z^p d_0 d_{-1} \cdots d_{-p+1} \frac{P^{(k)}_{1,k}(z) P^{(k)}_{k+p+2,k+h+1}(z)}{P^{(k)}_{1,k+h+1}(z)} \quad \text{if } p \in [1:h],$$

where the $P^{(k)}_{r,s}(z)$ are polynomials in $z$ satisfying the recurrence

$$P^{(k)}_{r,s}(z) = \delta_{r-1,s} \quad \text{for } s \leqslant r - 1$$

$$P^{(k)}_{r,s}(z) = [1 - e_{k-s+1}z] P^{(k)}_{r,s-1}(z) - u_{k-s+1} d_{k-s+2} z^2 P^{(k)}_{r,s-2}(z) \quad \text{for } s \geqslant r. \quad \blacksquare$$

This theorem gives us a constructive method for computing the generating function $E_{p,k,h}(z)$. It should be clear that the generating function of the total weights $w(\mathbb{P}^{\varphi}_{k,h}(n, i, p))$ of the uniform set of all $(k, h)$-bounded, $\mathbb{R}$-weighted random walks $\rho$ of length $n$ from $i$ to $p$ can be derived from $E_{p,k,h}(z)$, because such a $\rho$ is transformable into a random walk from 0 to $(p - i)$; we have only to change the parameters $p, k, h$ and the indices of the labels.

### 4.2.2 (d, e, u)-*Random Walks*

In this subsection we consider an important special case of weighted random walks. Choose $e_\lambda = e$ for $-h \leqslant \lambda \leqslant k$, $u_\lambda = u$ for $-h \leqslant \lambda \leqslant k - 1$, and $d_\lambda = d$ for $-h + 1 \leqslant \lambda \leqslant k$. In other words, the segments of types ↑, ↓, and ↕ of the random walks in $\mathbb{P}_{k,h}^\varphi(n, p)$ are labelled by $u$, $d$, and $e$ respectively. A uniform set $\mathbb{P}_{k,h}^\varphi(n, p)$ with this specification $\varphi$ is called a $(d, e, u)$-*set* and is denoted by $DEU_{k,h}(n, p)$. An element of $DEU_{k,h}(n, p)$ is said to be a $(d, e, u)$-random walk.

The formulae given in Theorem 4.2 yield the homogeneous linear recurrence

$$P_{r,s}^{(k)}(z) = \delta_{r-1,s} \quad \text{for } s \leqslant r - 1$$

$$P_{r,s}^{(k)}(z) = [1 - ez]P_{r,s-1}^{(k)}(z) - udz^2 P_{r,s-2}^{(k)}(z) \quad \text{for } s \geqslant r.$$

Using Appendix A, 4, we obtain the characteristic equation $q_r^2(z) - (1 - ez)q_r(z) + udz^2 = 0$, which has the solution

$$q_\pm(z) := q_r^\pm(z) = [1 - ez \pm \sqrt{(1 - ez)^2 - 4udz^2}]/2.$$

Thus $P_{r,s}^{(k)}(z)$ can be expressed in the form $Aq_+^n(z) + Bq_-^n(z)$, where $n$ depends on $r, s$ and $A, B$ are constants which are determined by the initial conditions. Computing $A$ and $B$, we find

$$P_{r,s}^{(k)}(z) = [(1 - ez)^2 - 4udz^2]^{-1/2}[(q_+(z))^{s-r+2} - (q_-(z))^{s-r+2}]$$

for $s \geqslant r - 2$ and $P_{r,s}^{(k)}(z) = 0$ for $s \leqslant r - 3$. We have now to insert the corresponding expressions for $P_{r,s}^{(k)}(z)$ into the formulae for $E_{p,k,h}(z)$ given in Theorem 4.2. Choosing the abbreviation $Q_m(z) := P_{r,m+r-2}^{(k)}(z)$, we obtain, after some simplifications

$$E_{p,k,h}(z) = z^p u^p \frac{Q_{k-p+1}(z)Q_{h+1}(z)}{Q_{k+h+2}(z)} \quad \text{for } p \in [0:k]$$

and

$$E_{-p,k,h}(z) = z^p d^p \frac{Q_{k+1}(z)Q_{h-p+1}(z)}{Q_{k+h+2}(z)} \quad \text{for } p \in [0:h].$$

Thus it is sufficient to restrict our further considerations to the case $E_{p,k,h}(z)$ for $p \in [0:k]$, because $E_{-p,k,h}(z)$, $p \in [0:h]$, arises from $E_{p,k,h}(z)$ by the replacing of $k, h, u$ by $h, k, d$ respectively. Now we have to compute the coefficient $\langle z^n \rangle E_{p,k,h}(z) = w(DEU_{k,h}(n, p))$. Let us first consider the case $ud = 0$. We get $Q_m(z) = (1 - ez)^{m-1}$ and therefore with (A12)

$$E_{p,k,h}(z) = z^p u^p/(1 - ez)^{p+1} = u^p \sum_{\lambda \geqslant 0} \binom{\lambda + p}{p} e^\lambda z^{\lambda+p}.$$

Hence for $p \in [0:k]$

$$w(DEU_{k,h}(n, p)) = \begin{cases} 0 & \text{if } p > n \\ \binom{n}{p} u^p e^{n-p} & \text{if } p \leqslant n. \end{cases}$$

To obtain $w(DEU_{k,h}(n, -p))$, $p \in [0:h]$, we have to replace $u$ by $d$. Next, we shall consider the case $ud \neq 0$. As mentioned above, the functions $Q_m(z)$ are polynomials in $z$ satisfying the recurrence

$$Q_0(z) = 0, \qquad Q_1(z) = 1$$

$$Q_m(z) = (1 - ez)Q_{m-1}(z) - udz^2 Q_{m-2}(z), \qquad m \geqslant 2.$$

These equations are a reminder of the recurrences of orthogonal polynomials. Indeed, $Q_m(z) = z^{m-1}(ud)^{(m-1)/2}U_{m-1}((1 - ez)/(2z\sqrt{ud}))$, $m \geqslant 1$, where $U_m(z)$ is the $m$-th *Chebyshev polynomial of the second kind* (see Appendix B, 2.5). In principle, there are two different ways to compute the coefficient $\langle z^n \rangle E_{p,k,h}(z)$:

(1) *The computation of $w(DEU_{k,h}(n, p))$ by partial fraction expansion*
Some reflection shows that the degree of the polynomial $z^p Q_{k-p+1}(z)Q_{h+1}(z)$ appearing in the numerator of $E_{p,k,h}(z)$ is strictly less than the degree of the polynomial $Q_{k+h+2}(z)$ appearing in the denominator. Now it is well known that the Chebyshev polynomial $U_m(z)$ has only simple zeros at $z_m(\lambda) = \cos(\pi\lambda/(m+1))$, $1 \leqslant \lambda \leqslant m$, that is

$$U_m(z) = 2^m \prod_{1 \leqslant \lambda \leqslant m} (z - z_m(\lambda)).$$

Therefore,

$$Q_m(z) = \prod_{1 \leqslant \lambda \leqslant m-1} (1 - [e + 2\sqrt{ud}\, z_{m-1}(\lambda)]z).$$

Hence

$$E_{p,k,h}(z) = \frac{u^p z^p Q_{k-p+1}(z)Q_{h+1}(z)}{Q_{k+h+2}(z)} = \sum_{1 \leqslant \lambda \leqslant k+h+1} \frac{\alpha_\lambda}{1 - v_\lambda z},$$

where the $\alpha_\lambda$, $1 \leqslant \lambda \leqslant k+h+1$, are constants and $v_\lambda$ is an abbreviation of $[e + 2\sqrt{ud}\, z_{k+h+1}(\lambda)]$. As usual, we obtain $\alpha_\lambda$, $\lambda \in [1 : k+h+1]$, by multiplying the last equation by $(1 - v_\lambda z)$ and by setting $z := v_\lambda^{-1}$. Thus

$$w(DEU_{k,h}(n, p)) = \langle z^n \rangle E_{p,k,h}(z)$$

$$= \langle z^n \rangle \sum_{n \geqslant 0} z^n \sum_{1 \leqslant \lambda \leqslant k+h+1} v_\lambda^n \alpha_\lambda$$

$$= \sum_{1 \leqslant \lambda \leqslant k+h+1} \alpha_\lambda v_\lambda^n,$$

where

$$\alpha_\lambda = \left. \frac{u^p z^p Q_{k-p+1}(z)Q_{h+1}(z)[1 - v_\lambda z]}{Q_{k+h+2}(z)} \right|_{z = v_\lambda^{-1}}.$$

The value of $\alpha_\lambda$ can be determined by L'Hospital's rule; we obtain

$$\alpha_\lambda = -u^p v_\lambda^{-p+1} \frac{Q_{k-p+1}(v_\lambda^{-1})Q_{h+1}(v_\lambda^{-1})}{Q'_{k+h+2}(v_\lambda^{-1})}.$$

Using the explicit expression for $Q_m(z)$ (or well-known formulae for $U_m(z)$ and $U'_m(z)$), we find with $\eta_\lambda = \lambda/(k + h + 2)$

$$Q_m(v_\lambda^{-1}) = (ud)^{(m-1)/2} \sin(\pi m \eta_\lambda)/(v_\lambda^{m-1} \sin(\pi \eta_\lambda))$$

and

$$Q'_{k+h+2}(v_\lambda^{-1}) = (-1)^\lambda (k + h + 2)(ud)^{(k+h)/2}/(2v_\lambda^{k+h-1} \sin^2(\pi \eta_\lambda)).$$

Thus

$$\alpha_\lambda = \frac{2}{k + h + 2}\left(\frac{u}{d}\right)^{\frac{1}{2}p} \sin((h + p + 1)\pi \eta_\lambda) \sin((h + 1)\pi \eta_\lambda).$$

Summarizing our results, we have proved the following theorem.

THEOREM 4.3   Let $ud \neq 0$. The total weight of the set $DEU_{k,h}(n, p)$, $p \in [0:k]$, is given by

$$w(DEU_{k,h}(n, p)) = \frac{2}{k + h + 2}\left(\frac{u}{d}\right)^{\frac{1}{2}p} \sum_{1 \leqslant \lambda \leqslant k+h+1} f_n(\lambda),$$

where

$$f_n(\lambda) = \sin\left(\frac{(h + p + 1)\pi\lambda}{k + h + 2}\right) \sin\left(\frac{(h + 1)\pi\lambda}{k + h + 2}\right)\left[e + 2\sqrt{ud}\, \cos\left(\frac{\pi\lambda}{k + h + 2}\right)\right]^n.$$

The weight $w(DEU_{k,h}(n, -p))$, $p \in [0:h]$, is obtained by the replacing of $k, h, u$ by $h, k, d$, respectively.   ■

This result is rather remarkable, because the expression appearing on the right-hand side of the above equation must always be an integer, provided that $u, d, e$ are integers with $ud \neq 0$. An equivalent relation was derived in [21] for $e = h = p = 0$, $u = d = 1$ and in [62] for $e = h = 0$, $u = d = 1$ and $p \geqslant 0$.

(2) *The computation of $w(DEU_{k,h}(n, p))$ by Cauchy's formula*
Let us return to the explicit expression for $E_{p,k,h}(z)$ given by

$$E_{p,k,h}(z) = z^p u^p \frac{Q_{k-p+1}(z)Q_{h+1}(z)}{Q_{k+h+2}(z)}, \qquad p \in [0:k].$$

The substitution $z = v/(v^2 + ev + ud)$ leads immediately to

$$Q_m(z) = \frac{v^{2m} - (ud)^m}{(v^2 - ud)(v^2 + ev + ud)^{m-1}}.$$

Hence

$$E_{p,k,h}(z) = v^p u^p (v^2 + ev + ud) \frac{[v^{2h+2} - (ud)^{h+1}][v^{2k-2p+2} - (ud)^{k-p+1}]}{[v^2 - ud][v^{2k+2h+4} - (ud)^{h+k+2}]}.$$

Therefore, we obtain with this expression and (A11)

$$w(DEU_{k,h}(n, p)) = \frac{1}{2\pi i} \int_C z^{-n-1} E_{p,k,h}(z) \, dz$$

$$= \frac{1}{2\pi i} \int_C \frac{dv}{v^{n+1}} I_{n,p,k,h}(v),$$

where

$$I_{n,p,k,h}(v) = u^p v^p [v^2 + ev + ud]^n \frac{[(ud)^{h+1} - v^{2h+2}][(ud)^{k-p+1} - v^{2k-2p+2}]}{(ud)^{k+h+2} - v^{2k+2h+4}}.$$

In other words, $w(DEU_{k,h}(n, p))$, $p \in [0:k]$, is the coefficient of $v^n$ in the expansion of $I_{n,p,k,h}(v)$. This coefficient can now be computed by means of the binomial theorem and the geometric series; generally, it is a sum whose terms are products of binomial coefficients. Since this expression is not informative in the general case, its computation is left to the reader; we shall consider two important special cases:

(a) $(1, 1, 1)$-Random walks. We obtain

$$I_{n,p,k,h}(v) = v^p [v^2 + v + 1]^n \frac{[1 - v^{2h+2}][1 - v^{2k-2p+2}]}{1 - v^{2k+2h+4}}$$

$$= \sum_{\lambda \geq 0} \sum_{j \geq 0} \binom{n, 3}{\lambda} v^{2(k+h+2)j + \lambda + p} [1 - v^{2h+2}][1 - v^{2k-2p+2}],$$

where $\binom{n, 3}{\lambda}$ are the *trinomial coefficients* (see Appendix B, 1). Hence for $p \in [0:k]$,

$$w(DEU_{k,h}(n, p)) = \binom{n, 3}{n-p} - \binom{n, 3}{n - p - 2h - 2} + \psi_p(n, k, h)$$

$$- \psi_{p+2h+2}(n, k, h),$$

where

$$\psi_a(n, k, h) = \sum_{j \geq 1} \left[ \binom{n, 3}{n + a - 2(k + h + 2)j} + \binom{n, 3}{n - a - 2(k + h + 2)j} \right].$$

For $w(DEU_{k,h}(n, -p))$, $p \in [0:h]$, we have to replace $k, h, u$ by $h, k, d$, respectively. In this case, $w(DEU_{k,h}(n, p))$ is equal to the number of all paths from $(0, 0)$ to $(n, p)$ in the diagram given in Figure 9. This result was proved in [96] for $p = h = 0$.

(b) $(1, 0, 1)$-Random walks. We obtain

$$I_{n,p,k,h}(v) = v^p[v^2 + 1]^n \frac{[1 - v^{2h+2}][1 - v^{2k-2p+2}]}{1 - v^{2k+2h+4}}$$

$$= \sum_{\lambda \geq 0} \sum_{j \geq 0} \binom{n}{\lambda} v^{2(k+h+2)j + 2\lambda + p}[1 - v^{2h+2}][1 - v^{2k-2p+2}].$$

Hence for $p \in [0:k]$,

$$w(DEU_{k,h}(n, p)) = \begin{cases} 0 & \text{if } n + p \equiv 1 \bmod(2) \\ \binom{n}{(n-p)/2} - \binom{n}{(n-p)/2 - h - 1} \\ \quad + \psi_{p/2}(n, k, h) - \psi_{p/2+h+1}(n, k, h) \\ & \text{if } n + p \equiv 0 \bmod(2); \end{cases}$$

where

$$\psi_a(n, k, h) = \sum_{j \geq 1}\left[\binom{n}{n/2 + a - (k + h + 2)j} + \binom{n}{n/2 - a - (k + h + 2)j}\right].$$

$w(DEU_{k,h}(n, -p))$, $p \in [0:h]$, arises from this expression by the replacing of $k, h, u$ by $h, k, d$ respectively. In this case, $w(DEU_{k,h}(n, p))$ gives the number of all paths from $(0, 0)$ to $(n, p)$ in the diagram given in Figure 9, if we eliminate all horizontal segments. This result was implicitly proved in [21] for $p = h = 0$ and in [66], [95] for $p \geq 0$ and $h = 0$. The generating functions $E_{0,k,h}(z)$ and $E_{p,h,h}(z)$ were derived in [98]. Non-negative $(1, 0, 1)$-random walks of length $n$ from $0$ to $0$ are related to ordered trees and stacks (see section 4.3 and Chapter 5).

We can also ask for the total weight of the sets $DEU_{\infty,\infty}(n, p)$, $\bigcup_{-h \leq p \leq k} DEU_{k,h}(n, p)$ or $\bigcup_{-\infty \leq p \leq \infty} DEU_{\infty,\infty}(n, p)$. Considering only $(1, 1, 1)$-random walks, $w(DEU_{\infty,\infty}(n, p))$ is the number of all paths from $(0, 0)$ to $(n, p)$ in the diagram given in Figure 9, where the boundaries at $y = k$ and $y = -h$ are eliminated. Similar interpretations can be given for the weights of the two other sets.

THEOREM 4.4

(a) Let $ud \neq 0$.

(a1) $w(DEU_{\infty,\infty}(n, p)) = \begin{cases} d^{-p}\langle v^{n-p}\rangle f(v) & \text{if } p \geq 0 \\ u^{-p}\langle v^{n-p}\rangle f(v) & \text{if } p \leq 0, \end{cases}$

where $f(v) = (v^2 + ev + ud)^n$.

(a2) $\quad w\left(\bigcup_{-h \leqslant p \leqslant k} DEU_{k,h}(n, p)\right) = \langle v^n \rangle \dfrac{(v^2 + ev + ud)^n}{(v - d)(v - u)} f_{k,h}(v),$

where

$$f_{k,h}(v) = \frac{a_1(v)[(vd)^{h+1}a_{k+1}(v) + (vu)^{k+1}a_{h+1}(v) - a_{k+h+2}(v)]}{a_{k+h+2}(v)}$$

and

$$a_m(v) = v^{2m} - (ud)^m.$$

(a3) $\quad w\left(\bigcup_{-\infty \leqslant p \leqslant \infty} DEU_{\infty,\infty}(n, p)\right) = \langle v^n \rangle \dfrac{ud - v^2}{(d - v)(u - v)}[v^2 + ev + ud]^n.$

(b) Let $ud = 0$.

(b1) $\quad w(DEU_{\infty,\infty}(n, p)) = \begin{cases} \dbinom{n}{p} u^p e^{n-p} & \text{if } p \in [0:k] \\ 0 & \text{if } p > n \end{cases}$

For $w(DEU_{\infty,\infty}(n, -p))$, $p \in [0:h]$, replace $u$ by $d$.

(b2)

$$w\left(\bigcup_{-h \leqslant p \leqslant k} DEU_{k,h}(n, p)\right) = \begin{cases} (n - h)\dbinom{n}{h} I_{d,e}(h) \\ \quad + (n - k)\dbinom{n}{k} I_{u,e}(k) - e^n \\ \qquad\qquad \text{if } k \neq n \wedge h \neq n \\[2mm] (e + u)^n - e^n + (n - h)\dbinom{n}{h} I_{d,e}(h) \\ \qquad\qquad \text{if } k = n \wedge h \neq n \\[2mm] (e + d)^n - e^n + (n - k)\dbinom{n}{k} I_{u,e}(k) \\ \qquad\qquad \text{if } k \neq n \wedge h = n \\[2mm] (e + u)^n + (e + d)^n - e^n \\ \qquad\qquad \text{if } k = h = n \end{cases}$$

where $I_{x,y}(z) = \int_x^{x+y} t^z(x + y - t)^{n-z-1} \, dt$.

(b3) $\quad w\left(\bigcup_{-\infty \leqslant p \leqslant \infty} DEU_{\infty,\infty}(n, p)\right) = (e + u)^n + (e + d)^n - e^n.$

*Proof*

(a) We have always $-n \leqslant p \leqslant n$ by definition of a random walk of length $n$ from 0 to $p$. This fact implies $DEU_{n,n}(n,p) = DEU_{\infty,\infty}(n,p)$. Using the general expression for $w(DEU_{k,h}(n,p))$ obtained above by Cauchy's formula, we find $w(DEU_{n,n}(n,p)) = \langle v^n \rangle I_{n,p,n,n}(v)$, where

$$I_{n,p,n,n}(v) = u^p v^p [v^2 + ev + ud]^n \frac{(ud)^{n-p+1} - v^{2n-2p+2}}{(ud)^{n+1} + v^{2n+2}}$$

for $p \geqslant 0$. In the case $p \leqslant 0$, we have to replace $u$ by $d$. The exponents of $v^j$ appearing in the expansion of $(v^2 + ev + ud)^n$ are all non-negative.

Considering

$$v^p \frac{(ud)^{n-p+1} - v^{2n-2p+2}}{(ud)^{n+1} + v^{2n+2}} = (ud)^{-p} \sum_{\lambda \geqslant 0} (-1)^\lambda \frac{v^{(2n+2)\lambda + p}}{(ud)^{(n+1)\lambda}}$$

$$- \sum_{\lambda \geqslant 0} (-1)^\lambda \frac{v^{(2n+2)(\lambda+1)-p}}{(ud)^{(n+1)(\lambda+1)}},$$

we see that only the term for $\lambda = 0$ in the first sum generates an exponent less than or equal to $n$. Hence

$$w(DEU_{\infty,\infty}(n,p)) = d^{-p} \langle v^{n-p} \rangle (v^2 + ev + ud)^n$$

for $p \geqslant 0$. This proves part (a1).

Since the sets $DEU_{k,h}(n,p)$ are mutually disjoint, we have

$$w\left( \bigcup_{-h \leqslant p \leqslant k} DEU_{k,h}(n,p) \right) = \sum_{-h \leqslant p \leqslant k} w(DEU_{k,h}(n,p))$$

$$= \langle v^n \rangle \left( \sum_{0 \leqslant p \leqslant h} I'_{n,p,k,h}(v) + \sum_{1 \leqslant p \leqslant k} I_{n,p,k,h}(v) \right),$$

where $I_{n,p,k,h}(v)$ is our general expression given above, and $I'_{n,p,k,h}(v)$ arises from $I_{n,p,k,h}(v)$ by replacing $k, h, u$ by $h, k, d$, respectively. The two sums correspond to geometric series; a lengthy, but elementary calculation leads to the result given in part (a2).

Using the arguments presented in the proof for (a1), we have

$$w\left( \bigcup_{-\infty \leqslant p \leqslant \infty} DEU_{\infty,\infty}(n,p) \right) = w\left( \bigcup_{-n \leqslant p \leqslant n} DEU_{n,n}(n,p) \right).$$

Hence this part is a special case of (a2).

(b) In the first part of this subsection we have derived an explicit expression for $w(DEU_{k,h}(n,p))$ in the case $ud = 0$. Applying the same arguments as in (a), we obtain the desired result. In (b2) we have used Exercise 1.4(a). ∎

Let us consider some examples.

EXAMPLE 4.1 Let $DEU_{\infty,\infty}(n,p)$ be the set of all $(d,e,u)$-random walks of length $n$ from 0 to $p$. We will compute the total weight $w(DEU_{\infty,\infty}(n,p))$ in the general case for $ud \neq 0$. An inspection of Theorem 4.4 shows that we have to determine a coefficient in the evaluation of a power of a function $f(v)$. In such cases, the *Lagrange–Bürmann formula* calls for application; it can be stated as follows:

Let $y = xf(y)$ be an equation defining implicitly $y$ as a function of $x$, where $f$ is a power series with $f(0) \neq 0$. The coefficients of $y^p$ can be expressed in terms of those of the powers of $f$ by $\langle x^n \rangle y^p = (p/n)\langle y^{n-p}\rangle f^n$.

Let us apply this formula to our problem. For this purpose, set $x := z$, $y := v$ and $f(v) := v^2 + ev + ud$. By our substitution, we have $z = v/(v^2 + ev + ud)$ and therefore $v = zf(v)$ and $v = (2z)^{-1}[1 - ez - \sqrt{(1-ez)^2 - 4udz^2}]$. (It is left to the reader to motivate the minus sign of the root!) Hence

$$\langle z^n \rangle v^p = \frac{p}{n}\langle v^{n-p}\rangle f^n.$$

In other words, $\langle v^{n-p}\rangle (v^2 + ev + ud)^n$ is equal to $n/p$ times the coefficient of $z^n$ in the expansion of $v^p$. This coefficient can easily be determined by a further application of the Lagrange–Bürmann formula. An elementary computation shows that

$$v = z^{-1}(1 - ez)C\left(\frac{udz^2}{(1-ez)^2}\right),$$

where $C(\alpha) = \frac{1}{2}(1 - \sqrt{1-4\alpha})$. Thus, if we know the coefficients in the evaluation of a power of $C$, then we can also compute the coefficients in the evaluation of a power of $v$. It is now easily verified that $C^2(\alpha) = C(\alpha) - \alpha$, or equivalently, $C(\alpha) = \alpha/(1 - C(\alpha))$. Using the Lagrange–Bürmann formula with $y := C$, $x := \alpha$ and $f(y) = (1 - y)^{-1}$, we obtain immediately for $n \geq p \geq 1$

$$\langle \alpha^n \rangle C^p = \frac{p}{n}\langle y^{n-p}\rangle f^n$$

$$= \frac{p}{n}\langle y^{n-p}\rangle (1 - y)^{-n}$$

$$= \frac{p}{n}\langle y^{n-p}\rangle \sum_{\lambda \geq 0}\binom{n-1+\lambda}{\lambda}y^\lambda$$

$$= \frac{p}{n}\binom{2n-p-1}{n-1}.$$

Since $C(0) = 0$, we have always $\langle \alpha^n \rangle C^p(\alpha) = 0$ for $n < p$. Hence

$$\langle z^n \rangle v^p = \langle z^n \rangle z^{-p}(1 - ez)^p C^p\left(\frac{udz^2}{(1-ez)^2}\right)$$

$$= \sum_{\lambda \geq 0} (\langle \alpha^{\lambda} \rangle C^p) \frac{(ud)^{\lambda} z^{2\lambda - p}}{(1 - ez)^{2\lambda - p}}$$

$$= \sum_{\lambda \geq 1} \frac{p}{\lambda} \binom{2\lambda - p - 1}{\lambda - 1} (ud)^{\lambda} \sum_{k \geq 0} \binom{2\lambda - p - 1 + k}{k} e^k z^{2\lambda - p + k}$$

$$= p e^{n + p} \sum_{\lambda \geq 1} \frac{1}{\lambda} \binom{2\lambda - p - 1}{\lambda - 1} \binom{n - 1}{2\lambda - p - 1} (ude^{-2})^{\lambda}.$$

Thus for $p \geq 0$

$$w(DEU_{\infty,\infty}(n, p)) = d^{-p} \frac{n}{p} \langle z^n \rangle v^p$$

$$= ne^n \left( \frac{e}{d} \right)^p \sum_{\lambda \geq 1} \frac{1}{\lambda} \binom{2\lambda - p - 1}{\lambda - 1} \binom{n - 1}{2\lambda - p - 1} (ude^{-2})^{\lambda}.$$

For $p \leq 0$, we have to replace $d$ by $u$.

EXAMPLE 4.2    Let $DEU_{\infty,\infty}(n, p)$ be the set of all $(1, 1, 1)$-random walks of length $n$ from 0 to $p$. We obtain, by Theorem 4.4(a1),

$$w(DEU_{\infty,\infty}(n, p)) = \langle v^{n - p} \rangle (1 + v + v^2)^n = \binom{n, 3}{n - p}.$$

Our general formula derived in Example 4.1 leads to the alternative expression

$$w(DEU_{\infty,\infty}(n, p)) = n \sum_{\lambda \geq 1} \frac{1}{\lambda} \binom{2\lambda - p - 1}{\lambda - 1} \binom{n - 1}{2\lambda - p - 1}.$$

Note that we have derived the identity

$$\binom{n, 3}{n - p} = n \sum_{\lambda \geq 1} \frac{1}{\lambda} \binom{2\lambda - p - 1}{\lambda - 1} \binom{n - 1}{2\lambda - p - 1}.$$

Thus, eliminating the boundaries in the diagram given in Figure 9, there are $\binom{n, 3}{n - p}$ paths from $(0, 0)$ to the point $(n, p)$.

By part (a2) of Theorem 4.4, we get

$$w \left( \bigcup_{-h \leq p \leq h} DEU_{h,h}(n, p) \right) = \langle v^n \rangle (1 + v + v^2)^n \frac{1 + v}{1 - v} \frac{(1 - v^{h + 1})^2}{1 + v^{2h + 2}}.$$

The expansion of the denominator leads to

$$(1 - v)^{-1} (1 + v^{2h + 2})^{-1} = \sum_{\lambda \geq 0} \sum_{0 \leq j \leq 2h + 1} v^{4\lambda(h + 1) + j}.$$

Hence, by an elementary computation,

$$w\left(\bigcup_{-h \leqslant p \leqslant h} DEU_{h,h}(n,p)\right)$$

$$= 3^n - 2 \sum_{\lambda \geqslant 0} \sum_{0 \leqslant j \leqslant h} [a_{n,h,j}(4\lambda + 1) + a_{n,h,j}(4\lambda + 2)],$$

where

$$a_{n,h,j}(m) = \binom{n,3}{n - m(h+1) \div j} + \binom{n,3}{n - m(h+1) - j - 1}.$$

Choosing $k = h$ in Figure 9, this expression gives the number of all paths with $n$ segments which start in the point $(0,0)$, or equivalently, the number of all unweighted random walks of length $n$ (from 0) having a maximal deviation less than or equal to $h$.

An application of part (a3) of Theorem 4.4 leads to

$$w\left(\bigcup_{-\infty \leqslant p \leqslant \infty} DEU_{\infty,\infty}(n,p)\right) = \langle v^n \rangle \frac{1+v}{1-v}(1 + v + v^2)^n$$

$$= \langle v^n \rangle (1 + v) \sum_{\lambda \geqslant 0} \sum_{s \geqslant 0} \binom{n,3}{s} v^{s+\lambda}$$

$$= \sum_{0 \leqslant s \leqslant n} \binom{n,3}{s} + \sum_{0 \leqslant s \leqslant n-1} \binom{n,3}{s}$$

$$= 3^n.$$

This result is evident: for each $f(t)$, $t \in [0:n-1]$, appearing in a $(1,1,1)$-random walk, there are exactly three possibilities of defining $f(t+1)$.

EXAMPLE 4.3  Let $DEU_{\infty,\infty}(n,p)$ be the set of all $(1,0,1)$-random walks of length $n$ from 0 to $p$. By a similar computation as in the previous examples, we find

$$w(DEU_{\infty,\infty}(n,p)) = \langle v^{n-p} \rangle (1 + v^2)^n$$

$$= \begin{cases} \binom{n}{(n-p)/2} & \text{if } (n+p) \equiv 0 \bmod(2) \\ 0 & \text{if } (n+p) \equiv 1 \bmod(2) \end{cases}.$$

An application of part (a2) of Theorem 4.4 yields

$$w\left(\bigcup_{-h \leqslant p \leqslant h} DEU_{h,h}(n,p)\right) = \langle v^n \rangle (1 + v^2)^n \frac{1+v}{1-v} \frac{(1 - v^{h+1})^2}{1 + v^{2h+2}}.$$

This function can be expanded in the same way as in the case of $(1,1,1)$-random walks. We obtain

$$w\left(\bigcup_{-h \leqslant p \leqslant h} DEU_{h,h}(n,p)\right) = 2^n - 2 \sum_{\lambda \geqslant 0} \sum_{0 \leqslant j \leqslant h} b_{n,h,j}(\lambda),$$

where

$$b_{n,h,j}(\lambda) = \left(\left\lceil \frac{n-h-2}{2}\right\rceil - 2\lambda(h+1) - j\right)^n$$

$$+ \left(\left\lfloor \frac{n-h-2}{2}\right\rfloor - 2\lambda(h+1) - j\right)^n.$$

Obviously, this expression gives the number of all simple unweighted random walks of length $n$ (from 0) having a maximal deviation less than or equal to $h$. This result is derived in [98]. The weight $w(\bigcup_{0 \leqslant p \leqslant k} DEU_{0,k}(n, p))$ is computed in [66]; it can be shown that the $(1, 0, 1)$-random walks in $\bigcup_{0 \leqslant p \leqslant k} DEU_{0,k}(n, p)$ correspond to all prefixes of length $n$ of the Dycklanguage $DY_1$ having a depth less than or equal to $k$ (see [66] and Exercise 5.20). Finally, an application of part (a3) of Theorem 4.4 leads to the evident result

$$w\left(\bigcup_{-\infty \leqslant p \leqslant \infty} DEU_{\infty,\infty}(n, p)\right) = 2^n.$$

It is interesting to note that the techniques given in this section lead to very nice combinatorial identities. Computing the weight of a class of random walks, we have two possibilities to obtain an explicit expression: on the one hand, we can evaluate a function by means of the binomial theorem and/or the geometric series, and on the other, we can derive this evaluation by partial fraction expansion. Here are two examples.

EXAMPLE 4.4  Considering $(1, 1, 1)$-random walks, we have proved

$$w(DEU_{\infty,\infty}(n, p)) = w(DEU_{n,n}(n, p)) = \binom{n, 3}{n - p}$$

for $|p| \leqslant n$.

Using Theorem 4.3, we obtain

$$w(DEU_{n,n}(n, p)) = \frac{1}{n+1} \sum_{1 \leqslant \lambda \leqslant 2n+1} \sin\left(\frac{\pi\lambda}{2}\right)\sin\left(\frac{\pi\lambda}{2} + \frac{\pi\lambda p}{2n+2}\right)$$

$$\times \left[1 + 2\cos\left(\frac{\pi\lambda}{2n+2}\right)\right]^n.$$

Since $\quad \sin\left(\frac{\pi\lambda}{2}\right)\sin\left(\frac{\pi\lambda}{2} + \frac{\pi\lambda p}{2n+2}\right) = \begin{cases} 0 & \text{if } \lambda \text{ even} \\ \cos\left(\dfrac{\pi\lambda p}{2n+2}\right) & \text{if } \lambda \text{ odd} \end{cases}$,

we obtain the identity

$$\binom{n, 3}{n - p} = \frac{1}{n+1} \sum_{0 \leqslant \lambda \leqslant n} \cos\left(\frac{(2\lambda+1)p\pi}{2n+2}\right)\left[1 + 2\cos\left(\frac{(2\lambda+1)\pi}{2n+2}\right)\right]^n$$

for $|p| \leqslant n$.

Furthermore, since

$$\sum_{0 \leqslant p \leqslant 2n} \binom{n, 3}{p} = 3^n,$$

$$3^n = \frac{1}{n+1} \sum_{1 \leqslant p \leqslant 2n+1} \sum_{0 \leqslant \lambda \leqslant n} (-1)^\lambda \sin\left(\frac{(2\lambda + 1)p\pi}{2n + 2}\right)$$

$$\times \left[1 + 2\cos\left(\frac{(2\lambda + 1)\pi}{2n + 2}\right)\right]^n.$$

EXAMPLE 4.5   In the case of $(1, 0, 1)$-random walks, we have proved

$$w(DEU_{\infty,\infty}(n, p)) = w(DEU_{n,n}(n, p))$$

$$= \begin{cases} \binom{n}{(n-p)/2} & \text{if } (n + p) \equiv 0 \bmod(2) \\ 0 & \text{if } (n + p) \equiv 1 \bmod(2) \end{cases}$$

for $|p| \leqslant n$. An application of Theorem 4.3 yields

$$w(DEU_{n,n}(n, p)) = \frac{2^n}{n+1} \sum_{0 \leqslant \lambda \leqslant n} \cos\left(\frac{(2\lambda + 1)p\pi}{2n + 2}\right)\cos^n\left(\frac{(2\lambda + 1)\pi}{2n + 2}\right).$$

Hence we obtain the identities

$$\binom{n}{(n-p)/2} = \frac{2^n}{n+1} \sum_{0 \leqslant \lambda \leqslant n} \cos\left(\frac{(2\lambda + 1)p\pi}{2n + 2}\right)\cos^n\left(\frac{(2\lambda + 1)\pi}{2n + 2}\right)$$

if $|p| \leqslant n$, $(n + p) \equiv 0 \bmod(2)$, and

$$0 = \sum_{0 \leqslant \lambda \leqslant n} \cos\left(\frac{(2\lambda + 1)p\pi}{2n + 2}\right)\cos^n\left(\frac{(2\lambda + 1)\pi}{2n + 2}\right)$$

if $|p| \leqslant n$, $(n + p) \equiv 1 \bmod(2)$.

For the derivation of similar results see Exercises 4.2 and 4.3. In this section we have investigated $(k, h)$-bounded, $(d, e, u)$-random walks, where $k$ and $h$ are constants. For the sake of completeness, we will quote a nice result concerning $(k, h)$-bounded, $(d, 0, u)$-random walks, where now $k, h: \mathbb{N}_0 \to \mathbb{Z}$ are functions. In our notation, the result can be stated as follows (for a proof see [10], [88]).

THEOREM 4.5   Let $h: \mathbb{N}_0 \to \mathbb{Z}$ be a function satisfying $h(0) = 0$, $|h(t) - h(t - 1)| < 1$ and let $\mathbb{P}_n$ be the set of all $(d, 0, u)$-random walks $\rho_f = (f(0), \ldots, f(n); \pi(\rho_f^1), \ldots, \pi(\rho_f^n))$ from $f(0) = 0$ to $f(n) = h(n)$ with $h(t) \leqslant f(t) \leqslant t$, $t \in \mathbb{N}_0$. The total weight $w(\mathbb{P}_n)$ is given by

$$w(\mathbb{P}_n) = \frac{(ud)^m}{d^{h(n)}} \det \begin{bmatrix} \binom{g(0)}{1} & \binom{g(1)}{0} & & & \\ \binom{g(0)}{2} & \binom{g(1)}{1} & \binom{g(2)}{0} & & 0 \\ \binom{g(0)}{3} & \binom{g(1)}{2} & \binom{g(2)}{1} & \binom{g(3)}{0} & \\ \vdots & \vdots & \vdots & & \binom{g(m-1)}{1} \\ \binom{g(0)}{m} & \binom{g(1)}{m-1} & \binom{g(2)}{m-2} & ------ & \binom{g(m-1)}{1} \end{bmatrix}$$

where $m = (n + h(n))/2$ and $g(t) = \text{MIN}\{j \mid t < h(t+j) + j\}$, $t \in \mathbb{N}_0$.

Note that $m$ is always a natural number by definition of the boundary $h(t)$. This theorem is a slight generalization of an equivalent result given in [10], [88] for $(1, 0, 1)$-random walks. The proof consists essentially of the derivation of a recurrence for $w(\mathbb{P}_n)$ which leads to a system of linear equations having a special form. Choosing $u = d = 1$, $w(\mathbb{P}_n)$ is the number of all paths from $(0, 0)$ to the point $(n, h(n))$ in a diagram such as given in Figure 10. For example, let $h(0) = h(4) = h(6) = h(8) = 0$, $h(5) = -1$, $h(1) = h(3) = h(7) = 1$, $h(2) = 2$ and $h(t) = h(t \bmod(8))$ for $t \geqslant 9$ (see Figure 10). We find

$$g(0) = \text{MIN}\{j \mid 0 < h(j) + j\} = 1,$$

$$g(1) = \text{MIN}\{j \mid 1 < h(1 + j) + j\} = 1,$$

$$g(2) = \text{MIN}\{j \mid 2 < h(j + 2) + j\} = 4$$

and generally, $g(4t) = g(4t + 1) = 4t + 1$, $g(4t + 2) = g(4t + 3) = 4t + 4$ for $t \in \mathbb{N}_0$. Choosing $n = 8$, we get $m = (8 + 0)/2 = 4$ and therefore

$$w(\mathbb{P}_8) = \det \begin{bmatrix} \binom{1}{1} & \binom{1}{0} & 0 & 0 \\ \binom{1}{2} & \binom{1}{1} & \binom{4}{0} & 0 \\ \binom{1}{3} & \binom{1}{2} & \binom{4}{1} & \binom{4}{0} \\ \binom{1}{4} & \binom{1}{3} & \binom{4}{2} & \binom{4}{1} \end{bmatrix} = \det \begin{bmatrix} 1 & 1 & 0 & 0 \\ 0 & 1 & 1 & 0 \\ 0 & 0 & 4 & 1 \\ 0 & 0 & 6 & 4 \end{bmatrix} = 10.$$

### 4.2.3 Non-negative Closed Random Walks

This section is devoted to the class of the so-called non-negative closed random walks which is more relevant to the analysis of algorithms than random walks

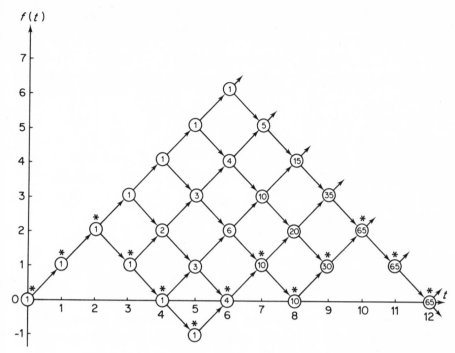

FIGURE 10. Graphical representation of the set $\mathbb{P}_n$. (The starred points correspond to the values $h(t)$ of the boundary; each point $(t, s)$ is labelled by the number of paths from $(0, 0)$ to this point.)

in their general form (see Chapter 5). A (weighted) random walk $\rho_f = (f(0), \ldots, f(n); \pi(\rho_f^1), \ldots, \pi(\rho_f^n))$ is called *closed* if $f(0) = f(n) = 0$. First, let us specify the result obtained in Theorem 4.2 to non-negative random walks. Note that a non-negative random walk is always $(k, 0)$-bounded for some $k \in \mathbb{N}_0$.

THEOREM 4.6    Let $NC_k^\varphi(n)$ be the uniform set (with respect to the specification $\varphi$ given in section 4.2.1) of all $(k, 0)$-bounded, $\mathbb{R}$-weighted, closed random walks of length $n$. The generating function

$$G_k(z) = \sum_{n \geqslant 0} w(NC_k^\varphi(n))z^n$$

of the total weights $w(NC_k^\varphi(n))$ is given by

$$G_k(z) = P_{1,k}^{(k)}(z)/P_{1,k+1}^{(k)}(z),$$

where $P_{1,s}^{(k)}(z)$ is a polynomial in $z$ recursively defined by

$$P_{1,-1}^{(k)}(z) = 0, \qquad P_{1,0}^{(k)}(z) = 1$$

$$P_{1,s}^{(k)}(z) = (1 - e_{k-s+1}z)P_{1,s-1}^{(k)}(z) - u_{k-s+1}d_{k-s+2}z^2 P_{1,s-2}^{(k)}(z)$$

for $s \geqslant 1$.    ∎

Obviously, $G_k(z)$ is always a quotient of two polynomials. Omitting the first lower index in $P_{1,s}^{(k)}(z)$, the above recurrence implies

$$\zeta_z^{(k,s)} = \frac{P_s^{(k)}(z)}{P_{s+1}^{(k)}(z)}$$

$$= \frac{1}{1 - e_{k-s}z - u_{k-s}d_{k-s+1}z^2\zeta_z^{(k,s-1)}}$$

and further by iteration

$$\zeta_z^{(k,s)} = \cfrac{1}{1 - e_{k-s}z - \cfrac{u_{k-s}d_{k-s+1}z^2}{1 - e_{k-s+1}z - \cfrac{u_{k-s+1}d_{k-s+2}z^2}{1 - e_{k-s+2}z - \cfrac{u_{k-s+2}d_{k-s+3}z^2}{1 - \cfrac{\phantom{x}}{1 - e_kz}}}}}$$

Thus we obtain a *continued fraction*. Generally, this is 'an expression of the form'

$$\eta = \cfrac{a_1}{b_1 + \cfrac{a_2}{b_2 + \cfrac{a_3}{b_3 + \cfrac{a_4}{\phantom{x}}}}}$$

which it has become customary to write in a typographically more convenient form as follows:

$$\eta = \frac{a_1|}{|b_1} + \frac{a_2|}{|b_2} + \frac{a_3|}{|b_3} + \cdots.$$

Here, $\eta$ is called *terminating* if there is an index $j$ such that $a_i \neq 0$, $1 \leq i \leq j-1$, $a_j = 0$ and $b_{j-1} \neq 0$. It is well known ([94]) that the *n-th approximant*

$$\eta(n) = \frac{a_1|}{|b_1} + \frac{a_2|}{|b_2} + \frac{a_3|}{|b_3} + \cdots + \frac{a_n|}{|b_n}$$

is given by $\eta(n) = A_n/B_n$, where

$$\begin{bmatrix} A_{-1} \\ B_{-1} \end{bmatrix} = \begin{bmatrix} 1 \\ 0 \end{bmatrix}, \quad \begin{bmatrix} A_0 \\ B_0 \end{bmatrix} = \begin{bmatrix} 0 \\ 1 \end{bmatrix}$$

$$\begin{bmatrix} A_n \\ B_n \end{bmatrix} = \begin{bmatrix} A_{n-1} & A_{n-2} \\ B_{n-1} & B_{n-2} \end{bmatrix} \begin{bmatrix} b_n \\ a_n \end{bmatrix} \quad \text{for } n \geq 1.$$

Furthermore, it is easily verified that

$$A_n B_{n-1} - A_{n-1} B_n = (-1)^{n-1} \prod_{1 \leqslant k \leqslant n} a_k.$$

Now using the notation of continued fractions, we can reformulate the result stated in Theorem 4.6 as follows.

THEOREM 4.7   The generating function

$$G_k(z) = \sum_{n \geqslant 0} w(NC_k^\varphi(n)) z^n$$

of the total weights $w(NC_k^\varphi(n))$ is given by $G_k(z) = \xi_z(k+1)$, where $\xi_z$ is the continued fraction defined by

$$\xi_z = \cfrac{1}{\left| 1 - e_0 z \right.} + \cfrac{-u_0 d_1 z^2}{\left| 1 - e_1 z \right.} + \cfrac{-u_1 d_2 z^2}{\left| 1 - e_2 z \right.} + \cdots + \cfrac{-u_{i-1} d_i z^2}{\left| 1 - e_i z \right.} + \cdots$$

$\xi_z(k+1)$ has a representation of the form $\xi_z(k+1) = A_k(z)/B_k(z)$, where $A_k(z)$ and $B_k(z)$ are polynomials satisfying the recurrences

$$A_{-1}(z) = 0, \qquad A_0(z) = 1$$

$$A_k(z) = [1 - e_k z] A_{k-1}(z) - u_{k-1} d_k z^2 A_{k-2}(z), \qquad k \geqslant 1$$

and

$$B_{-1}(z) = 1, \qquad B_0(z) = 1 - e_0 z$$

$$B_k(z) = [1 - e_k z] B_{k-1}(z) - u_{k-1} d_k z^2 B_{k-2}(z), \qquad k \geqslant 1. \quad \blacksquare$$

Letting $k$ go to infinity, we obtain a corollary to this theorem.

COROLLARY   The generating function

$$G_\infty(z) = \sum_{n \geqslant 0} w(NC_\infty^\varphi(n)) z^n$$

of the total weights of the sets $NC_\infty^\varphi(n)$ is given by $G_\infty(z) = \xi_z$, where $\xi_z$ is the continued fraction defined in Theorem 4.7.   $\blacksquare$

The representation of the function $G_k(z)$ $(G_\infty(z))$ by a continued fraction has been discovered in [29]; it was extensively studied in the subsequent paper [32]. Let us now consider some examples.

EXAMPLE 4.6   Consider the set $NCDEU_k^\varphi(n)$ consisting of all $(k, 0)$-bounded, closed $(d, e, u)$-random walks of length $n$. We obtain immediately

$$G_k(z) = \sum_{n \geqslant 0} w(NCDEU_k^\varphi(n)) z^n = \xi_z(k+1)$$

where

$$\xi_z = \frac{1}{\lfloor 1 - ez} + \frac{-udz^2 \rfloor}{\lfloor 1 - ez} + \frac{-udz^2 \rfloor}{\lfloor 1 - ez} + \cdots$$

To compute an explicit expression for $\xi_z(k+1) = A_k(z)/B_k(z)$, we have to solve the above recurrences for $A_k(z)$ and $B_k(z)$. This has already been done in section 4.2.2; we obtain $B_k(z) = A_{k+1}(z)$ and

$$A_k(z) = \begin{cases} (1 - ez)^k & \text{if } ud = 0 \\ z^k(ud)^{k/2} U_k\left(\dfrac{1 - ez}{2z\sqrt{ud}}\right) & \text{if } ud \neq 0 \end{cases},$$

where $U_k(z)$ is the $k$-th Chebyshev polynomial of the second kind.
Thus we obtain our old result (for $p = h = 0$):

$$\begin{aligned} G_k(z) &= A_k(z)/B_k(z) \\ &= \begin{cases} (1 - ez)^{-1} & \text{if } ud = 0 \\ z^{-1}(ud)^{-1/2} U_k\left(\dfrac{1 - ez}{2z\sqrt{ud}}\right) \Big/ U_{k+1}\left(\dfrac{1 - ez}{2z\sqrt{ud}}\right) & \text{if } ud \neq 0 \end{cases}. \end{aligned}$$

An expansion of these functions has already been computed in section 4.2.2.
Obviously, if $ud \neq 0$, $\xi_z$ satisfies the relation

$$\xi_z = \frac{1}{1 - ez - udz^2\xi_z},$$

which leads to a quadratic equation. Using the fact that $\xi_0 = 1$, we find the solution

$$\begin{aligned} G_\infty(z) &= \xi_z \\ &= (2udz^2)^{-1}\left[1 - ez - \sqrt{(1 - ez)^2 - 4udz^2}\right] \\ &= (udz^2)^{-1}(1 - ez)C\left(\frac{udz^2}{(1 - ez)^2}\right), \end{aligned}$$

where $C(\alpha)$ is the function introduced in Example 4.1. Since

$$C(\alpha) = \sum_{\lambda \geqslant 1} \frac{1}{\lambda}\binom{2\lambda - 2}{\lambda - 1}\alpha^\lambda$$

is the generating function of the Catalan numbers (see Example 4.1), we further obtain

$$\begin{aligned} G_\infty(z) &= \sum_{\lambda \geqslant 1} \frac{1}{\lambda}\binom{2\lambda - 2}{\lambda - 1}\frac{(udz^2)^{\lambda - 1}}{(1 - ez)^{2\lambda - 1}} \\ &= \sum_{\lambda \geqslant 0}\sum_{j \geqslant 0} \frac{1}{\lambda + 1}\binom{2\lambda}{\lambda}\binom{2\lambda + j}{j}(ud)^\lambda e^j z^{2\lambda + j}. \end{aligned}$$

Hence $\qquad w(NC^\varphi_\infty(n)) = \langle z^n \rangle G_\infty(z)$

$$= e^n \sum_{0 \leqslant \lambda \leqslant \lfloor n/2 \rfloor} \frac{1}{\lambda + 1} \binom{2\lambda}{\lambda} \binom{n}{2\lambda} \left(\frac{ud}{e^2}\right)^\lambda.$$

Choosing $e = 0$, this sum collapses and we find (convention $0^0 \equiv 1$)

$$w(NC^\varphi_\infty(n)) = \begin{cases} \dfrac{1}{N+1} \dbinom{2N}{N} u^N d^N & \text{if } n = 2N \\ 0 & \text{if } n = 2N+1 \end{cases}.$$

Thus the Catalan numbers were rediscovered.

Considering $(1, 1, 1)$-random walks, we obtain

$$w(NC^\varphi_\infty(n)) = \sum_{0 \leqslant \lambda \leqslant \lfloor n/2 \rfloor} \frac{1}{\lambda + 1} \binom{2\lambda}{\lambda} \binom{n}{2\lambda}.$$

These numbers are well known under the name *Motzkin numbers*. The first few values are $1, 1, 2, 4, 9, 21, \ldots$; they correspond to the number of paths from $(0, 0)$ to $(n, 0)$ in the diagram given in Figure 9, where the boundaries are $h = 0$ and $k = \infty$.

EXAMPLE 4.7 Let us consider the set $NC^\varphi_k(n)$ of all $(k, 0)$-bounded, $\mathbb{N}_0$-weighted, closed random walks of length $n$ with the labels $e_i = 2i + 1$ and $u_i d_{i+1} = (i + 1)^2$, $i \in \mathbb{N}_0$. By Theorem 4.7 the generating function of the weights $w(NC^\varphi_k(n))$ is given by the $(k + 1)$-th approximant of the continued fraction

$$\xi_z = \frac{1}{\lfloor 1 - z} + \frac{-1^2 z^2}{\lfloor 1 - 3z} + \frac{-2^2 z^2}{\lfloor 1 - 5z} + \frac{-3^2 z^2}{\lfloor 1 - 7z} + \cdots$$

To obtain an explicit expression for $\xi_z(k + 1)$, we have to solve the recurrences

$$A_{-1}(z) = 0, \qquad A_0(z) = 1$$

$$A_k(z) = [1 - (2k + 1)z]A_{k-1}(z) - k^2 z^2 A_{k-2}(z), \qquad k \geqslant 1$$

and

$$B_{-1}(z) = 1, \qquad B_0(z) = 1 - z$$

$$B_k(z) = [1 - (2k + 1)z]B_{k-1}(z) - k^2 z^2 B_{k-2}(z), \qquad k \geqslant 1.$$

For this purpose, let

$$F_A(z, t) = \sum_{k \geqslant 0} A_{k-1}(z)t^k/k! \quad \text{and} \quad F_B(z, t) = \sum_{k \geqslant 0} B_{k-1}(z)t^k/k!$$

be the exponential generating functions of the polynomials $A_k(z)$ and $B_k(z)$. The above recurrences imply immediately the following differential equations:

$$(1 + zt)^2 \frac{\partial}{\partial t} F_A(z, t) = 1 + (1 - z - z^2 t)F_A(z, t)$$

and

$$(1 + zt)^2 \frac{\partial}{\partial t} F_B(z, t) = (1 - z - z^2 t) F_B(z, t).$$

First, we consider the last equation. Obviously,

$$\frac{\partial}{\partial t} F_B(z, t) / F_B(z, t) = (1 - z - z^2 t)/(1 + zt)^2$$

and therefore,

$$\ln(F_B(z, t)) = R(z) + \int \frac{1 - z - z^2 t}{(1 + zt)^2} dt$$

$$= R(z) - \ln(1 + tz) + \frac{t}{1 + tz}.$$

The function $R(z)$ is determined by the initial condition $F_B(z, 0) = B_{-1}(z) = 1$; this fact implies $R(z) = 0$. Hence

$$F_B(z, t) = (1 + tz)^{-1} \exp(t/(1 + tz)).$$

An inspection of (B88) shows that the function $F_B(z^{-1}, -tz)$ is equal to the generating function of the Laguerre polynomial $L_n^{(0)}(z)$. Thus $L_n^{(0)}(z) = n!^{-1}(-1)^n z^n B_{n-1}(z^{-1})$ or equivalently

$$B_k(z) = (k + 1)! (-1)^{k+1} z^{k+1} L_{k+1}^{(0)}(z^{-1}).$$

As usual, to obtain the solution of the non-homogeneous differential equation for $F_A(z, t)$, we can use the solution $F_B(z, t)$ of the homogeneous equation. We find

$$F_A(z, t) = F_B(z, t) H(z, t),$$

where

$$\frac{\partial}{\partial t} H(z, t) = \frac{1}{1 + zt} \exp(-t/(1 + zt)).$$

Unfortunately, the integral of the function appearing on the right-hand side of this equation is not elementary, because the substitution $t := (1 - uz)/(uz^2)$ leads to

$$-z^{-1} \exp(-z^{-1}) \int u^{-1} \exp(u) \, du.$$

On the other hand, it is easily verified that

$$\frac{\partial}{\partial t} H(z, t) = F_B(-z, -t).$$

Thus

$$\frac{\partial}{\partial t} H(z, t) = \sum_{k \geqslant 0} B_{k-1}(-z)(-1)^k t^k / k!$$

or equivalently

$$H(z, t) = Y(z) + \sum_{k \geqslant 0} (-1)^k (k + 1)^{-1} t^{k+1} z^k L_k^{(0)}(-z^{-1}),$$

where the function $Y(z)$ is defined by the initial condition

$$F_A(z, 0) = A_{-1}(z) = 0;$$

we find immediately that $Y(z) = 0$. Therefore,

$$F_A(z, t) = F_B(z, t) H(z, t)$$

$$= \sum_{k \geqslant 0} t^{k+1} z^k (-1)^k \sum_{0 \leqslant i \leqslant k} \frac{1}{i + 1} L_i^{(0)}(-z^{-1}) L_{k-i}^{(0)}(z^{-1}).$$

Thus

$$A_k(z) = (k + 1)! \, z^k (-1)^k \sum_{0 \leqslant \mu \leqslant k} \frac{1}{\mu + 1} L_\mu^{(0)}(-z^{-1}) L_{k-\mu}^{(0)}(z^{-1}).$$

Combining these results, we have proved that the generating function $G_k(z)$ of the weights $w(NC_k^\varphi(n))$ is given by

$$G_k(z) = \xi_z(k + 1)$$

$$= A_k(z)/B_k(z)$$

$$= -z^{-1} \left[ \sum_{0 \leqslant \mu \leqslant k} \frac{1}{\mu + 1} L_\mu^{(0)}(-z^{-1}) L_{k-\mu}^{(0)}(z^{-1}) \right] \bigg/ L_{k+1}^{(0)}(z^{-1}),$$

where $L_k^{(0)}(z)$ is the $k$-th Laguerre polynomial. In order to compute the generating function $G_\infty(z) = \xi_z$ of the weights $w(NC_\infty^\varphi(n))$, we cannot use the same procedure as in the previous example because there is no evident functional equation for $\xi_z$. However, in the present case, we can apply a classical result ([115]) which can be stated as follows:

Let $\xi(z) = \sum_{n \geqslant 0} \xi_n z^n$ be a generating function which has the continued fraction expansion

$$\xi_z = \frac{1}{\underline{|1 - a_0 z|}} + \frac{-b_1 z^2}{\underline{|1 - a_1 z|}} + \frac{-b_2 z^2}{\underline{|1 - a_2 z|}} + \cdots,$$

and let $\xi_z(k + 1) = A_k(z)/B_k(z)$ be the $(k + 1)$-th approximant of $\xi_z$; furthermore, let $\langle \ \rangle_{\xi_n}$ be a linear form over polynomials $P(x) = \sum_{0 \leqslant i \leqslant k} p_i x^i$ defined by $\langle P(x) \rangle_{\xi_n} = \sum_{i \geqslant 0} p_i \xi_i$. The polynomials $\mathbf{B}_k(z) = z^{k+1} B_k(z^{-1})$ satisfy the orthogonality relations

$$\langle z^i | \mathbf{B}_{k-1}(z) \rangle_{\xi_n} = \langle \mathbf{B}_{i-1}(z) | \mathbf{B}_{k-1}(z) \rangle_{\xi_n} = \delta_{k,i} b_1 b_2 \ldots b_k$$

for $0 \leqslant i \leqslant k$, where $\langle P(x) | Q(x) \rangle_{\xi_n}$ is the scalar product defined by $\langle P(x) | Q(x) \rangle_{\xi_n} = \langle P(x) Q(x) \rangle_{\xi_n}$.

This result enables us to compute $G_\infty(z)$, because the generating function

$\mathbf{F}_B(z, t)$ of the polynomials $\mathbf{B}_{k-1}(z)$ is known; we have

$$\mathbf{F}_B(z, t) = \sum_{k \geqslant 0} \mathbf{B}_{k-1}(z) t^k / k!$$

$$= F_B(z^{-1}, zt)$$

$$= (1 + t)^{-1} \exp(zt/(1 + t))$$

and therefore (we omit the index $w(NC_\infty^\varphi(n))$ in the forms $\langle \ \rangle$)

$$\langle \mathbf{F}_B(z, t) \rangle = \langle (1 + t)^{-1} \exp(zt/(1 + t)) \rangle$$

$$= (1 + t)^{-1} \left\langle \sum_{\lambda \geqslant 0} \frac{1}{\lambda!} z^\lambda \left( \frac{t}{1 + t} \right)^\lambda \right\rangle$$

$$= (1 + t)^{-1} \sum_{\lambda \geqslant 0} \frac{1}{\lambda!} \left( \frac{t}{1 + t} \right)^\lambda w(NC_\infty^\varphi(\lambda)).$$

On the other hand, we obtain

$$\langle \mathbf{F}_B(z, t) \rangle = \left\langle \sum_{k \geqslant 0} \mathbf{B}_{k-1}(z) t^k / k! \right\rangle$$

$$= \sum_{k \geqslant 0} \langle \mathbf{B}_{k-1}(z) \rangle t^k / k!$$

$$= \sum_{k \geqslant 0} \langle \mathbf{B}_{-1}(z) \mathbf{B}_{k-1}(z) \rangle t^k / k!$$

$$= \sum_{k \geqslant 0} \langle \mathbf{B}_{-1}(z) | \mathbf{B}_{k-1}(z) \rangle t^k / k!$$

$$= \sum_{k \geqslant 0} \delta_{k,0} k!^2 t^k / k!$$

$$= 1.$$

Choosing $z = t/(1 + t)$, we find immediately that

$$(1 - z) \sum_{\lambda \geqslant 0} \frac{z^\lambda}{\lambda!} w(NC_\infty^\varphi(\lambda)) = 1$$

or equivalently that

$$\sum_{\lambda \geqslant 0} \frac{z^\lambda}{\lambda!} w(NC_\infty^\varphi(\lambda)) = \frac{1}{1 - z}.$$

Therefore, $w(NC_\infty^\varphi(n)) = n!$.

## 4.3 One-to-one Correspondences

### 4.3.1 Random Walks–Ordered Trees

DEFINITION 4.6    An (*unordered*) *tree* is a rooted digraph $T = (V, A)$ with one root $r(T) \in V$ such that out$(r(T)) = 0$ and out$(v) = 1$ for all $v \in V\backslash\{r(T)\}$. If $(v_1, v_2) \in A$, we say that $v_1$ ($v_2$) is the *son* (*father*) of $v_2$ ($v_1$). A node $v_1$ is the *brother* of a node $v_2$ if $v_1$ and $v_2$ have the same father; a node $v_1$ ($v_2$) is the *ancestor* (*descendant*) of $v_2$ ($v_1$) if there is a path from $v_2$ to $v_1$. A *leaf* (*interior node*) is a node $v \in V$ with in$(v) = 0$ (in$(v) > 0$). A *subtree* of a tree $T$ is any tree $T' = (V', A')$ such that $V' \neq \varnothing$, $V' \subseteq V$, $A' = (V' \times V') \cap A$ and no node of $V\backslash V'$ is a descendant of a node in $V'$. If $(v_1, v_2) \in A$, then each subtree $T'$ with $r(T') = v_1$ is called a *subtree of* $v_2$. The tree $T$ is a *r-tree* if in$(r(T)) = r$; $T$ is an *extended binary tree* if either in$(v) = 0$ or in$(v) = 2$ for all $v \in V$; $T$ is an *t-ary tree*, if each node in $T$ has the in-degree $t \in \mathbb{N}$ or zero. The *level* of a node $v \in V$ is the number of nodes on the path from $v$ to the root $r(T)$ including $r(T)$ and $v$. The *height* $h(T)$ of a tree $T$ is the maximum level of a node $v \in V$ appearing in $T$. We say the tree $T$ has a *height of order r*, $r \in \mathbb{N}$, if there are exactly $r$ nodes in $T$ with maximum level. The binary tree is called *complete* if all leaves have the same level.

For example, let $V = \{v_0, v_1, v_2, v_3, v_4, v_5, v_6\}$ and $A = \{(v_1, v_0), (v_2, v_0), (v_3, v_1), (v_4, v_3), (v_5, v_3), (v_6, v_2)\}$. We shall follow the convention of drawing trees with the root on top and having all edges directed downward. Figure 11(a) represents the tree $T = (V, A)$. Adopting the above convention, we can omit the arrowheads and obtain the graph given in Figure 11(b). Figure 11(c) represents the same tree. Obviously, $v_3$ is the father of the nodes $v_4, v_5$ and $v_1, v_2$ are sons of the root $r(T) = v_0$; $v_1$ ($v_4$) is the brother of $v_2$ ($v_5$). The node $v_0$ is an ancestor of $v_3$, and $v_6$ is a descendant of $v_0$. The leaves of $T$ are $v_4, v_5, v_6$, the interior nodes $v_0, v_1, v_2, v_3$. The tree $T' = (V', A')$ with $V' = \{v_1, v_3, v_4, v_5\}$ and $A' = \{(v_3, v_1), (v_4, v_3), (v_5, v_3)\}$ is a subtree of $T$ with root $v_1$; the tree $T'' = (V'', A'')$ with $V'' = \{v_1, v_3, v_4\}$ and $A'' = \{(v_3, v_1), (v_4, v_3)\}$ is not a subtree of $T$, because

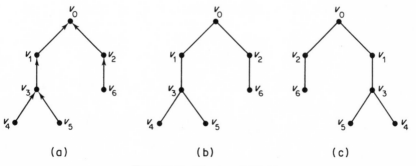

(a)                    (b)                    (c)

FIGURE 11. The tree $T(V, A)$.

$v_5 \in V \backslash V''$ is a descendant of $v_3 \in V''$. Obviously, $T$ is a 2-tree; it is not an extended binary tree. The root $v_0$ has level 1, $v_1, v_2$ have level 2, $v_3, v_6$ have level 3, and $v_4, v_5$ have level 4. The tree $T$ has the height $h(T) = 4$ which is of order 2.

DEFINITION 4.7  Let $T = (V, A)$ be a tree, $v \in V$ and $R_v = A \cap (V \times \{v\})$. Here, $T$ is called an *ordered tree* if there is a linear order $\prec$ on each non-empty $R_v$, $v \in V$; $T$ is called a *labelled tree* if there is a (total) mapping $f: V \to L$ for some set $L$ of labels; and $T$ is called an *unlabelled tree* if the labelling function $f$ has a range with one element.

Evidently, if $(v_1, v)$ is the $i$-th element in $R_v$ with respect to $\prec$, it makes sense to call the tree $T'$ with $r(T') = v_1$ the '$i$-th subtree' at node $v$. For example, consider the tree given in Figure 11. We have $R_{v_0} = \{(v_1, v_0), (v_2, v_0)\}$, $R_{v_1} = \{(v_3, v_1)\}$, $R_{v_2} = \{(v_6, v_2)\}$, $R_{v_3} = \{(v_4, v_3), (v_5, v_3)\}$, and $R_v = \varnothing$ for $v \in \{v_4, v_5, v_6\}$. Unless otherwise stated, we shall assume that the sons of a node $v$ are always linearly ordered from left to right in the graphical representation of a tree. Choosing the orderings $(v_1, v_0) \prec (v_2, v_0)$ in $R_{v_0}$ and $(v_4, v_3) \prec (v_5, v_3)$ in $R_{v_3}$, we obtain the tree of Figure 11(a); if the orderings are defined by $(v_2, v_0) \prec (v_1, v_0)$ and $(v_5, v_3) \prec (v_4, v_3)$, then the resulting ordered tree is drawn in Figure 11(c). Thus the trees given in Figure 11(a) and 11(c) are identical as unordered trees, but not as ordered trees. Similarly, the trees drawn in Figure 12 are distinct if they are considered as ordered labelled trees. As ordered unlabelled trees, the first and the second one are identical; as unordered labelled trees, the first and the third one are the same. Finally, as unordered unlabelled trees, (a), (b), and (c) represent the same tree. Henceforth, we will assume that *all trees we discuss are ordered unlabelled trees, unless it is explicitly stated otherwise.* Sometimes, ordered unlabelled trees are also called *plane trees*, since they are embedded in the plane so that the relative order of subtrees at each node is part of their structure.

DEFINITION 4.8  Let $T = (V, A)$ be a tree. The *post-order* (*pre-order, level-order*) of the nodes of $T$ is the word $PO(T) \in V^*$ ($PRO(T) \in V^*$, $LO(T) \in V^*$) recursively defined by:

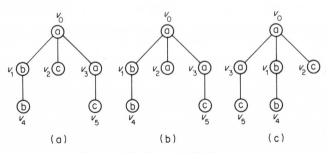

(a)    (b)    (c)

FIGURE 12. Three labelled trees.

(1) If $T$ has a root with no subtree, then $PO(T) = PRO(T) = LO(T) = r(T)$.
(2) If $T$ has a root $r(T)$ with the subtrees $T_1, T_2, \ldots, T_k$, then $PO(T) = PO(T_1)PO(T_2) \ldots PO(T_k)r(T)$ $(PRO(T) = r(T)PRO(T_1)PRO(T_2) \ldots PRO(T_k)$, $LO(T) = r(T)LO(T_1)r(T)LO(T_2)r(T) \ldots r(T)LO(T_k)r(T))$.

Thus the post-order, pre-order, and level-order of the nodes of the tree given in Figure 11(a) is $PO(T) = v_4 v_5 v_3 v_1 v_6 v_2 v_0$, $PRO(T) = v_0 v_1 v_3 v_4 v_5 v_2 v_6$, and $LO(T) = v_0 v_1 v_3 v_4 v_3 v_5 v_3 v_1 v_0 v_2 v_6 v_2 v_0$, respectively.

There are well-known one-to-one correspondences between classes of trees and unweighted non-negative closed random walks introduced in section 4.2.

(a) *Ordered trees with n nodes—closed* $(1, 0, 1)$-*random walks*
    *of length* $2n - 2$

Let $LO(T) = v_0 v_1 \ldots v_{2n-2}$ be the level order of $T$. We define the random walk $\rho_f^T = (f(0), \ldots, f(2n - 2))$ by $f(i) = \text{level}(v_i) - 1, 0 \leqslant i \leqslant 2n - 2$, where $\text{level}(v)$ denotes the level of the node $v$. It is easy to see that this sets up a one-to-one correspondence between all ordered trees with $n$ nodes and all non-negative closed $(1, 0, 1)$-random walks of length $2n - 2$. For example, consider all trees with four nodes illustrated in Figure 13. The level-order of the nodes and the corresponding random walks are given in the third and second columns. The last column shows the graphical representation of these random walks. The present one-to-one correspondence transforms some quantities defined on trees into those defined on non-negative closed random walks. For example, the height $h(T)$ is equal to the maximal deviation of $\rho_f^T$ increased by one, the order $p$ of the height is equal to the number of segments with level $d(\rho_f^T)$ appearing in $\rho_f^T$ and the in-degree of the root of $T$ is equal to the number of segments with level 0.

(b) *Ordered binary trees with n leaves—closed* $(1, 0, 1)$-*random walks*
    *of length* $2n - 2$

Let $PO(T) = v_0 v_1 \ldots v_{2n-2}$ be the post-order of the binary tree $T$ with the set of leaves $L$ and the set of interior nodes $I$. We define the random walk $\rho_f^T = (f(0), \ldots, f(2n - 2))$ by

$$f(0) = 0$$

$$f(i) = \begin{cases} f(i - 1) + 1 & \text{if } v_i \in L \\ f(i - 1) - 1 & \text{if } v_i \in I \end{cases} \quad 1 \leqslant i \leqslant 2n - 2.$$

It is not hard to see that this defines a one-to-one correspondence between all binary trees with $2n + 1$ nodes and all non-negative, closed $(1, 0, 1)$-random walks of length $2n$. Figure 14 illustrates this relation for $n = 3$.

The defined correspondence plays an important part in the analysis of algorithms that traverse a binary tree using a stack (see section 5.1.1). The maximal deviation of the random walk $\rho_f^T$ increased by one represents the maximum size of the stack; the number of segments with level $d(\rho_f^T)(0)$

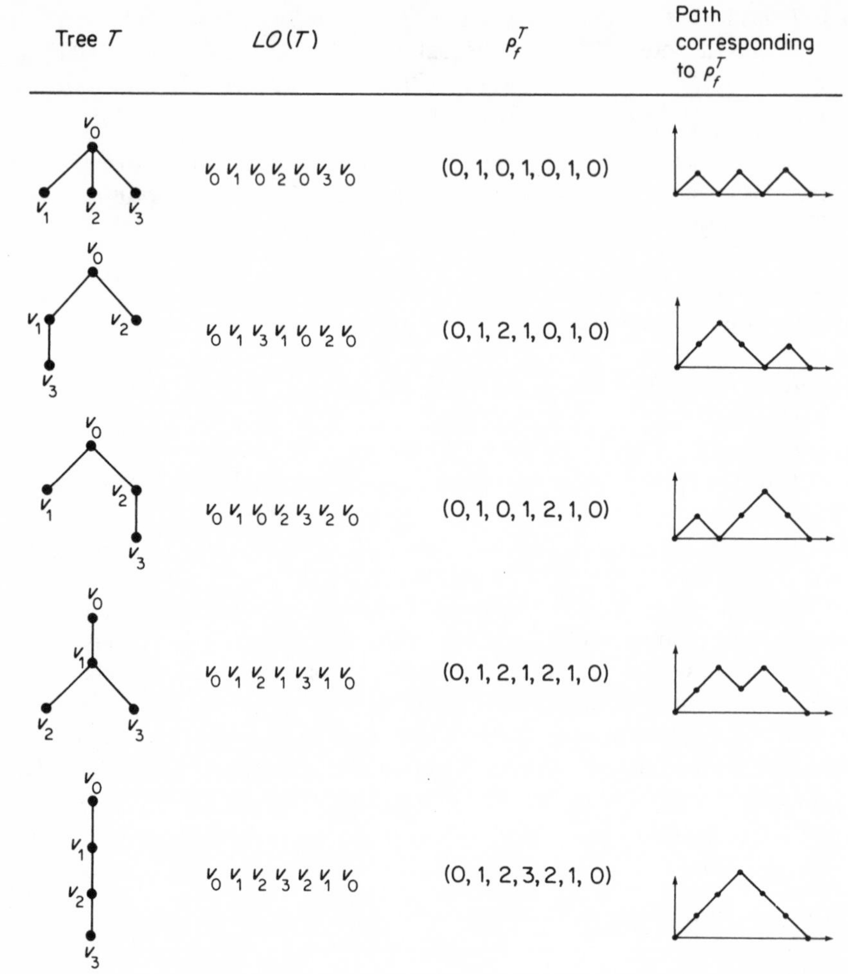

| Tree $T$ | $LO(T)$ | $P_f^T$ | Path corresponding to $P_f^T$ |
|---|---|---|---|
| $v_0$ / $v_1$ $v_2$ $v_3$ | $v_0\,v_1\,v_0\,v_2\,v_0\,v_3\,v_0$ | $(0, 1, 0, 1, 0, 1, 0)$ | |
| $v_0$ / $v_1$ $v_2$ / $v_3$ | $v_0\,v_1\,v_3\,v_1\,v_0\,v_2\,v_0$ | $(0, 1, 2, 1, 0, 1, 0)$ | |
| $v_0$ / $v_1$ $v_2$ / $v_3$ | $v_0\,v_1\,v_0\,v_2\,v_3\,v_2\,v_0$ | $(0, 1, 0, 1, 2, 1, 0)$ | |
| $v_0$ / $v_1$ / $v_2$ $v_3$ | $v_0\,v_1\,v_2\,v_1\,v_3\,v_1\,v_0$ | $(0, 1, 2, 1, 2, 1, 0)$ | |
| $v_0$ / $v_1$ / $v_2$ / $v_3$ | $v_0\,v_1\,v_2\,v_3\,v_2\,v_1\,v_0$ | $(0, 1, 2, 3, 2, 1, 0)$ | |

FIGURE 13. All ordered trees with four nodes and the corresponding random walks.

corresponds to the number of configurations in which the stack has maximum size (is empty).

Note that (a) and (b) also induce a one-to-one correspondence between the set of all ordered trees with $n$ nodes and the set of all ordered binary trees with $2n - 1$ nodes. This relationship was discovered in [50]. It can be checked that our correspondence is (apart from the notation) identical to that described in [20].

### 4.3.2 Random Walks–Dynamic Data Structures

A *data type* consists of a set of objects (its *domain*) and a set of operations to be done on these objects. Using the 'operational specification', the domain and

| Binary tree $T$ | $PO(T)$ | $\rho_f^T$ | Path corresponding to $\rho_f^T$ |
|---|---|---|---|

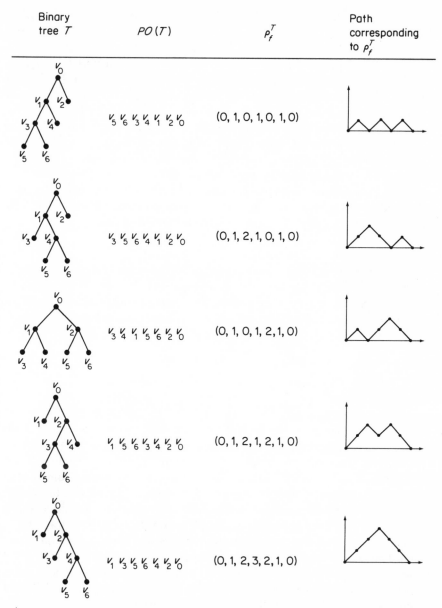

FIGURE 14. All ordered binary trees with seven nodes and the corresponding random walks.

operations of a type can be described by the domain and operations of some previously defined type; in our case, this basic type is a 'file' (standing for a set or a sequence) together with the operations 'insertion' ($I$), 'deletion' ($D$), 'successful search' ($S^+$) and 'negative search' ($S^-$). It is assumed that these basic types are intuitively clear so that we can renounce a formal definition.

A *history of length* $n$ (see [34], [43]) is a sequence of operations $O_1(k_1)$, $O_2(k_2)$, ..., $O_n(k_n)$, where $k_i$ is a *key* (an element of a finite set) and $O_i \in \{I, D, S^+, S^-\}$, $1 \leqslant i \leqslant n$. We shall describe the performance of an operation $O$ in terms of their effect on the files. Given a history $O_1(k_1)$, $O_2(k_2)$, ..., $O_n(k_n)$, the *content* $f_i$ of the file at *stage i* is recursively defined by $f_0 = \varnothing$ and $f_i$ is the result of performing $O_i(k_i)$ on $f_{i-1}$, $2 \leqslant i \leqslant n$. A history of length $n$ is called *closed* if $f_n = \varnothing$; it is called *feasible* if the result of performing $O_i(k_i)$ on $f_{i-1}$ is always defined. For example, the deletion of a key in an empty file leads to a history which is not feasible. Finally, a history of length $n$ is said to be of *size k* if $\text{MAX}_{0 \leqslant i \leqslant n} (|f_i|) = k$, where $|f_i|$ denotes the number of elements appearing in the file at stage $i$.

We shall now give some one-to-one correspondences between classes of data types and $\mathbb{N}_0$-weighted random walks. These correspondences were first introduced in [29], [43]. They are extensively studied in [34].

### (a) *Stacks—(1, 0, 1)-random walks*

The domain of the data-type *stack* consists of all sequences (=files) on a set of keys which are accessed by position. The operations are $I$ and $D$ which can be performed only at one end ('top') of the file. Formally, the performance of an operation $O(k)$ on the content of a file $f = (a_1, a_2, \ldots, a_r)$ leads to an $f'$ defined by

$$f' = \begin{cases} (a_1, a_2, \ldots, a_r, k) & \text{if } O = I \\ (a_1, a_2, \ldots, a_{r-1}) & \text{if } O = D \text{ and } r \geqslant 1. \\ \text{undefined} & \text{otherwise} \end{cases}$$

There is exactly one possibility of inserting or deleting a key. Forgetting about the key values and retaining only the information relative to the position of keys, we are interested in the set of all closed histories of length $n$ (with maximum size $k$). For example, the paths from (i.e. random walks) from $(0, 0)$ to $(6, 0)$ in the diagram drawn in Figure 15 correspond to all feasible closed histories of length 6 with maximum size 3. The set of histories of odd length is empty; the five closed histories of length 6 are $I, D, I, D, I, D$ (of size 1), $I, D, I, I, D, D$; $I, I, D, D, I, D$; $I, I, D, I, D, D$ (all of size 2) and $I, I, I, D, D, D$ (of size 3). The one-to-one correspondence between the closed histories of length $n$ induced by a stack and the set of all closed non-negative $(1, 0, 1)$-random walks of length $n$ should be obvious; the history has the maximum size $k$ if and only if the corresponding random walk has a maximal deviation $k$.

### (b) *Deques—(2, 0, 2)-random walks*

The domain of the data type *deque* consists of all sequences (=files) on a set of keys which are accessed by position. The operations are $I$ and $D$ which can be performed at the ends of the file. Thus we have to distinguish between two types of insertions $I_l, I_r$ and deletions $D_l, D_r$; the operation $I_l$ $(D_l)$ describes the insertion (deletion) of a key at the left-hand end, $I_r$ $(D_r)$ the same operation at

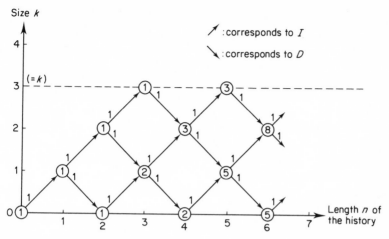

FIGURE 15. A diagram representing histories induced by a stack. (The number of possibilities of performing an operation is indicated by the label of the segments; the encircled numbers correspond to the number of histories.)

the right-hand end of the file. Formally, performing an operation $O(k)$ on the content of a file $f = (a_1, a_2, \ldots, a_r)$ leads to a file $f'$ defined by

$$
f' = \begin{cases}
(a_1, a_2, \ldots, a_r, k) & \text{if } O = I_r \\
(k, a_1, a_2, \ldots, a_r) & \text{if } O = I_l \\
(a_1, a_2, \ldots, a_{r-1}) & \text{if } O = D_r \wedge r \geqslant 1. \\
(a_2, a_3, \ldots, a_r) & \text{if } O = D_l \wedge r \geqslant 1 \\
\text{undefined} & \text{otherwise}
\end{cases}
$$

Thus there are two possibilities of inserting or deleting a key. Similar to (a), omitting the key values and retaining only the information relative to the position of the keys, we will consider the set of all closed histories of length $n$ (with maximum size $k$). The number of all feasible closed histories of length 6 with maximum size 3 are represented by the total weight of the set consisting of all paths (i.e. random walks) from $(0, 0)$ to $(6, 0)$ drawn in Figure 16. For example, there are four histories of length 2, namely $I_l, D_l$; $I_r, D_r$; $I_l, D_r$ and $I_r, D_l$ (all of size 1). The one-to-one correspondence between the closed histories of length $n$ (with maximum size $k$) and the set of all $((k, 0)$-bounded) closed non-negative $(2, 0, 2)$-random walks of length $n$ is evident.

In a similar way as in (a) and (b), we can define further one-to-one correspondences between histories induced by a queue, by an input-restricted deque, or by an output-restricted deque and the set of all closed $(1, 0, 1)$-, $(2, 0, 1)$-, and $(1, 0, 2)$-random walks, respectively (see Exercise 4.15).

88

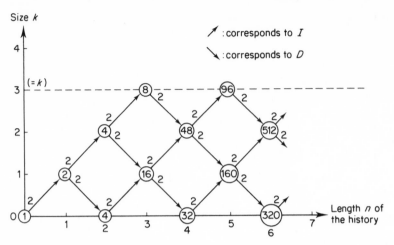

FIGURE 16. A diagram representing histories induced by a deque. (The number of possibilities of performing an operation is indicated by the label of the segments; the encircled numbers correspond to the number of histories.)

(c) *Linear lists—weighted random walks with* $e_i = 0$,
$u_i = d_{i+1} = i + 1, i \in \mathbb{N}_0$

The elements of the domain of the data type *linear list* are all sequences ($=$files) on a set of keys which are accessed by position. The operations are $I$ and $D$ which can be performed without restriction; therefore, we have to distinguish between the types of insertions $I_1, I_2, I_3, \ldots$ (deletions $D_1, D_2, D_3, \ldots$) according to the position in the file where the operation must be performed. Formally, an operation $O(k)$ made on the content of a file $f = (a_1, a_2, \ldots, a_r)$ yields a file $f'$ defined by

$$f' = \begin{cases} (a_1, \ldots, a_{p-1}, k, a_p, \ldots, a_r) & \text{if } O = I_p \wedge p \in [1:r+1] \\ (a_1, \ldots, a_{p-1}, a_{p+1}, \ldots, a_r) & \text{if } O = D_p \wedge r \geqslant 1 \\ \text{undefined} & \text{otherwise} \end{cases}$$

Thus if a file consists of $r$ keys, there are $(r + 1)$ possible operations $I$ and $r$ possible operations $D$. The number of all feasible closed histories of length 6 with maximum size 3 are represented by the total weight of the set of all paths (i.e. random walks) from $(0, 0)$ to $(6, 0)$ drawn in Figure 17. For example, there are five closed histories of length 4, namely $I_1, D_1, I_1, D_1$ (of size 1) and $I_1, I_1, D_1, D_1; I_1, I_1, D_2, D_1; I_1, I_2, D_1, D_1; I_1, I_2, D_2, D_1$ (all of size 2). The one-to-one correspondence between the closed histories of length $n$ (with maximum size $k$) and the set of all weighted ($(k, 0)$-bounded) closed non-negative random walks of length $n$ is obvious; using the notation introduced in section 4.2.1, the weights are $e_i = 0$, $u_i = i + 1$, and $d_{i+1} = i + 1$ for $i \in \mathbb{N}_0$.

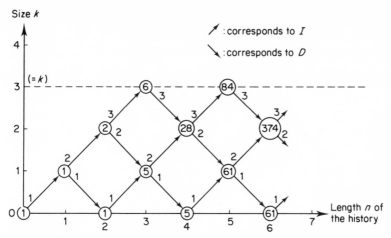

FIGURE 17. A diagram representing histories induced by a linear list. (The number of possibilities of performing an operation is indicated by the label of the segments; the encircled numbers correspond to the number of histories.)

**(d)** *Priority queues—weighted random walks with $e_i = 0$,*
$$u_i = i + 1, d_{i+1} = 1, i \in \mathbb{N}_0$$

The domain of the data-type *priority queue* consists of all finite subsets (=files) of a totally ordered set $K$ of keys which are accessed by value. The operations are $I$ and $D$; deletion $D$ is performed only on the key of minimal value. Here, we have to distinguish between the types of insertions $I_1, I_2, I_3, \ldots$ according to the relative rank (with respect to the order on $K$) of the key $k$ which is to insert in a file $f$. Formally, if $f = \{b_1, b_2, \ldots, b_r\}$ denotes the file $f = \{a_1, a_2, \ldots, a_r\}$, where $b_1 < b_2 < \cdots < b_r$, then, performing an operation $O(k)$ on the content of $f$ leads to a file $f'$ defined by

$$f' = \begin{cases} f \cup \{k\} & \text{if } O = I_s \wedge k \notin f \\ f \backslash \{b_1\} & \text{if } O = D \\ \text{undefined} & \text{otherwise} \end{cases},$$

where $b_s \leqslant k < b_{s+1}$, $s \in [0:r]$, with the convention $b_0 < k \leqslant b_{r+1}$. Thus, if a file has $r$ keys, we have $(r+1)$ possible operations $I$ and one operation $D$. Retaining only the relative rank of a key which is operated upon, the number of all feasible closed histories of length 6 with maximum size 3 are represented by the total weight of the set of all paths (i.e. random walks) from $(0, 0)$ to $(6, 0)$ drawn in Figure 18. For example, there are three closed histories of length 4, namely $I_1, D, I_1, D$ (of size 1) and $I_1, I_1, D, D$; $I_1, I_2, D, D$ (of size 2). Thus we have a one-to-one correspondence between the closed histories of length $n$ (with maximum size $k$) and the set of all weighted $((k, 0)$-bounded) closed non-negative random walks of length $n$, where the weights are $e_i = 0$, $u_i = i + 1$ and $d_{i+1} = 1$, $i \in \mathbb{N}_0$.

90

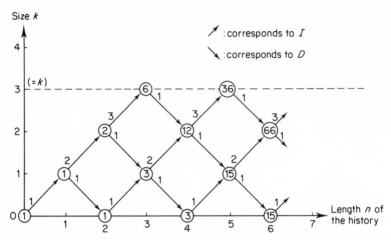

FIGURE 18. A diagram representing histories induced by a priority queue. (The number of possibilities of performing an operation is indicated by the label of the segments; the encircled numbers correspond to the number of histories.)

(e) *Symbol tables—weighted random walks with $e_i = i$,*
  $u_i = i + 1, d_{i+1} = 1, i \in \mathbb{N}_0$

The domain of the data type *symbol table* consists of all sequences (=files) on a set of keys which are accessed by value. The operations are $I$, $D$, and $S^+$. A deletion $D$ operates always on the key last inserted in the file; the operation $S^+$ does not change the content of the file. Similar to the above cases (see also [34]), we obtain a one-to-one correspondence between the closed histories of length $n$ (with maximum size $k$) and the set of all weighted ($(k, 0)$-bounded) closed non-negative random walks of length $n$, where the weights are $e_i = i$, $u_i = i + 1$, and $d_{i+1} = 1, i \in \mathbb{N}_0$. The number of all feasible closed histories of length 6 with maximum size 3 are represented by the total weight of the set of all paths (i.e. random walks) from $(0, 0)$ to $(6, 0)$ drawn in Figure 19. For example, there are four closed histories of length 4, namely $I_1, D, I_1, D$; $I_1, S_1^+, S_1^+, D$ (of size 1) and $I_1, I_1, D, D$; $I_1, I_2, D, D$ (of size 2).

(f) *Dictionaries—weighted random walks with $e_i = 2i + 1$,*
  $u_i = d_{i+1} = i + 1, i \in \mathbb{N}_0$

The domain of the data-type *dictionary* consists of all finite subsets (=files) of a totally ordered set of keys which are accessed by value. All operations $I, D, S^+, S^-$ are allowed without any restriction. This data type leads to a one-to-one correspondence between the closed histories of length $n$ (with maximum size $k$) and the set of all weighted ($(k, 0)$-bounded) closed non-negative random walks of length $n$, where the weights are $e_i = 2i + 1$, $u_i = d_{i+1} = i + 1, i \in \mathbb{N}_0$ (see [34]).

In this section we have given several examples of one-to-one correspondences between (weighted) random walks and other mathematical objects

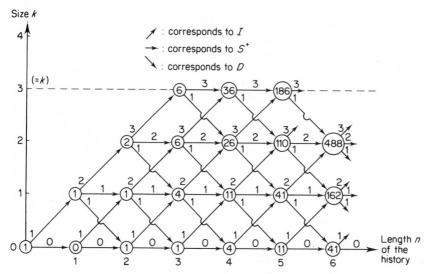

FIGURE 19. A diagram representing histories induced by a symbol table. (The number of possibilities of performing an operation is indicated by the label of the segments; the encircled numbers correspond to the number of histories.)

(trees, data types). Indeed, there are many other correspondences of this kind; here is a short list (see [32], [44], [45]):

—The set of all partitions (or equivalence relations) of a set with $n$ elements—the set of all non-negative closed weighted random walks of length $n$, where the weights are $e_i = d_{i+1} = i + 1$ and $u_i = 1, i \in \mathbb{N}_0$.

—The set of all permutations in $\mathfrak{S}(\mathbb{N}_{n+1})$—the set of all non-negative weighted random walks of length $n$, where the weights are $e_i = 2i + 2$, $d_{i+1} = i + 1$, and $u_i = i + 2, i \in \mathbb{N}_0$.

—The set of involutions appearing in $\mathfrak{S}(\mathbb{N}_n)$—the set of all non-negative weighted random walks of length $n$, where the weights are $e_i = u_i = 1$, and $d_{i+1} = i + 1, i \in \mathbb{N}_0$.

—The set of involutions without fixed points in $\mathfrak{S}(\mathbb{N}_n)$—the set of all non-negative weighted random walks of length $n$, where the weights are $e_i = 0$, $u_i = 1$, and $d_{i+1} = i + 1, i \in \mathbb{N}_0$.

—The set of alternating permutations in $\mathfrak{S}(\mathbb{N}_{2n+1})$—the set of all non-negative closed weighted random walks of length $n$, where the weights are $e_i = 0$, $u_i = i + 1$, and $d_{i+1} = i + 2, i \in \mathbb{N}_0$.

—The set of derangements in $\mathfrak{S}(\mathbb{N}_n)$—the set of all non-negative closed weighted random walks of length $n$, where the weights are $e_i = 2i$, $u_i = d_{i+1} = i + 1, i \in \mathbb{N}_0$.

## 4.4 Exact and Asymptotical Enumeration Results

### 4.4.1 Useful Techniques for Determining Asymptotics From Generating Functions

In preceding sections (e.g. 3.2, 4.2) we have established explicit formulae for the number of certain objects. Sometimes, the computation of such an explicit expression is complicated and if it is possible, then no information about its (asymptotical) behaviour can be derived, because its efficiency is low. The same intricate problem appears in situations where the generating function of the objects which we want to count is known, but explicit expressions of the coefficients are not available (e.g. the generating function satisfies a quadratic recurrence $f_{n+1}(z) = 1 + zf_n^2(z)$ or a quadratic functional equation $f(z) = 1 + zf(z)f(z^2)$). In this section we shall present some tools for obtaining estimates of the coefficients of a given generating function. No proof will be given, but some applications of the stated results. (General methods for handling sums are discussed in [17]). The following theorem is sometimes useful for simplifying a problem.

THEOREM 4.8  Let $A(z) = \sum_{n \geqslant 0} a_n z^n$ and $B(z) = \sum_{n \geqslant 0} b_n z^n$ be two power series with radii of convergence $\rho(A) > \rho(B) \geqslant 0$, respectively, and let $A(z)B(z) = \sum_{n \geqslant 0} c_n z^n$ be the product of $A(z)$ and $B(z)$. Assuming that $\lim_{n \to \infty} (b_{n-1}/b_n) = b$ exists and that $A(b) \neq 0$, then $c_n \sim A(b)b_n$.  ∎

The proof of this theorem is standard; it consists of a repeated application of the triangle inequality to the difference $|A(b) - c_n/b_n|$. Let us determine the asymptotic behaviour of the sum $S_n$ of the first $(n + 1)$ Catalan numbers, that is

$$S_n = \sum_{0 \leqslant \lambda \leqslant n} \frac{1}{\lambda + 1} \binom{2\lambda}{\lambda}.$$

We know that the generating function $C(z)$ of the Catalan numbers is given by

$$C(z) = z \sum_{n \geqslant 0} \frac{1}{n + 1} \binom{2n}{n} z^n = (1 - \sqrt{1 - 4z})/2$$

(Example 4.1 and Example 4.6). Choosing $A(z) = (1 - z)^{-1}$ and $B(z) = (1 - \sqrt{1 - 4z})/(2z)$, we immediately obtain

$$A(z)B(z) = \sum_{n \geqslant 0} S_n z^n.$$

Obviously, $\rho(A) = 1$ and $\rho(B) = \frac{1}{4}$. Moreover,

$$\lim_{n \to \infty} \left[ \frac{1}{n} \binom{2n - 2}{n - 1} \right] \Big/ \left[ \frac{1}{n + 1} \binom{2n}{n} \right] = \frac{1}{4},$$

and therefore $b = \frac{1}{4}$. Since $\rho(A) > \rho(B) > 0$ and $A(b) = \frac{4}{3} \neq 0$, by Theorem 4.8

we obtain

$$S_n \sim \tfrac{4}{3}(n+1)^{-1}\binom{2n}{n}.$$

If the radii of convergence $\rho(A)$ and $\rho(B)$ are equal, Theorem 4.8 cannot be applied. The following result can be helpful in such cases.

THEOREM 4.9 ([85], [86])   Let $A(z) = \sum_{n \geqslant 0} a_n z^n$ and $B(z) = \sum_{n \geqslant 0} b_n z^n$ be two power series and let $A(z)B(z) = \sum_{n \geqslant 0} c_n z^n$ be the product of $A(z)$ and $B(z)$. Assuming that there exist constants $\alpha$, $\beta$, $a$, $b$, and $\rho$, where $a > 0$, $b > 0$, and $\rho > 0$, such that $a_n \sim a\rho^{-n}n^{-\alpha}$ and $b_n \sim b\rho^{-n}n^{-\beta}$ for $n \to \infty$, then

$$c_n \sim \begin{cases} 2ab\rho^{-n}\sqrt{n} & \text{if } \alpha = 0 \wedge \beta = \tfrac{1}{2} \\ \pi ab\rho^{-n} & \text{if } \alpha = \beta = \tfrac{1}{2} \\ A(\rho)b_n + B(\rho)a_n & \text{if } \alpha = \beta = \tfrac{3}{2} \\ A(\rho)b_n & \text{if } \alpha = \tfrac{3}{2} \wedge \beta = \tfrac{1}{2} \end{cases}$$

The last case also holds if the assumption about $a_n$ is replaced by $a_n = O(\rho^{-n}n^{-3/2})$ or by $A(z)$ is regular for $|z| < \rho + \varepsilon$ for some $\varepsilon > 0$. ∎

For example, let $A(z) = B(z)$ be the generating function $\mathbf{C}(z)$ of the Catalan numbers given by

$$\mathbf{C}(z) = \sum_{n \geqslant 0} \frac{1}{n+1}\binom{2n}{n}z^n = (1 - \sqrt{1-4z})/(2z).$$

By Stirling's formula, we immediately obtain

$$a_n = b_n = \frac{1}{n+1}\binom{2n}{n} \sim 4^n/(n\sqrt{\pi n}).$$

Choosing $\alpha = \beta = \tfrac{3}{2}$, $a = b = 1/\sqrt{\pi}$ and $\rho = \tfrac{1}{4}$, we obtain, by the third case of Theorem 4.9,

$$c_n = \sum_{0 \leqslant \lambda \leqslant n} \frac{1}{\lambda+1}\binom{2\lambda}{\lambda}\frac{1}{n-\lambda+1}\binom{2n-2\lambda}{n-\lambda}$$

$$\sim 2\mathbf{C}(\tfrac{1}{4})a_n = 4^{n+1}/(n\sqrt{\pi n}).$$

Indeed, $c_n = a_{n+1} = b_{n+1} = \dfrac{1}{n+2}\dbinom{2n+2}{n+1}$, because $z\mathbf{C}^2(z) = \mathbf{C}(z) - 1$.

If we choose

$$A(z) = B(z) = \sum_{n \geqslant 0}\binom{2n}{n}z^n = (1-4z)^{-1/2},$$

then $a_n = b_n \sim 4^n/\sqrt{\pi n}$. Thus with $a = b = 1/\sqrt{\pi}$, $\rho = \tfrac{1}{4}$, and $\alpha = \beta = \tfrac{1}{2}$, the second case of Theorem 4.9 leads to

$$c_n = \sum_{0 \leqslant \lambda \leqslant n} \binom{2\lambda}{\lambda}\binom{2n - 2\lambda}{n - \lambda} \sim \pi a b \rho^{-n} = 4^n.$$

In fact, we have $c_n = 4^n$, because $A(z)B(z) = (1 - 4z)^{-1}$.

THEOREM 4.10 ([5])  Let $A(z) = \sum_{n \geqslant 1} a_n z^n$ and $B(z) = \sum_{n \geqslant 0} b_n z^n$ be two power series with $B(z) = F(z, A(z))$, where

$$F(z, y) = \sum_{\lambda \geqslant 0} \sum_{k \geqslant 0} f_{\lambda,k} z^\lambda y^k.$$

Assuming that $F$ is analytic in $(0, 0)$ and $a_{n-1} = o(a_n)$ and

$$\sum_{r \leqslant k \leqslant n-r} |a_k a_{n-k}| = O(a_{n-r}) \quad \text{for some } r > 0,$$

then

$$b_n = \sum_{0 \leqslant k \leqslant r-1} d_k a_{n-k} + O(a_{n-r}),$$

where

$$d_k = \langle z^k \rangle \left[ \frac{\partial}{\partial y} F(z, y)|_{y = A(z)} \right]. \quad \blacksquare$$

For example, consider the power series $A(z) = \sum_{n \geqslant 1} n! \, z^n$ which has a radius of convergence $\rho(A) = 0$. Obviously, $a_{n-1} = o(a_n)$, because $a_{n-1}/a_n = 1/n$. Since

$$\sum_{r \leqslant k \leqslant n-r} \frac{|a_k a_{n-k}|}{|a_{n-r}|} = \sum_{r \leqslant k \leqslant n-r} \frac{k! \, (n-k)!}{(n-r)!}$$

$$\leqslant 2 \sum_{r \leqslant k \leqslant n/2} \frac{k! \, (n-k)!}{(n-r)!}$$

$$\leqslant 2r! + 2 \sum_{r+1 \leqslant k \leqslant n/2} \frac{(r+1)! \, (n-r-1)!}{(n-r)!}$$

$$\leqslant (r+3)r!,$$

we have also $\sum_{r \leqslant k \leqslant n-r} |a_k a_{n-k}| = O(a_{n-r})$ for all $r > 0$. If we want to compute the asymptotic behaviour of the coefficients $b_n$ in $B(z) = \sum_{n \geqslant 0} b_n z^n$ defined by $B(z) = [\sum_{n \geqslant 0} n! \, z^n]^{-1}$, we have to choose $F(z, y) = (1 + y)^{-1}$ because $B(z) = F(z, A(z))$. Obviously, $F(z, y)$ is analytic near zero. Since

$$\frac{\partial}{\partial y} F(z, y)|_{y = A(z)} = -(1 + A(z))^{-2},$$

we obtain immediately by Theorem 4.10

$$b_n = - \sum_{0 \leqslant k \leqslant r-1} (n - k)! \, \langle z^k \rangle (1 + A(z))^{-2} + O((n-r)!)$$

for $r > 0$. Choosing $r = 4$, we find by an elementary computation

$$b_n = -[n! \langle z^0 \rangle f(z) + (n-1)! \langle z^1 \rangle f(z) + (n-2)! \langle z^2 \rangle f(z) + (n-3)! \langle z^3 \rangle f(z)]$$
$$+ O((n-4)!)$$

where $f(z) = 1 - 2z - z^2 + 4z^3$. Hence

$$b_n = -n(n-3)! (n^3 - 5n^2 + 7n - 6)(1 + O(n^{-4})).$$

THEOREM 4.11 ([54])   Let $A(z) = \sum_{n \geq 0} a_n z^n$ be a meromorphic function with simple poles at the points $z_s$, $s = 1, 2, 3, \ldots$, where $|z_{s+1}| \geq |z_s|$, $s = 1, 2, 3, \ldots$. We have

$$a_n \sim - \sum_{s \geq 1} \operatorname*{Res}_{z=z_s} (A(z)) z_s^{-n-1}. \quad \blacksquare$$

For example, consider the function $A(z) = \cos^{-1}(z)$. Obviously, $z_m = (2m+1)\pi/2$, $m \in \mathbb{Z}$. Since

$$\operatorname*{Res}_{z=z_m} (A(z)) = \lim_{z \to (2m+1)\pi/2} \frac{z - \dfrac{2m+1}{2}\pi}{\cos(z)} = \lim_{z \to (2m+1)\pi/2} \frac{-1}{\sin(z)}$$

$$= -\sin^{-1}\left(\frac{2m+1}{2}\pi\right) = (-1)^{m+1},$$

we find

$$a_n \sim \sum_{m \in \mathbb{Z}} 2^{n+1} \pi^{-n-1} (2m+1)^{-n-1} (-1)^m$$

$$= 2^{n+1} \pi^{-n-1} [1 + (-1)^n] \sum_{m \geq 0} (-1)^m (2m+1)^{-n-1}.$$

Therefore, $a_{2n+1} \sim 0$ and

$$a_{2n} \sim 4^{n+1} \pi^{-2n-1} \sum_{m \geq 0} (-1)^m (2m+1)^{-2n-1}.$$

Indeed, (B38) shows that

$$\cos^{-1}(z) = \sum_{n \geq 0} E_{2n} z^{2n} (-1)^n / (2n)!$$

where $E_n$ is the $n$-th Euler number. Hence $a_{2n+1} = 0$ and by (B40)

$$a_{2n} = E_{2n}(-1)^n/(2n)! = 4^{n+1} \pi^{-2n-1} \sum_{k \geq 0} (-1)^k (2k+1)^{-2n-1}.$$

If a generating function has singularities other than poles on the boundary of its disk of convergence, then Theorem 4.10 cannot be applied because there is no partial fraction expansion in such cases. However, if the generating function has only a finite number of algebraic singularities on its circle of convergence, then asymptotic expansions can frequently be obtained by a result due to Darboux. The following special case is convenient for handling many generating functions.

THEOREM 4.12 Let $A(z) = \sum_{n \geq 0} a_n z^n$ be a function with the radius of convergence $\rho(A) > 0$ and with a finite number of singularities $z_\lambda, \lambda \in [1:m]$, on the circle of convergence $|z| = \rho(A)$. Suppose that in a neighbourhood of each of these singularities $z_\lambda$, $A(z)$ has an expansion of the form $A(z) = f_\lambda(z) + (1 - z/z_\lambda)^{-\omega_\lambda} g_\lambda(z)$, $\lambda \in [1:m]$, where $f_\lambda$ and $g_\lambda$ are analytic near $z_\lambda$, $g_\lambda$ is non-zero near $z_\lambda$, and $-\omega_\lambda \in \mathbb{C} \setminus \mathbb{N}_0$. Then

$$a_n = \frac{1}{n} \sum_{1 \leq \lambda \leq m} \frac{g_\lambda(z_\lambda) n^{\omega_\lambda}}{\Gamma(\omega_\lambda) z_\lambda^n} + o(\rho(A)^{-n} n^{w-1}),$$

where $w = \text{MAX}_{1 \leq \lambda \leq m} \, \text{Re}(\omega_\lambda)$, and $\Gamma$ denotes the gamma function (Appendix B, 2.11). ∎

For example, consider the function $A(z) = (1 - z)^{-1/2} \exp(-z/2)$ which is the exponential generating function of the numbers $P(n, 2)$ of all 2-permutations of $\mathbb{N}_n$ (Exercise 3.6). Here, $A(z)$ has only one singularity at $z = 1$. Thus $m = 1$, $z_1 = \rho(A) = 1$, $f_1(z) = 0$, $\omega_1 = \frac{1}{2}$, and $g_1(z) = \exp(-z/2)$. Hence by Theorem 4.12

$$P(n, 2)/n! = \frac{1}{n} g_1(z_1) n^{1/2} / \Gamma(\tfrac{1}{2}) + o(n^{-1/2})$$

or equivalently

$$P(n, 2) = n! / \sqrt{\pi e n} + o(n! \, n^{-1/2})$$

$$= n^n e^{-n-1/2} \sqrt{2} + o(n^n e^{-n})$$

by Stirling's formula.

The exponential generating function of the numbers $a_n(S)$ of permutations $\sigma \in \mathfrak{S}(\mathbb{N}_n)$ such that all the cycle lengths belong to a set $S \subseteq \mathbb{N}$ is given by $A(z) = \exp(\sum_{k \in S} z^k/k)$ (Exercise 3.7). Assume that $\mathbb{N} \setminus S$ is finite. We immediately obtain

$$A(z) = \exp\left(\sum_{k \geq 1} z^k/k - \sum_{k \notin S} z^k/k\right) = (1 - z)^{-1} \exp\left(-\sum_{k \notin S} z^k/k\right).$$

Here, $A(z)$ has only one singularity at $z = 1$. Thus $m = 1$, $z_1 = \rho(A) = 1$, $f_1(z) = 0$, $\omega_1 = 1$, and $g_1(z) = \exp(-\sum_{k \notin S} z^k/k)$. Hence, by Theorem 4.12,

$$a_n(S)/n! = \frac{1}{n} g_1(z_1) n / \Gamma(1) + o(1),$$

that is
$$a_n(S) = n! \exp\left(-\sum_{k \notin S} \frac{1}{k}\right) + o(n!).$$

Finally, let us consider the generating function $A(z) := E_{p,k,h}(z)$ of the total weights $w(DEU_{k,h}^{\varphi}(n,p))$ for $e = 0$ (see section 4.2.2). We had shown that

$$A(z) = \sum_{1 \leqslant \lambda \leqslant k+h+1} \alpha_\lambda / (1 - v_\lambda z),$$

where
$$v_\lambda = 2\sqrt{ud} \cos\left(\frac{\pi\lambda}{k+h+2}\right)$$

and
$$\alpha_\lambda = \frac{2}{k+h+2} \left(\frac{u}{d}\right)^{p/2} \sin\left(\frac{(h+p+1)\pi\lambda}{k+h+2}\right) \sin\left(\frac{(h+1)\pi\lambda}{k+h+2}\right).$$

Here, $A(z)$ has simple poles at $z_\lambda = v_\lambda^{-1}$, $1 \leqslant \lambda \leqslant k+h+1$. Since $z_{\lambda+1} \geqslant z_\lambda$, $\lambda = 1, 2, \ldots, k+h+1$, we have $\rho(A) = z_1$. To obtain all singularities on the circle of convergence, we have to find all $\lambda \in [1 : k+h+1]$ satisfying

$$\left|2\sqrt{ud} \cos\left(\frac{\pi\lambda}{k+h+2}\right)\right| = 2\sqrt{ud} \cos\left(\frac{\pi}{k+h+2}\right).$$

This implies $\lambda = 1$ and $\lambda = k+h+1$. Thus $m = 2$,

$$z_1 = \left[2\sqrt{ud} \cos\left(\frac{\pi}{k+h+2}\right)\right]^{-1}, \qquad z_2 = \left[-2\sqrt{ud} \cos\left(\frac{\pi}{k+h+2}\right)\right]^{-1},$$

$$f_1(z) = \sum_{2 \leqslant \lambda \leqslant k+h+1} \alpha_\lambda / (1 - v_\lambda z),$$

$\omega_1 = 1$, $g_1(z_1) = \alpha_1$,

$$f_2(z) = \sum_{1 \leqslant \lambda \leqslant k+h} \alpha_\lambda / (1 - v_\lambda z),$$

$\omega_2 = 1$ and $g_2(z_2) = \alpha_{k+h+1}$. Hence for fixed $k, h, p$

$$w(DEU_{k,h}^{\varphi}(n,p)) = \frac{1}{n} g_1(z_1) n z_1^{-n} / \Gamma(1) + \frac{1}{n} g_2(z_2) n z_2^{-n} / \Gamma(1) + o(z_1^{-n})$$

or equivalently

$$w(DEU_{k,h}^{\varphi}(n,p)) = 2^{n+1} [1 + (-1)^n] \frac{(ud)^{n/2}}{k+h+2} \left(\frac{u}{d}\right)^{p/2} \sin\left(\frac{(h+p+1)\pi}{k+h+2}\right)$$

$$\times \sin\left(\frac{(h+1)\pi}{k+h+2}\right) \cos^n\left(\frac{\pi}{k+h+2}\right)$$

$$+ o\left(2^n (ud)^{n/2} \cos^n\left(\frac{\pi}{k+h+2}\right)\right).$$

Sometimes an explicit expression for a generating function $A(z)$ is unknown, but a functional equation for $A(z)$ is available. In such cases, the following result can be useful for determining the asymptotic behaviour of the coefficient $\langle z^n \rangle A(z)$.

THEOREM 4.13 ([6])  Assume that the power series $A(z) = \sum_{n \geqslant 0} a_n z^n$ with non-negative coefficients satisfies $F(z, A(z)) \equiv 0$. Suppose there exist real numbers $r > 0$ and $s > a_0$ such that

(i) for some $\delta > 0$, $F(z, y)$ is analytic for $|z| < r + \delta$ and $|y| < s + \delta$;

(ii) $F(r, s) = \dfrac{\partial}{\partial y} F(z, y)|_{(z,y) = (r,s)} = 0$;

(iii) $\dfrac{\partial}{\partial z} F(z, y)|_{(z,y) = (r,s)} \neq 0$, and $\dfrac{\partial^2}{\partial y^2} F(z, y)|_{(z,y) = (r,s)} \neq 0$;

(iv) if $|z| \leqslant r$, $|y| \leqslant s$, and $F(z, y) = \dfrac{\partial}{\partial y} F(z, y) = 0$, then $z = r$ and $y = s$.

Then $a_n \sim \sqrt{C(r, s)}\, n^{-3/2} r^{-n}$, where

$$C(r, s) = r \frac{\partial}{\partial z} F(z, y)|_{(z,y) = (r,s)} \bigg/ \left( 2\pi \frac{\partial^2}{\partial y^2} F(z, y)|_{(z,y) = (r,s)} \right). \quad \blacksquare$$

Generally, condition (iv) is not easy to verify directly; an alternate is given in [6]. Let us consider a simple example.

We will compute the asymptotic behaviour of the coefficient of the generating function $A(z) = \sum_{n \geqslant 0} a_n z^n$ defined by the functional equation $A(z) = z + f(z) + zA^t(z)$, where $f(z) = z + zf^t(z)$, $t \geqslant 1$. It can be shown (Exercise 4.11) that $a_n$ is the number of the ordered $t$-ary trees with $n$ nodes which are monotonously labelled by 1 and 2; that is, whenever a node $v$ is a son of $v'$ then the label of $v$ is greater than or equal to the label of $v'$. It is not hard to see that $a_n = 0$ if $t$ is not a divisor of $(n - 1)$. The first few values are $a_1 = 2$ and $a_{t+1} = 2^t + 1$. To apply Theorem 4.13, we define $B(z) = z^{-1/t} A(z^{1/t})$ and $h(z) = z^{-1/t} f(z^{1/t})$. This substitution leads to

$$B(z) = \sum_{n \geqslant 0} a_n z^{n/t - 1/t} = \sum_{n \geqslant 0} a_{tn+1} z^n, \qquad B(z) = 1 + h(z) + zB^t(z)$$

and $h(z) = 1 + zh^t(z)$. Now for the asymptotics.

We have to choose $F(z, y) = 1 + h(z) + zy^t - y$ which implies $(\partial/\partial y)F(z, y) = zty^{t-1} - 1$. By condition (iv), the numbers $r$ and $s$ are determined by the equations $h(r) + 1 + rs^t = s$ and $rts^{t-1} = 1$. Hence $r = t^{-1}s^{-t+1}$ and $h(r) = s(t - 1)t^{-1} - 1$. Inserting these relations into the functional equation for $h(z)$, we find that $s$ is determined by the equation

$$s^t t^t (t - 1) - 2t^{t+1} s^{t-1} - [s(t - 1) - t]^t = 0.$$

Since $r = t^{-1}s^{-t+1}$, $r$ is also known. With this choice of $s$ and $r$, the conditions (i)–(iv) are easily verified. Hence

$$C(r, s) = [h'(r) + s^t]/[2\pi t(t-1)s^{t-2}].$$

Since $h'(z) = h^t(z) + zth^{t-1}(z)h'(z)$, we immediately obtain

$$h'(r) = h^t(r)/[1 - rth^{t-1}(r)]$$
$$= r^{-1}h(r)[h(r) - 1]/[t + (1-t)h(r)]$$
$$= (tr)^{-1}[s(t-1) - 2t][s(t-1) - t]/[2t^2 - t - s(t-1)^2].$$

Therefore, $a_{tn+1} \sim C(t)^{1/2}n^{-3/2}r^{-n}$, where

$$C(t) = s \frac{2t - s(t-2)}{2\pi(t-1)[2t^2 - t - s(t-1)^2]}, \qquad r = t^{-1}s^{-t+1}$$

and $s$ is the solution of the equation

$$s^t t^t(t-1) - 2t^{t+1}s^{t-1} - [s(t-1) - t]^t = 0.$$

For example, if $t = 2$ (binary trees), we find $s = 2(2\sqrt{3} + 3)/3$, $r = (2\sqrt{3} - 3)/4$, and $C(2) = (3\sqrt{3} + 5)/(2\pi)$. Thus

$$a_{2n+1} \sim \sqrt{(3\sqrt{3} + 5)/(2\pi)}\, n^{-3/2}(4(2\sqrt{3} + 3)/3)^n.$$

If a generating function $A(z)$ satisfies a functional equation of the form $A(z) = z\theta(A(z))$, then the following result can be established as a special case of Theorem 4.13.

THEOREM 4.14 ([86])  Suppose $F(y) = 1 + \sum_{i \geq 1} c_i y^i$ is a regular function of $y$ when $|y| < R \leqslant +\infty$ and let $A(z) = z + \sum_{i \geq 2} a_i z^i$ denote the solution of $A(z) = zF(A(z))$ in the neighbourhood of $z = 0$. If

(i) $c_1 > 0$ and $c_j > 0$ for some $j \geqslant 2$;
(ii) $c_i \geqslant 0$ for $i \geqslant 2$;
(iii) $\tau F'(\tau) = F(\tau)$ for some $\tau$, where $0 < \tau < R$,

then

$$a_n \sim \left[\frac{F(\tau)}{2\pi F''(\tau)}\right]^{1/2} n^{-3/2}[F(\tau)/\tau]^n. \quad \blacksquare$$

For example, consider again the generating function

$$A(z) = C(z) = \sum_{n \geq 1} \frac{1}{n}\binom{2n-2}{n-1}z^n$$

of the Catalan numbers. We know that $A(z) = (1 - \sqrt{1 - 4z})/2$ and $A^2(z) = A(z) - z$. Choosing $F(y) = (1 - y)^{-1}$, then $A(z) = zF(A(z))$. Conditions (i) and

(ii) are easily verified. To determine $\tau$, we obtain by (iii) the equation $\tau(1 - \tau)^{-2} = (1 - \tau)^{-1}$; its solution is $\tau = \frac{1}{2}$. Since $F(\frac{1}{2}) = 2$ and $F''(\frac{1}{2}) = 16$, we immediately obtain our old result

$$a_n = \frac{1}{n}\binom{2n - 2}{n - 1} \sim 4^{n-1}/(n\sqrt{\pi n}).$$

Let us now consider the number of all unordered labelled trees with $n$ nodes and labels $1, 2, \ldots, n$, where the root is labelled by 1. The generating function $A(z) = \sum_{n \geqslant 1} a_n z^n/(n - 1)!$ satisfies the functional equation $A(z) = z \exp(A(z))$ (see [102]). Choosing $F(y) = \exp(y)$, condition (iii) leads to $\tau e^\tau = e^\tau$, that is $\tau = 1$. Hence $a_n/(n - 1)! \sim n^{-3/2}e^n/\sqrt{2\pi}$, or equivalently by Stirling's formula $a_n \sim n^{n-2}$. Indeed, $a_n = n^{n-2}$ according to the classical result given in [12].

Let us conclude this section by an interesting theorem which has been proved in [92].

THEOREM 4.15  Let $P(z)$ and $Q(z) = \sum_{0 \leqslant \lambda \leqslant N} q_\lambda z^{e_\lambda}$, $N \geqslant 1$, be two non-zero polynomials with real, non-negative coefficients satisfying $P(0) = Q(0) = Q'(0) = 0$. Assume further that $2 \leqslant e_\lambda < e_{\lambda+1}, 0 \leqslant \lambda \leqslant N - 1, q_j > 0, 0 \leqslant j \leqslant N$, and that the greatest common divisor of the numbers $(e_\lambda - e_0)$, $1 \leqslant \lambda \leqslant N$, is equal to one. If the generating function $A(z) = \sum_{n \geqslant 1} a_n z^n$ satisfies the functional equation $A(z) = P(z) + A(Q(z))$, then

$$a_n = n^{-1}\alpha^{-n}u(\ln(n)) + O(n^{-2}\alpha^{-n}),$$

where $\alpha$ is the (unique) positive root of $Q(z) = z$ and $u(x)$ is a non-constant, positive, continuous function which is periodic with period $\ln(Q'(\alpha))$. ∎

For example, let $P(z) = z^2 + z^5$ and $Q(z) = z^2 + z^5 + z^7$. We have $\alpha \approx 0.68233$, and therefore, $a_n \sim n^{-1}(1.465\,57)^n u(\ln(n))$, where $u(x)$ is a non-constant positive continuous function with period $\approx 1.148\,95$. Functional equations of this type are of interest in the enumeration of trees. In [92] the above theorem was proved in order to determine the asymptotic behaviour of the number of all balanced 2, 3-trees with $n$ leaves; a balanced 2, 3-tree is an unlabelled ordered tree each of whose interior nodes has either two or three sons, and all of whose paths from a leaf to the root have the same length. It is easy to see that the generating function of the numbers $a_n$ of these trees satisfies the functional equation $A(z) = z + A(z^2 + z^3)$; the above theorem implies that $a_n = n^{-1}\varphi^n u(\ln(n))$, where $\varphi = (1 + \sqrt{5})/2$ and $u(x)$ is a positive, non-constant, continuous function with period $\ln(4 - \varphi)$.

In this section we have presented some useful techniques for determining the asymptotic behaviour of numbers $a_n$ from their generating function $A(z)$. The stated theorems can easily be applied in many cases; nevertheless, such a list must be incomplete. Further useful methods are discussed in [6], along with interesting applications. Very little is known about obtaining asymptotics from multivariate generating functions (for a class of bivariate generating functions see [7]).

### 4.4.2 Ordered Trees

In section 4.3.1 we have presented a one-to-one correspondence between the set of all ordered trees with $n$ nodes and the set of all closed non-negative $(1, 0, 1)$-random walks of length $(2n - 2)$. This connection implies immediately the following enumeration results:

—Let $t(n)$ be the number of all ordered trees with $n$ nodes.

$$t(n) = w(NCDEU_\infty^\varphi(2n - 2)) = \frac{1}{n}\binom{2n - 2}{n - 1} \quad \text{(see Example 4.6)}.$$

—Let $t(n, k)$ be the number of all ordered trees with $n$ nodes and height less than or equal to $k$.

● $t(n, k) = w(NCDEU_{k-1}^\varphi(2n - 2))$

$\quad = w(DEU_{k-1,0}^\varphi(2n - 2, 0))$

$\quad = 2^{2n-1}(k + 1)^{-1} \sum_{1 \leqslant \lambda \leqslant k} \sin^2\left(\frac{\pi\lambda}{k + 1}\right)\cos^{2n-2}\left(\frac{\pi\lambda}{k + 1}\right)$

$\hfill \text{(see Theorem 4.3)}.$

● $t(n, k) = \binom{2n - 2}{n - 1} - \binom{2n - 2}{n - 2} + \psi_0(2n - 2, k - 1, 0)$

$\quad - \psi_1(2n - 2, k - 1, 0)$

$\quad = t(n) - \sum_{j \geqslant 1}\left[\binom{2n - 2}{n - (k + 1)j} - 2\binom{2n - 2}{n - 1 - (k + 1)j}\right.$

$\qquad\qquad \left. + \binom{2n - 2}{n - 2 - (k + 1)j}\right]$

$\hfill \text{(see special case (b) in section 4.2.2)}.$

● $t(n, k) = 4^n(k + 1)^{-1}\cos^{2n}\left(\frac{\pi}{k + 1}\right)\text{tg}^2\left(\frac{\pi}{k + 1}\right)$

$\quad + o\left(4^n \cos^{2n}\left(\frac{\pi}{k + 1}\right)\right)$

$\hfill \text{(see remark following Theorem 4.12)}.$

Naturally, these results can be easily derived without use of random walks. The approach given in section 4.2.1 is an obvious and elegant technique for counting classes of trees. We will consider some examples.

EXAMPLE 4.8  Let $X = \{g_i | i \geqslant 0\}$ be a countable set and let $\mathscr{L}$ be the set of all words which can be derived from $S$ using the following context-free

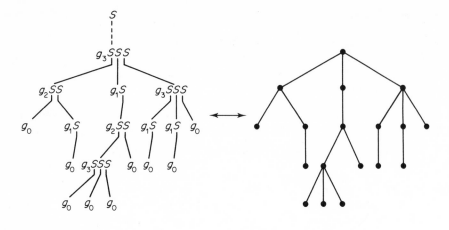

$$w = g_3 g_2 g_0 g_1 g_0 g_1 g_2 g_3 g_0 g_0 g_0 g_0 g_3 g_1 g_0 g_1 g_0 g_0$$

FIGURE 20. Representation of an ordered tree by the corresponding word $w$.

unambiguous substitution scheme

$$S \to g_0 \qquad\qquad\qquad \text{(rule } f_0)$$

$$S \to g_k \underbrace{SSS \ldots SS}_{k\text{-times}}, k \geqslant 1 \quad \text{(rule } f_k)$$

Some reflection shows that each word $w \in \mathscr{L} \cap X^n$ is a coding of an ordered tree $T$ with $n$ nodes. Here, $T$ is essentially the tree structure induced by the derivation tree of $w \in \mathscr{L} \cap X^n$. For example, Figure 20 shows an ordered tree with 18 nodes together with the corresponding word $w \in \mathscr{L} \cap X^{18}$. The broken line is not part of the tree; it only designates the root. Note that we have put some redundant information in the coding, namely each $g_i$ appearing in $w \in \mathscr{L} \cap X^n$ corresponds to a node with in-degree $i$. The system of formal equations induced by the substitution scheme is

$$S = g_0 + \sum_{k \geqslant 1} g_k \underbrace{SSS \ldots SSS}_{k\text{-times}}$$

Let $S = \sum_{w \in \mathscr{L}} w$ be the solution in the ring of formal power series over $X^*$. We have now to specify the homomorphism $\theta$ representing the property by which we wish to enumerate the trees. Here are some possibilities.

(a) Let $\theta$ be defined by $\theta(g_i) = z, i \geqslant 0$, and let $t(n)$ be the number of all ordered trees with $n$ nodes. We find

$$\theta(S) = \sum_{n \geqslant 1} \sum_{w \in \mathscr{L} \cap X^n} \theta(w) = \sum_{n \geqslant 1} z^n \operatorname{card}(\mathscr{L} \cap X^n) = \sum_{n \geqslant 1} t(n) z^n.$$

Thus, taking the image of the above formal equation, the generating function $A(z) = \theta(S)$ is given by

$$A(z) = z + \sum_{k \geqslant 1} zA^k(z) = z/(1 - A(z)).$$

Hence we find the quadratic equation $A^2(z) - A(z) + z = 0$ whose solution is the generating function of the Catalan numbers.

(b) Let $\theta$ be defined by $\theta(g_0) = uz$, $\theta(g_i) = z$, $i \geqslant 1$, and let $t_m(n)$ be the number of all ordered trees with $n$ nodes and $m$ leaves. We find

$$\theta(S) = \sum_{n \geqslant 1} \sum_{w \in \mathscr{L} \cap X^n} \theta(w) = \sum_{n \geqslant 1} z^n \sum_{w \in \mathscr{L} \cap X^n} u^{\#_0(w)},$$

where $\#_0(w)$ is the number of $g_0$ appearing in $w$. Since each $g_0$ corresponds to a leaf in the corresponding tree, we obtain

$$\theta(S) = \sum_{n \geqslant 1} \sum_{m \geqslant 1} t_m(n)z^n u^m.$$

Thus, taking the image of the above formal equation, we see that the generating function $F(z, u) = \theta(S)$ satisfies the relation

$$F(z, u) = uz + \sum_{k \geqslant 1} zF^k(z, u)$$

$$= uz + zF(z, u)/(1 - F(z, u))$$

which leads to $F^2(z, u) - (1 + uz - z)F(z, u) + uz = 0$. Hence

$$F(z, u) = \tfrac{1}{2}[1 + uz - z - \sqrt{(1 + uz - z)^2 - 4uz}]$$

$$= (1 + uz - z)C\left(\frac{uz}{(1 + uz - z)^2}\right),$$

where $C(z)$ is again the generating function of the Catalan numbers satisfying $C^2(z) - C(z) + z = 0$. Therefore,

$$(1 + uz - z)C\left(\frac{uz}{(1 + uz - z)^2}\right)$$

$$= \sum_{i \geqslant 1} \frac{1}{i}\binom{2i - 2}{i - 1} \frac{u^i z^i}{(1 + z(u - 1))^{2i - 1}}$$

$$= \sum_{i \geqslant 1} \frac{1}{i}\binom{2i - 2}{i - 1} u^i z^i \sum_{\lambda \geqslant 0} \binom{2i + \lambda - 2}{\lambda} z^\lambda (1 - u)^\lambda$$

$$= \sum_{i \geqslant 1} \sum_{\lambda \geqslant 0} \sum_{p \geqslant 0} \frac{1}{i}\binom{2i - 2}{i - 1}\binom{2i + \lambda - 2}{\lambda}\binom{\lambda}{p}(-1)^{\lambda - p} z^{\lambda + i} u^{i + \lambda - p}.$$

This implies

$$t_m(n) = \sum_{i \geq 1} \frac{1}{i} \binom{2i-2}{i-1} \binom{n+i-2}{n-i} \binom{n-i}{n-m} (-1)^{m-i}$$

$$= \frac{1}{n} \binom{n}{m} \sum_{i \geq 1} (-1)^{m-i} \binom{m}{i} \binom{n+i-2}{n-1}.$$

Using the general identity

$$\sum_{k \geq 0} \binom{r}{k} \binom{s+k}{p} (-1)^k = (-1)^r \binom{s}{p-r}, \qquad r \geq 0, s \geq 0, p \geq 0$$

with $r := m$, $s := n-2$, and $p := n-1$, we find for $n \geq 2$ the closed expression

$$t_m(n) = \frac{1}{n} \binom{n}{m} \binom{n-2}{m-1}.$$

For $n = 1$, we immediately obtain $t_m(1) = \delta_{1,m}$. For a generalization see [67].

(c) Let $\theta$ be defined by $\theta(g_t) = uz$, $\theta(g_i) = z$, $i \geq 0$, $i \neq t$, and let $d_{t,m}(n)$ be the number of all ordered trees with $n$ nodes having $m$ nodes of in-degree $t$. Note that $d_{0,m}(n) = t_m(n)$. We find

$$\theta(S) = \sum_{n \geq 1} \sum_{w \in \mathcal{L} \cap X^n} \theta(w) = \sum_{n \geq 1} z^n \sum_{w \in \mathcal{L} \cap X^n} u^{\#_t(w)},$$

where $\#_t(w)$ is the number of $g_t$ appearing in $w$. Since each $g_t$ corresponds to a node of in-degree $t$, we obtain

$$\theta(S) = \sum_{n \geq 1} \sum_{m \geq 0} d_{t,m}(n) z^n u^m.$$

Thus the generating function $T(z, u) = \theta(S)$ satisfies the induced equation

$$T(z, u) = z + \sum_{\substack{k \geq 1 \\ k \neq t}} z T^k(z, u) + uz T^t(z, u)$$

$$= z[(1 - T(z, u))^{-1} - (1 - u)T^t(z, u)]$$

for $t \geq 1$. Obviously, this relation also holds for $t = 0$. To get $d_{t,m}(n) = \langle z^n u^m \rangle T(z, u)$, we shall apply the Lagrange–Bürmann formula (see Example 4.1). We obtain $\langle z^n \rangle T(z, u) = (1/n) \langle y^{n-1} \rangle f^n(y)$, where $f(y) = (1 - y)^{-1} - (1 - u)y^t$. Using the binomial theorem and the geometric series, we find

$$\langle y^{n-1} \rangle f^n(y) = \sum_{\lambda \geq 0} \binom{n}{\lambda} (1 - u)^\lambda (-1)^\lambda \binom{2n-2-\lambda(t+1)}{n-\lambda-1}.$$

Hence

$$d_{t,m}(n) = \left\langle u^m \right\rangle \left( \frac{1}{n} \sum_{\lambda \geq 0} \binom{n}{\lambda}(1-u)^\lambda (-1)^\lambda \binom{2n-2-\lambda(t+1)}{n-\lambda-1} \right)$$

$$= \frac{1}{n} \sum_{\lambda \geq 0} (-1)^{\lambda+m} \binom{n}{\lambda}\binom{\lambda}{m}\binom{2n-2-\lambda(t+1)}{n-\lambda-1}.$$

Let us assume that all trees with $n$ nodes are equally likely. What is the average number of nodes of in-degree $t$ appearing in a $n$-node tree? We have to compute the expected value

$$\mathbf{d}_t(n) = t^{-1}(n) \sum_{m \geq 1} m d_{t,m}(n).$$

Let $t \geq 1$ and $D_t(z) = \sum_{n \geq 1} \mathbf{d}_t(n)t(n)z^n$ be the generating function of the numbers $\mathbf{d}_t(n)t(n)$. Since

$$\sum_{m \geq 1} m d_{t,m}(n) = \left\langle z^n \right\rangle \frac{\partial}{\partial u} T(z,u)\big|_{u=1},$$

we immediately obtain $D_t(z) = (\partial/\partial u)T(z,u)\big|_{u=1}$.

On the other hand, we have

$$\frac{\partial}{\partial u} T(z,u) = z\left[ \frac{1}{(1-T(z,u))^2} \frac{\partial}{\partial u} T(z,u) + T^t(z,u) \right.$$

$$\left. - (1-u)tT^{t-1}(z,u)\frac{\partial}{\partial u} T(z,u) \right]$$

which implies

$$\frac{\partial}{\partial u} T(z,u)\big|_{u=1} = zT^t(z,1)[1 - z/(1-T(z,1))^2]^{-1}.$$

Since $T(z,1) = z/(1-T(z,1))$, we find $T(z,1) = C(z) = (1-\sqrt{1-4z})/2$ and further

$$D_t(z) = z^2 C^{t-1}(z)/\sqrt{1-4z} = t^{-1}z^2 \frac{\mathrm{d}}{\mathrm{d}z} C^t(z).$$

Hence

$$\frac{t}{n-1} \mathbf{d}_t(n)t(n) = \left\langle z^{n-1} \right\rangle C^t(z).$$

The coefficient of $z^n$ in the expansion of $C^t(z)$ was already computed in Example 4.1. Therefore, we obtain finally

$$\mathbf{d}_t(n) = t^{-1}(n)(n-1)t^{-1}\left\langle z^{n-1} \right\rangle C^t(z) = n\binom{2n-t-3}{n-2} \bigg/ \binom{2n-2}{n-1}$$

for $t \geq 1$. It can be easily verified that this expression is also valid for $t = 0$. Thus an ordered tree has $n/2$ nodes of in-degree 0 (leaves), about $n/4$ nodes of in-degree 1, etc. on average.

It should be clear that further enumeration results depending on the in-degrees of the nodes can be derived in a similar way; we have only to change the homomorphism $\theta$. For example, the homomorphism $\theta(g_0) = \theta(g_1) = \theta(g_2) = z$, $\theta(g_i) = 0$ for $i \in \mathbb{N}\setminus\{1,2\}$ leads to the generating function of the number of all ordered binary trees with $n$ nodes, and the homomorphism $\theta(g_0) = \theta(g_t) = z$, $\theta(g_i) = 0$ for $i \in \mathbb{N}\setminus\{t\}$ to the generating function of all ordered $t$-ary trees with $n$ nodes.

Unfortunately, the context-free unambiguous substitution scheme given in Example 4.8 is not appropriate for determining enumeration results depending on the height of the trees. For this purpose, we have to generalize this substitution scheme.

EXAMPLE 4.9 Let $\mathfrak{S} = \{S_i | i \geq 0\}$ and $X = \{g_{ij} | i \geq 0 \wedge j \geq 1\}$ are two countable sets and let $\mathscr{L}$ be the set of all words $w$ which can be derived from $S_0$ using the following context-free unambiguous substitution scheme:

$$S_i \to g_{0(i+1)} \qquad \qquad \text{(rule } f_{0,(i+1)})$$
$$S_i \to g_{\lambda(i+1)}\underbrace{S_{i+1}\cdots S_{i+1}}_{\lambda\text{-times}} \qquad \text{(rule } f_{\lambda,(i+1)})$$
$$\lambda\text{-times} \qquad i = 0, 1, 2, \ldots.$$

This scheme is similar to that given in Example 4.8. Each word $w \in \mathscr{L} \cap X^n$ is a coding of an ordered tree $T$ with $n$ nodes, but we have now put some more information in the coding: each $g_{ij}$ appearing in $w \in \mathscr{L} \cap X^n$ corresponds to a node at level $j$ with in-degree $i$. For example, the tree drawn in Figure 20 is now represented by the word

$$w = g_{31}g_{22}g_{03}g_{13}g_{04}g_{12}g_{23}g_{34}g_{05}g_{05}g_{05}g_{04}g_{32}g_{13}g_{04}g_{13}g_{04}g_{03}.$$

The above scheme induces the following formal equations:

$$S_i = g_{0(i+1)} + \sum_{\lambda \geq 1} g_{\lambda(i+1)}\underbrace{S_{i+1}\cdots S_{i+1}}_{\lambda\text{-times}}$$

for $i \geq 0$. Let $S_0 = \sum_{w \in \mathscr{L}} w$ be the solution in the ring of formal power series over $X^*$. The specification of the homomorphism $\theta$ again leads to several enumeration results. We will consider some cases.

(a) Let $k \in \mathbb{N}$ and let $\theta$ be defined by

$$\theta(g_{ij}) = \begin{cases} z & \text{if } i \geq 0 \wedge j \in [1:k-1+\delta_{i,0}] \\ 0 & \text{otherwise} \end{cases}.$$

Furthermore, let $t(n, k)$ be the number of all ordered trees with $n$ nodes and height less than or equal to $k$. We find with

$$X_k = \{g_{ij} \in X \mid \theta(g_{ij}) = z\}$$

$$\theta(S_0) = \sum_{n \geqslant 1} \sum_{w \in \mathscr{L} \cap X^n} \theta(w) = \sum_{n \geqslant 1} \sum_{w \in \mathscr{L} \cap X_k^n} \theta(w) = \sum_{n \geqslant 1} z^n \operatorname{card}(\mathscr{L} \cap X_k^n)$$

$$= \sum_{n \geqslant 1} z^n t(n, k).$$

Thus, taking the image of the above equations, the generating function $A_k(z) = \theta(S_0)$ is given by $A_1(z) = z$ and for $k \geqslant 2$ by

$$A_k(z) = z + z \sum_{\lambda \geqslant 1} F_1^\lambda(z) = z/(1 - F_1(z)),$$

where

$$F_i(z) = z + z \sum_{\lambda \geqslant 1} F_{i+1}^\lambda(z) = z/(1 - F_{i+1}(z)), \qquad 1 \leqslant i \leqslant k - 2,$$

$$F_{k-1}(z) = z.$$

Hence $A_k(z)$ is the $k$-th approximant of the continued fraction

$$\psi_z = \frac{z}{|1|} + \frac{-z}{|1|} + \frac{-z}{|1|} + \frac{-z}{|1|} + \cdots$$

Choosing $e = 0$, $ud = 1$ in Example 4.6, we further obtain

$$\psi_z(k) = \xi_{\sqrt{z}}(k) = \sqrt{z}\, U_{k-1}(2z^{-1/2})/U_k(2z^{-1/2}),$$

where $U_k(z)$ is the $k$-th Chebyshev polynomial of the second kind. In section 4.2.2 we had found $U_k((2z)^{-1}) = z^{-k}Q_{k+1}(z)$, where $Q_k(z)$ is the polynomial

$$Q_k(z) = 2^{-k}[(1 + \sqrt{1 - 4z^2})^k - (1 - \sqrt{1 - 4z^2})^k]/\sqrt{1 - 4z^2}.$$

Hence an explicit expression for $A_k(z)$ is given by

$$A_k(z) = 2z \frac{(1 + \sqrt{1 - 4z})^k - (1 - \sqrt{1 - 4z})^k}{(1 + \sqrt{1 - 4z})^{k+1} - (1 - \sqrt{1 - 4z})^{k+1}}, \qquad k \geqslant 1.$$

This function satisfies some nice properties (Exercise 4.12) which we shall use in Chapter 5. The coefficients $t(n, k) = \langle z^n \rangle A_k(z)$ were computed in section 4.2.2; they correspond to the number of all closed non-negative $(1, 0, 1)$-random walks of length $2n - 2$ and height less than or equal to $k - 1$. Taking $p := 0$, $h := 0$, $n := 2n - 2$, $k := k - 1$, $e := 0$, $u := 1$, and $d := 1$ in the expression for $I_{n,p,k,h}(v)$ derived by Cauchy's formula, we find

$$t(n+1, k-1) = \frac{1}{n+1}\binom{2n}{n}$$

$$- \sum_{j \geqslant 1}\left[\binom{2n}{n+1-jk} - 2\binom{2n}{n-jk} + \binom{2n}{n-1-jk}\right].$$

(b) Let $k \in \mathbb{N}$ and let $\theta$ be defined by

$$\theta(g_{ij}) = \begin{cases} uz & \text{if } i = 0 \wedge j \in [1:k] \\ z & \text{if } i \geqslant 1 \wedge j \in [1:k-1]. \\ 0 & \text{otherwise} \end{cases}$$

Furthermore, let $h_k(n, m)$ be the number of all ordered trees with $n$ nodes, $m$ leaves, and height less than or equal to $k$. Choosing

$$X_k = \{g_{ij} \in X | \theta(g_{ij}) \in \{z, uz\}\},$$

we obtain

$$\theta(S_0) = \sum_{n \geqslant 1} \sum_{w \in \mathscr{L} \cap X^n} \theta(w) = \sum_{n \geqslant 1} \sum_{w \in \mathscr{L} \cap X_k^n} \theta(w) = \sum_{n \geqslant 1} z^n \sum_{w \in \mathscr{L} \cap X_k^n} u^{\#_0(w)},$$

where $\#_0(w)$ is the number of $g_{0,j}, j \geqslant 1$, appearing in $w$. Since each $g_{0,j}$ corresponds to a leaf in the corresponding tree, we obtain

$$\theta(S_0) = \sum_{n \geqslant 1} \sum_{m \geqslant 1} h_k(n, m) z^n u^m.$$

Thus, taking the image of the above equations, we see that the generating function $F_k(z, u) = \theta(S_0)$ satisfies the relations $F_1(z, u) = zu$ and for $k \geqslant 2$

$$F_k(z, u) = zu + z \sum_{\lambda \geqslant 1} H_1^\lambda(z, u) = zu + \frac{zH_1(z, u)}{1 - H_1(z, u)},$$

where

$$H_i(z, u) = zu + z \sum_{\lambda \geqslant 1} H_{i+1}^\lambda(z, u) = zu + \frac{zH_{i+1}(z, u)}{1 - H_{i+1}(z, u)}, \qquad 1 \leqslant i \leqslant k-2,$$

and $H_{k-1}(z, u) = zu$. Hence $F_k(z, u) = zu + \psi_{z,u}$, where $\psi_{z,u}$ is the $(2k-2)$-th approximant of the continued fraction

$$\psi_{z,u} = \frac{-z|}{|1} + \frac{-1|}{|zu} + \frac{-z|}{|1} + \frac{-1|}{|zu} + \frac{-z|}{|1} + \cdots$$

Solving the linear recurrences for the numerator and the denominator of the $k$-th approximant of $\psi_{z,u}$ (section 4.2.3), we find

$$\psi_{z,u}(2k-2) = -z + 2zP_{k-2}(z, u)/P_{k-1}(z, u),$$

where

$$P_k(z, u) = (1 - zu - z + W)[1 - zu + z + W]^k$$

$$- (1 - zu - z - W)[1 - zu + z - W]^k$$

and $W = [(1 + z - zu)^2 - 4z]^{1/2}$. Therefore,

$$F_k(z, u) = z(u - 1) + 2zP_{k-2}(z, u)/P_{k-1}(z, u).$$

To obtain $h_k(n, m) = \langle z^n u^m \rangle F_k(z, u)$, we have to evaluate the function $F_k(z, u)$. A lengthy, but elementary, computation (see [68]) leads to the closed expression (Exercise 4.13)

$$h_k(1, m) = \delta_{m,1}, \qquad h_1(n, m) = \delta_{n,m}\delta_{n,1}$$

$$h_k(n, m) = \frac{1}{n}\binom{n}{m}\binom{n-2}{m-1} - [R_1(n, m, k) - 2R_0(n, m, k) + R_{-1}(n, m, k)],$$

$n \geqslant 2, k \geqslant 2$, where

$$R_a(n, m, k) = \sum_{s \geqslant 1} \binom{n - s(k-1) - 2}{m + s + a - 1}\binom{n + s(k-1) - 2}{m - s - a - 1}.$$

(c) Let $k \in \mathbb{N}$ and let $\theta$ be defined by

$$\theta(g_{ij}) = \begin{cases} z & \text{if } i \in \mathbb{N}_0\backslash\{t\} \wedge j \in \mathbb{N}\backslash\{k\} \\ zu & \text{if } i = t \wedge j = k \end{cases}.$$

Furthermore, let $d_t(n, m, k)$ be the number of all ordered trees with $n$ nodes and $m$ nodes of in-degree $t$ on level $k$. We find by the same procedure as in the above cases that the generating function

$$H_{t,k}(z, u) = \sum_{n \geqslant 1} \sum_{m \geqslant 0} d_t(n, m, k)z^n u^m$$

satisfies the equations

$$H_{t,1}(z, u) = z(u - 1)G_1^t(z, u) + z/(1 - G_1(z, u))$$

$$G_i(z, u) = z/(1 - G_{i+1}(z, u)), \qquad i \in \mathbb{N},$$

and for $k \geqslant 2$

$$H_{t,k}(z, u) = z/(1 - G_1(z, u))$$

$$G_i(z, u) = z/(1 - G_{i+1}(z, u)), \qquad i \in \mathbb{N}\backslash\{k - 1\}$$

$$G_{k-1}(z, u) = z(u - 1)G_k^t(z, u) + z/(1 - G_k(z, u)).$$

Let us first consider the case $k \geqslant 2$. Obviously,

$$G_k(z, u) = \frac{z|}{|1} + \frac{-z|}{|1} + \frac{-z|}{|1} + \frac{-z|}{|1} + \cdots$$

Thus $G_k^2(z, u) - G_k(z, u) + z = 0$, that is $G_k(z, u) = C(z)$, where $C(z)$ is the generating function of the Catalan numbers given by $C(z) = (1 - \sqrt{1 - 4z})/2$. Hence $G_{k-1}(z, u) = z(u - 1)C^t(z) + C(z)$, because $1 - C(z) = z/C(z)$. Therefore,

$$H_{t,k}(z, u) = \left.\frac{z}{|1}\right. + \left.\frac{-z}{|1}\right. + \left.\frac{-z}{|1}\right. + \left.\frac{-z}{|1}\right. + \cdots + \left.\frac{-z}{|1}\right. + \left.\frac{-G_{k-1}(z, u)}{|1}\right..$$

$$\underbrace{\qquad\qquad\qquad\qquad\qquad\qquad\qquad}_{(k-1)\text{-terms}}$$

Solving the linear recurrences for the numerator and the denominator of the $k$-th approximant of this continued fraction (section 4.2.3), we find $H_{t,k}(z, u) = 2zR^{(t)}_{k-2}(z, u)/R^{(t)}_{k-1}(z, u)$, where

$$R^{(t)}_k(z, u) = w(1 + w)^k - z(u - 1)[(1 + w)^k - (1 - w)^k]C^t(z), \quad w = \sqrt{1 - 4z}.$$

It is easily checked that this solution is also valid for $k = 1$. Using the substitution $z = v/(1 + v)^2$, we obtain by a simple computation

$$H_{t,k}(z, u) = \frac{v}{1 + v} \frac{(1 - v)(1 + v)^{t+1} - (u - 1)v^{t+1}[1 - v^{k-2}]}{(1 - v)(1 + v)^{t+1} - (u - 1)v^{t+1}[1 - v^{k-1}]}.$$

Let us discuss an application. Assuming that all ordered trees with $n$ nodes are equally likely, we will compute the average number of nodes of indegree $t$ on level $k$. We have to compute the expected value

$$N_{t,k}(n) = t^{-1}(n) \sum_{m \geqslant 1} md_t(m, n, k).$$

For this purpose, let $N_{t,k}(z) = \sum_{n \geqslant 1} t(n)N_{t,k}(n)z^n$ be the generating function of the numbers $N_{t,k}(n)t(n)$. Since

$$\sum_{m \geqslant 1} md_t(m, n, k) = \langle z^n \rangle \frac{\partial}{\partial u} H_{t,k}(z, u)|_{u=1},$$

we immediately obtain $N_{t,k}(z) = (\partial/\partial u)H_{t,k}(z, u)|_{u=1}$. On the other hand, we have

$$\frac{\partial}{\partial u} H_{t,k}(z, u)|_{u=1} = v^{t+k}/(1 + v)^{t+2}.$$

Therefore by Cauchy's formula

$$N_{t,k}(n)t(n) = \frac{1}{2\pi i} \int^{(0+)} \frac{dz}{z^{n+1}} N_{t,k}(z)$$

$$= \frac{1}{2\pi i} \int^{(0+)} \frac{dv}{v^{n+1}} (1 - v)(1 + v)^{2n-1} \frac{\partial}{\partial u} H_{t,k}(z, u)|_{u=1}$$

$$= \frac{1}{2\pi i} \int^{(0+)} \frac{dv}{v^{n+1}} (1 - v)v^{t+k}(1 + v)^{2n-t-3}.$$

In other words, $N_{t,k}(n)t(n)$ is the coefficient $\langle v^n \rangle((1 - v)v^{t+k}(1 + v)^{2n-t-3})$. An application of the binomial theorem leads directly to

$$N_{t,k}(n) = n \frac{2k + t - 2}{2n - t - 2} \binom{2n - t - 2}{n - t - k} \Big/ \binom{2n - 2}{n - 1}.$$

This result appears in [72]. Since there is only the root at level one, $N_{t,0}(n)$ is equal to the probability that an ordered tree with $n$ nodes is a $t$-tree. This fact has been proved in [64].

In this subsection we have discussed a general approach to the counting of classes of ordered trees by several parameters. Choosing other substitution schemes and other homomorphisms, further enumeration results can be derived.

### 4.4.3 Derivation Trees of Context-free Grammars

We have seen in section 4.4.2 that context-free unambiguous substitution schemes are appropriate for enumerating ordered trees. Let us briefly discuss an application to the derivation trees of context-free grammars.

Let $G_i = (V_N, V_T, P, X_i)$ be a context-free grammar in Chomsky-normal form (see Appendix A, 2.1) with the set of non-terminals $V_N = \{X_j | 0 \leqslant j \leqslant N\}$, the set of terminals $V_T = \{a_j | 0 \leqslant j \leqslant t\}$, the start symbol $X_i \in V_N$ and the production system $P \subseteq V_N \times (V_N V_N \cup V_T)$. The set of derivation trees with root $X_i \in V_N$ and $n$ leaves that are labelled by terminals is denoted by $T_i(n)$. Note that the tree $\tau$ arising from $\tau \in T_i(n)$ by eliminating the leaves is a labelled binary tree with labels $X \in V_N$. The *stack size* $S_i(\tau)$, $\tau \in T_i(n)$, is recursively defined by

$$S_i(\tau) := if \ |\tau| = 2 \ then \ 1$$
$$else \ if \ S_l(\tau_1) > S_r(\tau_2) \ then \ S_l(\tau_1)$$
$$else \ S_r(\tau_2) + 1;$$

where $(X_i, X_l X_r) \in P$ and $\tau_1 \in T_l(m)$ (resp. $\tau_2 \in T_r(n - m)$), $m \in [1 : n - 1]$, is the left (resp. right) subtree of $\tau$; $|\tau|$ denotes the number of nodes of the tree $\tau$. Here, $S_i(\tau)$ is the maximum number of nodes stored in the stack during post-order traversing of $\tau \in T_i(n)$ (see Chapter 5) or, in other words, the height of the ordered tree $\tau'$ corresponding to $\tau$ according to the one-to-one correspondence discussed in section 4.3.1. For example, consider the following context-free grammers $G_i = (V_N, V_T, P, X_i)$, $0 \leqslant i \leqslant 6$, with $V_N = \{X_i | 0 \leqslant i \leqslant 6\}$, $V_T = \{a, b, c\}$ and $P = \{X_0 \rightarrow X_1 X_2, \ X_1 \rightarrow X_3 X_4, \ X_1 \rightarrow X_3 X_6, \ X_2 \rightarrow X_5 X_2, \ X_2 \rightarrow c, \ X_3 \rightarrow a, \ X_4 \rightarrow b, \ X_5 \rightarrow c, \ X_6 \rightarrow X_1 X_4\}$. A derivation tree $\tau \in T_0(10)$ together with $\tau$ and the corresponding ordered tree $\tau'$ are drawn in Figure 21. Obviously, $S_0(\tau) = 4$.

The following theorem describes a general method for the enumeration of derivation trees by the parameter $S_i(\tau)$ (see [59], [63]).

THEOREM 4.16 Let $G_i = (V_N, V_T, P, X_i)$ be a context-free grammar in Chomsky-normal form and let $X_i \rightarrow X_{l_j} X_{r_j}$, $X_i \rightarrow a_{t_j}$, $1 \leqslant j \leqslant n_i$, $1 \leqslant j \leqslant m_i$, are all productions in $P$ with the left-hand side $X_i$. Furthermore, let $H_i(n, j)$ and $B_i(n, k)$ be the set of all derivation trees $\tau \in T_i(n)$ with $S_i(\tau) = j$ and $S_i(\tau) \leqslant k$,

112

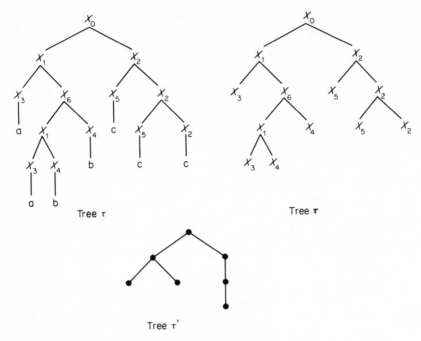

FIGURE 21. The derivation tree $\tau \in T_0(20)$.

respectively. The generating function

$$G_i(z, k) = \sum_{n \geqslant 1} z^n \, \text{card}(B_i(n, k))$$

is given by

$$G_i(z, 1) = n_i z$$

$$G_i(z, k) = n_i z + \sum_{1 \leqslant j \leqslant m_i} G_{l_j}(z, k) G_{r_j}(z, k - 1), \qquad k \geqslant 2.$$

*Proof* Since $\tau \in H_i(n, \lambda)$ if and only if $X_i \to X_l X_r \in P$, $\tau_l \in H_l(n - m, j)$, $\tau_r \in H_r(m, s)$ with $j = \lambda$ and $1 \leqslant s \leqslant \lambda - 1$ or $1 \leqslant j \leqslant \lambda - 1$ and $s = \lambda - 1$, $1 \leqslant m \leqslant n - 1$, for all productions with the left-hand side $X_i$, we obtain all derivation trees $\tau$ with $S_i(\tau) \leqslant k$ by taking (a) all trees $\tau \in T_i(1)$, giving the contribution $n_i z$, and (b) all trees $\tau \in H_i(n, \lambda)$, $2 \leqslant \lambda \leqslant k$, giving the contribution

$$\sum_{2 \leqslant \lambda \leqslant k} \sum_{1 \leqslant j \leqslant m_i} [G_{l_j}(z, \lambda) - G_{l_j}(z, \lambda - 1)] G_{r_j}(z, \lambda - 1)$$

$$+ \sum_{2 \leqslant \lambda \leqslant k} \sum_{1 \leqslant j \leqslant m_i} G_{l_j}(z, \lambda - 1) [G_{r_j}(z, \lambda - 1) - G_{r_j}(z, \lambda - 2)].$$

The sum of these contributions yields our statement. ∎

Let $F_i(z) = \sum_{n\geq 1} \mathrm{card}(T_i(n))z^n$ be the generating function of the number of all derivation trees $\tau \in T_i(n)$. Since $F_i(z) = \lim_{k\to\infty} G_i(z,k)$, we find by Theorem 4.16

$$F_i(z) = n_i z + \sum_{1 \leq j \leq m_i} F_{l_j}(z)F_{r_j}(z).$$

If the grammar $G_i$ is unambiguous, then $F_i(z)$ is also the generating function of the number of all words of length $n$ which can be derived from $X_i$ according to the productions in $P$. In this case, $F_i(z)$ is the *structure-generating function* of the language $\mathscr{L}(G_i)$ defined by

$$F_i(z) = \sum_{n \geq 1} \mathrm{card}(\mathscr{L}(G_i) \cap V_T^n)z^n.$$

For example, consider the above grammar $G_0$. We immediately find the following system of equations:

$G_0(z,1) = 0$

$G_0(z,k) = G_1(z,k)G_2(z,k-1), \qquad k \geq 2$

$G_1(z,1) = 0$

$G_1(z,k) = G_3(z,k)G_4(z,k-1) + G_3(z,k)G_6(z,k-1), \qquad k \geq 2$

$G_2(z,1) = z$

$G_2(z,k) = z + G_5(z,k)G_2(z,k-1), \qquad k \geq 2$

$G_3(z,k) = z, \quad k \geq 1$

$G_4(z,k) = z, \quad k \geq 1$

$G_5(z,k) = z, \quad k \geq 1$

$G_6(z,1) = 0$

$G_6(z,k) = G_1(z,k)G_4(z,k-1), \qquad k \geq 2.$

Solving this system, we find for $k \geq 1$

$$G_0(z,k) = z^3(1 - z^{k-1})(1 - z^{2k-2})/[(1+z)(1-z)^2].$$

Computing the expansion of this function, we obtain

$$\mathrm{card}(B_0(n,k)) = \begin{cases} 0 & \text{if } k \leq \frac{1}{3}(n+2) \\ \frac{1}{2}(3k-n) - \frac{1}{4}(-1)^{n+k} - \frac{3}{4} & \text{if } \frac{1}{3}(n+3) \leq k \leq \frac{1}{2}(n+1) \\ \frac{1}{2}(k-1) - \frac{1}{4}(-1)^n - \frac{1}{4}(-1)^{n+k} & \text{if } \frac{1}{2}(n+2) \leq k \leq n \\ \frac{1}{2}n - \frac{1}{4}(-1)^k - \frac{3}{4} & \text{if } k \geq n+1 \end{cases}$$

Since $F_0(z) = \lim_{k\to\infty} G_0(z,k)$, we further obtain

$$F_0(z) = z^3/[(1+z)(1-z)^2]$$

and therefore

$$\text{card}(T_0(n)) = \tfrac{1}{2}n - \tfrac{1}{4}(-1)^n - \tfrac{3}{4}.$$

Let us now assume that all derivation trees with $n$ leaves are equally likely. What is the average maximum stack size $S_i(n)$ of a tree $\tau \in T_i(n)$? To answer this question we have to compute the expected value

$$S_i(n) := if \ T_i(n) = \varnothing \ then \ 0$$

$$else \ [\text{card}(T_i(n))]^{-1} \sum_{1 \leqslant k \leqslant n} k \ \text{card}(H_i(n, k)).$$

Since $B_i(n, n) = T_i(n)$ and $\text{card}(B_i(n, k)) = \sum_{1 \leqslant \lambda \leqslant k} \text{card}(H_i(n, \lambda))$, we find for $T_i(n) \neq \varnothing$

$$S_i(n) = (n + 1) - [\text{card}(T_i(n))]^{-1} \sum_{1 \leqslant k \leqslant n} \text{card}(B_i(n, k))$$

$$= (n + 1) - [\text{card}(T_i(n))]^{-1} \langle z^n \rangle \sum_{1 \leqslant k \leqslant n} G_i(z, k).$$

Let us determine $S_0(n)$ for the above grammar $G_0$. We obtain

$$\sum_{1 \leqslant k \leqslant n} G_0(z, k) = \frac{z^3}{(1 + z)(1 - z)^2} \left[ n - \frac{1 - z^n}{1 - z} - \frac{1 - z^{2n}}{1 - z^2} + \frac{1 - z^{3n}}{1 - z^3} \right]$$

and therefore by an elementary computation

$$S_0(n) = n + 1 - [\text{card}(T_0(n))]^{-1} \langle z^n \rangle F_0(z) \left[ n - \frac{1}{1 - z} - \frac{1}{1 - z^2} + \frac{1}{1 - z^3} \right]$$

$$= \tfrac{7}{12}n + \tfrac{5}{8} + \tfrac{1}{24}(-1)^n - \tfrac{4}{9} \left[ 1 + 2 \cos\left( \frac{2(n - 3)\pi}{3} \right) \right] \Big/ [2n - 3 - (-1)^n]$$

$$= \tfrac{7}{12}n + \tfrac{5}{8} + \tfrac{1}{24}(-1)^n + O(n^{-1}).$$

Thus $S_0(n)$ is an oscillating function in $n$.

Restricting the above considerations to the subclass of linear context-free grammars, an exact expression for $S_i(n)$ in terms of matrices associated with the given grammar is derived in [59], [63] (see Exercise 4.14). The asymptotic behaviour of $S_i(n)$ can be described by $g(n) \cdot n + f(n)$, where $g(n)$ and $f(n)$ are bounded periodic functions (see [78], [79], [80]). In these papers, a generalization to context-free grammars with infinite parallel control languages in non-cyclic form is also given.

### 4.4.4 Dynamic Data Structures

In section 4.3.2 we have discussed some one-to-one correspondences between classes of data types and $\mathbb{N}_0$-weighted non-negative closed random walks. In this section we will enumerate the number of histories of length $n$ for each such data type. We shall see that these data types can be characterized by a family of orthogonal polynomials. Most of the material of this subsection is taken from [34].

Since the set of all closed histories of length $n$ induced by a data type corresponds to a uniform set consisting of $\mathbb{N}_0$-weighted non-negative closed random walks, the generating function of the number of these histories is given by a continued fraction (see section 4.2.3). Henceforth, let $c_{DT}(n)$ be the number of all closed histories of length $n$ induced by the data type DT, and $c_{DT}(n, k)$ the number of these histories of size $k$. The corresponding ordinary generating functions are denoted by $F_{DT}(z)$ and $F_{DT}^{(k)}(z)$, respectively. As we have seen in section 4.2.3, $F_{DT}(z) = \lim_{k \to \infty} F_{DT}^{(k)}(z)$. The function $F_{DT}^{(k)}(z)$ is the $(k+1)$-th approximant of a continued fraction and can be expressed by $A_k^{DT}(z)/B_k^{DT}(z)$, where $A_k^{DT}(z)$ and $B_k^{DT}(z)$ are polynomials satisfying the recurrences given in Theorem 4.7. We prove now the following theorem.

THEOREM 4.17 Let $F_{DT}^{(k)}(z) = A_k^{DT}(z)/B_k^{DT}(z)$ and $\mathbf{B}_k^{DT}(z) = z^{k+1}B_k^{DT}(1/z)$ be the reciprocal polynomial of $B_k^{DT}(z)$. Each data type DT introduced in section 4.3.2 can be characterized by the polynomial $\mathbf{B}_k^{DT}(z)$ as follows:

| DT | Polynomial $\mathbf{B}_k^{DT}(z)$ | $a_k$ | $H_B^{DT}(z, t)$ |
|---|---|---|---|
| Stack | $U_{k+1}(z/2)$ (Chebyshev) | 1 | $(1 - tz + t^2)^{-1}$ |
| Deque | $2^{k+1}U_{k+1}(z/4)$ (Chebyshev) | 1 | $(1 - tz + 4t^2)^{-1}$ |
| Linear list | $M_{k+1}(z)$ (Meixner) | $k!^{-1}$ | $(1 + t^2)^{-1/2} \exp(z \operatorname{arctg}(t))$ |
| Priority queue | $2^{-(k+1)/2}H_{k+1}(z/\sqrt{2})$ (Hermite) | $k!^{-1}$ | $\exp(zt - t^2/2)$ |
| Symbol table | $C_{k+1}(z + 1)$ (Poisson–Charlier) | $k!^{-1}$ | $(1 + t)^{z+1} \exp(-t)$ |
| Dictionary | $(k+1)!(-1)^{k+1}L_{k+1}^{(0)}(z)$ (Laguerre) | $k!^{-1}$ | $(1 + t)^{-1} \exp(zt/(1 + t))$ |

$H_B^{DT}(z, t)$ is the generating function of the polynomials $\mathbf{B}_k^{DT}(z)$ given by

$$H_B^{DT}(z, t) = \sum_{k \geqslant 0} a_k \mathbf{B}_{k-1}^{DT}(z)t^k.$$

*Proof*

(a) DT = stack. The one-to-one correspondence between histories induced by a stack and $(1, 0, 1)$-random walks implies the recurrence

$$B_{-1}^{DT}(z) = 1, \qquad B_0^{DT}(z) = 1$$

$$B_k^{DT}(z) = B_{k-1}^{DT}(z) - z^2 B_{k-2}^{DT}(z), \qquad k \geqslant 1.$$

Translating these relations into terms of $\mathbf{B}_k^{\mathrm{DT}}(z)$, we find

$$\mathbf{B}_{-1}^{\mathrm{DT}}(z) = 1, \qquad \mathbf{B}_0^{\mathrm{DT}}(z) = z$$

$$\mathbf{B}_k^{\mathrm{DT}}(z) = z\mathbf{B}_{k-1}^{\mathrm{DT}}(z) - \mathbf{B}_{k-2}^{\mathrm{DT}}(z), \qquad k \geqslant 1.$$

Introducing the generating function $H_B^{\mathrm{DT}}(z,t) = \sum_{\lambda \geqslant 0} \mathbf{B}_{\lambda-1}^{\mathrm{DT}}(z)t^\lambda$, this recurrence implies $H_B^{\mathrm{DT}}(z,t) = (1 - tz + t^2)^{-1}$. An inspection of (B76) shows that $H_B^{\mathrm{DT}}(2z,t)$ is equal to the generating function of the Chebyshev polynomials of the second kind. Hence, $\mathbf{B}_k^{\mathrm{DT}}(z) = U_{k+1}(z/2)$. In view of the general result discussed in Example 4.6, this relation does not surprise.

(b) DT = deque. In this case, we find

$$B_{-1}^{\mathrm{DT}}(z) = 1, \qquad B_0^{\mathrm{DT}}(z) = 1$$

$$B_k^{\mathrm{DT}}(z) = B_{k-1}^{\mathrm{DT}}(z) - 4z^2 B_{k-2}^{\mathrm{DT}}(z), \qquad k \geqslant 1.$$

A similar computation as in (a) leads to $H_B^{\mathrm{DT}}(z,t) = (1 - tz + 4t^2)^{-1}$. Hence $H_B^{\mathrm{DT}}(4z,t/2)$ is equal to the generating function of the Chebyshev polynomials of the second kind. Therefore, $\mathbf{B}_k^{\mathrm{DT}}(z) = 2^{k+1}U_{k+1}(z/4)$.

(c) DT = linear list. Using the one-to-one correspondence between histories induced by a linear list and weighted random walks with weights $e_i = 0$, $u_i = i + 1$, $d_{i+1} = i + 1$, $i \in \mathbb{N}_0$, we get the following recurrence:

$$B_{-1}^{\mathrm{DT}}(z) = 1, \qquad B_0^{\mathrm{DT}}(z) = 1$$

$$B_k^{\mathrm{DT}}(z) = B_{k-1}^{\mathrm{DT}}(z) - k^2 z^2 B_{k-2}^{\mathrm{DT}}(z), \qquad k \geqslant 1,$$

or equivalently

$$\mathbf{B}_{-1}^{\mathrm{DT}}(z) = 1, \qquad \mathbf{B}_0^{\mathrm{DT}}(z) = z$$

$$\mathbf{B}_k^{\mathrm{DT}}(z) = z\mathbf{B}_{k-1}^{\mathrm{DT}}(z) - k^2 \mathbf{B}_{k-2}^{\mathrm{DT}}(z), \qquad k \geqslant 1.$$

Translating these equations into terms of the generating function $H_B^{\mathrm{DT}}(z,t)$, we find the differential equation

$$(1 + t^2)\frac{\partial}{\partial t} H_B^{\mathrm{DT}}(z,t) = (z - t)H_B^{\mathrm{DT}}(z,t)$$

whose solution is

$$H_B^{\mathrm{DT}}(z,t) = (1 + t^2)^{-1/2} \exp(z \operatorname{arctg}(t)).$$

This is the generating function of the *Meixner polynomials* $M_{k+1}(z)$ given in (B99).

(d) DT = priority queue. In this case, we find the recurrence

$$\mathbf{B}_{-1}^{\mathrm{DT}}(z) = 1, \qquad \mathbf{B}_0^{\mathrm{DT}}(z) = z$$

$$\mathbf{B}_k^{\mathrm{DT}}(z) = z\mathbf{B}_{k-1}^{\mathrm{DT}}(z) - k\mathbf{B}_{k-2}^{\mathrm{DT}}(z), \qquad k \geqslant 1.$$

These relations imply the differential equation

$$\frac{\partial}{\partial t} H_B^{DT}(z, t) = (z - t)H_B^{DT}(z, t)$$

which has the solution

$$H_B^{DT}(z, t) = \exp(zt - t^2/2).$$

Hence $H_B^{DT}(\sqrt{2}\, z, \sqrt{2}\, t)$ is the generating function of the *Hermite polynomials* $H_k(z)$ given by (B83). Therefore,

$$\mathbf{B}_k^{DT}(z) = 2^{-(k+1)/2} H_{k+1}(z/\sqrt{2}).$$

(e) DT = symbol table. The recurrence for $\mathbf{B}_k^{DT}(z)$ has the following form:

$$\mathbf{B}_{-1}^{DT}(z) = 1, \qquad \mathbf{B}_0^{DT}(z) = z$$

$$\mathbf{B}_k^{DT}(z) = [z - k]\mathbf{B}_{k-1}^{DT}(z) - k\mathbf{B}_{k-2}^{DT}(z), \qquad k \geqslant 1.$$

Thus $H_B^{DT}(z)$ satisfies the differential equation

$$(1 + t)\frac{\partial}{\partial t} H_B^{DT}(z, t) = (z - t)H_B^{DT}(z, t)$$

whose solution is $H_B^{DT}(z, t) = (1 + t)^{z+1} \exp(-t)$. $H_B^{DT}(z - 1)$ is the generating function of the *Poisson–Charlier polynomials* $C_k(z)$ given by (B103).

(f) DT = dictionary. We obtain

$$B_{-1}^{DT}(z) = 1, \qquad B_0^{DT}(z) = 1 - z$$

$$B_k^{DT}(z) = [1 - (2k + 1)z]B_{k-1}^{DT}(z) - k^2 z^2 B_{k-2}^{DT}(z), \qquad k \geqslant 1.$$

This recurrence was extensively studied in Example 4.7. We find $H_B^{DT}(z, t) = (1 + t)^{-1} \exp(zt/(1 + t))$ and therefore $\mathbf{B}_k^{DT}(z) = (k + 1)! \, (-1)^{k+1} L_{k+1}^{(0)}(z)$, where $L_k^{(0)}(z)$ is the $k$-th Laguerre polynomial given by (B87). ∎

An inspection of Theorem 4.7 shows that the recurrences for the polynomials $\mathbf{A}_k^{DT}(z) = z^{k+1} A_k^{DT}(1/z)$ and $\mathbf{B}_k^{DT}(z)$ differ only in the initial conditions. As a consequence of this observation, the generating function

$$H_A^{DT}(z, t) = \sum_{k \geqslant 0} a_k \mathbf{A}_{k-1}^{DT}(z)t^k$$

of the polynomials $\mathbf{A}_k^{DT}(z)$ satisfies a non-homogeneous differential equation; the corresponding homogeneous equation is identical to the differential equation satisfied by the generating function $H_B^{DT}(z, t)$. Therefore, using the technique discussed in Example 4.7, we can derive explicit expressions for the polynomials $\mathbf{A}_k^{DT}(z)$. The following theorem summarizes these results. It is left for the exercises to prove these relations (Exercise 4.16).

THEOREM 4.18   Let $F_{\text{DT}}^{(k)}(z) = A_k^{\text{DT}}(z)/B_k^{\text{DT}}(z)$ and $\mathbf{A}_k^{\text{DT}}(z) = z^{k+1}A_k^{\text{DT}}(1/z)$ be the reciprocal polynomial of $A_k^{\text{DT}}(z)$. We have

(a)  DT = stack: $\mathbf{A}_k^{\text{DT}}(z) = zU_k(z/2)$.

(b)  DT = deque: $\mathbf{A}_k^{\text{DT}}(z) = z2^kU_k(z/4)$.

(c)  DT = linear list:
$$\mathbf{A}_k^{\text{DT}}(z) = z \sum_{0 \leqslant \mu \leqslant k} \binom{k+1}{\mu+1} M_\mu(-z)M_{k-\mu}(z).$$

(d)  DT = priority queue:
$$\mathbf{A}_k^{\text{DT}}(z) = z2^{-k/2} \sum_{0 \leqslant \mu \leqslant k} \binom{k+1}{\mu+1} i^\mu H_\mu(iz/\sqrt{2})H_{k-\mu}(z/\sqrt{2}) \qquad (i^2 = -1).$$

(e)  DT = symbol table:
$$\mathbf{A}_k(z) = z \sum_{0 \leqslant \mu \leqslant k} \binom{k+1}{\mu+1} \sum_{0 \leqslant j \leqslant \mu} 2^j \binom{\mu}{j} C_{\mu-j}(-z-2)C_{k-\mu}(z+1).$$

(f)  DT = dictionary:
$$\mathbf{A}_k(z) = z(k+1)!\,(-1)^k \sum_{0 \leqslant \mu \leqslant k} \frac{1}{\mu+1} L_\mu^{(0)}(-z)L_{k-\mu}^{(0)}(z). \quad \blacksquare$$

Thus the generating functions $F_{\text{DT}}^{(k)}(z)$ of the numbers $c_{\text{DT}}(n, k)$ of all closed histories of length $n$ and size $k$ induced by each data type DT are determined by the results stated in the preceding two theorems. Let us now compute the number $c_{\text{DT}}(n)$ of all closed histories of length $n$ for each data type DT. Since the polynomials $\mathbf{B}_k^{\text{DT}}(z)$ together with their generating function $H_B^{\text{DT}}(z, t)$ are known, we can use the scalar product introduced in Example 4.7 in order to compute $c_{\text{DT}}(n)$ and the corresponding generating function $F_{\text{DT}}(z)$.

THEOREM 4.19   The number $c_{\text{DT}}(n)$ of all closed histories of length $n$ induced by the data type DT and the corresponding generating function $F_{\text{DT}}(z) = \sum_{n \geqslant 0} a_n c_{\text{DT}}(n)z^n$ are given by

| DT | $a_n$ | $F_{\text{DT}}(z)$ | $c_{\text{DT}}(n)$ |
|---|---|---|---|
| Stack | 1 | $(1 - \sqrt{1 - 4z^2})/(2z^2)$ | $(1 + (-1)^n)\binom{n}{n/2}\Big/(n+2)$ |
| Deque | 1 | $(1 - \sqrt{1 - 4z^2})/(8z^2)$ | $(1 + (-1)^n)2^n\binom{n}{n/2}\Big/(n+2)$ |
| Linear list | $n!^{-1}$ | $(\cos(z))^{-1}$ | $|E_n|$ |
| Priority queue | $n!^{-1}$ | $\exp(z^2/2)$ | $(1 + (-1)^n)n!\,2^{-n/2-1}/(n/2)!$ |
| Symbol table | $n!^{-1}$ | $\exp(\exp(z) - z - 1)$ | $(-1)^n\left[1 - \sum_{0 \leqslant i \leqslant n-1} (-1)^i\omega_i\right]$ |
| Dictionary | $n!^{-1}$ | $(1 - z)^{-1}$ | $n!$ |

*Proof*  Using the linear form $\langle\ \rangle_{c_{DT}(n)}$ introduced in Example 4.7, we obtain for all data types DT (omitting the index $c_{DT}(n)$)

$$
\begin{aligned}
\langle H_B^{DT}(z, t)\rangle &= \left\langle \sum_{k \geqslant 0} a_k \mathbf{B}_{k-1}^{DT}(z)t^k \right\rangle \\
&= \sum_{k \geqslant 0} a_k t^k \langle \mathbf{B}_{-1}^{DT}(z)\mathbf{B}_{k-1}^{DT}(z)\rangle \\
&= \sum_{k \geqslant 0} a_k t^k \langle \mathbf{B}_{-1}^{DT}(z)\,|\,\mathbf{B}_{k-1}^{DT}(z)\rangle \\
&= \sum_{k \geqslant 0} a_k t^k \delta_{k,0} u_0 \ldots u_{k-1} d_1 \ldots d_k \\
&= 1.
\end{aligned}
$$

On the other hand, we obtain by Theorem 4.17

(a) DT = stack.

$$
\begin{aligned}
\langle H_B^{DT}(z, t)\rangle &= \langle (1 - zt + t^2)^{-1}\rangle \\
&= (1 + t^2)^{-1}\langle (1 - zt/(1 + t^2))^{-1}\rangle \\
&= (1 + t^2)^{-1} \left\langle \sum_{n \geqslant 0} z^n \left(\frac{t}{1 + t^2}\right)^n \right\rangle \\
&= (1 + t^2)^{-1} \sum_{n \geqslant 0} c_{DT}(n)\left(\frac{t}{1 + t^2}\right)^n \\
&= (1 + t^2)^{-1} F_{DT}(t/(1 + t^2)).
\end{aligned}
$$

Thus $F_{DT}(t/(1 + t^2)) = 1 + t^2$. Choosing $t = (1 - \sqrt{1 - 4z^2})/(2z)$, we find

$$
\begin{aligned}
F_{DT}(z) &= \frac{1}{2z^2}\,(1 - \sqrt{1 - 4z^2}) \\
&= \sum_{n \geqslant 1} \frac{1}{n}\binom{2n - 2}{n - 1} z^{2n - 2}
\end{aligned}
$$

Hence

$$
c_{DT}(n) = \begin{cases} \dfrac{1}{1 + n/2}\dbinom{n}{n/2} & \text{if } n \equiv 0 \bmod (2) \\ 0 & \text{if } n \equiv 1 \bmod (2) \end{cases}
$$

(b) DT = deque.

$$
\begin{aligned}
\langle H_B^{DT}(z, t)\rangle &= \langle (1 - tz + 4t^2)^{-1}\rangle \\
&= (1 + 4t^2)^{-1} \sum_{n \geqslant 0} c_{DT}(n)\left(\frac{t}{1 + 4t^2}\right)^n \\
&= (1 + 4t^2)^{-1} F_{DT}(t/(1 + 4t^2)).
\end{aligned}
$$

Hence $F_{DT}(t/(1 + 4t^2)) = 1 + 4t^2$ or equivalently

$$F_{DT}(z) = \frac{1}{8z^2}\left(1 - \sqrt{1 - 16z^2}\right)$$

$$= \sum_{n \geq 1} \frac{1}{n}\binom{2n-2}{n-1}(2z)^{2n-2}.$$

(c) DT = linear list.

$$\langle H_B^{DT}(z, t)\rangle = \langle (1 + t^2)^{-1/2}\exp(z\,\text{arctg}(t))\rangle$$

$$= (1 + t^2)^{-1/2}\sum_{n \geq 0} c_{DT}(n)\,\text{arctg}^n(t)/n!$$

$$= (1 + t^2)^{-1/2}F_{DT}(\text{arctg}(t)).$$

Thus $F_{DT}(\text{arctg}(t)) = (1 + t^2)^{1/2}$. Choosing $t = \text{tg}(z)$, we find

$$F_{DT}(z) = \cos^{-1}(z) = \sum_{n \geq 0} |E_{2n}|z^{2n}/(2n)!,$$

where $E_{2n}$ is the $2n$-th Euler number (see Exercise 3.13(c)).

(d) DT = priority queue.

$$\langle H_B^{DT}(z, t)\rangle = \langle \exp(zt - t^2/2)\rangle$$

$$= \exp(-t^2/2)\sum_{n \geq 0} c_{DT}(n)t^n/n!$$

$$= \exp(-t^2/2)F_{DT}(t).$$

Therefore,

$$F_{DT}(z) = \exp(z^2/2) = \sum_{n \geq 0} \frac{1}{n!}2^{-n}z^{2n}.$$

Thus

$$c_{DT}(n) = \begin{cases} 2^{-n/2}\dfrac{n!}{(n/2)!} & \text{if } n \equiv 0 \bmod (2) \\ 0 & \text{if } n \equiv 1 \bmod (2) \end{cases}$$

(e) DT = symbol table.

$$\langle H_B^{DT}(z, t)\rangle = \langle (1 + t)^{z+1}\exp(-t)\rangle$$

$$= (1 + t)\exp(-t)\langle \exp(z\ln(1 + t))\rangle$$

$$= (1 + t)\exp(-t)\sum_{n \geq 0} c_{DT}(n)\ln^n(1 + t)/n!$$

$$= (1 + t)\exp(-t)F_{DT}(\ln(1 + t)).$$

Hence $F_{DT}(z) = \exp(\exp(z) - z - 1)$. Using (B47), it is easily verified that

$$c_{DT}(n) = (-1)^n \left[ 1 - \sum_{0 \leqslant i \leqslant n-1} (-1)^i \omega_i \right],$$

where $\omega_n$ is the $n$-th *Bell number*.

(f) DT = dictionary. The corresponding relations have been derived in Example 4.7. ∎

In section 4.3.2 we have described further one-to-one correspondences between weighted random walks and partitions, involutions in $\mathfrak{S}(\mathbb{N}_n)$, etc. It stands to reason that the same methods described in this section lead to enumeration results for these mathematical objects.

## Exercises

**4.1** (a) Let $M_n = (m_{ij})$ be the $n \times n$-matrix defined by $m_{ij} = \binom{j}{i-j+1}$. Prove the identity $\det(M_n) = \dfrac{1}{n+1}\binom{2n}{n}$ for $n \geqslant 1$.

(b) Let $M_n = (m_{ij})$ be the $n \times n$-matrix defined by $m_{ij} = \binom{n+1}{i-j+1}$. Prove the identity $\det(M_n) = \binom{2n}{n}$ for $n \geqslant 1$.

**4.2** In section 4.2.1 we have derived a general result for the number of all simple $(k, h)$-bounded $(1, 0, 1)$-random walks of length $n$ from 0 to $p$. We had shown that this number is equal to

$$\langle v^n \rangle (v^p (1 + v^2)^n (1 - v^{2h+2})(1 - v^{2k-2p+2})/(1 - v^{2k+2h+4})).$$

(a) Show that the number of all simple $(k, 0)$-bounded $(1, 0, 1)$-random walks of length $n$ from 0 to $p$ is given by

$$\frac{2^{n+2}}{k+2} \sum_{1 \leqslant \lambda \leqslant \lfloor (k+1)/2 \rfloor} \sin\left(\frac{\pi\lambda}{k+2}\right) \sin\left(\frac{(p+1)\pi\lambda}{k+2}\right) \cos^n\left(\frac{\pi\lambda}{k+2}\right),$$

where $(n + p) \equiv 0 \bmod (2)$, $1 \leqslant p \leqslant k \leqslant n$.

(b) Deduce from (a) the identity

$$\sum_{1 \leqslant \lambda \leqslant \lfloor (n+1)/2 \rfloor} \sin\left(\frac{\pi\lambda}{n+2}\right) \sin\left(\frac{(p+1)\pi\lambda}{n+2}\right) \cos^n\left(\frac{\pi\lambda}{n+2}\right)$$

$$= 2^{-n-1} \frac{(n+2)(p+1)}{n+p+2}\binom{n}{(n-p)/2},$$

where $(n + p) \equiv 0 \bmod (2)$, $1 \leqslant p \leqslant n$.

**4.3** In section 4.2.1 we have computed the number of all simple (unweighted) random walks of length $n$ (from 0) having a maximal deviation less than or equal to $h$. We had proved that this number is given by

$$\langle v^n \rangle ((1 + v^2)^n (1 + v)(1 - v^{h+1})^2 / [(1 - v)(1 + v^{2h+2})]).$$

(a) Show that this coefficient is equal to

$$\frac{2^n}{h+1}\sum_{0\le\lambda\le h}(-1)^\lambda\,\mathrm{tg}^{-1}\!\left(\frac{(2\lambda+1)\pi}{4(h+1)}\right)\cos^n\!\left(\frac{(2\lambda+1)\pi}{2(h+1)}\right)$$

(b) Deduce from (a) the identity

$$\sum_{0\le\lambda\le h}(-1)^\lambda\,\mathrm{tg}^{-1}\!\left(\frac{(2\lambda+1)\pi}{4(h+1)}\right)\cos^n\!\left(\frac{(2\lambda+1)\pi}{2(h+1)}\right)=h+1,\qquad h\ge n.$$

**4.4** Let $\sigma = i_1, i_2, \ldots, i_n \in \mathfrak{S}(\mathbb{N}_n)$ be a permutation in linear notation. Here, $\sigma$ is called *2-ordered* if $i_j < i_{j+2}$, $1 \le j \le n-2$.

(a) Show that there is a one-to-one correspondence between the set of all 2-ordered permutations in $\mathfrak{S}(\mathbb{N}_n)$ and the set of all simple (unweighted) random walks of length $n$ from 0 to $((-1)^n - 1)/2$.
(b) Deduce from (a) that the number of all 2-ordered permutations in $\mathfrak{S}(\mathbb{N}_n)$ is equal to
$$\binom{n}{\lfloor n/2\rfloor}.$$
(c) Assume that all 2-ordered permutations in $\mathfrak{S}(\mathbb{N}_n)$ are equally likely. Show that the average number of inversions appearing in a 2-ordered permutation $\sigma \in \mathfrak{S}(\mathbb{N}_n)$ is equal to $\lfloor n/2\rfloor 2^{n-2}\Big/\binom{n}{\lfloor n/2\rfloor} \sim \sqrt{\pi/128}\,n^{3/2}$. Prove that the maximum number of inversions in a 2-ordered permutation of $\mathfrak{S}(\mathbb{N}_n)$ is equal to $\frac{1}{2}\lfloor n/2\rfloor(\lfloor n/2\rfloor + 1)$.

**4.5** The generating function of the average length $l_k$ of the $k$-th run appearing in a permutation $\sigma \in \mathfrak{S}(\mathbb{N}_n)$ is given by $(1-x)x/[\exp(x-1)-x]-x$ (see section 3.2.6). Show that $l_k = 2 + o(1)$ for $k \to \infty$.

**4.6** Consider the sum

$$D_n(m) = \sum_{0\le\lambda\le n-1}\frac{1}{n-\lambda}\binom{2n-2\lambda-2}{n-\lambda-1}\binom{\lambda}{m}\binom{\lambda+1}{m}.$$

Note that $D_n(m) = \langle z^n\rangle C(z)g_m(z)$, where

$$g_m(z) = \sum_{k\ge 0}\binom{k}{m}\binom{k+1}{m}z^k \quad\text{and}\quad C(z) = (1-\sqrt{1-4z})/2.$$

(a) Prove that

$$C(z)g_m(z) = \begin{cases}(1-z)^{-1}C(z) & \text{if } m = 0 \\[2mm] 2m^{-1}(1-z)^{-m-2}z^m C(z)\dfrac{\mathrm d}{\mathrm dx}P_m(x)\big|_{(1+z)/(1-z)} & \text{if } m \ge 1\end{cases},$$

where $P_m(z)$ is the $m$-th Legendre polynomial. (*Hint:* Use the recurrences (B95) and (B96) and Murphy's formula.)
(b) Deduce from (a) that the asymptotic behaviour of $D_n(m)$ is given by

$$D_n(m) = \begin{cases}\dfrac{2}{3}\binom{2n}{n}\Big/(2n-1)+o(4^n) & \text{if } m = 0 \\[3mm] \dfrac{16}{9m}3^{-m}\binom{2n}{n}P_m'(\tfrac{5}{3})/(2n-1)+o(4^n) & \text{if } m\ge 1\end{cases}$$

for fixed $m \in \mathbb{N}_0$.

**4.7** In [86] the notion of a *simply generated family of trees* is introduced. Let $T$ be a family of trees and let $t(n)$ be the number of trees in $T$ with $n$ nodes. Here, $T$ is called 'simply generated' if the generating function $T(z) = \sum_{n\ge 1}a_n t(n)z^n$, $a_i \in \mathbb{R}$, satisfies a relation of the type $T(z) = zF(T(z))$, where $F(y)$ is a power series in $y$ with $F(0) = 1$.

Examples of simply generated families of trees are ordered trees ($a_n = 1$ and $F(y) = (1 - y)^{-1}$), binary trees ($a_n = 1$ and $F(y) = 1 + y^2$), $t$-ary ordered trees ($a_n = 1$ and $F(y) = 1 + y^t$) or unordered labelled trees with distinct labels ($a_n = n!^{-1}$ and $F(y) = \exp(y)$).

(a) Show that the number $t(n)$ of all trees in a simply generated family of trees is asymptotically given by

$$t(n) \sim \begin{cases} \delta C n^{-3/2} \left( \dfrac{F(\tau)}{\tau} \right)^n & \text{if } n \equiv 1 \bmod (\delta) \\ 0 & \text{otherwise} \end{cases},$$

where $\tau$ is the smallest positive root of the equation $F(\tau) = \tau F'(\tau)$; furthermore, $C = [F(\tau)/(2\pi F''(\tau))]^{1/2}$ and $\delta$ is the greatest common divisor of the numbers in $\{n \,|\, \langle y^n \rangle F(y) \neq 0\}$.

(b) Let $t_{i,j}(n)$ be the number of ordered trees with $n$ nodes having in-degree $i$ or $j$ or zero. Show that $t_{1,2}(n) \sim [3/(4\pi)]^{1/2} n^{-3/2} 3^n$, $t_{2,3}(n) \sim 0.214\,358\ldots n^{-3/2}(2.610\,719\ldots)^n$. Give an asymptotic expression for $t_{1,k}(n)$ and $t_{k,k}(n)$. (Note that $t_{1,2}(n)$ is equal to the $n$-th Motzkin number.)

**4.8** Let $T$ be a simply generated family of trees and let $T(z) = \sum_{n \geq 1} t(n)z^n$ be the generating function of the number $t(n)$ of all trees in $T$ with $n$ nodes satisfying the functional equation $T(z) = F(T(z))$, where $F(y)$ is a power series in $y$ with $F(0) = 1$ (see Exercise 4.7).

(a) Let $t_m(n)$ be the number of trees in $T$ with $n$ nodes and $m$ leaves and let $L(z,u) = \sum_{n \geq 1} \sum_{m \geq 1} t_m(n)z^n u^m$ be the generating function of the numbers $t_m(n)$. Show that $L(z,u) = z(u - 1) + zF(L(z,u))$.

(b) Let $\mathbf{t}(n)$ be the number of all $n$-node trees in $T$ with exactly one leaf labelled, and let $\mathbf{T}(z) = \sum_{n \geq 1} \mathbf{t}(n)z^n$ be the generating function of these numbers. Show that $\mathbf{T}(z) = z^2 (d/dz) \ln(T(z))$.

(c) Let $\tau \in T$ be a tree with $n$ nodes and $\tau' \in T$ be a tree with $i$ interior nodes and $l$ leaves. The tree $\tau'$ is an 'occurrence' in $\tau$, if $\tau$ can be split in $(l + 2)$ subtrees $\tau_0, \tau', \tau_1, \ldots, \tau_l$ such that the root of $\tau'$ is a leaf in $\tau_0$ and the roots of $\tau_k$, $1 \leq k \leq l$, are the leaves of $\tau'$. Figure 22 illustrates the general situation and shows two trees $\tau$ and $\tau'$, where the number of occurrences of $\tau'$ in $\tau$ is three (marked by *); the number of occurrences of $\tau'$ in $\tau''$ is zero. Let $occ_{i,l}(n)$ be the number of all occurrences of a fixed tree $\tau' \in T$ with $i$ interior nodes and $l$ leaves in all trees $\tau \in T$ with $n$ nodes and let

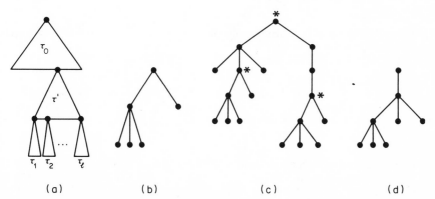

(a)          (b)          (c)          (d)

FIGURE 22. (a) The general situation; (b) the tree $\tau'$; (c) the tree $\tau$; (d) the tree $\tau''$.

$O(z) = \sum_{n \geq 1} \mathrm{occ}_{i,l}(n) z^n$ be the generating function of the numbers $\mathrm{occ}_{i,l}(n)$. Show that $O(z) = z^{i+1} l^{-1} (d/dz) T^l(z)$.

(d) Prove that $\mathrm{occ}_{i,l}(n) = \langle y^{n-i-l} \rangle F^{n-i}(z)$.

(e) Prove the following explicit results:

| Family $T$ | $i$ | $l$ | $n$ | $\mathrm{occ}_{i,l}(n)$ |
|---|---|---|---|---|
| Ordered trees | $I$ | $L$ | $N$ | $\binom{2N - 2I - L - 1}{N - I - 1}$ |
| Extended binary ordered trees | $I$ | $I+1$ | $2N+1$ | $\binom{2N - I + 1}{N + 1}$ |
| Ordered trees whose nodes have an in-degree 0, 1, or 2 | $I$ | $L$ | $N$ | $\binom{N - I, 3}{N - I - L}$ |

**4.9** Let $T$ be a simply generated family of trees and let $T(z) = \sum_{n \geq 1} t(n) z^n$ be the generating function of the number $t(n)$ of trees in $T$ with $n$ nodes satisfying the functional equation $T(z) = zF(T(z))$, where $F(y)$ is a power series in $y$ with $F(0) = 1$.

(a) The *external path length of a tree* $\tau \in T$ is defined to be the sum—taken over all leaves—of the lengths of the paths from a leaf to the root. Let $t_{\mathrm{ep}}(n, m, w)$ be the number of all trees $\tau \in T$ with $n$ nodes, $m$ leaves and an external path length $w$ and let

$$P_e(z, u, t) = \sum_{n \geq 1} \sum_{m \geq 1} \sum_{w \geq 0} t_{\mathrm{ep}}(n, m, w) z^n u^m t^w$$

be the generating function of the numbers $t_{\mathrm{ep}}(n, m, w)$. Show that $P_e(z, u, t)$ satisfies the functional equation

$$P_e(z, u, t) = z(u - 1) + zF(P_e(z, ut, t)).$$

(b) The *internal path length* of a tree $\tau \in T$ is the sum—taken over all interior nodes—of the lengths of the paths from an interior node to the root. Let $t_{\mathrm{ip}}(n, m, w)$ be the number of all trees $\tau \in T$ with $n$ nodes, $m$ leaves and an internal path length $w$ and let

$$P_i(z, u, t) = \sum_{n \geq 1} \sum_{m \geq 1} \sum_{w \geq 0} t_{\mathrm{ip}}(n, m, w) z^n u^m t^w$$

be the generating function of the numbers $t_{\mathrm{ip}}(n, m, w)$. Show that $P_i(z, u, t)$ satisfies the functional equation

$$P_i(z, u, t) = z(u - 1) + zF(P_i(zt, ut^{-1}, t)).$$

(c) The *degree path length* of a tree $\tau \in T$ is the sum—taken over all leaves—of the in-degrees of the interior nodes on the path from a leaf to the root. Let $t_{\mathrm{dp}}(n, m, w)$ be the number of all trees $\tau \in T$ with $n$ nodes and a degree path length $w$ and let

$$P_d(z, u, t) = \sum_{n \geq 1} \sum_{m \geq 1} \sum_{w \geq 0} t_{\mathrm{dp}}(n, m, w) z^n u^m t^w$$

be the generating function of the numbers $t_{\mathrm{dp}}(n, m, w)$. Show that $P_d(z, u, t)$ satisfies the functional equation

$$P_d(z, u, t) = z(u - 1) + z \sum_{r \geq 0} P_d^r(z, ut^r, t) \langle y^r \rangle F(y).$$

(d) Let $L(z, u) = \sum_{n \geqslant 1} \sum_{m \geqslant 1} t_m(n) z^n u^m$ be the generating function of the numbers of all trees in $T$ with $n$ nodes and $m$ leaves (Exercise 4.8(a)) and let ep$(n, m)$ (ip$(n, m)$, dp$(n, m)$) be the sum of all external (internal, degree) path lengths of these trees, respectively. Denote the corresponding generating function by $EP(z, u) = \sum_{n \geqslant 1} \sum_{m \geqslant 1} \text{ep}(n, m) z^n u^m$, $IP(z, u) = \sum_{n \geqslant 1} \sum_{m \geqslant 1} \text{ip}(n, m) z^n u^m$, and $DP(z, u) = \sum_{n \geqslant 1} \sum_{m \geqslant 1} \text{dp}(n, m) z^n u^m$. Prove the following relations

(i) $EP(z, u) = uz^2 L_z(z, u)[zL_z(z, u) - L(z, u)]L^{-2}(z, u);$

(ii) $IP(z, u) = zL_z(z, u)[zL_z(z, u) - L(z, u)][L(z, u) - uz]L^{-2}(z, u);$

(iii) $DP(z, u) = uz[zL_z(z, u) - 2L(z, u)][zL_z(z, u) - L(z, u)]L^{-2}(z, u)$
$\qquad\qquad + uz^2 L_{zz}(z, u)L_z^{-1}(z, u).$

(e) Deduce from (d):

(i) The sum of all external (internal, degree) path lengths of all extended binary ordered trees with $(2n + 1)$ nodes is equal to

$$4^n - \binom{2n}{n}\left(4^n - \frac{3n+1}{n+1}\binom{2n}{n}, \quad 2 \cdot 4^n - 2\binom{2n}{n}\right),$$

respectively.

(ii) The sum of all external (internal, degree) path lengths of all ordered trees with $n$ $(\geqslant 2)$ nodes is equal to

$$4^{n-2}\left(4^{n-2} - \frac{1}{2}\binom{2n-2}{n-1}, \quad 3 \cdot 4^{n-2} - \binom{2n-2}{n-1}\right),$$

respectively.

(iii) The sum of all external (internal, degree) path lengths of all ordered trees with $n$ nodes and $m$ leaves is given by

$$\text{ep}(n, m) = \frac{1}{2}\binom{2n-2}{2m-1}$$

$$\left(\text{ip}(n, m) = \frac{1}{2}\binom{2n-2}{2m} + \frac{1}{2}(-1)^{n-m}\sum_{k \geqslant 0}\binom{n-1}{k}\binom{n-1+k}{k}\binom{n-1-k}{m}(-1)^k,\right.$$

$$\text{dp}(n, m) = \frac{1}{2}\binom{2n}{2m-1} - \frac{1}{2}\binom{2n-2}{2m-3}$$

$$+ (-1)^{n-m+1}\sum_{k \geqslant 0}\binom{n-1}{k}\binom{n-1+k}{k}\binom{n-1-k}{m-1}(-1)^k,$$

respectively. (*Hint:* Use the generating function of the Chebyshev and Legendre polynomials and apply Murphy's formula.)

**4.10** Let $B(n, k, r)$ be the number of all $r$-tuply rooted ordered trees with $n$ nodes and height less than or equal to $k$ and let $Q(n, k, r)$ be the number of all ordered trees with $n$ nodes and height $k$ of order $r$.

(a) Prove that

$$B(n, k, r) = \sum_{\lambda \geqslant 0} \sum_{p \geqslant 0} (-1)^{\lambda}\binom{r}{\lambda}\binom{r-1+p}{r-1}$$

$$\times \left[\binom{2n-r-3}{n-r-1-\lambda(k-1)-pk} - \binom{2n-r-3}{n-r-2-\lambda(k-1)-pk}\right]$$

for $n \geqslant r + 1 \geqslant 2$.

(b) Show that for fixed $k, r \in \mathbb{N}$

$$B(n, k, r) = 4^{n-1} k^{-r} \frac{n^{r-1}}{(r-1)!} \cos^{2n-2}\left(\frac{\pi}{k}\right) \mathrm{tg}^{2r}\left(\frac{\pi}{k}\right)$$

$$+ 4^{n-2} k^{-r} \frac{n^{r-2}}{(r-2)!} u_{k,r} \cos^{2n-4}\left(\frac{\pi}{k}\right) \mathrm{tg}^{2r-2}\left(\frac{\pi}{k}\right)$$

$$+ o\left(n^{r-2} 4^n \cos^{2n}\left(\frac{\pi}{k}\right)\right),$$

where $u_{k,r} = 2kr - 3r - (2kr + 2r + 4)\sin^2\left(\frac{\pi}{k}\right)$.

(c) Prove the identity

$$Q(n, k, r) = B(n+1, k, r+1) - B(n+1, k, r) + B(n, k, r-1)$$

for $n, k, r \geqslant 1$.

**4.11** Let $T = (V, A)$ be an ordered tree and $f: V \to \mathbb{N}_k$ be a function. Here, $T$ is *monotonously labelled* ([99], [100]) if whenever $v$ is a son of $v'$, then $f(v) \geqslant f(v')$. Let $t_j(n)$ be the number of all ordered trees with $n$ nodes monotonously labelled by $1, 2, 3, \ldots, j$ and let $T_j(z) = \sum_{n \geqslant 1} t_j(n) z^n$ be the generating function of the numbers $t_j(n)$.

(a) Show $T_0(z) = 0$ and $T_j(z) = T_{j-1}(z) + z/(1 - T_j(z))$ for $j \geqslant 1$.

(b) Prove that $T_2(z) = C(z) + zC(C^2(z)/z)/C(z)$, where $C(z) = (1 - \sqrt{1-4z})/2$ is the generating function of the Catalan numbers. Deduce from this equation that

$$t_2(n) = 2t_1(n) + \sum_{1 \leqslant \lambda < n} t_1(n - \lambda)\left[\binom{2n-2}{\lambda} - \binom{2n-2}{\lambda-1}\right],$$

where $t_1(n) = \dfrac{1}{n}\binom{2n-2}{n-1}$ is a Catalan number.

(c) Introduce $F_j(z, y) = T_{j-1}(z) + z/(1-y) - y$ and let $r_j, s_j$ be the numbers defined in Theorem 4.13 (with respect to $F_j(z, y)$). Prove the following relations: $r_j = (1 - s_j)^2$, $j \geqslant 1$, and $r_j/(1 - s_j) + T_{j-1}(r_j) = s_j, j \geqslant 1$.

(d) Deduce from (a) and (c) that $T_p(r_k) = 1 - (1 - s_k)x_{k-p}, p \leqslant k$, where $x_m$ satisfies the recurrence $x_0 = 1, x_{m+1} = x_m + x_m^{-1}$. (Recurrences of this type are handled in [17]; in our case, we obtain $x_m^2 = 2m + \ln(\sqrt{m}) + C + O(\ln(m)/m)$.)

(e) Prove that $t_1(n) \sim (4\pi)^{-1/2} n^{-3/2} 4^n$, $t_2(n) \sim (15\pi)^{-1/2} n^{-3/2}(\frac{25}{4})^n$, $t_3(n) \sim (125/(1827\pi))^{-1/2} n^{-3/2}(\frac{841}{100})^n$, and generally

$$t_k(n) \sim \sqrt{\frac{T'_{k-1}(x_k^{-2}) + x_k}{4\pi x_k^3}} \, n^{-3/2} x_k^{2n}$$

for fixed $k$. Note that $x_k^2 \sim 2k$ for $k \to \infty$.

**4.12** Let $A_k(z)$ be the function

$$A_k(z) = 2z \frac{(1+u)^k - (1-u)^k}{(1+u)^{k+1} - (1-u)^{k+1}}, \qquad u = \sqrt{1-4z}, k \geqslant 1.$$

(a) Prove that

$$A_{2k+1}(z) - A_k(z) = [A_k^2(z) - A_k(z)A_{k-1}(z)]/[1 - 2A_k(z)], \qquad k \geqslant 1.$$

(b) Prove that

$$A_{(i+1)(k+1)-1}(z) - A_{i(k+1)-1}(z)$$

$$= \frac{[A_{i(k+1)-1}(z) - A_{(i-1)(k+1)-1}(z)][A_{i(k+1)-1}(z) - A_k(z)]}{[1 - A_k(z) - A_{i(k+1)-1}(z)]}$$

for $k \geqslant 1$, $i \geqslant 2$.

**4.13** In section 4.4.2 we have computed an explicit expression for the generating function $F_k(z, u) = \sum_{n \geqslant 1} \sum_{m \geqslant 1} h_k(n, m) z^n u^m$ of the number of all ordered trees with $n$ nodes, $m$ leaves, and a height less than or equal to $k$. Show that $h_k(1, m) = \delta_{m,1}$, $h_1(n, m) = \delta_{n,m} \delta_{n,1}$, and

$$h_k(n, m) = \frac{1}{n} \binom{n}{m} \binom{n-2}{m-1} - [R_1(n, m, k) - 2R_0(n, m, k) + R_{-1}(n, m, k)],$$

$n \geqslant 2$, $k \geqslant 2$, where

$$R_a(n, m, k) = \sum_{s \geqslant 1} \binom{n - s(k-1) - 2}{m + s + a + 1} \binom{n + s(k-1) - 2}{m - s - a - 1}.$$

**4.14** Let $G_i = (V_N, V_T, P, X_i)$ be a linear context-free grammar with $V_N = \{X_i \mid 1 \leqslant i \leqslant N\}$, $V_T = \{a_j \mid 1 \leqslant j \leqslant t\}$, and $P \subseteq V_N \times (V_T V_N \cup V_N V_T \cup V_T)$. The right (left) transition matrix $A_r = (r_{ij})$ $(A_l = (l_{ij}))$ is a $N \times N$-matrix defined by

$$r_{ij} = \text{card}\{(X_i, AX_j) \in P \mid A \in V_T \wedge X_i, X_j \in V_N\}$$

$$(l_{ij} = \text{card}\{(X_i, X_j A) \in P \mid A \in V_T \wedge X_i, X_j \in V_N\}).$$

Moreover, let $A = A_r + A_l$ and let

$$\overrightarrow{t(n)} = \begin{bmatrix} \text{card}(T_0(n)) \\ \vdots \\ \text{card}(T_N(n)) \end{bmatrix} \quad \text{and} \quad \overrightarrow{S(n)} = \begin{bmatrix} \bar{S}_0(n) \\ \vdots \\ \bar{S}_N(n) \end{bmatrix},$$

where $\text{card}(T_i(n))$ is the number of all derivation trees with $n$ leaves having a root $X_i \in V_N$, and $\bar{S}_i(n)$ is the average maximum stack size of a tree $T \in T_i(n)$. Obviously, $\text{card}(T_i(1)) = \text{card}\{(X_i, a) \in P \mid a \in V_T\}$.

(a) Show that $\overrightarrow{t(n)} = A^{n-1} \overrightarrow{t(1)}$ and

$$\overrightarrow{S(n)} = \left[ nA^{n-1}\overrightarrow{t(1)} - \sum_{0 \leqslant i \leqslant n-3} A^i A_l A^{n-i-2} \overrightarrow{t(1)} \right] \Big/ A^{n-1} \overrightarrow{t(1)}, \quad n \geqslant 1,$$

where the quotient $\vec{p}/\vec{q}$ of two vectors

$$\vec{p} = \begin{bmatrix} p_1 \\ \vdots \\ p_m \end{bmatrix} \quad \text{and} \quad \vec{q} = \begin{bmatrix} q_1 \\ \vdots \\ q_m \end{bmatrix}$$

is defined by

$$\vec{p}/\vec{q} = \begin{bmatrix} c_1 \\ \vdots \\ c_m \end{bmatrix}$$

with $c_i = p_i/q_i$, if $q_i \neq 0$, and $c_i = 0$, if $q_i = 0$, $1 \leqslant i \leqslant m$.

(b) Consider the grammar $G_0 = (V_N, V_T, P, X_0)$ with $V_N = \{X_0, X_1, X_2\}$, $V_T = \{a, b, c\}$

and the productions

$$X_0 \to X_1 c \qquad X_2 \to c X_1$$
$$X_0 \to X_0 a \qquad X_2 \to a X_0$$
$$X_0 \to a \qquad X_2 \to c$$
$$X_1 \to a X_2$$
$$X_1 \to b$$

Show that

$$\overrightarrow{t(n)} = \begin{bmatrix} \text{Fib}(n) \\ \text{Fib}(n-1) \\ \text{Fib}(n) \end{bmatrix}, \, n \geqslant 1 \quad \text{and} \quad \overrightarrow{S(n)} = \tfrac{1}{5}(5 - \sqrt{5})n \begin{bmatrix} 1 \\ 1 \\ 1 \end{bmatrix} + \begin{bmatrix} 9\sqrt{5} - 19 \\ 10\sqrt{5} - 14 \\ 9\sqrt{5} - 14 \end{bmatrix},$$

where $\text{Fib}(n)$ is the $(n+1)$-th *Fibonacci* number defined by $\text{Fib}(k) = 0$ for $k < 0$, $\text{Fib}(0) = \text{Fib}(1) = 1$, $\text{Fib}(n+2) = \text{Fib}(n+1) + \text{Fib}(n)$ for $n \geqslant 0$.

(c) Show that $S_i(n)$, $i \in [0:N]$, is either a linear function in $n$ or a constant, if the matrix $A$ has only one dominant eigenvalue.

(d) Let $F \subseteq V_T^*$, $d_n(F) = \text{card}\{w \in V_T^* \mid w \in F \backslash V_T^* V_T^{n+1}\}$, and $L \subseteq V_T^*$. If the limit $d(L) = \lim_{n \to \infty} d_n(L)/d_n(V_T^*)$ exists, $d(L)$ is called the density of the language $L$ ([8]). Let $G = (V_N, V_T, P, X)$ be a linear context-free grammar which generates the language $L(G)$ and assume that $A$ possesses the dominant eigenvalue $l_1 < \text{card}(V_T)$. Show that $d(L(G)) = 0$.

**4.15** Let us define the domain of a data-type *simple linear list* by the set of all sequences (=files) on a set of keys which are accessed by position. The operations are $I$ and $D$, where $D$ can be performed without any restriction and $I$ only at one end of the file.

(a) Characterize the weighted random walks corresponding to this data type.
(b) Compute the generating functions $F_{\text{DT}}^{(k)}(z)$, $H_B^{\text{DT}}(z, t)$, and $F_{\text{DT}}(z)$ introduction in section 4.4.4 for this data type.
(c) Solve (b) for the data types *queue*, *input-restricted deque*, and *output-restricted deque*. (A queue is a linear list for which all insertions are made at one end of the list, all deletions at the other end. An input-restricted (output-restricted) deque is a linear list in which keys may be inserted (deleted) at one end but deleted (inserted) at either end.)

**4.16** Prove Theorem 4.18.

**4.17** Let $NC^\varphi(h, k, n)$ be the uniform set (with respect to the specification $\varphi$ given in section 4.2.1) of all non-negative weighted random walks of length $n$ from $h$ to $k$ and let $N_{h,k}(z) = \sum_{n \geqslant 0} w(NC^\varphi(h, k, n))z^n$ be the generating function of the total weights of the sets $NC^\varphi(h, k, n)$.

(a) Using the notation given in Theorem 4.7, show that

$$N_{h,k}(z) = [u_0 \ldots u_{h-1} d_1 \ldots d_k] z^{-k-h} [B_{m-1}(z)\xi_z - A_{m-1}(z)] B_{q-1}(z),$$

where $q = \text{MIN}(h, k)$ and $m = \text{MAX}(h, k)$.
(b) Making use of the scalar product $\langle \ \rangle$ introduced in Example 4.7, show that

$$w(NC^\varphi(h, k, n)) = [u_0 \ldots u_{h-1} d_1 \ldots d_k] \langle \mathbf{B}_{h-1}(z) \mid \mathbf{B}_{k-1}(z) z^n \rangle_{w(NC^\varphi(h,k,n))},$$

where $\mathbf{B}_k(z) = z^{k+1} B_k(1/z)$ is the reciprocal polynomial of $B_k(z)$ given in Theorem 4.7.
(c) Let DT be a data type and $c_{\text{DT}}(n, h, k)$ be the number of all induced histories of length $n$ starting with a file containing $h$ elements and finishing with a file containing $k$ elements. Prove that the generating function

$$I^{\mathrm{DT}}(z, y, t) = \sum_{n \geqslant 0} \sum_{h \geqslant 0} \sum_{k \geqslant 0} c_{\mathrm{DT}}(n, h, k) s_{n,h,k} y^h t^k z^n$$

satisfies the following relations:

| DT | $s_{n,h,k}$ | $I^{\mathrm{DT}}(z, y, t)$ |
|---|---|---|
| Linear list | $n!^{-1}$ | $[(1 - yt)\cos(z) - (y + t)\sin(z)]^{-1}$ |
| Priority queue | $k!^{-1}n!^{-1}$ | $\exp(zy + zt + yt + z^2/2)$ |
| Symbol table | $k!^{-1}n!^{-1}$ | $\exp((1 + y)(1 + t)\exp(z)) - 1 - z - y - t)$ |
| Dictionary | $n!^{-1}$ | $[(1 - z(1 + y)(1 + t) - yt]^{-1}$ |

# 5

# *Applications*

## 5.1 Reduction of Binary Trees

The evaluation of expressions plays an important part in the compilers for programming languages. An expression may be represented by an ordered binary tree provided that it consists of brackets, binary operators, and operands; the operators correspond to the interior nodes and the operands to the leaves. For example, the arithmetical expression $E = x_1/((x_2 - x_3) \uparrow ((x_4 + x_5) * x_6))$ corresponds to the binary tree (*syntax tree*) drawn in Figure 23.

The evaluation of an expression is equivalent to the reduction of the corresponding tree according to its structure. These reductions are closely related to the process of code generation in compilers. For example, in order to evaluate $E$ for given values $x_1, x_2, x_3, x_4, x_5, x_6$, we have to use *registers* $R_j, j = 1, 2, 3, \ldots$, and produce codes such as

$$
\begin{array}{lll}
R_1 \leftarrow x_1 & & R_1 \leftarrow x_6 \\
R_2 \leftarrow x_2 & & R_2 \leftarrow x_5 \\
R_3 \leftarrow x_3 & & R_3 \leftarrow x_4 \\
R_2 \leftarrow R_2 - R_3 & & R_2 \leftarrow R_3 + R_4 \\
R_3 \leftarrow x_4 & & R_1 \leftarrow R_2 * R_1 \\
R_4 \leftarrow x_5 & \text{or} & R_2 \leftarrow x_3 \\
R_3 \leftarrow R_4 + R_5 & & R_3 \leftarrow x_2 \\
R_4 \leftarrow x_6 & & R_2 \leftarrow R_2 - R_3 \\
R_3 \leftarrow R_3 * R_4 & & R_1 \leftarrow R_2 \uparrow R_1 \\
R_2 \leftarrow R_2 \uparrow R_3 & & R_2 \leftarrow x_1 \\
R_1 \leftarrow R_1/R_2 & & R_1 \leftarrow R_2/R_1
\end{array}
$$

which leaves the desired result in registers $R_1$, using the registers $R_2, R_3, R_4$ and $R_2, R_3$, respectively, for storing intermediate values. Obviously, the second

130

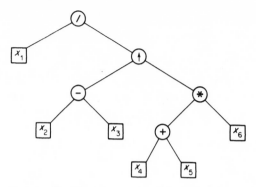

FIGURE 23. The syntax tree of the expression $E$.

code is better than the previous one, since it uses one less register. There are well-known strategies for the computation of expressions formed with binary operators:

(a) 'Left-to-right' strategy based on a stack (see section 5.1.1).
(b) 'Optimal' (with respect to the number of registers) strategy (see section 5.1.2).
(c) 'Left-to-right' strategy based on an input-restricted deque (see section 5.1.3).

Before analysing the algorithms induced by these strategies, we will briefly formalize the concept of the *reduction* of a binary tree $T$ with the set of interior nodes $I$, the set of leaves $L$, and the root $r \in I$. An *instruction* $Q$ is a string of symbols of one of the following three types:

(a) $A \leftarrow w, w \in L$;
(b) $A \leftarrow A'A''i, i \in I$;
(c) $A \leftarrow A'$.

In these instructions, $A$, $A'$, and $A''$ are *intermediate variables* (possibly the same). The *value* of an intermediate variable is always a string over $(I \cup L)^*$. We assume that the variables are numbered $A_1, A_2, \ldots$ in some order for identification. Instructions of type (a) replace the value of $A$ by $w$, and instructions of type (b) replace the value of $A$ by the concatenation of the values of $A'$, $A''$, and node $i$. If $A'$ or $A''$ is undefined, then $A$ is also undefined. Instructions of type (c) replace the value of $A$ by the value of $A'$. A *program* $\pi$ is a sequence of instructions $\pi = Q_1; Q_2; \ldots; Q_m;$. Here, $\pi$ is called a *k-program*, if there are $k$ distinct variables appearing in $\pi$. The *value of the variable $A$ after instruction $Q_t$*, denoted by $v_t(A)$, is recursively defined by:

(1) $v_0(A)$ is undefined for all variables $A$.
(2) If $Q_t$ is of type (a), then $v_t(A) = w$.
(3) If $Q_t$ is of type (b), then $v_t(A) = v_{t-1}(A')v_{t-1}(A'')i$.
(4) If $Q_t$ is of type (c), then $v_t(A) = v_{t-1}(A')$.
(5) If $v_t(A)$ is not defined by (3)–(4), but $v_{t-1}(A)$ has been defined, then $v_t(A) = v_{t-1}(A)$. Otherwise, $v_t(A)$ is undefined.

We say that a program $\pi$ *evaluates* a binary tree $T$ if after the last instruction of $\pi$, the variable $A_1$ has the value $PO(T)$. Furthermore, the tree $T$ *can be reduced by a given algorithm ALG*, if $ALG$ with input $PO(T)$ computes a program which evaluates $T$. Obviously, if $\pi$ is a program evaluating $T$, then $\pi$ describes the reduction of $T$ according to its structure. The relationship of the reduction of a binary tree $T$ with the evaluation of an expression formed with binary operators should be evident: given an expression $E$, $PO(T)$ corresponds to the post-fix notation of $E$, $T$ is the syntax tree of $E$, the algorithm $ALG$ describes the strategy for the computation of the value of $E$ and the intermediate variables of the program $\pi$ produced by $ALG$ correspond to the registers appearing in the code for $E$.

### 5.1.1 The Reduction of Binary Trees by a Stack

A customary method for the reduction of a tree $T$ with the set of interior nodes $I$, the set of leaves $L$, and the root $r \in I$ is as follows.

ALGORITHM $S$
Input: $PO(T) \subseteq (I \cup L)^*$.
Output: A program which evaluates $T$.
Method:

(1) A triple $(j, \gamma, \rho)$ will be used to denote a *configuration* of the algorithm:

  (a) $j \in \mathbb{N}$ represents the location of the input pointer; we assume that the first 'input symbol' is the leftmost symbol in $PO(T)$;
  (b) $\gamma \in (I \cup L)^*$ represents the stack list; the 'top' is assumed to be at the right of $\gamma$;
  (c) $\rho$ is a sequence of instructions of types (a) and (b).

(2) If $j$ is the location of the input pointer, then $c(j)$ is the 'current' input symbol.
(3) The initial configuration of the algorithm is $C_0 = (1, \varepsilon, \varepsilon)$.
(4) There are two types of steps. These steps will be described in terms of their effect on the configurations of the algorithm. The heart of the algorithm is to compute successive configurations defined by a 'goes to' relation $\perp$. The notation $(j, \gamma, \rho) \perp (j', \gamma', \rho')$ means that if the current configuration is $(j, \gamma, \rho)$, then we are to go next into configuration $(j', \gamma', \rho')$. The two types of move are as follows:

  (4.1) Let $c(j) \in L$. Then

$$(j, \gamma, \rho) \perp (j + 1, \gamma c(j), \rho A_{l(\gamma)+1} \leftarrow c(j);)$$

  (4.2) Let $c(j) \in I$ and $\gamma = \gamma' ab$. Then

$$(j, \gamma, \rho) \perp (j + 1, \gamma' c(j), \rho A_{l(\gamma)-1} \leftarrow A_{l(\gamma)-1} A_{l(\gamma)} c(j);)$$

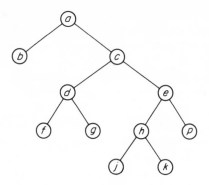

FIGURE 24. An ordered binary tree $T$.

The execution of algorithm $S$ is as follows:

*Step 1* Starting in the initial configuration, compute successive configurations $C_0 \perp C_1 \perp C_2 \perp \ldots \perp C_i \perp \ldots$ until no further configuration can be computed.

*Step 2* If the last configuration is $(l(PO(T)) + 1, r, \pi)$, emit $\pi$ and halt; $\pi$ is a program which evaluates $T$.

Obviously, if we number the stack list cells by $1, 2, 3, \ldots$ from the bottom, then the variable $A_m$ corresponds to the $m$-th cell.

Let us consider the binary tree $T$ drawn in Figure 24. We have $I = \{a, c, d, e, h\}$, $L = \{b, f, g, j, k, p\}$, and $PO(T) = bfgdjkhpeca$. The algorithm $S$ computes the following 4-program which evaluates the tree $T$. For typographical reasons, we omit the third component in the configurations and give only the current instruction in each move.

| Configuration | Current instruction | Move |
|---|---|---|
| $(1, \varepsilon) \perp (2, b)$ | $A_1 \leftarrow b;$ | (4.1) |
| $\perp (3, bf)$ | $A_2 \leftarrow f;$ | (4.1) |
| $\perp (4, bfg)$ | $A_3 \leftarrow g;$ | (4.1) |
| $\perp (5, bd)$ | $A_2 \leftarrow A_2 A_3 d;$ | (4.2) |
| $\perp (6, bdj)$ | $A_3 \leftarrow j;$ | (4.1) |
| $\perp (7, bdjk)$ | $A_4 \leftarrow k;$ | (4.1) |
| $\perp (8, bdh)$ | $A_3 \leftarrow A_3 A_4 h;$ | (4.2) |
| $\perp (9, bdhp)$ | $A_4 \leftarrow p;$ | (4.1) |
| $\perp (10, bde)$ | $A_3 \leftarrow A_3 A_4 e;$ | (4.2) |
| $\perp (11, bc)$ | $A_2 \leftarrow A_2 A_3 c;$ | (4.2) |
| $\perp (12, a)$ | $A_1 \leftarrow A_1 A_2 a;$ | (4.2) |

Thus algorithm $S$ reduces the tree $T$ using a stack list of maximum length four. Note that we obtain the first code given in section 5.1, if we replace each variable $A_j$ by the register $R_j$, each $a \in I \cup L$ by the corresponding operator or operand, and each instruction $A_i \leftarrow A_r A_s a$ by $R_i \leftarrow R_r a R_s$.

Let us now consider the number of intermediate variables appearing in a program $\pi$ produced by algorithm $S$; in other words, we are interested in the number of registers required for evaluating an arithmetical expression formed with $(n-1)$ binary operators by the left-ro-right strategy induced by algorithm $S$.

For this purpose, let $t(n, k)$ be the number of all ordered binary trees with $n$ leaves (i.e. $(n-1)$ interior nodes) which can be reduced by algorithm $S$ requiring less than or equal to $k$ variables. Using the one-to-one correspondence between all binary trees with $n$ leaves and all closed non-negative $(1, 0, 1)$-random walks of length $(2n - 2)$, we obtain immediately (see sections 4.3.1 and 4.4.2)

$$\sum_{n \geqslant 1} t(n, k)z^n = 2z \frac{(1 + \sqrt{1 - 4z})^k - (1 - \sqrt{1 - 4z})^k}{(1 + \sqrt{1 - 4z})^{k+1} - (1 - \sqrt{1 - 4z})^{k+1}} \qquad k \geqslant 1,$$

and

$$t(n + 1, k - 1) = t(n + 1) - \sum_{j \geqslant 1} \left[ \binom{2n}{n + 1 - jk} - 2\binom{2n}{n - jk} \right.$$
$$\left. + \binom{2n}{n - 1 - jk} \right], \qquad k \geqslant 2,$$

where

$$t(n + 1) = t(n + 1, n + 1) = \frac{1}{n + 1}\binom{2n}{n}$$

is the number of all binary trees with $(n + 1)$ leaves. Furthermore, the minimum (maximum) number of variables appears in the program evaluating the tree drawn in Figures 25(a) and (b), respectively; it is given by two and $n$ for $n \geqslant 2$.

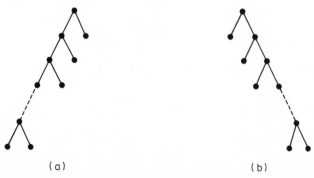

(a)                                   (b)

FIGURE 25. The two binary trees requiring a minimum ((a)) and maximum ((b)) number of variables.

Assuming that all binary trees with $n$ leaves are equally likely, the quotient $p(n, k) = [t(n, k) - t(n, k - 1)]/t(n, n)$ is the probability that a program evaluating such a tree requires $k$ variables. Therefore, the $s$-th moment about the origin is given by $m_s(n) = \sum_{1 \leqslant k \leqslant n} k^s p(n, k)$. Using the above definition of $p(n, k)$ and the fact $t(n, 0) = 0$ for $n \geqslant 1$, this expression can be easily transformed into

$$m_s(n) = n^s - t^{-1}(n) \sum_{1 \leqslant k \leqslant n-1} [(k + 1)^s - k^s] t(n, k).$$

Plugging the explicit expression for $t(n, k)$ into this equation, we find

$$m_s(n + 1) = 1 + t^{-1}(n + 1) \sum_{k \geqslant 1} [(k + 1)^s - k^s] \psi(n, k),$$

where

$$\psi(n, k) = \psi_1(n, k) - 2\psi_0(n, k) + \psi_{-1}(n, k)$$

and

$$\psi_a(n, k) = \sum_{j \geqslant 1} \binom{2n}{n + a - j(k + 1)}.$$

Let us now consider the sum

$$\beta_a^{(s)}(n) = \sum_{k \geqslant 1} [(k + 1)^s - k^s] \psi_a(n, k).$$

We obtain

$$\beta_a^{(s)}(n) = \sum_{k \geqslant 1} [(k + 1)^s - k^s] \sum_{j \geqslant 1} \binom{2n}{n + a - j(k + 1)}$$

$$= \sum_{k \geqslant 1} [k^s - (k - 1)^s] \sum_{j \geqslant 1} \binom{2n}{n + a - jk} - \sum_{j \geqslant 1} \binom{2n}{n + a - j}$$

$$= \sum_{k \geqslant 1} \binom{2n}{n + a - k} \sum_{d \mid k} [d^s - (d - 1)^s] - \psi_a(n, 0),$$

and therefore

$$m_s(n + 1) = 1 + t^{-1}(n + 1)[\beta_1^{(s)}(n) - 2\beta_0^{(s)}(n) + \beta_{-1}^{(s)}(n)]$$

$$= 1 + t^{-1}(n + 1) \sum_{k \geqslant 1} \delta_s(k) \left[ \binom{2n}{n + 1 - k} - 2\binom{2n}{n - k} \right.$$

$$\left. + \binom{2n}{n - 1 - k} \right]$$

$$- t^{-1}(n + 1)[\psi_1(n, 0) - 2\psi_0(n, 0) + \psi_{-1}(n, 0)],$$

where

$$\delta_s(n) = \sum_{d \mid n} [d^s - (d - 1)^s].$$

Since

$$\psi_1(n, 0) - 2\psi_0(n, 0) + \psi_{-1}(n, 0)$$

$$= \sum_{j \geqslant 1} \left\{ \left[ \binom{2n}{n-j-1} - \binom{2n}{n-j} \right] - \left[ \binom{2n}{n-j} - \binom{2n}{n-j+1} \right] \right\}$$

$$= \binom{2n}{n} - \binom{2n}{n-1} = t(n+1),$$

we have proved the following theorem.

THEOREM 5.1   Assume that all binary trees with $(n + 1)$ leaves are equally likely and let $p(n, k)$ be the probability that a program produced by algorithm $S$ requires $k$ variables. The $s$-th moment about the origin of the random variable which takes on the value $k$ with probability $p(n, k)$ is given by

$$m_s(n + 1) = t^{-1}(n + 1) \sum_{k \geqslant 1} \delta_s(k) \left[ \binom{2n}{n+1-k} - 2\binom{2n}{n-k} \right.$$

$$\left. + \binom{2n}{n-1-k} \right],$$

where $\delta_s(n)$ is the arithmetical function defined by

$$\delta_s(n) = \sum_{d \mid n} [d^s - (d-1)^s]. \quad \blacksquare$$

Choosing $s = 1$, we obtain the following corollary as a special case.

COROLLARY   Assuming that all binary trees with $(n + 1)$ leaves are equally likely, the average number of variables appearing in a program produced by algorithm $S$ is given by

$$m_1(n + 1) = t^{-1}(n + 1) \sum_{k \geqslant 1} d(k) \left[ \binom{2n}{n+1-k} - 2\binom{2n}{n-k} + \binom{2n}{n-1-k} \right],$$

where $d(n)$ is the number of all positive divisors of the natural number $n \in \mathbb{N}$.   $\blacksquare$

Let us first derive an asymptotic equivalent for $m_1(n)$. For this purpose, we shall concentrate on evaluating the sum

$$\varphi_a(n) = \sum_{k \geqslant 1} d(k) \binom{2n}{n+a-k} \Big/ \binom{2n}{n}.$$

After we have computed an asymptotic expression for $\varphi_a(n)$, $a$ fixed, we shall easily be able to deal with $m_1(n + 1)$ because

$$m_1(n + 1) = (n + 1)[\varphi_1(n) - 2\varphi_0(n) + \varphi_{-1}(n)].$$

Sums of the above type appear relatively frequently in combinatorial analysis and the analysis of algorithms. They can be evaluated by the so-called *gamma-function method* which is attributed to N. G. de Bruijn (e.g. [16]). We will present this method in some detail.

The first step is to use Stirling's approximation to express the quotient of the binomial coefficients appearing in the above sum in terms of the exponential function.

**THEOREM 5.2** Let $R \in \mathbb{Q}$, $k \in \mathbb{N}_0$, and $a \in \mathbb{Z}$. We have for all $\varepsilon > 0$ and all $\delta > (R + 6)\varepsilon$

$$\binom{2n}{n + a - k} \bigg/ \binom{2n}{n} = \exp\left(-\frac{(k - a)^2}{n}\right) f_a^{[2 + R/2]}(n, k),$$

where $k \leqslant n^{1/2 + \varepsilon} + a$ and

$$f_a^{[2 + R/2]}(n, k) = 1 + \sum_{\lambda \geqslant 1} (k - a)^{2\lambda} \sum_{\lfloor (3\lambda + 1)/2 \rfloor \leqslant i < \lambda + 2 + R/2} c_{i,\lambda} n^{-i} + O(n^{-2 - R/2 + \delta}).$$

Here the $c_{i,\lambda}$ are numbers independent of $n$, $k$, and $a$. If $k > n^{1/2 + \varepsilon} + a$, the quotient $\binom{2n}{n + a - k} \bigg/ \binom{2n}{n}$ is exponentially small.

*Proof* Stirling's approximation says that for fixed $M \geqslant 0$

$$\ln(n!) = (n + \tfrac{1}{2}) \ln(n) - n + \tfrac{1}{2} \ln(2\pi) + \sum_{1 \leqslant m \leqslant M} \frac{B_{2m}}{2m(2m - 1)} n^{-2m + 1} + O(n^{-2M - 1}),$$

where $B_m$ is the $m$-th Bernoulli number (see Appendix B, 2.11). Applying this approximation to the quotient of the two binomial coefficients we obtain

$$\binom{2n}{n + a - k} \bigg/ \binom{2n}{n} = \exp[2 \ln(n!) - \ln((n + a - k)!) - \ln((n - a + k)!)]$$

$$= \exp\bigg[ 2(n + \tfrac{1}{2}) \ln(n) - (n + \tfrac{1}{2})$$

$$\times \{\ln(n + a - k) + \ln(n - a + k)\}$$

$$- (k - a)\{\ln(n - a + k) - \ln(n + a - k)\}$$

$$+ \sum_{1 \leqslant m \leqslant M} \frac{B_{2m}}{2m(2m - 1)} \bigg\{ \frac{2}{n^{2m - 1}} - \frac{1}{(n + a - k)^{2m - 1}}$$

$$- \frac{1}{(n - a + k)^{2m - 1}} \bigg\} + O(n^{-2M - 1})$$

$$+ O((n + a - k)^{-2M - 1}) + O((n - a + k)^{-2M - 1}) \bigg].$$

Let us now restrict the value of $k$. First we consider the case $k \leqslant n^{1/2+\varepsilon} + a$ for some small positive constant $\varepsilon > 0$. With this restriction, we can replace $O((n + a - k)^{-2M-1})$ and $O((n - a + k)^{-2M-1})$ by $O(n^{-2M-1})$. Furthermore, using the well-known expansions of $\ln(1 + x)$, $\ln(1 - x)$, and $(1 + x)^{-m}$, $m \geqslant 1$, (see (A14), (A15), and (B2)), we obtain immediately by an elementary computation for fixed $R \geqslant 0$

$$\binom{2n}{n+a-k} \bigg/ \binom{2n}{n} = \exp\left[ -\frac{(k-a)^2}{n} + (k-a)^2 \left\{ \frac{1}{2n^2} - \sum_{1 \leqslant m < 1 + R/4} B_{2m} n^{-2m-1} \right\} \right.$$

$$+ \sum_{2 \leqslant i < 3 + R/2} (k-a)^{2i} \left\{ \frac{1}{2i} n^{-2i} - \frac{1}{i(2i-1)} n^{-2i+1} \right\}$$

$$- 2 \sum_{2 \leqslant i < 3 + R/2} \sum_{1 \leqslant m < (R - 2i + 6)/4} \binom{2m - 2 + 2i}{2i}$$

$$\left. \times \frac{B_{2m}}{2m(2m-1)} (k-a)^{2i} n^{-2m-2i+1} + O(n^{-2-R/2+\delta}) \right]$$

where $\delta > (R + 6)\varepsilon$. Therefore, we obtain with some numbers $b_{i,\lambda}$ independent of $n$, $k$, and $a$

$$\binom{2n}{n+a-k} \bigg/ \binom{2n}{n} = \exp\left[ -\frac{(k-a)^2}{n} + W_{k,n} \right],$$

where

$$W_{k,n} = (k-a)^2 \sum_{2 \leqslant i < 3 + R/2} b_{i,1} n^{-i} + \sum_{\lambda \geqslant 2} (k-a)^{2\lambda} \sum_{2\lambda - 1 \leqslant i < \lambda + 2 + R/2} b_{i,\lambda} n^{-i}$$

$$+ O(n^{-2-R/2+\delta}).$$

Now a simple induction proof over $p$ shows that the powers of $W_{k,n}$ have for $p \geqslant 1$ the following form:

$$W_{k,n}^p = \sum_{p \leqslant \lambda \leqslant 2p-1} (k-a)^{2\lambda} \sum_{p+\lambda \leqslant i < \lambda + 2 + R/2} f_{i,\lambda,p} n^{-i}$$

$$+ \sum_{\lambda \geqslant 2p} (k-a)^{2\lambda} \sum_{2\lambda - p \leqslant i < \lambda + 2 + R/2} f_{i,\lambda,p} n^{-i} + O(n^{-2-R/2+\delta}),$$

where the $f_{i,\lambda,p}$ are independent of $n$, $k$, and $a$. Using this relation together with the expansion of $\exp(x)$, we can compute an asymptotic equivalent of $\exp(W_{k,n})$. We obtain

$$\exp(W_{k,n}) = 1 + \sum_{1 \leqslant p < 2 + R/2} W_{k,n}^p / p! + O(n^{-2-R/2+\delta})$$

$$= 1 + \sum_{\lambda \geqslant 1} (k-a)^{2\lambda} \sum_{p_\lambda \leqslant i < \lambda + 2 + R/2} c_{i,\lambda} n^{-i} + O(n^{-2-R/2+\delta}),$$

where

$$p_\lambda = \text{MIN}(\text{MIN}\{\lambda + j \,|\, \tfrac{1}{2}(\lambda + 1) \leqslant j \leqslant \lambda \wedge \lambda \in \mathbb{N}\},$$

$$\text{MIN}\{2\lambda - j \,|\, j \leqslant \tfrac{1}{2}\lambda \wedge \lambda \in \mathbb{N}\})$$

and the $c_{i,\lambda}$ are numbers independent of $n$, $k$, and $a$. An elementary computation shows that $p_\lambda = \lfloor (3\lambda + 1)/2 \rfloor$. Hence

$$\binom{2n}{n + a - k} \bigg/ \binom{2n}{n} = \exp\left(-\frac{(k - a)^2}{n}\right) f_a^{[2 + R/2]}(n, k),$$

where

$$f_a^{[2 + R/2]}(n, k) = 1 + \sum_{\lambda \geqslant 1} (k - a)^{2\lambda} \sum_{\lfloor (3\lambda + 1)/2 \rfloor \leqslant i < \lambda + 2 + R/2} c_{i,\lambda} n^{-i} + O(n^{-2 - R/2 + \delta}),$$

$k - a \leqslant n^{1/2 + \varepsilon}$ and $\delta > \varepsilon(R + 6)$.

Next let us consider the case $k - a > n^{1/2 + \varepsilon}$. Obviously,

$$\binom{2n}{n + a - k} < \binom{2n}{n - n^{1/2 + \varepsilon}}$$

for $k - a > n^{1/2 + \varepsilon}$. Therefore, the above approximation implies that

$$\binom{2n}{n + a - k} \bigg/ \binom{2n}{n} = \exp(-n^{2\varepsilon}) \left[ 1 + \sum_{\lambda \geqslant 1} n^{(1 + 2\varepsilon)\lambda} \sum_{\lfloor (3\lambda + 1)/2 \rfloor \leqslant i < \lambda + 2 + R/2} c_{i,\lambda} n^{-i} \right.$$

$$\left. + O(n^{-2 - R/2 + \delta}) \right]$$

for $k - a > n^{1/2 + \varepsilon}$ and this is exponentially small, being $O(n^{-m})$ for all $m > 0$. ∎

Using the procedure just described in the proof of Theorem 5.2, we obtain the following explicit approximations:

$$\binom{2n}{n + a - k} \bigg/ \binom{2n}{n} = \exp(-k^2/n) f_a^{[p]}(n, k),$$

where

$$f_a^{[2.5]}(n, k) = 1 + \frac{a^2 + a^4}{2n^2} - \frac{a^2}{n} + \left[\frac{2a}{n} - \frac{2a^3 + a}{n^2}\right] k + \left[\frac{4a^2 + 1}{2n^2} - \frac{12a^4 + 21a^2 + 1}{6n^3}\right] k^2$$

$$+ \frac{4a^3 + 5a}{3n^3} k^3 + \left[\frac{16a^4 + 60a^2 + 9}{24n^4} - \frac{1}{6n^3}\right] k^4 - \frac{a}{3n^4} k^5$$

$$- \frac{20a^2 + 9}{60n^5} k^6 + \frac{1}{72n^6} k^8 + O(n^{-2.5 + \delta}) \tag{F1}$$

and

$$f_a^{[2]}(n,k) = 1 - \frac{a^2}{n} + \left[\frac{2a}{n} - \frac{2a^3 + a}{n^2}\right]k + \frac{4a^2 + 1}{2n^2}k^2 + \frac{4a^3 + 5a}{3n^3}k^3$$

$$- \frac{1}{6n^3}k^4 - \frac{a}{3n^4}k^5 + O(n^{-2+\delta}) \tag{F2}$$

and

$$f_a^{[1.5]}(n,k) = 1 - \frac{a^2}{n} + \frac{2a}{n}k + \frac{4a^2 + 1}{2n^2}k^2 - \frac{1}{6n^3}k^4 + O(n^{-1.5+\delta}) \tag{F3}$$

and

$$f_a^{[1]}(n,k) = 1 + \frac{2a}{n}k + O(n^{-1+\delta}) \tag{F4}$$

and

$$f_a^{[0.5]}(n,k) = 1 + O(n^{-0.5+\delta}). \tag{F5}$$

The general result stated in Theorem 5.2 has been proved in [64]. The explicit approximation given in (F1) has been given in [64]; (F2) is proved in [21] and (F5) in [27].

Let us now return to the computation of an asymptotic expression for $\varphi_a(n)$. Applying the above approximation (F2), we immediately obtain

$$\varphi_a(n) = \sum_{k \geqslant 1} d(k)\binom{2n}{n + a - k} \Big/ \binom{2n}{n}$$

$$= \sum_{k \geqslant 1} d(k)\exp(-k^2/n)f_a^{[2]}(n,k).$$

The terms for which the approximation (F2) is not valid are exponentially small, as is $\exp(-k^2/n)$; therefore, it does not matter which we use for the terms $k > n^{1/2+\varepsilon} + a$.

Now the computation of an asymptotic equivalent of $\varphi_a(n)$ is reduced to the analogous problem for the sum

$$g_p(n) = \sum_{k \geqslant 1} \exp(-k^2/n)\,d(k)k^p, \quad p \text{ fixed},$$

because

$$\varphi_a(n) = \left(1 - \frac{a^2}{n}\right)g_0(n) + \left(\frac{2a}{n} - \frac{2a^3 + a}{n^2}\right)g_1(n) + \frac{4a^2 + 1}{2n^2}g_2(n)$$

$$+ \frac{4a^3 + 5a}{3n^3}g_3(n) - \frac{1}{6n^3}g_4(n) - \frac{a}{3n^4}g_5(n) + O(n^{-2+\delta}g_0(n)).$$

Since there is no precise equation for the number of divisors $d(k)$ of the natural number $k$, we need to resort to more advanced techniques to get an accurate estimate for $g_p(n)$ and $\varphi_a(n)$. The idea is to express $\exp(-k^2/n)$ as an integral in the complex plane involving the *gamma function* (see Appendix B, 2.11), then interchange the order of integration and summation. Choosing this procedure, we shall be able to express the resulting complex series involving $d(k)$ in terms of classical analytic functions. An asymptotic equivalent is then found by computing residues within an appropriate contour of integration. Let us start with the identity

$$\exp(-x) = \frac{1}{2\pi i} \int_{c-i\infty}^{c+i\infty} \Gamma(z) x^{-z} \, dz, \qquad c > 0, \, x > 0, \, i^2 = -1,$$

which is the so-called Mellin transform of $\exp(-x)$ (see [24], [54]), a special case of Fourier inversion. It can also be easily proved (see [76]) by an application of Cauchy's residue theorem (see Appendix A, 6). Applying this identity to our formula for $g_p(n)$, we have

$$g_p(n) = \sum_{k \geq 1} d(k) k^p \frac{1}{2\pi i} \int_{c-i\infty}^{c+i\infty} \Gamma(z) \left( \frac{k^2}{n} \right)^{-z} dz$$

$$= \frac{1}{2\pi i} \int_{c-i\infty}^{c+i\infty} \Gamma(z) n^z \sum_{k \geq 1} d(k) k^{-2z+p} \, dz, \qquad c > \tfrac{1}{2}(p+1).$$

Note that the interchange of summation and integration is justified because of absolute convergence which can be easily checked. In order to proceed further we need to know the properties of the function $\sum_{k \geq 1} d(k) k^{-2z+p}$. This is a *Dirichlet series* with coefficients $d(k)$ (see Appendix A, 5). The Dirichlet series with all coefficients equal to one, that is, $\zeta(z) = \sum_{k \geq 1} k^{-z}$, is called the *Riemann zeta function* and plays an important part in analytic number theory. Using the Dirichlet convolution theorem (see Appendix A, 5) with $f(n) = 1$ and $g(n) = n^\alpha$, we obtain

$$h(n) = \sum_{d \mid n} f(d) g(n/d) = \sum_{d \mid n} (n/d)^\alpha = \sum_{d \mid n} d^\alpha = \sigma_\alpha(n)$$

and

$$H(z) = \sum_{k \geq 1} \sigma_\alpha(k) k^{-z} = \zeta(z) \zeta(z - \alpha),$$

because

$$\sum_{k \geq 1} f(k) k^{-z} = \zeta(z) \quad \text{and} \quad \sum_{k \geq 1} g(k) k^{-z} = \zeta(z - \alpha).$$

Since $d(n) = \sigma_0(n)$, the above expression for $g_p(n)$ is equivalent to

$$g_p(n) = \frac{1}{2\pi i} \int_{c-i\infty}^{c+i\infty} \Gamma(z) n^z \zeta^2(2z - p) \, dz, \qquad c > \tfrac{1}{2}(p+1).$$

To evaluate this integral, we have to use Cauchy's residue theorem (see Appendix A, 6). For this purpose, we first approximate $g_p(n)$ by integrating

142

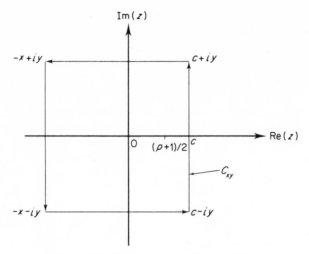

FIGURE 26. Contour $C_{xy}$ of integration for $g_p(z)$.

around the contour $C_{xy}$ shown in Figure 26 and letting $x$ and $y$ go to infinity. The value of the integral around the contour $C_{xy}$ is equal to the sum of the residues of $\Gamma(z)n^z\zeta^2(2z-p)$ within $C_{xy}$. There is a double pole at $z_0 = (p+1)/2$ contributed by $\zeta^2(2z-p)$ and possibly simple poles at $z_{r+1} = -r, 0 \leqslant r < x$, contributed by $\Gamma(z)$ (see Appendix B, 2.11 and 2.13). Thus

$$\frac{1}{2\pi i} \int_{C_{xy}} \Gamma(z)n^z\zeta^2(2z-p)\,\mathrm{d}z = \sum_{0 \leqslant m < x+1} \operatorname*{Res}_{z=z_m} (\Gamma(z)n^z\zeta^2(2z-p)).$$

On the other hand, we have

$$\frac{1}{2\pi i} \int_{C_{xy}} \Gamma(z)n^z\zeta^2(2z-p)\,\mathrm{d}z$$

$$= I(c-iy, c+iy) + I(c+iy, -x+iy)$$

$$+ I(-x+iy, -x-iy) + I(-x-iy, c-iy),$$

where

$$I(a, b) = \frac{1}{2\pi i} \int_a^b \Gamma(z)n^z\zeta^2(2z-p)\,\mathrm{d}z.$$

Considering the integrals $I(c+iy, -x+iy)$ and $I(-x-iy, c-iy)$ along the top and bottom lines of $C_{xy}$, we find with the bounds on the $\Gamma$ and $\zeta$ function given in (B114) and (B130) that the values of these integrals are exponentially small for $x, y \to \infty$, being $O(n^{-s})$ for all $s > 0$. Similarly, the value of $I(-x+iy, -x-iy)$ along the left line of $C_{xy}$ vanishes exponentially as $x$ and $y$ go to infinity. Therefore,

$$\frac{1}{2\pi i} \int_{c-i\infty}^{c+i\infty} \Gamma(z)n^z\zeta^2(2z-p)\,\mathrm{d}z = \sum_{m \geqslant 0} \operatorname*{Res}_{z=z_m} (\Gamma(z)n^z\zeta^2(2z-p)) + O(n^{-s})$$

for all $s > 0$. Thus we have to compute the residues appearing in the above sum in order to obtain an asymptotic expression for $g_p(n)$.

Let us first consider the double pole $z_0 = (p + 1)/2$. An application of the Laurent series expansions given in (B128) leads to $(u = z - (p + 1)/2)$

$$\Gamma(z)n^z\zeta^2(2z - p) = [\Gamma(\tfrac{1}{2}(p + 1)) + \Gamma'(\tfrac{1}{2}(p + 1))u + O(u^2)]n^{(p+1)/2}$$

$$\times [1 + u\ln(n) + O(u^2)]\left[\frac{1}{2u} + \gamma + O(u)\right]^2$$

$$= au^{-2} + bu^{-1} + O(1),$$

where

$$a = \tfrac{1}{4}n^{(p+1)/2}\Gamma(\tfrac{1}{2}(p + 1))$$

and

$$b = n^{(p+1)/2}[\tfrac{1}{4}\ln(n)\Gamma(\tfrac{1}{2}(p + 1)) + \tfrac{1}{4}\Gamma'(\tfrac{1}{2}(p + 1)) + \gamma\Gamma(\tfrac{1}{2}(p + 1))].$$

Therefore,

$$\operatorname*{Res}_{z=z_0}\,(\Gamma(z)n^z\zeta^2(2z-p)) = n^{(p+1)/2}\Gamma(\tfrac{1}{2}(p+1))[\tfrac{1}{4}\ln(n) + \tfrac{1}{4}\psi(\tfrac{1}{2}(p+1)) + \gamma],$$

where $\psi(z) = (d/dz)\ln(\Gamma(z))$ is the *psi-function* (see Appendix B, 2.12). Next we consider the poles $z_{r+1} = -r$, $r \in \mathbb{N}_0$. Since these poles are simple, we obtain with (B115)

$$\operatorname*{Res}_{z=z_{r+1}}\,(\Gamma(z)n^z\zeta^2(2z - p)) = n^{-r}\zeta^2(-2r - p)\operatorname*{Res}_{z=z_{r+1}}\,(\Gamma(z))$$

$$= (-1)^r n^{-r}\zeta^2(-2r - p)/r!.$$

Summarizing our results, we have proved that

$$g_p(n) = n^{(p+1)/2}\Gamma(\tfrac{1}{2}(p + 1))[\tfrac{1}{4}\ln(n) + \tfrac{1}{4}\psi(\tfrac{1}{2}(p + 1)) + \gamma]$$

$$+ \sum_{r \geq 0} (-1)^r n^{-r}\zeta^2(-2r - p)/r! + O(n^{-s})$$

for all $s > 0$. Substituting the equivalents of $\Gamma(\tfrac{1}{2}(p + 1))$, $\psi(\tfrac{1}{2}(p + 1))$, and $\zeta^2(-2r - p)$ given in (B109), (B112), (B118), (B119), and (B126), we finally obtain for all $p \geqslant 0$ and $s > 0$

$$g_{2p}(n) = \frac{(2p)!}{p!\,4^{p+1}}\,n^p\sqrt{\pi n}\left[\ln(n) + 3\gamma - 2\ln(2) + 2\sum_{0 \leqslant \lambda \leqslant p-1}(2\lambda + 1)^{-1}\right]$$

$$+ \tfrac{1}{4}\delta_{p,0} + O(n^{-s})$$

$$g_{2p+1}(n) = \tfrac{1}{4}n^{p+1}p!\left[\ln(n) + 3\gamma + \sum_{1 \leqslant \lambda \leqslant p}\lambda^{-1}\right] + \tfrac{1}{4}B^2_{2p+2}/(p + 1)^2 + O(n^{-1}),$$

where $B_p$ is the $p$-th Bernoulli number and $\gamma$ is Euler's constant. For example, we have

$$g_0(n) = \tfrac{1}{4}\sqrt{\pi n}\,[\ln(n) + 3\gamma - 2\ln(2)] + \tfrac{1}{4} + O(n^{-s})$$

$$g_2(n) = \tfrac{1}{8}n\sqrt{\pi n}\,[\ln(n) + 3\gamma - 2\ln(2) + 2] + O(n^{-s})$$

$$g_4(n) = \tfrac{3}{16}n^2\sqrt{\pi n}\,[\ln(n) + 3\gamma - 2\ln(2) + \tfrac{8}{3}] + O(n^{-s})$$

and

$$g_1(n) = \tfrac{1}{4}n[\ln(n) + 3\gamma] + \tfrac{1}{144} + O(n^{-1})$$

$$g_3(n) = \tfrac{1}{4}n^2[\ln(n) + 3\gamma + 1] + \tfrac{1}{14400} + O(n^{-1})$$

$$g_5(n) = \tfrac{1}{2}n^3[\ln(n) + 3\gamma + \tfrac{3}{2}] + \tfrac{1}{63504} + O(n^{-1}).$$

Table 1 shows that the above expressions are very good approximations, even for small values of $n$.

We are now ready to prove the following theorem.

THEOREM 5.3  Assuming that all ordered binary trees with $(n + 1)$ leaves are equally likely, the average number of variables appearing in a program produced by algorithm $S$ is for all $\delta > 0$ given by

$$m_1(n + 1) = \sqrt{\pi n} - 0.5 + O(\ln(n)/n^{0.5-\delta}).$$

*Proof*  Using the corollary following Theorem 5.2, the definition of the sum $\varphi_a(n)$ and its approximation by $g_p(n)$, we find

$$m_1(n + 1) = (n + 1)[\varphi_1(n) - 2\varphi_0(n) + \varphi_{-1}(n)]$$

$$= (n + 1)[4n^{-2}g_2(n) - 2n^{-1}g_0(n) + O(n^{-2+\delta}g_0(n))].$$

Inserting the derived approximations for $g_p(n)$ into this relation, we get $m_1(n + 1) = (1 + n^{-1})(\sqrt{\pi n} - \tfrac{1}{2}) + O(\ln(n)/n^{1/2-\delta})$ which is equivalent to our stated result.  ∎

In section 4.3.1 we have described a one-to-one correspondence between the set of all ordered trees with $n$ nodes and the set of all ordered binary trees with $(2n - 1)$ nodes. This observation shows that $m_1(n)$ is equal to the average height of an ordered tree with $n$ nodes. The result given in Theorem 5.3 was first stated in these terms in [21]. Note that $m_1(n)$ may be also interpreted as the average length of the stack required for computing a program for a binary tree with $n$ leaves by algorithm $S$. The derivation presented uses the explicit approximation (F2) of the binomial coefficients; if we make the same computation with the approximation (F1), we get

$$m_1(n + 1) = \sqrt{\pi n} - \tfrac{1}{2} + 11\sqrt{\pi/n}/24 + O(\ln(n)/n^{1-\delta}) \quad \text{for all } \delta > 0 \text{ ([61])}.$$

Let us now compute the higher moments $m_s(n + 1)$.

THEOREM 5.4  Assume that all ordered binary trees with $(n + 1)$ leaves are

TABLE 1. Exact (first column) and asymptotic values (second column) for $g_p(n)$, $0 \le p \le 5$, $n = 2, 4, 6$.

| n | $g_0(n)$ Ex. | $g_0(n)$ As. | $g_1(n)$ | | $g_2(n)$ | | $g_3(n)$ | | $g_4(n)$ | | $g_5(n)$ | |
|---|---|---|---|---|---|---|---|---|---|---|---|---|
| 2 | 0.9008 | 0.9004 | 1.2193 | 1.2186 | 1.9041 | 1.9044 | 3.4249 | 3.4371 | 6.9656 | 6.9993 | 15.6992 | 15.7213 |
| 4 | 1.7846 | 1.7847 | 3.1249 | 3.1248 | 6.6142 | 6.6130 | 16.4718 | 16.4658 | 46.7748 | 46.7697 | 147.7741 | 147.892 |
| 6 | 2.5696 | 2.5696 | 5.2920 | 5.2920 | 13.4713 | 13.4720 | 40.7107 | 40.7144 | 140.7788 | 140.7907 | 542.5279 | 542.464 |

145

equally likely and let $p(n, k)$ be the probability that a program produced by algorithm $S$ requires $k$ variables. The $s$-th moment $(s \geq 2)$ about the origin of the random variable which takes on the value $k$ with probability $p(n, k)$ is given by

$$m_2(n+1) = \tfrac{1}{3}n\pi^2 - \sqrt{\pi n} + \tfrac{1}{3} + \tfrac{5}{18}\pi^2 - \tfrac{11}{24}\sqrt{\pi/n} + O(n^{-1/2+\delta})$$

$$m_s(n+1) = 2\binom{s}{2}\zeta(s)\Gamma(\tfrac{1}{2}s)n^{s/2} - 3\binom{s}{3}\zeta(s-1)\Gamma(\tfrac{1}{2}(s-1))n^{(s-1)/2} + O(n^{(s-2)/2})$$

for all $\delta > 0$ and $s \geq 3$.

*Proof* An inspection of Theorem 5.2 shows that

$$m_s(n+1) = (n+1)[\Phi_1^{(s)}(n) - 2\Phi_0^{(s)}(n) + \Phi_{-1}^{(s)}(n)],$$

where

$$\Phi_a^{(s)}(n) = \sum_{k \geq 1} \delta_s(k)\binom{2n}{n+a-k} \bigg/ \binom{2n}{n} \quad \text{and} \quad \delta_s(k) = \sum_{d \mid k}[d^s - (d-1)^s].$$

Using the approximation (F1), we obtain by the same procedure as in the derivation of $m_1(n+1)$

$$\Phi_1^{(s)}(n) - 2\Phi_0^{(s)}(n) + \Phi_{-1}^{(s)}(n) = \left[\frac{2}{n^2} - \frac{2}{n}\right]g_0^{(s)}(n) + \left[\frac{4}{n^2} - \frac{11}{n^3}\right]g_2^{(s)}(n) + \frac{19}{3n^4}g_4^{(s)}(n)$$

$$- \frac{2}{3n^5}g_6^{(s)}(n) + O(n^{-2.5+\delta}g_0^{(s)}(n)),$$

where

$$g_p^{(s)}(n) = \sum_{k \geq 1} \exp(-k^2/n)\delta_s(k)k^p.$$

Thus the computation of an asymptotic equivalent of $m_s(n+1)$ is reduced to the analogous problem for the sum $g_p^{(s)}(n)$. Its asymptotic behaviour can be determined by the gamma function method described above. An application of the Mellin transform of $\exp(-x)$ yields

$$g_p^{(s)}(n) = \frac{1}{2\pi i} \int_{c-i\infty}^{c+i\infty} \Gamma(z)n^z D(2z-p)\, dz, \qquad c > \tfrac{1}{2}(p+1),$$

where $D(z)$ is the Dirichlet series with the coefficients $\delta_s(n)$, that is,

$$D(z) = \sum_{k \geq 1} \delta_s(k)k^{-z}.$$

Since $\sum_{k \geq 1} \sigma_\alpha(k)k^{-z} = \zeta(z)\zeta(z-\alpha)$, $D(z)$ can be transformed as follows:

$$D(z) = \sum_{k \geq 1} \sum_{d \mid k} [d^s - (d-1)^s]k^{-z}$$

$$= \sum_{k \geqslant 1} k^{-z} \sum_{d|k} \left[ d^s - \sum_{0 \leqslant \lambda \leqslant s} \binom{s}{\lambda}(-1)^{s-\lambda}d^\lambda \right]$$

$$= -\zeta(z) \sum_{0 \leqslant \lambda < s} \binom{s}{\lambda}(-1)^{s-\lambda}\zeta(z-\lambda).$$

Hence

$$g_p^{(s)}(n) = - \sum_{0 \leqslant \lambda \leqslant s} \binom{s}{\lambda}(-1)^{s-\lambda}I_{p,\lambda}(n),$$

where

$$I_{p,\lambda}(n) = \frac{1}{2\pi i} \int_{c-i\infty}^{c+i\infty} n^z \Gamma(z)\zeta(2z - p)\zeta(2z - p - \lambda)\,dz.$$

The evaluation of this integral is similar to that of $g_p(n) = I_{p,0}(n)$. We can shift the line of integration to the left as far as we please if we only take the residues into account. The case $\lambda = 0$ leads to the approximation of $g_p(n)$ given before Theorem 5.3. If $\lambda \geqslant 1$, there are simple poles at $z = (p+1)/2$, $z = (p+\lambda+1)/2$ and possibly at $z = -r$, $r \in \mathbb{N}_0$, with the residues

$$\operatorname*{Res}_{z=(p+1)/2} (n^z\Gamma(z)\zeta(2z-p)\zeta(2z-p-\lambda)) = \tfrac{1}{2}n^{(p+1)/2}\Gamma(\tfrac{1}{2}(p+1))\zeta(1-\lambda)$$

$$\operatorname*{Res}_{z=(p+\lambda+1)/2} (n^z\Gamma(z)\zeta(2z-p)\zeta(2z-p-\lambda)) = \tfrac{1}{2}n^{(p+\lambda+1)/2}\Gamma(\tfrac{1}{2}(p+\lambda+1))\zeta(1+\lambda)$$

$$\operatorname*{Res}_{z=-r} (n^z\Gamma(z)\zeta(2z-p)\zeta(2z-p-\lambda)) = (-1)^r n^{-r}\zeta(-2r-p)\zeta(-2r-p-\lambda)/r!.$$

Therefore, for all $m > 0$

$$g_p^{(s)}(n) = (-1)^{s+1}[n^{(p+1)/2}\Gamma(\tfrac{1}{2}(p+1))\{\tfrac{1}{4}\ln(n) + \tfrac{1}{4}\psi(\tfrac{1}{2}(p+1)) + \gamma\}]$$

$$+ (-1)^{s+1} \sum_{k \geqslant 0} \zeta^2(-2k-p)(-1)^k n^{-k}/k!$$

$$+ \tfrac{1}{2}n^{(p+1)/2} \sum_{1 \leqslant \lambda < s} (-1)^{s-\lambda+1} \binom{s}{\lambda}[\Gamma(\tfrac{1}{2}(p+1))\zeta(1-\lambda)$$

$$+ n^{\lambda/2}\Gamma(\tfrac{1}{2}(p+\lambda+1))\zeta(1+\lambda)]$$

$$+ \sum_{1 \leqslant \lambda < s} (-1)^{s-\lambda+1} \binom{s}{\lambda} \sum_{k \geqslant 0} \zeta(-2k-p)\zeta(-2k-p-\lambda)(-1)^k n^{-k}/k!$$

$$+ O(n^{-m}).$$

Choosing $s = 2$ and using some special values of $\Gamma(z)$, $\zeta(z)$, and $\psi(z)$ (see Appendix B, 2.11, 2.12, 2.13), we obtain our expressions for $m_s(n+1)$ by an elementary computation. ∎

Since the variance is given by $\sigma^2(n+1) = m_2(n+1) - m_1^2(n+1)$, we further obtain the following corollary.

TABLE 2. The variance $\sigma^2(n)$ and the average number $m_1(n)$ of variables appearing in a program produced by algorithm $S$ for a binary tree with $n$ leaves. The numbers of the first (second) column correspond to the exact (asymptotical) values.

| $n$ | $m_1(n)$ | | $\sigma^2(n)$ | |
|----|---------|---------|---------|---------|
| 1 | 1.000 | — | 0.0000 | — |
| 2 | 2.000 | 2.0848 | 0.0000 | 0.0934 |
| 3 | 2.5000 | 2.5810 | 0.2500 | 0.2416 |
| 4 | 3.0000 | 3.0390 | 0.4000 | 0.3900 |
| 5 | 3.4286 | 3.4511 | 0.5306 | 0.5382 |
| 8 | 4.4849 | 4.4965 | 0.9817 | 0.9830 |
| 10 | 5.0802 | 5.0882 | 1.2782 | 1.2796 |
| 12 | 5.6176 | 5.6235 | 1.5743 | 1.5761 |
| 14 | 6.1114 | 6.1160 | 1.8712 | 1.8727 |

COROLLARY   The variance of the random variable defined in Theorem 5.1 is

$$\sigma^2(n+1) = \left(\frac{\pi}{3} - 1\right)\pi n + \tfrac{1}{12} + \tfrac{5}{18}\pi^2 - \tfrac{11}{12}\pi + O(\ln(n)/n^{1/2-\delta})$$

for all $\delta > 0$. ∎

The results stated in Theorem 5.4 were proved in [61]. An inspection of the above corollary shows that the variance is very large. The first few values of $m_1(n)$ and $\sigma^2(n)$ are summarized in Table 2.

Let us conclude this section by computing the cumulative distribution function $V_n(x) = t(n, x)/t(n, n)$; by definition, $V_n(x)$ is the probability that a program produced by algorithm $S$ has less than or equal to $k$ variables, or in other words, that a binary tree with $n$ leaves can be reduced by algorithm $S$ with a stack of length less than or equal to $k$.

THEOREM 5.5   The cumulative distribution function $V_n(x)$ is given by

$$V_n(x) = 1 - \sum_{k \geqslant 1}\left[4\frac{k^2(x+1)^2}{n} - 2\right]\exp(-k^2(x+1)^2/n) + O(n^{-1/2+\delta}),$$

or alternatively by

$$V_n(x) = 4\pi\left[\frac{\sqrt{\pi n}}{x+1}\right]^3 \sum_{k \geqslant 1} k^2 \exp(-k^2\pi^2 n/(x+1)^2) + O(n^{-1/2+\delta})$$

for all $\delta > 0$.

Proof   Using the explicit expression $t(n, k)$ for the number of all ordered binary trees with $n$ leaves which can be reduced by algorithm $S$ requiring less than or equal to $k$ variables, we find immediately that

$$V_n(x) = 1 - \sum_{1 \leqslant k \leqslant \lfloor n/(x+1) \rfloor} \left[ 4 \frac{k^2(x+1)^2}{n} - 2 \right] \binom{2n}{n-k(x+1)} \Big/ \binom{2n}{n}.$$

Hence

$$V_n(x) = 1 - \sum_{k \geqslant 1} \left[ 4 \frac{k^2(x+1)^2}{n} - 2 \right] \binom{2n}{n-k(x+1)} \Big/ \binom{2n}{n}$$

$$+ \sum_{k > n^{1/2+\varepsilon}/(x+1)} \left[ 4 \frac{k^2(x+1)^2}{n} - 2 \right] \binom{2n}{n-k(x+1)} \Big/ \binom{2n}{n}$$

$$- \sum_{n^{1/2+\varepsilon}/(x+1) \leqslant k \leqslant \lfloor n/(x+1) \rfloor} \left[ 4 \frac{k^2(x+1)^2}{n} - 2 \right] \binom{2n}{n-k(x+1)} \Big/ \binom{2n}{n}$$

$$= 1 - [1 + O(n^{-1/2+\delta})] \sum_{k \geqslant 1} \left[ 4 \frac{k^2(x+1)^2}{n} - 2 \right]$$

$$\times \exp(-k^2(x+1)^2/n) + O(n^{-m})$$

for all $\delta > 0$ and $m > 0$. Here we have used the approximation (F5) of the quotient $\binom{2n}{n-k(x+1)} \Big/ \binom{2n}{n}$ and the fact that this quotient is exponentially small for $k > n^{1/2+\varepsilon}/(x+1)$. This implies the first part of our theorem. To obtain the second part, let us introduce the function $\theta(z) = \sum_{k \geqslant 1} \exp(-k^2 \pi z)$. A simple computation shows that part (a) is equivalent to

$$V_n(x) = 1 + 2[\theta(t) + 2t\theta'(t)] + O(n^{-1/2+\delta})$$

where $t = (x+1)^2/(\pi n)$. Now, the function $\theta$ satisfies a well-known relation, the so-called *theta-relation* given by ([13])

$$\theta(z) = \frac{1}{\sqrt{z}} \theta\left(\frac{1}{z}\right) + \frac{1}{2\sqrt{z}} - \frac{1}{2}.$$

This relation implies that

$$2[\theta(z) + 2z\theta'(z)] = -4z^{-3/2}\theta'(z^{-1}) - 1.$$

Thus

$$V_n(x) = -4t^{-3/2}\theta'(t^{-1}) + O(n^{-1/2+\delta}) \quad \text{for all } \delta > 0.$$

This expression is identical to the expression stated in the second part. ■

Some values of $V_n(x)$ with $x = c\sqrt{n} - 1$, $c$ fixed, are given in Table 3. For example, 74.35 per cent of all ordered binary trees with 100 leaves can be reduced by algorithm $S$ using a stack of length less than or equal to 19, and 99.62 per cent of all trees can be reduced with a stack of length less than or equal to 29. In the asymptotic case, 74.36 percent of all trees with $n$ leaves can be reduced by algorithm $S$ with a stack of maximum length $2\sqrt{n} - 1$ and 99.58 per cent with a stack of maximum length $3\sqrt{n} - 1$. Note that there is exactly one tree which uses a stack of length $n$; its probability is exponentially small, being $t^{-1}(n) = O(n^{3/2}4^{-n})$.

TABLE 3. Some values of $V_n(c\sqrt{n}-1)$. The last row represents the asymptotic values for $n \to \infty$.

| | | | $c$ | | | |
|---|---|---|---|---|---|---|
| $n$ | 0.5 | 1 | 1.5 | 2 | 2.5 | 3 |
| 9 | | 0.0007 | | 0.7650 | | 0.9993 |
| 16 | 0.0000 | 0.0017 | 0.2467 | 0.7550 | 0.9653 | 0.9980 |
| 25 | | 0.0023 | | 0.7507 | | 0.9972 |
| 36 | 0.0000 | 0.0027 | 0.2532 | 0.7485 | 0.9598 | 0.9968 |
| 49 | | 0.0029 | | 0.7471 | | 0.9966 |
| 100 | 0.0000 | 0.0033 | 0.2563 | 0.7453 | 0.9571 | 0.9962 |
| $\infty$ | 0.0000 | 0.0036 | 0.2580 | 0.7436 | 0.9556 | 0.9958 |

### 5.1.2 The Reduction of Binary Trees by an Optimal Algorithm

Another type of algorithm for evaluating a given ordered binary tree $T$ is a procedure consisting in the main of the following two steps:

(A) Attach additional labels to the nodes of the tree.
(B) Convert the labelled tree into a program $\pi$ which evaluates $T$.

The following algorithm is of this type and represents an optimal strategy (with respect to the number of variables appearing in $\pi$) for the reduction of ordered binary trees ([90], [110]).

ALGORITHM $OP$
Input: A binary tree $T$ with a set of interior nodes $I$, a set of leaves $L$, and a root $r \in I$.
Output: An optimal program $\pi$ which evaluates $T$.
Method:
(A) Attach additional labels to the nodes of $T$. The labels are integers which can be recursively computed by the labelling function $f: I \cup L \to \mathbb{N}$ defined by

$f(x) := if\ x \in L\ then\ 1$
$\qquad else\ \text{MIN}(\text{MAX}(f(y), f(z)+1), \text{MAX}(f(y)+1, f(z)));,$

where $y$ $(z)$ is the root of the left (right) subtree of the node $x$.
(B) The computation of the program $\pi$ is as follows:
(B1) One starts from the root of the labelled tree. Scanning is performed from those nodes which have a larger integer label. If both have the same label, one begins on the right node.
(B2) One continues scanning until a leaf or a node with sons labelled zero is reached. This node is 'evaluated' and is substituted by the resulting variable name (zero is substituted for its label). Then one returns to the father of this node and continues scanning. The evaluation of a node $x$

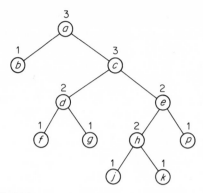

FIGURE 27. Labelled binary tree. The number at node $x$ represents $f(x)$.

means that the instruction '$A \leftarrow x$;' is emitted, if $x \in L$, and the instruction '$A_m \leftarrow A_r A_s x$;' with $m = \text{MIN}(r, s)$, if $x \in I$ has the left son $A_r$ and the right son $A_s$. In each step, the result appears as the value of the available variable with lowest index.

For clarity, we have not described the algorithm in terms of operations on the post-order $PO(T)$. Let us consider the binary tree $T$ drawn in Figure 24. The corresponding labelled tree is given in Figure 27. Performing step (B), we have first to evaluate node $k \in L$. Thus the instruction '$A_1 \leftarrow k$;' is emitted, the label $f(k)$ is replaced by 0 and the node $k$ by the variable name $A_1$. We have to return to node $h$ and to continue scanning. Again performing step (B), we have now to evaluate node $j \in L$; the instruction '$A_2 \leftarrow j$;' is emitted, the label $f(j)$ is substituted by 0 and node $j$ by $A_2$. Scanning is continued at node $h$ itself. The instruction '$A_1 \leftarrow A_2 A_1 h$;' is emitted, the label $f(h)$ is substituted by 0 and node $h$ by the variable name $A_1$. Returning to node $e$, we have next to evaluate node $p \in L$. Finally, after the evaluation of root $a$, the following 3-program is computed:

$$A_1 \leftarrow k;$$
$$A_2 \leftarrow j;$$
$$A_1 \leftarrow A_2 A_1 h;$$
$$A_2 \leftarrow p;$$
$$A_1 \leftarrow A_1 A_2 e;$$
$$A_2 \leftarrow g;$$
$$A_3 \leftarrow f;$$
$$A_2 \leftarrow A_3 A_2 d;$$
$$A_1 \leftarrow A_2 A_1 c;$$
$$A_2 \leftarrow b;$$
$$A_1 \leftarrow A_2 A_1 a;$$

This program is optimal; that is, the tree cannot be evaluated by a $k$-program $\pi$, where $k \leqslant 2$.

A lower bound of the number of variables appearing in a program $\pi$ produced by algorithm $OP$ for an ordered binary tree with $n$ ($\geqslant 2$) leaves is equal to two; for example, a binary tree with $n$ leaves and height $n$ can always be reduced by a 2-program. A simple induction argument suffices to prove that an upper bound of the number of variables is given by $\lfloor \mathrm{ld}(2n) \rfloor$; complete trees with $n$ leaves can always be evaluated by a $\lfloor \mathrm{ld}(2n) \rfloor$-program (Exercise 5.3). Let us now assume that all ordered binary trees with $n$ leaves are equally likely. We shall compute the average number of variables appearing in a program produced by algorithm $OP$, that is, the average minimum number of registers required for evaluating a tree. We first prove the following theorem.

THEOREM 5.6  Let $q(n, k)$ be the number of all binary trees with $n$ leaves which can be reduced by algorithm $OP$ requiring less than or equal to $k$ variables and let $Q_k(z) = \sum_{k \geqslant 1} q(n, k)z^n$ be the generating function of these numbers. We have

$$Q_1(z) = z$$

$$Q_{k+1}(z) = [Q_k^2(z) - z]/[2Q_k(z) - 1], \qquad k \geqslant 1.$$

*Proof*  Obviously, only the one-node tree can be reduced by a 1-program. Thus $Q_1(z) = z$. The labelling function $f$ defined in algorithm $OP$ can also be written in the form

$$f(x) = \begin{cases} 1 & \text{if } x \in L \\ f(z) + 1 & \text{if } f(y) = f(z), \\ \mathrm{MAX}(f(y), f(z)) & \text{if } f(y) \neq f(z) \end{cases}$$

where $y$ ($z$) is the root of the left (right) subtree of $x$. Therefore, we obtain all binary trees requiring less than or equal to $(k + 1)$ variables by taking

(a)  the one-node tree (giving the contribution $z$); or
(b)  a tree with subtrees requiring less than or equal to $k$ variables (giving the contribution $Q_k^2(z)$); or
(c)  a tree, where one subtree requires $(k + 1)$ variables and the other less than or equal to $k$ variables (giving the contribution $2Q_k(z)[Q_{k+1}(z) - Q_k(z)]$).

Hence

$$Q_{k+1}(z) = z + Q_k^2(z) + 2Q_k(z)[Q_{k+1}(z) - Q_k(z)]. \quad \blacksquare$$

We have now to solve the recurrence given in Theorem 5.6. We obtain the following theorem.

THEOREM 5.7  The generating function $Q_k(z)$ of the numbers $q(n, k)$ is given by

$$Q_k(z) = 2z \, \frac{(1 + \sqrt{1 - 4z})^{2^{k-1}} - (1 - \sqrt{1 - 4z})^{2^{k-1}}}{(1 + \sqrt{1 - 4z})^{2^k} - (1 - \sqrt{1 - 4z})^{2^k}}.$$

*Proof*  Naturally, this result can be easily proved by induction on $k$ using the recurrence for $Q_k(z)$. Another method consists of solving this recurrence directly. Substituting $Q_k(z) = (1 + \sqrt{1 - 4z}\, H_k(z))/2$, the recurrence for $Q_k(z)$ can be translated into

$$H_1(z) = (2z - 1)(1 - 4z)^{-1/2}$$

$$H_{k+1}(z) = \frac{H_k^2(z) + 1}{2H_k(z)}.$$

Note that $H_k^2(z) + 1 + 2H_k(z) = (H_k(z) + 1)^2$ and $H_k^2(z) + 1 - 2H_k(z) = (H_k(z) - 1)^2$. Thus replacing $H_k(z)$ by $P_k(z)/Q_k(z)$ and splitting the resulting expression into a recurrence for the numerator and denominator, we obtain

$$P_1(z) = 2z - 1, \qquad Q_1(z) = \sqrt{1 - 4z}$$

$$P_{k+1}(z) + Q_{k+1}(z) = [P_k(z) + Q_k(z)]^2$$

$$P_{k+1}(z) - Q_{k+1}(z) = [P_k(z) - Q_k(z)]^2.$$

These recurrences can easily be solved. We obtain

$$P_{k+1}(z) + Q_{k+1}(z) = [P_1(z) + Q_1(z)]^{2^k} = [2z - 1 + \sqrt{1 - 4z}]^{2^k}$$

$$P_{k+1}(z) - Q_{k+1}(z) = [P_1(z) - Q_1(z)]^{2^k} = [2z - 1 - \sqrt{1 - 4z}]^{2^k}.$$

Since $(1 + \sqrt{1 - 4z})^2 = -2(2z - 1 - \sqrt{1 - 4z})$ and $(1 - \sqrt{1 - 4z})^2 = -2(2z - 1 + \sqrt{1 - 4z})$, we find by addition and subtraction of these equations

$$2P_{k+1}(z) = 2^{-2^k}[(1 - \sqrt{1 - 4z})^{2^{k+1}} + (1 + \sqrt{1 - 4z})^{2^{k+1}}]$$

$$2Q_{k+1}(z) = 2^{-2^k}[(1 - \sqrt{1 - 4z})^{2^{k+1}} - (1 + \sqrt{1 - 4z})^{2^{k+1}}].$$

Using these explicit expressions, we obtain our result with $H_k(z) = P_k(z)/Q_k(z)$. ∎

The expansion of the function $Q_k(z)$ has been computed in section 4.2.2. We have

$$q(n+1, k) = \langle z^{n+1} \rangle Q_k(z)$$

$$= t(n+1) - \sum_{j \geqslant 1} \left[ \binom{2n}{n+1-j2^k} - 2\binom{2n}{n-j2^k} + \binom{2n}{n-1-j2^k} \right].$$

A comparison of this formula with $t(n, k)$ given in section 5.1.1 leads immediately to $q(n + 1, k) = t(n + 1, 2^k - 1)$. Hence we have the following theorem.

THEOREM 5.8  The number of ordered binary trees with $n$ leaves which can be reduced by algorithm $S$ requiring less than or equal to $2^k - 1$ variables is equal to the number of binary trees with $n$ leaves which can be reduced by the optimal algorithm $OP$ requiring less than or equal to $k$ variables. ∎

Note that this fact is only a connection between the cardinalities of the corresponding classes of trees. In general, the corresponding sets are different. It would be nice to have an explicit correspondence between the sets of these trees. Translating the problem into terms of random walks, a one-to-one correspondence between these random walks is given in [42].

Assuming that all ordered binary trees with $n$ leaves are equally likely, the quotient $p(n, k) = [q(n, k) - q(n, k - 1)]/t(n)$ is the probability that a program produced by algorithm $OP$ has $k$ variables. Therefore, the $s$-th moment about the origin is given by

$$m_s(n) = \sum_{1 \leqslant k \leqslant \lfloor \mathrm{ld}(2n) \rfloor} k^s p(n, k).$$

Using the above definition of $p(n, k)$, the facts $q(n, 0) = 0$ for $n \geqslant 1$ and $q(n, \lfloor \mathrm{ld}(2n) \rfloor) = t(n)$, this expression can be transformed into

$$m_s(n) = \lfloor \mathrm{ld}(2n) \rfloor^s - t^{-1}(n) \sum_{1 \leqslant k < \lfloor \mathrm{ld}(2n) \rfloor} [(k + 1)^s - k^s] q(n, k).$$

Inserting the explicit expression for $q(n, k)$ into this equation, we find

$$m_s(n + 1) = 1 + t^{-1}(n + 1) \sum_{k \geqslant 1} [(k + 1)^s - k^s] \psi(n, k),$$

where

$$\psi(n, k) = \psi_1(n, k) - 2\psi_0(n, k) + \psi_{-1}(n, k)$$

with

$$\psi_a(n, k) = \sum_{j \geqslant 1} \binom{2n}{n + a - j2^k}.$$

Let us now consider the sum

$$\beta_a^{(s)}(n) = \sum_{k \geqslant 1} [(k + 1)^s - k^s] \psi_a(n, k).$$

We get

$$\beta_a^{(s)}(n) = \sum_{k \geqslant 1} [(k + 1)^s - k^s] \sum_{j \geqslant 1} \binom{2n}{n + a - j2^k}$$

$$= \sum_{k \geqslant 1} \binom{2n}{n + a - k} \alpha_s(k),$$

where

$$\alpha_s(k) = \sum_{1 \leqslant i \leqslant r(k)} [(i + 1)^s - i^s] \quad \text{with} \quad r(k) = \mathrm{card}(\{d \mid d|k \wedge d = 2^r \wedge r \in \mathbb{N}\}).$$

Note that $r(n)$ is the number of all positive divisors of $n \in \mathbb{N}$ which are a power of two. Thus $\alpha_s(k) = 0$ if $k$ is odd.

Summarizing the above results, we have proved the following theorem.

THEOREM 5.9 Assume that all ordered binary trees with $(n + 1)$ leaves are equally likely and let $p(n, k)$ be the probability that a program produced by algorithm $OP$ requires $k$ variables. The $s$-th moment about the origin of the random variable which takes on the value $k$ with probability $p(n, k)$ is given by

$$m_s(n+1) = 1 + t^{-1}(n+1) \sum_{k \geqslant 1} \alpha_s(k) \left[ \binom{2n}{n+1-k} - 2\binom{2n}{n-k} + \binom{2n}{n-1-k} \right],$$

where $\alpha_s(n)$ is the arithmetical function defined by

$$\alpha_s(n) = \sum_{1 \leqslant i \leqslant r(n)} [(i+1)^s - i^s]$$

and $r(n)$ is the number of all positive divisors of $n$ which are a power of two.

Choosing $s = 1$, we obtain the following corollary as a special case.

COROLLARY  Assuming that all ordered binary trees with $(n+1)$ leaves are equally likely, the average number of variables appearing in a program produced by algorithm $OP$ is equal to

$$m_1(n+1) = 1 + t^{-1}(n+1) \sum_{k \geqslant 1} r(k) \left[ \binom{2n}{n+1-k} - 2\binom{2n}{n-k} + \binom{2n}{n-1-k} \right],$$

where $r(n)$ is the number of all positive divisors of $n$ of the form $2^r$, $r \in \mathbb{N}$.  ■

Let us now derive an asymptotic equivalent of $m_1(n+1)$. This can be done by the gamma function method presented in section 5.1.1. Using the approximation (F2) (see section 5.1.1), an analogous computation to that in section 5.1.1 leads to

$$m_1(n+1) = 1 + (n+1)[4n^{-2}h_2(n) - 2n^{-1}h_0(n) + O(n^{-2+\delta}h_0(n))]$$

for all $\delta > 0$, where

$$h_p(n) = \sum_{k \geqslant 1} \exp(-k^2/n) r(k) k^p.$$

If we are able to compute a closed expression for the Dirichlet series with coefficients $r(k)$, then the sum $h_p(n)$ can be transformed into an integral. Indeed, we find

$$\sum_{k \geqslant 1} r(k) k^{-z} = \sum_{k \geqslant 1} r(2k)(2k)^{-z}$$

$$= \sum_{j \geqslant 1} \sum_{k \geqslant 1} (2^j k)^{-z}$$

$$= \zeta(z)[2^z - 1]^{-1},$$

where $\zeta(z)$ is Riemann's zeta function. Therefore, by Mellin's transform of

$\exp(-x)$

$$h_p(n) = \frac{1}{2\pi i} \int_{c-i\infty}^{c+i\infty} \Gamma(z) n^z \zeta(2z - p) [2^{2z-p} - 1]^{-1} \, dz, \qquad c > \tfrac{1}{2}(p + 1).$$

Again, we can shift the line of integration to the left as far as we please if we only take the residues into account. For $p = 0$, there is a double pole at $z = 0$ (contributed by $\Gamma(z)[2^{2z} - 1]^{-1}$) and simple poles at $z = \pi i k/\ln(2)$, $k \in \mathbb{Z}\backslash\{0\}$, (contributed by $[2^{2z} - 1]^{-1}$) and $z = \tfrac{1}{2}$ (contributed by $\zeta(2z)$). For $p \geqslant 1$, there are only simple poles at $z = p/2 + \pi i k/\ln(2)$ (contributed by $[2^{2z-p} - 1]^{-1}$), at $z = (p + 1)/2$ (contributed by $\zeta(2z - p)$), and possibly at $z = -r$, $r \in \mathbb{N}_0$ (contributed by $\Gamma(z)$). Let us first consider the case $p = 0$.

(a) Double pole at $z = 0$.
  Since $\Gamma(z + 1) = z\Gamma(z)$, we obtain

$$\frac{\Gamma(z)n^z\zeta(2z)}{2^{2z} - 1} = \frac{\Gamma(z+1)n^z\zeta(2z)}{z[2^{2z} - 1]}$$

$$= z^{-2} \frac{n^z\Gamma(z+1)\zeta(2z)}{2\ln(2)F(z)}$$

$$= \frac{1}{2z^2\ln(2)}\left[\frac{\Gamma(1)\zeta(0)}{F(0)} + z\frac{d}{dz}\left(\frac{n^z\Gamma(z+1)\zeta(2z)}{F(z)}\right)\Bigg|_{z=0} + O(z^2)\right],$$

where

$$F(z) = \sum_{j\geqslant 1} 2^{j-1}\ln^{j-1}(2)z^{j-1}/j!.$$

Hence

$$\operatorname*{Res}_{z=0}\left(\frac{\Gamma(z)n^z\zeta(2z)}{2^{2z} - 1}\right) = \frac{1}{2\ln(2)}\frac{d}{dz}\left(\frac{n^z\Gamma(z+1)\zeta(2z)}{F(z)}\right)\Bigg|_{z=0}$$

$$= \frac{F(0)[\ln(n)\Gamma(1)\zeta(0) + \Gamma'(1)\zeta(0) + 2\Gamma(1)\zeta'(0)] - \Gamma(1)\zeta(0)F'(0)}{2\ln(2)F^2(0)}.$$

Using the special values for $\Gamma'(1)$, $\zeta(0)$, and $\zeta'(0)$ given in (B113), (B126), and (B127), we find

$$\operatorname*{Res}_{z=0}\left(\frac{\Gamma(z)n^z\zeta(2z)}{2^{2z} - 1}\right) = -\tfrac{1}{4}\operatorname{ld}(n) + \frac{\gamma}{4\ln(2)} - \tfrac{1}{2}\operatorname{ld}(2\pi) + \tfrac{1}{4}.$$

(b) Simple pole at $z = \pi i k/\ln(2)$, $k \in \mathbb{Z}\backslash\{0\}$.
  We immediately obtain

$$\operatorname*{Res}_{z=\pi i k/\ln(2)}\left(\frac{\Gamma(z)n^z\zeta(2z)}{2^{2z} - 1}\right) = \frac{1}{2\ln(2)}n^{\pi i k/\ln(2)}\Gamma\left(\frac{\pi i k}{\ln(2)}\right)\zeta\left(2\frac{\pi i k}{\ln(2)}\right).$$

(c) Simple pole at $z = \tfrac{1}{2}$.

$$\operatorname*{Res}_{z=1/2}\left(\frac{\Gamma(z)n^z\zeta(2z)}{2^{2z} - 1}\right) = \Gamma(\tfrac{1}{2})n^{1/2}\operatorname*{Res}_{z=1/2}(\zeta(2z)) = \tfrac{1}{2}\sqrt{\pi n}.$$

Thus for all $m > 0$

$$h_0(n) = \tfrac{1}{2}\sqrt{\pi n} - \tfrac{1}{4}\operatorname{ld}(4\pi^2 n) + \frac{\gamma}{4\ln(2)} + \tfrac{1}{4} + H(n) + O(n^{-m}),$$

where

$$H(n) = \frac{1}{2\ln(2)} \sum_{\substack{-\infty \leqslant k \leqslant \infty \\ k \neq 0}} \exp(\pi i k \operatorname{ld}(n)) \Gamma\left(\frac{\pi i k}{\ln(2)}\right) \zeta\left(2\frac{\pi i k}{\ln(2)}\right).$$

Let us now consider the case $p \geqslant 1$.

(a) Simple pole at $z = p/2 + \pi i k/\ln(2)$, $k \in \mathbb{Z}$.

$$\operatorname*{Res}_{z = p/2 + \pi i k/\ln(2)} \left( \frac{\Gamma(z)n^z \zeta(2z - p)}{2^{2z-p} - 1} \right) = \frac{1}{2\ln(2)} n^{\frac{1}{2}p + (\pi i k/\ln(2))} \Gamma\left(\tfrac{1}{2}p + \frac{\pi i k}{\ln(2)}\right) \zeta\left(2\frac{\pi i k}{\ln(2)}\right).$$

(b) Simple pole at $z = (p + 1)/2$.

$$\operatorname*{Res}_{z = (p+1)/2} \left( \frac{\Gamma(z)n^z \zeta(2z - p)}{2^{2z-p} - 1} \right) = \tfrac{1}{2}n^{(p+1)/2}\Gamma(\tfrac{1}{2}(p + 1)).$$

(c) Simple pole at $z = -r$, $r \in \mathbb{N}_0$.

$$\operatorname*{Res}_{z = -r} \left( \frac{\Gamma(z)n^z \zeta(2z - p)}{2^{2z-p} - 1} \right) = (-1)^r \frac{1}{r!} n^{-r} \zeta(-2r - p)[2^{-2r-p} - 1]^{-1}.$$

Hence for all $m > 0$ and $p \geqslant 1$,

$$h_p(n) = \tfrac{1}{2}n^{(p+1)/2}\Gamma(\tfrac{1}{2}(p + 1)) + \sum_{r \geqslant 0} (-1)^r n^{-r} \zeta(-2r - p)[2^{-2r-p} - 1]^{-1}/r!$$

$$+ G_p(n) + O(n^{-m}),$$

where

$$G_p(n) = \frac{1}{2\ln(2)} n^{p/2} \sum_{-\infty \leqslant k \leqslant \infty} \exp(\pi i k \operatorname{ld}(n)) \Gamma\left(\tfrac{1}{2}p + \frac{\pi i k}{\ln(2)}\right) \zeta\left(2\frac{\pi i k}{\ln(2)}\right).$$

We are now ready to prove the following theorem.

THEOREM 5.10  Assuming that all ordered binary trees with $(n + 1)$ leaves are equally likely, the average number of variables appearing in a program produced by the optimal algorithm $OP$ is given by

$$m_1(n + 1) = \tfrac{1}{2}\operatorname{ld}(8\pi^2 n) - \frac{\gamma + 2}{2\ln(2)} + F(n) + O(n^{-1/2 + \delta})$$

for all $\delta > 0$, where

$$F(n) = \frac{1}{\ln(2)} \sum_{\substack{-\infty \leqslant k \leqslant +\infty \\ k \neq 0}} \left[ 2\frac{\pi i k}{\ln(2)} - 1 \right] \Gamma\left(\frac{\pi i k}{\ln(2)}\right) \zeta\left(2\frac{\pi i k}{\ln(2)}\right) \exp(\pi i k \operatorname{ld}(n)).$$

*Proof* Using the above approximation for $h_p(n)$, we find with the expression for $m_1(n+1)$ given in the corollary following Theorem 5.9

$$m_1(n+1) = 1 + (n+1)[4n^{-2}h_2(n) - 2n^{-1}h_0(n) + O(n^{-2+\delta}h_0(n))]$$

$$= \tfrac{1}{2}\,\mathrm{ld}(4\pi^2 n) + \tfrac{1}{2} - \frac{\gamma}{2\ln(2)} - \frac{1}{\ln(2)} + F(n) + O(n^{-1/2+\delta}),$$

where

$$F(n) = \frac{1}{\ln(2)} \sum_{\substack{-\infty \leqslant k \leqslant \infty \\ k \neq 0}} \left[ 2\Gamma\left(1 + \frac{\pi i k}{\ln(2)}\right) - \Gamma\left(\frac{\pi i k}{\ln(2)}\right) \right] \times \zeta\left(2\,\frac{\pi i k}{\ln(2)}\right) \exp(\pi i k\,\mathrm{ld}(n)).$$

Since $\Gamma(z+1) = z\Gamma(z)$, this expression is identical to that stated in our theorem. ∎

This result has first been proved in [58], [60] and [28], [31]; the latter papers give an alternative derivation. For further applications see [87], [111].

Since $\exp(\pi i k\,\mathrm{ld}(4n)) = \exp(\pi i k\,\mathrm{ld}(n))$, the above function $F(n)$ satisfies the relation $F(n) = F(4n)$ for all $n \in \mathbb{N}$. A detailed examination of $F(n)$ (see [58]) shows that

$$F(n) = \lfloor \tfrac{1}{2}\,\mathrm{ld}(\pi n) \rfloor - \tfrac{1}{2}\,\mathrm{ld}(\pi n) + C + f(n),$$

where

$$C = \frac{1}{2} + \frac{1}{\ln(2)} \int_1^\infty (x^{-1/2} + x^{-1}) \sum_{k \geqslant 1} \exp(-\pi x k^2)\,dx \approx 0.533\,32\ldots$$

and

$$f(n) = 2\left(\frac{8\pi}{\lambda} - 1\right)\exp\left(-\frac{4\pi}{\lambda}\right) + 4\left(\frac{32\pi}{\lambda} - 1\right)\exp\left(-\frac{16\pi}{\lambda}\right)$$

$$+ 2\left(\frac{72\pi}{\lambda} - 1\right)\exp\left(-\frac{36\pi}{\lambda}\right)$$

$$- 4\lambda\sqrt{\lambda}\,\pi[\exp(-\lambda\pi) + 12\exp(-4\lambda\pi) + 9\exp(-9\lambda\pi)] + C_1$$

with $\lambda = n\pi/2^{2\lfloor\mathrm{ld}(\sqrt{\pi n})\rfloor}$ and $|C_1| < 10^{-18}$. Table 4 summarizes the exact and the asymptotical values of $m_1(n+1)$.

The higher moments $m_s(n+1)$ defined in Theorem 5.9 can be computed in a similar way as $m_1(n+1)$ (see Exercise 5.5). The variance and the cumulative distribution function is derived in [32] and [87].

### 5.1.3 The Reduction of Binary Trees by an Input-restricted Deque

In this section we shall present an intermediate class of algorithms for the reduction of ordered binary trees. The algorithms use only a restricted deque and some auxiliary cells.

Let $T$ be an ordered binary tree with the set of interior nodes $I$, a set of

TABLE 4. The values of $m_1(n)$ for $1 \leqslant n \leqslant 14$. The numbers of the first (second) column correspond to the exact (asymptotical) values.

| $n$ | $m_1(n + 1)$ | |
|---|---|---|
| 1 | 1.0000 | — |
| 2 | 2.0000 | 1.2528 |
| 3 | 2.0000 | 1.8321 |
| 4 | 2.2000 | 2.0656 |
| 5 | 2.4286 | 2.2528 |
| 6 | 2.6191 | 2.4401 |
| 7 | 2.7576 | 2.6041 |
| 8 | 2.8531 | 2.7338 |
| 9 | 2.9203 | 2.8321 |
| 10 | 2.9716 | 2.9070 |
| 11 | 3.0157 | 2.9668 |
| 12 | 3.0585 | 3.0182 |
| 13 | 3.1020 | 3.0656 |
| 14 | 3.1474 | 3.1119 |

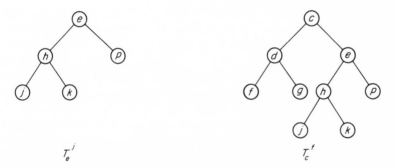

FIGURE 28. Two subtrees of the tree drawn in Figure 24.

leaves $L$ and a root $r \in I$. If $i \in I \cup L$ and $w \in L$, the tree $T_i^w$ is the binary tree with a set of interior nodes $I' \subseteq I$, a set of leaves $L' \subseteq L$ and a root $i$, where the leftmost leaf of $T_i^w$ is $w$. Obviously, a given tree $T$ and $i \in I \cup L$ define a uniquely determined tree $T_i^w$. For example, Figure 28 shows two such trees for the tree $T$ given in Figure 24.

We shall now turn to the presentation of the algorithm $D_k$ for the reduction of a binary tree $T$. The algorithm uses an auxiliary store $H$, an input-restricted deque of length $k \in \mathbb{N}$, a counter containing the current position of the input pointer, and an auxiliary cell $Z$. The deque list symbols are triples $(a, b, t) \in (I \cup L \times (I \cup L) \times \{0, 1\}$ representing the subtree $T_b^a$. If the reduction of the subtree $T_b^a$ has required an auxiliary cell in $H$, then $t = 1$; otherwise $t = 0$. A triple may be put on to the top of the deque and may be removed from the bottom or the top of the deque. The contents of an auxiliary cell in $H$ is a tuple $(a, b) \in (I \cup L) \times (I \cup L)$ representing the subtree $T_b^a$; the contents of the auxiliary cell $Z$ are always a node or the symbol \$. Henceforth, we say that the algorithm $D_k$ is in state $x$, if $x$ is the contents of the cell $Z$. Here, $D_k$ will always be in a state $x \in I \cup L$, if $(a, x, t)$ was the last triple which was removed from the bottom of the deque and was stored as the tuple $(a, x)$ in an empty auxiliary cell in $H$, provided that this cell was not cleared or no other triple was removed from the deque after the deletion of $(a, x, t)$. Otherwise, $D_k$ is in state \$.

Since the algorithm $D_k$ is rather complex, we shall first give an informal description. The algorithm reads the input $PO(T)$ from left to right and works as follows:

(1) If the current input symbol is a leaf $\omega \in L$ and there is a tuple $(a, b)$ in an auxiliary cell $h \in H$ with $a = \omega$, then we know that the tree $T_b^a$ ought to be reduced in the following steps. Since this reduction was made in earlier steps, the input pointer moves right until the symbol following $b$, the triple $(a, b, 1)$ is put on to the top of the deque, if the deque list has a length less than $k$, and the auxiliary cell $h$ is cleared. The state $z$ is unchanged, if $z \neq b$; otherwise, $D_k$ goes in state \$. If the deque list has a length equal to $k$, then the triple $(a, b, 1)$ cannot be inserted at the top of the deque. In this case, we have to consider the following two cases:

    (1.1) The input symbol $c$ following $b$ is an interior node. Then the triple $(x, y, t)$ at the top of the deque represents the left subtree $T_y^x$ and $(a, b)$ the right subtree $T_b^a$ of the tree $T_c^x$. In this case, the triple at the top of the deque is replaced by $(x, c, 1)$, the auxiliary cell $h$ is cleared, and the input pointer moves right. The state $z$ is unchanged, if $z \neq b$; otherwise, $D_k$ goes in state \$.

    (1.2) The input symbol $c$ following $b$ is a leaf. Let $(x, y, t)$ be the triple at the bottom of the deque. If $t = 0$, then the triple $(x, y, 0)$ is removed from the deque, $(a, b, 1)$ is inserted at the top of the deque, and the algorithm goes in state \$. If $t = 1$, the triple $(x, y, 1)$ is removed from the deque, the tuple $(x, y)$ is stored in an empty auxiliary cell, the triple $(a, b, 1)$ is put on to the top of the deque, and $D_k$ goes in state $y$.

(2) If the current input symbol is a leaf $\omega \in L$ and there is no tuple $(a, b)$ in an auxiliary cell $h \in H$ with $a = \omega$, then we know that we have to reduce a subtree in the subsequent steps which was not reduced in earlier steps or was reduced and then forgotten, because the corresponding triple was removed from the bottom of the deque. In this case, the triple $(\omega, \omega, 0)$ is inserted at the top of the deque, if the length of the deque list is less than $k$, the input pointer moves right and the state is unchanged. If the length of the deque list is equal to $k$ and the triple at the bottom of the deque is $(x, y, t)$, then $(x, y, t)$ is removed from the deque, $(x, y)$ is stored in an empty auxiliary cell, if $t = 1$, the triple $(\omega, \omega, 0)$ is put on to the top of the deque,

the input pointer moves right, and the algorithm goes in state $y$. If $t = 0$, the triple $(x, y, 0)$ will be forgotten, that is, the tuple $(x, y)$ is not stored in an auxiliary cell and the algorithm goes in state \$.

(3) If the current input symbol $i$ is an interior node of $T$, then we have to consider the following two cases:

    (3.1) If the length of the deque list is $d \in [2:k]$, then the string $(x, a, t_1)(y, b, t_2)$ at the top of the deque represents the left subtree $T_a^x$ and the right subtree $T_b^y$ of the tree $T_i^x$. At this stage, the input pointer moves right, the string at the top of the deque is replaced by $(x, i, t_1 \vee t_2)$, and the state is unchanged. Here, $t_1 \vee t_2$ is the disjunction of $t_1$ and $t_2$.

    (3.2) Let the length of the deque list equal one. The triple $(x, y, t)$ on the deque represents a subtree $T_y^x$. First let the algorithm in state $z \in I \cup L$. We know then that the last triple which was removed from the bottom of the deque and was stored as a tuple in an empty auxiliary cell $h$ has the form $(a, z, t')$. This triple represents a tree $T_z^a$. The node $z$ must be the left brother of $y$, because there is no other triple which was removed from the bottom of the deque after the deletion of $(a, z, t')$. Thus the input pointer moves right, the triple $(x, y, t)$ is replaced by $(a, i, 1)$, the auxiliary cell $h$ is cleared, and the algorithm goes in state \$. Next, if the algorithm is in state \$, then we do not know the left brother of $y$. In this case, the input pointer goes back to the first position of $PO(T)$, the triple $(x, y, t)$ is removed from the deque, $(x, y)$ is stored in an empty auxiliary cell, and the algorithm goes in state $y$.

To describe the algorithm $D_k$ precisely, we shall use the stylized notation similar to algorithm $S$ given in section 5.1.1.

ALGORITHM $D_k$
Input:    $PO(T) \subseteq (I \cup L)^*$.
Output:  A program which evaluates $T$.
Method:
(1) A 5-tuple $(z, j, \gamma, \mathbf{H}, \rho)$ will be used to denote a *configuration* of the algorithm:

    (a) $z \in I \cup L \cup \{\$\}, \$ \notin I \cup L$ denotes the contents of a special auxiliary cell; $z$ is called the state of the algorithm.
    (b) $j \in \mathbb{N}$ represents the location of the input pointer. We assume that the first 'input symbol' is the leftmost symbol in $PO(T)$.
    (c) $\gamma \in ((I \cup L) \times (I \cup L) \times \{0, 1\})^*$ represents the input-restricted deque list. The 'bottom' ('top') is assumed to be at the left (right) of $\gamma$. An item may be put on to the top and may be removed from the top or the bottom. The maximum length of the deque list is $k \in \mathbb{N}$. A deque list symbol $(a, b, t)$ represents the tree $T_b^a$.

(d) $\mathbf{H} \subseteq \{(a, b)_s \mid a, b \in I \cup L, \ s \in \mathbb{N}\}$ represents the contents of the non-empty cells in the auxiliary store. We assume that the cells are numbered $1, 2, 3, \ldots$ in some order for identification. The element $(a, b)_s \in \mathbf{H}$ indicates that the tuple $(a, b)$ representing the tree $T_b^a$ is stored in cell $s$. A tuple is always stored in the empty auxiliary cell with the lowest number.

(e) $\rho$ is a sequence of instructions of types (a), (b), and (c). The statement '$\mathrm{DO}\ A_{s-1} \leftarrow A_s\ s = \lambda, \eta;$' stands for a sequence of instructions of type (c), that is $A_{s-1} \leftarrow A_s$ for $\lambda \leqslant s \leqslant \eta$. If $\lambda > \eta$, this statement is to be interpreted as a dummy statement.

(2) If $(a, b, t)$ is a deque list symbol, then $t = 1$ $(t = 0)$ indicates that the reduction of the tree $T_b^a$ has required at least one (no) auxiliary cell. If $t = 0$, a triple $(a, b, t)$ deleted at the bottom of the deque will be 'forgotten'. If $t = 1$, the tuple $(a, b)$ will be stored in an empty auxiliary cell and the algorithm goes in state $b$. The algorithm will always be in state $z \in I \cup L$, if $(x, z, t)$ was the last triple which was removed from the bottom of the deque and was stored as the tuple $(x, z)$ in an empty auxiliary cell $h$, provided that $h$ was not cleared or no other triple was removed from the deque after the deletion of $(x, z, t)$. Otherwise, the algorithm is in state $.

(3) The contents of the first (second) component of an auxiliary cell with number $s$ is denoted by $pr_1(s)$ $(pr_2(s))$; if $j$ is the location of the input pointer, then $c(j)$ is the current input symbol. The notation '$\mathbf{H} \setminus \{s\}$' means that the auxiliary cell $s$ is cleared; similarly, '$\mathbf{H} \cup \{(x, y)_\eta\}$' indicates that the tuple $(x, y)$ is to be stored in the auxiliary cell $\eta$. Successive operations of this kind are performed from left to right.

(4) The initial configuration of the algorithm is $C_0 = (\$, 1, \varepsilon, \varnothing, \varepsilon)$.

(5) There are 10 types of steps. These steps will be described in terms of their effect on the configurations of the algorithm. The algorithm computes successive configurations defined by a 'goes to' relation $\perp$. The notation $(z, j, \gamma, \mathbf{H}, \rho) \perp (z', j', \gamma', \mathbf{H}', \rho')$ means that if the current configuration is $(z, j, \gamma, \mathbf{H}, \rho)$, then we are to go next into the configuration $(z', j', \gamma', \mathbf{H}', \rho')$. The 10 types of move are as follows:

(5.1) Let $c(j) \in L$.

    (5.1.1) There is an auxiliary cell $s$ with $pr_1(s) = c(j)$. Let $c(\mu) = pr_2(s)$.

        (5.1.1.1) If $l(\gamma) \leqslant k - 1$, then

$$(z, j, \gamma, \mathbf{H}, \rho) \perp$$
$$(\mathbf{z}, \mu + 1, \gamma(c(j), c(\mu), 1), \mathbf{H} \setminus \{s\}, \rho A_{l(\gamma)+1} \leftarrow M_s;)$$

(If $z = pr_2(s)$, then $\mathbf{z} = \$$; otherwise, $z = \mathbf{z}$.)

*Comment*: This move corresponds to (1) (with $l(\gamma) \leqslant k - 1$) in the informal description of the algorithm $D_k$.

        (5.1.1.2) If $l(\gamma) = k$ with $\gamma = \gamma'(x, y, t)$ and $c(\mu + 1) \in I$, then

$(z, j, \gamma, \mathbf{H}, \rho) \perp$

$\qquad (\mathbf{z}, \mu + 2, \gamma'(x, c(\mu + 1), 1), \mathbf{H}\backslash\{s\},$

$$\rho A_{l(\gamma)} \leftarrow A_{l(\gamma)} M_s c(\mu + 1);)$$

(If $z = pr_2(s)$, then $\mathbf{z} = \$$; otherwise, $z = \mathbf{z}$.)

*Comment:* This move corresponds to (1.1) in the informal description of the algorithm $D_k$.

(5.1.1.3) If $l(\gamma) = k$ with $\gamma = (x, y, 0)\gamma'$ and $c(\mu + 1) \in L$, then

$(z, j, \gamma, \mathbf{H}, \rho) \perp$

$\qquad (\$, \mu + 1, \gamma'(c(j), c(\mu), 1), \mathbf{H}\backslash\{s\},$

$\qquad\qquad \rho \text{ DO } A_{\lambda-1} \leftarrow A_\lambda \ \lambda = 2, k; A_k \leftarrow M_s;)$

*Comment:* This move corresponds to (1.2) (with $t = 0$) in the informal description of the algorithm $D_k$.

(5.1.1.4) If $l(\gamma) = k$ with $\gamma = (x, y, 1)\gamma'$ and $c(\mu + 1) \in L$, then

$(z, j, \gamma, \mathbf{H}, \rho) \perp$

$\qquad (y, \mu + 1, \gamma'(c(j), c(\mu), 1), \mathbf{H}\backslash\{s\} \cup \{(x, y)_\eta\},$

$\qquad\qquad \rho \ M_\eta \leftarrow A_1; \text{DO } A_{\lambda-1} \leftarrow A_\lambda \ \lambda = 2, k; A_k \leftarrow M_s;)$

*Comment:* This move corresponds to (1.2) (with $t = 1$) in the informal description of the algorithm $D_k$.

(5.1.2) There is no auxiliary cell $s$ with $pr_1(s) = c(j)$.

(5.1.2.1) If $l(\gamma) \leqslant k - 1$, then

$(z, j, \gamma, \mathbf{H}, \rho) \perp$

$\qquad (z, j + 1, \gamma(c(j), c(j), 0), \mathbf{H}, \rho \ A_{l(\gamma)+1} \leftarrow c(j);)$

*Comment:* This move corresponds to (2) (with $l(\gamma) \leqslant k - 1$) in the informal description of the algorithm $D_k$. Note also that this move corresponds to (4.1) in the definition of algorithm $S$ given in section 5.1.1.

(5.1.2.2) If $l(\gamma) = k$ with $\gamma = (x, y, 0)\gamma'$, then

$(z, j, \gamma, \mathbf{H}, \rho) \perp (\$, j + 1, \gamma'(c(j), c(j), 0), \mathbf{H},$

$\qquad\qquad \rho \text{ DO } A_{\lambda-1} \leftarrow A_\lambda \ \lambda = 2, k; A_k \leftarrow c(j);)$

*Comment:* This move corresponds to (2) (with $l(\gamma) = k$ and $t = 0$) in the informal description of the algorithm $D_k$.

(5.1.2.3) If $l(\gamma) = k$ with $\gamma = (x, y, 1)\gamma'$, then

$(z, j, \gamma, \mathbf{H}, \rho) \perp$

$\qquad (y, j + 1, \gamma'(c(j), c(j), 0), \mathbf{H} \cup \{(x, y)_\eta\},$

$\qquad\qquad \rho \ M_\eta \leftarrow A_1; \text{DO } A_{\lambda-1} \leftarrow A_\lambda \ \lambda = 2, k; A_k \leftarrow c(j);)$

*Comment:* This move corresponds to (2) (with $l(\gamma) = k$ and $t = 1$) in the informal description of the algorithm $D_k$.

(5.2) Let $c(j) \in I$.

    (5.2.1) If $2 \leqslant l(\gamma) \leqslant k$ with $\gamma = \gamma'(x, y, t_1)(a, b, t_2)$, then

$$(z, j, \gamma, \mathbf{H}, \rho) \perp (z, j+1, \gamma'(x, c(j), t_1 \vee t_2), \mathbf{H},$$
$$\rho \; A_{l(\gamma)-1} \leftarrow A_{l(\gamma)-1} A_{l(\gamma)} c(j);)$$

> *Comment:* This move corresponds to (3.1) in the informal description of the algorithm $D_k$. Note also that this move corresponds to (4.2) in the definition of algorithm $S$ given in section 5.1.1.

    (5.2.2) If $l(\gamma) = 1$ with $\gamma = (x, y, t)$ and there is an auxiliary cell $s$ with $pr_2(s) = z$, then

$$(z, j, \gamma, \mathbf{H}, \rho) \perp (\$, j+1, (pr_1(s), c(j), 1),$$
$$\mathbf{H} \backslash \{s\}, \rho \; A_1 \leftarrow M_s A_1 c(j);)$$

> *Comment:* This move corresponds to (3.2) (with $z \in I \cup L$) in the formal description of the algorithm $D_k$.

    (5.2.3) If $l(\gamma) = 1$ with $\gamma = (x, y, t)$ and $z = \$$, then

$$(z, j, \gamma, \mathbf{H}, \rho) \perp (y, 1, \varepsilon, \mathbf{H} \cup \{(x, y)_\eta\}, \rho \; M_\eta \leftarrow A_1;)$$

> *Comment:* This move corresponds to (3.2) (with $z = \$$) in the informal description of the algorithm $D_k$.

The execution of the algorithm $D_k$ is as follows:

*Step 1*    Starting in the initial configuration, compute successive configurations $C_0 \perp C_1 \perp C_2 \perp \cdots \perp C_i \perp \cdots$ until no further configuration can be computed.

*Step 2*    If the last computation is $(S, l(PO(T)) + 1, (x, r, t), \varnothing, \pi)$, emit $\pi$ and halt; $\pi$ is a program which evaluates $T = T_r^x$.

Note that the algorithm $D_k$ is deterministic for each $k \in \mathbb{N}$, that is, $D_k$ has at least one choice of move in any configuration. Obviously, if we number the deque list cells by $1, 2, 3, \ldots$ from the bottom, then the variable $A_m$ corresponds to the $m$-th cell; the variable $M_s$ corresponds to the auxiliary cell with number $s$.

    Let us consider the binary tree $T$ drawn in Figure 24. We have $I = \{a, c, d, e, h\}$, $L = \{b, f, g, j, k, p\}$, and $PO(T) = bfgdjkhpeca$. The algorithm $D_k$ computes the following sequence of configurations. For typographical reasons, we omit the fifth component in the configurations and give only the current instruction in each move.

165

(a) *Algorithm $D_1$*

| Configuration | Current instruction | Move |
|---|---|---|
| $(\$,1,\varepsilon,\varnothing) \perp (\$,2,(b,b,0),\varnothing)$ | $A_1 \leftarrow b;$ | (5.1.2.1) |
| $\perp (\$,3,(f,f,0),\varnothing)$ | $A_1 \leftarrow f;$ | (5.1.2.2) |
| $\perp (\$,4,(g,g,0),\varnothing)$ | $A_1 \leftarrow g;$ | (5.1.2.2) |
| $\perp (g,1,\varepsilon,\{(g,g)_1\})$ | $M_1 \leftarrow A_1;$ | (5.2.3) |
| $\perp (g,2,(b,b,0),\{(g,g)_1\})$ | $A_1 \leftarrow b;$ | (5.1.2.1) |
| $\perp (\$,3,(f,f,0),\{(g,g)_1\})$ | $A_1 \leftarrow f;$ | (5.1.2.2) |
| $\perp (\$,5,(f,d,1),\varnothing)$ | $A_1 \leftarrow A_1 M_1 d;$ | (5.1.1.2) |
| $\perp (d,6,(j,j,0),\{(f,d)_1\})$ | $M_1 \leftarrow A_1; A_1 \leftarrow j;$ | (5.1.2.3) |
| $\perp (\$,7,(k,k,0),\{(f,d)_1\})$ | $A_1 \leftarrow k;$ | (5.1.2.2) |
| $\perp (k,1,\varepsilon,\{(f,d)_1,(k,k)_2\})$ | $M_2 \leftarrow A_1;$ | (5.2.3) |
| $\perp (k,2,(b,b,0),\{(f,d)_1,(k,k)_2\})$ | $A_1 \leftarrow b;$ | (5.1.2.1) |
| $\perp (\$,5,(f,d,1),\{(k,k)_2\})$ | $A_1 \leftarrow M_1;$ | (5.1.1.3) |
| $\perp (d,6,(j,j,0),\{(f,d)_1,(k,k)_2\})$ | $M_1 \leftarrow A_1; A_1 \leftarrow j;$ | (5.1.2.3) |
| $\perp (d,8,(j,h,1),\{(f,d)_1\})$ | $A_1 \leftarrow A_1 M_2 h;$ | (5.1.1.2) |
| $\perp (h,9,(p,p,0),\{(f,d)_1,(j,h)_2\})$ | $M_2 \leftarrow A_1; A_1 \leftarrow p;$ | (5.1.2.3) |
| $\perp (\$,10,(j,e,1),\{(f,d)_1\})$ | $A_1 \leftarrow M_2 A_1 e;$ | (5.2.2) |
| $\perp (e,1,\varepsilon,\{(f,d)_1,(j,e)_2\})$ | $M_2 \leftarrow A_1;$ | (5.2.3) |
| $\perp (e,2,(b,b,0),\{(f,d)_1,(j,e)_2\})$ | $A_1 \leftarrow b;$ | (5.1.2.1) |
| $\perp (\$,5,(f,d,1),\{(j,e)_2\})$ | $A_1 \leftarrow M_1;$ | (5.1.1.3) |
| $\perp (\$,11,(f,c,1),\varnothing)$ | $A_1 \leftarrow A_1 M_2 c;$ | (5.1.1.2) |
| $\perp (c,1,\varepsilon,\{(f,c)_1\})$ | $M_1 \leftarrow A_1;$ | (5.2.3) |
| $\perp (c,2,(b,b,0),\{(f,c)_1\})$ | $A_1 \leftarrow b;$ | (5.1.2.1) |
| $\perp (\$,12,(b,a,1),\varnothing)$ | $A_1 \leftarrow A_1 M_1 a;$ | (5.1.1.2) |

(b) *Algorithm $D_2$*

| Configuration | Current instruction | Move |
|---|---|---|
| $(\$,1,\varepsilon,\varnothing) \perp (\$,2,(b,b,0),\varnothing)$ | $A_1 \leftarrow b;$ | (5.1.2.1) |
| $\perp (\$,3,(b,b,0)(f,f,0),\varnothing)$ | $A_2 \leftarrow f;$ | (5.1.2.1) |
| $\perp (\$,4,(f,f,0)(g,g,0),\varnothing)$ | $A_1 \leftarrow A_2; A_2 \leftarrow g;$ | (5.1.2.2) |
| $\perp (\$,5,(f,d,0),\varnothing)$ | $A_1 \leftarrow A_1 A_2 d;$ | (5.2.1) |
| $\perp (\$,6,(f,d,0)(j,j,0),\varnothing)$ | $A_2 \leftarrow j;$ | (5.1.2.1) |
| $\perp (\$,7,(j,j,0)(k,k,0),\varnothing)$ | $A_1 \leftarrow A_2; A_2 \leftarrow k;$ | (5.1.2.2) |
| $\perp (\$,8,(j,h,0),\varnothing)$ | $A_1 \leftarrow A_1 A_2 h;$ | (5.2.1) |
| $\perp (\$,9,(j,h,0)(p,p,0),\varnothing)$ | $A_2 \leftarrow p;$ | (5.1.2.1) |
| $\perp (\$,10,(j,e,0),\varnothing)$ | $A_1 \leftarrow A_1 A_2 e;$ | (5.2.1) |
| $\perp (e,1,\varepsilon,\{(j,e)_1\})$ | $M_1 \leftarrow A_1;$ | (5.2.3) |
| $\perp (e,2,(b,b,0),\{(j,e)_1\})$ | $A_1 \leftarrow b;$ | (5.1.2.1) |
| $\perp (e,3,(b,b,0)(f,f,0),\{(j,e)_1\})$ | $A_2 \leftarrow f;$ | (5.1.2.1) |
| $\perp (\$,4,(f,f,0)(g,g,0),\{(j,e)_1\})$ | $A_1 \leftarrow A_2; A_2 \leftarrow g;$ | (5.1.2.2) |
| $\perp (\$,5,(f,d,0),\{(j,e)_1\})$ | $A_1 \leftarrow A_1 A_2 d;$ | (5.2.1) |
| $\perp (\$,10,(f,d,0)(j,e,1),\varnothing)$ | $A_2 \leftarrow M_1;$ | (5.1.1.1) |

| | | |
|---|---|---|
| $\perp (\$, 11, (f, c, 1), \varnothing)$ | $A_1 \leftarrow A_1 A_2 c;$ | (5.2.1) |
| $\perp (c, 1, \varepsilon, \{(f, c)_1\})$ | $M_1 \leftarrow A_1;$ | (5.2.3) |
| $\perp (c, 2, (b, b, 0), \{(f, c)_1\})$ | $A_1 \leftarrow b;$ | (5.1.2.1) |
| $\perp (\$, 12, (b, a, 1), \varnothing)$ | $A_1 \leftarrow A_1 M_1 a;$ | (5.1.1.2) |

(c) *Algorithm* $D_3$

| Configuration | Current instruction | Move |
|---|---|---|
| $(\$, 1, \varepsilon, \varnothing) \perp (\$, 2, (b, b, 0), \varnothing)$ | $A_1 \leftarrow b;$ | (5.1.2.1) |
| $\perp (\$, 3, (b, b, 0)(f, f, 0), \varnothing)$ | $A_2 \leftarrow f;$ | (5.1.2.1) |
| $\perp (\$, 4, (b, b, 0)(f, f, 0)(g, g, 0), \varnothing)$ | $A_3 \leftarrow g;$ | (5.1.2.1) |
| $\perp (\$, 5, (b, b, 0)(f, d, 0), \varnothing)$ | $A_2 \leftarrow A_2 A_3 d;$ | (5.2.1) |
| $\perp (\$, 6, (b, b, 0)(f, d, 0)(j, j, 0), \varnothing)$ | $A_3 \leftarrow j;$ | (5.1.2.1) |
| $\perp (\$, 7, (f, d, 0)(j, j, 0)(k, k, 0), \varnothing)$ | $A_1 \leftarrow A_2; A_2 \leftarrow A_3;$ | (5.1.2.2) |
| | $A_3 \leftarrow k;$ | |
| $\perp (\$, 8, (f, d, 0)(j, h, 0), \varnothing)$ | $A_2 \leftarrow A_2 A_3 h;$ | (5.2.1) |
| $\perp (\$, 9, (f, d, 0)(j, h, 0)(p, p, 0), \varnothing)$ | $A_3 \leftarrow p;$ | (5.1.2.1) |
| $\perp (\$, 10, (f, d, 0)(j, e, 0), \varnothing)$ | $A_2 \leftarrow A_2 A_3 e;$ | (5.2.1) |
| $\perp (\$, 11, (f, c, 0), \varnothing)$ | $A_1 \leftarrow A_1 A_2 c;$ | (5.2.1) |
| $\perp (c, 1, \varepsilon, \{(f, c)_1\})$ | $M_1 \leftarrow A_1;$ | (5.2.3) |
| $\perp (c, 2, (b, b, 0), \{(f, c)_1\})$ | $A_1 \leftarrow b;$ | (5.1.2.1) |
| $\perp (\$, 11, (b, b, 0)(f, c, 1), \varnothing)$ | $A_2 \leftarrow M_1;$ | (5.1.1.1) |
| $\perp (\$, 12, (b, a, 1), \varnothing)$ | $A_1 \leftarrow A_1 A_2 a;$ | (5.2.1) |

Thus the reduction of the tree $T$ by algorithm $D_k$ requires a deque list of length one and two auxiliary cells; therefore, $D_1$ emits a 3-program which evaluates $T$. Similarly, algorithm $D_2$ ($D_3$) requires a deque list of length two (three) and one auxiliary cell; $D_2$ produces a 3-program, $D_3$ a 4-program for $T$. Obviously, $D_k$ is a possible generalization of algorithm $S$ given in section 5.1.1: $D_k$ with no auxiliary cell always reduces a given tree $T$, if the algorithm $S$ produces a program with $\lambda \leqslant k$ variables, because in this case algorithm $D_k$ is identical to algorithm $S$; in other words, the deque can be interpreted as a stack. Thus $D_k$ with $k \geqslant 4$ reduces the above tree $T$ with a deque list of length four and no auxiliary cell; the program for $T$ produced by these algorithms is identical to that produced by algorithm $S$ in section 5.1.1. Note that the tree cannot be reduced by $D_1$ with one auxiliary cell, because $D_1$ stops in configuration $(\$, 7, (k, k, 0), \{(f, d)_1\})$. Generally, $D_k$ with $i$ auxiliary cells reduces trees which cannot be reduced by $D_{k+i}$ and no auxiliary cell. Considering the execution of $D_k$, it is easy to see that a tree $T = T_r^y$ is reduced if the left subtree $T_1 = T_x^y$ and the right subtree $T_2 = T_a^b$ is already reduced. The correctness of algorithm $D_k$ should be obvious; the formal proof consists in the main of an induction proof on the length of $PO(T)$, because in general $PO(T) = PO(T_1)PO(T_2)r$. Finally, we will note that the use of the auxiliary cell

$Z$ representing the state of $D_k$ is not really necessary; $D_k$ also works correctly if we eliminate the first component of the configurations and all references to this component. However, on doing this, the following results become rather complicated.

Henceforth, we shall say that a binary tree $T$ is a $(k, i)$-*tree*, if $T$ can be reduced by algorithm $D_k$ with exactly $i$ auxiliary cells. The set of all $(k, i)$-trees is denoted by $T(k, i)$. The following lemma gives a characterization of the set $T(k, i)$. The simple proof is left to the reader (Exercise 5.6).

LEMMA 5.1 Let $T$ be an ordered binary tree with the left-hand subtree $T_1$ and the right-hand subtree $T_2$. We have

$$T \in T(k, 0) \Leftrightarrow T_1 \in T(k, 0) \wedge (\exists j \in [1:k-1])(T_2 \in T(j, 0))$$

$$\vee (\exists j \in [1:k-1])(T_1 \in T(j, 0)) \wedge T_2 \in T(k-1, 0). \tag{a}$$

$$T \in T(k, 1) \Leftrightarrow T_1 \in T(k, 1) \wedge (\exists j \in [1:k])(T_2 \in T(j, 0))$$

$$\vee (\exists j \in [1:k])(T_1 \in T(j, 0)) \wedge T_2 \in T(k, 1)$$

$$\vee (\exists j \in [1:k])(T_1 \in T(j, 0)) \wedge T_2 \in T(k, 0). \tag{b}$$

Let $i \geqslant 2$.

$$T \in T(k, i) \Leftrightarrow T_1 \in T(k, i) \wedge (\exists j \in [1:k-1])(\exists m \in [0:i-1])(T_2 \in T(j, 0) \cup T(k, m))$$

$$\vee (\exists j \in [1:k])(T_1 \in T(j, 0)) \wedge T_2 \in T(k, i)$$

$$\vee (\exists m \in [1:i-1])(T_1 \in T(k, m)) \wedge T_2 \in T(k, i-1). \quad \blacksquare \tag{c}$$

We are now ready to prove the following theorem.

THEOREM 5.11 Let $T(n, k, i)$ be the set of all $(k, i)$-trees with $n$ leaves and let $t(n, k, i) = \mathrm{card}(T(n, k, i))$. We have

$$t(n, k, i) = \sum_{1 \leqslant j \leqslant (i+1)(k+1)-1} t(n, j, 0) - \sum_{1 \leqslant j \leqslant i(k+1)-1} t(n, j, 0)$$

for $i \geqslant 1$ and $k \geqslant 1$.

*Proof* Let $H_n(k, i) = \sum_{1 \leqslant j \leqslant k} t(n, j, i)$ and let $F_i(k, z) = \sum_{n \geqslant 1} H_n(k, i)z^n$ be the generating function of the numbers $H_n(k, i)$. We have to prove

$$t(n, k, i) = H_n((i+1)(k+1)-1, 0) - H_n(i(k+1)-1, 0).$$

For this purpose, set $\Delta_i(k, z) = F_i(k, z) - F_i(k-1, z)$. Thus

$$\Delta_i(k, z) = \sum_{n \geqslant 1} t(n, k, i)z^n.$$

Translating the recurrences given in Lemma 5.1 into terms of these generating functions, we immediately find

$$\Delta_0(k, z) = F_0(k - 1, z)[\Delta_0(k, z) + \Delta_0(k - 1, z)]. \tag{a}$$

$$\Delta_1(k, z) = 2\Delta_1(k, z)F_0(k, z) + F_0(k, z)\Delta_0(k, z). \tag{b}$$

$$\Delta_i(k, z) = 2\Delta_i(k, z)F_0(k, z) + [\Delta_i(k, z) + \Delta_{i-1}(k, z)] \sum_{1 \leqslant r < i} \Delta_r(k, z),$$
$$i \geqslant 2. \tag{c}$$

Using the definition of $\Delta_0(k, z)$, relation (a) is equivalent to

$$F_0(k, z) - F_0(k, z)F_0(k - 1, z) = F_0(k - 1, z) - F_0(k - 1, z)F_0(k - 2, z).$$

Hence the sequence $F_0(k, z) - F_0(k, z)F_0(k - 1, z)$ is a constant sequence. Since $F_0(1, z) = z$, we find the recurrence $F_0(k, z) = z/[1 - F_0(k - 1, z)]$ which we have already studied in sections 4.3.1 and 4.4.2; as expected, $F_0(k, z)$ is the generating function of the number of all ordered binary trees with $n$ leaves which can be reduced by algorithm $S$ given in section 5.1.1 requiring less than or equal to $k$ variables. Hence

$$F_0(k, z) = 2z \frac{(1 + \sqrt{1 - 4z})^k - (1 - \sqrt{1 - 4z})^k}{(1 + \sqrt{1 - 4z})^{k+1} - (1 - \sqrt{1 - 4z})^{k+1}}, \qquad k \geqslant 1.$$

Inserting the definition of $\Delta_i(k, z)$ into equations (b) and (c), we obtain with Exercise 4.12

$$\Delta_1(k, z) = [F_0^2(k, z) - F_0(k, z)F_0(k - 1, z)]/[1 - 2F_0(k, z)]$$
$$= F_0(2k + 1, z) - F_0(k, z)$$

and

$$\Delta_i(k, z) = \frac{[F_0(i(k + 1) - 1, z) - F_0((i - 1)(k + 1) - 1, z)]}{1 - F_0(k, z) - F_0(i(k + 1) - 1, z)} [F_0(i(k + 1) - 1, z) - F_0(k, z)]$$
$$= F_0((i + 1)(k + 1) - 1, z) - F_0(i(k + 1) - 1, z)$$

for $i \geqslant 2$.

These relations imply the result stated in the theorem. ∎

COROLLARY  The number of all ordered binary trees with $n$ leaves which can be reduced by algorithm $D_k$ requiring a deque list of length $k$ and exactly $i$ ($\geqslant 1$) auxiliary cells is equal to the number of all ordered binary trees with $n$ leaves which can be reduced by algorithm $S$ requiring a stack list of length $m$, where $m \in [(k + 1)i:(k + 1)(i + 1) - 1]$. ∎

It is not hard to see that this fact is only a connection between the cardinalities of the corresponding classes of trees. In general, the corresponding sets are different. Since $\sum_{1 \leqslant j \leqslant k} t(n, j, 0)$ is the number of binary trees with $n$ leaves which can be reduced by $D_k$ without any auxiliary cell, that is, the number $t(n, k)$ of trees which can be reduced by algorithm $S$ with a stack of length less than or equal to $k$, we can use the expression for $t(n, k)$ given in section 5.1.1 in order to obtain an explicit expression for $t(n, k, i)$. With Theorem 5.11, we obtain the following theorem.

THEOREM 5.12   The number $t(n, k, i)$ of all $(k, i)$-trees with $n$ leaves is given by

$$t(n, k, i) = \psi_0(n, k, i) - 2\psi_1(n, k, i) + \psi_2(n, k, i),$$

where

$$\psi_a(n, k, i) = \sum_{\lambda \geqslant 1} \left[ \binom{2n - 2}{n - a - \lambda i(k + 1)} - \binom{2n - 2}{n - a - \lambda(i + 1)(k + 1)} \right]$$

and $n, k, i \in \mathbb{N}$.  ∎

Generally, the algorithm $D_k$ with $i$ auxiliary cells does not only reduce all ordered binary trees with $n$ leaves. We shall now derive a condition for $n, k, i$ such that $D_k$ with $i$ auxiliary cells reduces all trees with $n$ leaves. The algorithm $D_k$ with $i$ auxiliary cells reduces the trees in $T(k, i)$ and all trees which require a deque list of length less than $k$ or a deque list of length $k$ and less than or equal to $i$ auxiliary cells. Thus $D_k$ reduces all trees $T \in \bigcup_{1 \leqslant j \leqslant k} T(j, 0) \cup \bigcup_{1 \leqslant r \leqslant i} T(k, r)$.

Now let $\mathrm{RED}(n, k, i)$ be the number of these trees with $n$ leaves. Since the sets $T(n, 1, 0)$, $T(n, 2, 0)$, $\ldots$, $T(n, k, 0)$, $T(n, k, 1)$, $T(n, k, 2)$, $\ldots$, $T(n, k, i)$ are mutually disjoint, we immediately obtain

$$\mathrm{RED}(n, k, i) = \sum_{1 \leqslant j \leqslant k} t(n, j, 0) + \sum_{1 \leqslant \lambda \leqslant i} t(n, k, \lambda)$$

or with Theorem 5.11

$$\mathrm{RED}(n, k, i) = \sum_{1 \leqslant j \leqslant k} t(n, j, 0)$$

$$+ \sum_{1 \leqslant \lambda \leqslant i} \left[ \sum_{1 \leqslant j \leqslant (\lambda + 1)(k + 1) - 1} t(n, j, 0) - \sum_{1 \leqslant j \leqslant \lambda(k + 1) - 1} t(n, j, 0) \right]$$

$$= \sum_{1 \leqslant j \leqslant (i + 1)(k + 1) - 1} t(n, j, 0).$$

Hence we have proved the following theorem.

THEOREM 5.13   The number of ordered binary trees with $n$ leaves which can be reduced by algorithm $D_k$ requiring less than or equal to $i$ auxiliary cells is equal to the number of all ordered binary trees with $n$ leaves which can be reduced by algorithm $S$ requiring a stack of maximum length $(i + 1)(k + 1) - 1$.  ∎

Since $t(n, j, 0)$ is equal to the number $t(n, j)$ of trees which can be reduced by algorithm $S$ with a stack list of length less than or equal to $j$, we can use the explicit expression for $t(n, k)$, given in section 5.1.1, in order to obtain an explicit expression for $\mathrm{RED}(n, k, i)$.

COROLLARY We have

$$\text{RED}(n,k,i) = t(n) - [\xi_0(n,k,i) - 2\xi_1(n,k,i) + \xi_2(n,k,i)]$$

where

$$t(n) = \frac{1}{n}\binom{2n-2}{n-1} \quad \text{and} \quad \xi_a(n,k,i) = \sum_{\lambda \geqslant 1}\binom{2n-2}{n-a-\lambda(k+1)(i+1)}. \quad \blacksquare$$

If $k \geqslant n$, the sum $\sum_{1 \leqslant j \leqslant k} t(n,j,0)$ is the number $t(n)$ of all ordered binary trees with $n$ leaves. Since

$$\text{RED}(n,k,i) = \sum_{1 \leqslant j \leqslant (i+1)(k+1)-1} t(n,j,0),$$

we further obtain the following theorem.

THEOREM 5.14 For each $k \geqslant 1$, algorithm $D_k$ reduces all ordered binary trees with $n$ leaves if and only if $D_k$ has at least $\lfloor n/(k+1) \rfloor$ auxiliary cells. The computed programs have at most $k + \lfloor n/(k+1) \rfloor$ variables. $\quad \blacksquare$

Note that $D_n$ requires no auxiliary cell; in this case, $D_n$ is identical to algorithm $S$ given in section 5.1.1. Since the function $f(k) = k + \lfloor n/(k+1) \rfloor$ has surely a minimum at $k = \lfloor \sqrt{n} \rfloor$, we further obtain the corollary.

COROLLARY Among all algorithms $D_k$, $D_{\lfloor \sqrt{n} \rfloor}$ with $\lfloor n/(\lfloor \sqrt{n} \rfloor + 1) \rfloor$ auxiliary cells reduces all ordered binary trees with $n$ leaves and requires a minimum number of deque list and auxiliary cells. The programs have at most $\lfloor \sqrt{n} \rfloor + \lfloor n/(\lfloor \sqrt{n} \rfloor + 1) \rfloor$ variables. $\quad \blacksquare$

Let us now briefly discuss the average case behaviour of algorithm $D_k$. Since $t(n,k,0)$ is equal to $t(n,k)$, we can apply Theorems 5.5 and 5.13 in order to obtain an expression for the cumulative distribution function.

THEOREM 5.15 Assuming that all ordered binary trees with $n$ leaves are equally likely, the probability $V_n(k,i)$ that a tree can be reduced by algorithm $D_k$ with $i$ auxiliary cells is asymptotically given by

$$V_n(k,i) = 1 - \sum_{\lambda \geqslant 1}\left[4\lambda^2 \frac{(k+1)^2(i+1)^2}{n} - 2\right]$$
$$\times \exp(-\lambda^2(k+1)^2(i+1)^2/n) + O(n^{-1/2+\delta})$$

for all $\delta > 0$. $\quad \blacksquare$

For example, using the numerical values given in Table 3, we see that, in the average case, 99.58 per cent of all trees can be reduced by algorithm $D_k$ with $i$ auxiliary cells provided that $(i+1)(k+1) = 3\sqrt{n}$. Thus 99.58 per cent of all trees with $n$ leaves can be reduced by $D_1$ with approximately $\frac{3}{2}\sqrt{n} - 1$ auxiliary cells, or by $D_2$ with approximately $\sqrt{n} - 1$ auxiliary cells etc. Let us now assume that the algorithm $D_k$ has $\lfloor n/(k+1) \rfloor$ auxiliary cells, that is, $D_k$ can reduce all ordered binary trees with $n$ leaves. We now turn to the average number of auxiliary cells required by $D_k$ during the reduction of a tree with $n$ leaves. Assuming that all these trees are equally likely, the quotient $p_k(n,i) = t(n,k,i)/t(n)$ is the probability that the reduction of a $n$-node tree by $D_k$ uses exactly $i$ auxiliary cells. Therefore, the average number of auxiliary cells required by $D_k$ during the reduction of a tree with $n$ leaves is given by $h_k(n)$, where

$$h_k(n) = \sum_{1 \leqslant i \leqslant \lfloor n/(k+1) \rfloor} i p_k(n, i).$$

Using the definition of $p_k(n, i)$ and Theorem 5.11, this expression can be easily transformed into

$$h_k(n) = \lfloor n/(k+1) \rfloor - t^{-1}(n) \sum_{1 \leqslant i \leqslant \lfloor n/(k+1) \rfloor} \sum_{1 \leqslant j < i(k+1)} t(n, j, 0)$$

$$= \sum_{i \geqslant 1} \sum_{j \geqslant 1} \left[ 4 \frac{j^2 i^2 (k+1)^2}{n} - 2 \right] \binom{2n}{n - ji(k+1)} \bigg/ \binom{2n}{n},$$

because $t(n, j, 0) = t(n, j)$, where $t(n, j)$ is given in section 5.1.1. An application of the approximation (F5) (section 5.1.1) to the quotient $\binom{2n}{n - ji(k+1)} \big/ \binom{2n}{n}$ leads immediately to the following theorem (Exercise 5.8).

THEOREM 5.16 Assuming that all ordered binary trees with $n$ leaves are equally likely, the average number $h_k(n)$ of auxiliary cells used by algorithm $D_k$ during the reduction of a binary tree with $n$ leaves is asymptotically given by

$$h_k(n) = \begin{cases} O(\exp(-n^{2\beta})) & \text{if } k \geqslant n^{1/2+\varepsilon} \\[2mm] \sum_{R \geqslant 1} d(R)[4R^2 c^2 - 2] \exp(-R^2 c^2) + O(n^{-1/2+\delta}) & \text{if } k = c\sqrt{n},\, c > 0 \\[2mm] \sqrt{\pi n}/(k+1) - \frac{1}{2} + O(n^{-1/2+\delta}/(k+1)) & \text{if } k \leqslant n^{1/2-\varepsilon},\, 0 < \varepsilon \leqslant \frac{1}{2} \end{cases}$$

for all fixed $\varepsilon > 0$, $\delta > 0$, $\beta > 0$. The arithmetical function $d(n)$ is the number of all positive divisors of the natural number $n$. ∎

Let us now turn to the average number of auxiliary cells and deque list cells required by algorithm $D_k$ during the reduction of a binary tree with $n$ leaves. There are $t(n, j, 0)$, $1 \leqslant j \leqslant k$, trees using exactly $j$ deque list cells and no auxiliary cell; there are $t(n, k, i)$, $1 \leqslant i \leqslant \lfloor n/(k+1) \rfloor$, trees requiring exactly $k$ deque list cells and exactly $i$ auxiliary cells. Thus considering all binary trees with $n$ leaves to be equally likely, the average number of auxiliary cells and deque list cells required by $D_k$ during the reduction of a tree with $n$ leaves is given by

$$e_k(n) = t^{-1}(n)\left[\sum_{1 \leqslant j \leqslant k} jt(n, j, 0) + \sum_{1 \leqslant i \leqslant \lfloor n/(k+1)\rfloor} (k+i)t(n, k, i)\right].$$

Using the above formulas for $t(n, j, 0)$ and $t(n, k, i)$, this expression can be easily transformed into $e_k(n) = h_k(n) + q_k(n)$, where

$$q_k(n) = k - t^{-1}(n) \sum_{1 \leqslant \lambda \leqslant k-1} \sum_{1 \leqslant j \leqslant \lambda} t(n, j, 0)$$

$$= \sum_{1 \leqslant \lambda \leqslant k} \sum_{j \geqslant 1} \left[4\frac{j^2\lambda^2}{n} - 2\right]\binom{2n}{n-j\lambda} \bigg/ \binom{2n}{n}.$$

A similar proof to that of Theorem 5.17 leads to (Exercise 5.9) the following lemma.

LEMMA 5.2   The numbers $q_k(n)$ have the following asymptotic behaviour:

$$q_k(n) = \begin{cases} \sqrt{\pi n} - \frac{1}{2} + O(n^{-1+\delta}) & \text{if } k \geqslant n^{1/2+\varepsilon} \\ b\sqrt{n} + O(n^{-1/2+\delta}) & \text{if } k = c\sqrt{n}, c > 0 \\ k + O(kn^{-1+\delta}) & \text{if } k \leqslant n^{1/2-\varepsilon}, 0 < \varepsilon \leqslant \frac{1}{2} \end{cases}$$

for all fixed $\varepsilon > 0$ and $\delta > 0$. Here,

$$c \sum_{R \geqslant 1} (4R^2c^2 - 2)\exp(-R^2c^2) < b \leqslant c. \quad \blacksquare$$

Theorem 5.16 and Lemma 5.2 imply the following theorem.

THEOREM 5.17   Assuming that all ordered binary trees with $n$ leaves are equally likely, the average number $e_k(n)$ of auxiliary cells and deque list cells required by algorithm $D_k$ during the reduction of a tree with $n$ leaves is asymptotically given by

$$e_k(n) = \begin{cases} \sqrt{\pi n} - \frac{1}{2} + O(n^{-1+\delta}) & \text{if } k \geqslant n^{1/2+\varepsilon} \\ b\sqrt{n} + \sum_{R \geqslant 1} d(R)[4R^2c^2 - 2]\exp(-R^2c^2) + O(n^{-1/2+\delta}) & \\ & \text{if } k = c\sqrt{n}, c > 0 \\ k + \sqrt{\pi n}/(k+1) + O(n^{-1/2+\delta}) & \text{if } k \leqslant n^{1/2-\varepsilon}, 0 < \varepsilon \leqslant \frac{1}{2} \end{cases}$$

for all fixed $\varepsilon > 0$ and $\delta > 0$. Here,

$$c \sum_{R \geqslant 1} (4R^2c^2 - 2)\exp(-R^2c^2) < b \leqslant c. \quad \blacksquare$$

Since the function $f(k) = k + (k+1)^{-1}\sqrt{\pi n} - \frac{1}{2}$ has a minimum at $k = (\pi n)^{1/4} - 1$, Theorem 5.17 implies the following corollary.

COROLLARY  Assume that all ordered binary trees with $n$ leaves are equally likely. Among all algorithms $D_k$, $D_{k'}$ with $k' = (\pi n)^{1/4} - 1$ requires a minimum number of deque list and auxiliary cells, on average. The programs produced by $D_{k'}$ have $2(\pi n)^{1/4} - \frac{3}{2}$ variables, on average.  ■

In this chapter we have discussed three different strategies for the reduction of ordered binary trees. These reductions are closely related to the process of code generation in compilers and, in general, to the evaluation of a tree according to its structure. Although we have given a detailed analysis of the space complexity of these algorithms in the worst and average case, several questions are still waiting to be resolved (see Exercises). We have seen that the analysis of these algorithms has provided excellent examples of the application of the gamma function method of asymptotic analysis.

### 5.2 Two Algorithms for the Recognition of Dycklanguages

Let $B_k$, $\mathbf{B}_k$ be two finite sets with cardinality $k \in \mathbb{N}$ and let $\psi : B_k \to \bar{B}_k$ be a bijection. The *Dycklanguage* $DY_k$ with $k$ types of *brackets* is the formal language $DY_k \subseteq (B_k \cup \mathbf{B}_k)^*$ recursively defined by

(a) $\varepsilon \in DY_k$;
(b) $(\forall b \in B_k)(w \in DY_k \Rightarrow bw\psi(b) \in DY_k)$;
(c) $(\forall u, v \in DY_k)(uv \in DY_k)$;
(d) $DY_k$ is minimal with (a), (b), (c).

Here, $w \in DY_k$ is called a *Dyckword*. The set of all Dyckwords $w \in DY_k$ of length $2N$ is denoted by $DY_k(2N)$, the cardinality of $DY_k(2N)$ by $d_k(2N)$. Given $w \in DY_k$, the tuple $(b, \bar{b}) \in B_k \times \mathbf{B}_k$ is a *pair of brackets in* $w$ if and only if $w$ has the form $w = xby\bar{b}z$ with $\bar{b} = \psi(b)$ and $y \in DY_k$. Obviously, each Dyckword $w \in DY_k(2N)$ consists of $N$ pairs of brackets. Dycklanguages play an important part in the theory of formal languages ([53]).

Now let $\mathfrak{P}$ be an algorithm which needs $T_{\mathfrak{P}}(w)$ units of time and $L_{\mathfrak{P}}(w)$ units of space in order to scan $w \in DY_k$. We define the *maximum time* $T_{\mathfrak{P}}(2N)$ and the *maximum space* $L_{\mathfrak{P}}(2N)$ for the recognition of a Dyckword $w \in DY_k(2N)$ by $T_{\mathfrak{P}}(2N) = \text{MAX}_{w \in DY_k(2N)} (T_{\mathfrak{P}}(w))$ and $L_{\mathfrak{P}}(2N) = \text{MAX}_{w \in DY_k(2N)} (L_{\mathfrak{P}}(w))$. Assuming that all Dyckwords of length $2N$ are equally likely, the average time $\mathbf{T}_{\mathfrak{P}}(2N)$ and the average space $\mathbf{L}_{\mathfrak{P}}(2N)$ for the recognition of a Dyckword $w \in DY_k(2N)$ by algorithm $\mathfrak{P}$ is defined by

$$\mathbf{T}_{\mathfrak{P}}(2N) = d_k^{-1}(2N) \sum_{w \in DY_k(2N)} T_{\mathfrak{P}}(w)$$

and

$$\mathbf{L}_{\mathfrak{P}}(2N) = d_k^{-1}(2N) \sum_{w \in DY_k(2N)} L_{\mathfrak{P}}(w).$$

### 5.2.1 The Recognition by a Stack

A customary method for the recognition of the Dycklanguage $DY_k$ is the following algorithm $DS$ using a stack.

Algorithm $DS$

Input:   $w \in (B_k \cup \mathbf{B}_k)^{2N}$.

Output:  $w \in DY_k$ or $w \notin DY_k$.

Method:

(1) A triple $(q, j, \gamma)$ will be used to denote a configuration of the algorithm:

    (a) $q$ is a state of the algorithm.

    (b) $j \in \mathbb{N}$ represents the location of the input pointer. We assume that the first 'input symbol' is the leftmost symbol in $w$. The current input symbol is denoted by $c(j)$.

    (c) $\gamma \in (B_k \cup \mathbf{B}_k)^*$ represents the stack list. The 'top' is assumed to be at the right of $\gamma$.

(2) The initial configuration of the algorithm is $C_0 = (q_0, 1, \varepsilon)$.

(3) There are three types of steps. These steps will be described in terms of their effect on the configurations of the algorithm. The algorithm computes successive configurations defined by a 'goes to' relation $\perp$. The notation $(q, j, \gamma) \perp (q', j', \gamma')$ means that if the current configuration is $(q, j, \gamma)$, then we are to go next into the configuration $(q', j', \gamma')$. The three types of move are as follows:

    (3.1) Let $c(j) \in B_k$. Then $(q_0, j, \gamma) \perp (q_0, j + 1, \gamma c(j))$.

    (3.2) Let $c(j) \in \mathbf{B}_k$. Then $(q_0, j, \gamma) \perp (q_1, j + 1, \gamma c(j))$.

    (3.3) Let $\gamma = \gamma' b \psi(b)$ with $b \in B_k$. Then $(q_1, j, \gamma) \perp (q_0, j, \gamma')$.

The execution of the algorithm $DS$ is as follows:

*Step 1*   Starting in the initial configuration, compute successive configurations $C_0 \perp C_1 \perp \cdots \perp C_i \perp \cdots$ until no further configuration can be computed.

*Step 2*   If the last configuration is $(q_0, 2N + 1, \varepsilon)$, then $w \in DY_k$; otherwise, $w \notin DY_k$.

For example, let $N = 4$, $B_2 = \{[, \langle\}$, $\mathbf{B}_2 = \{], \rangle\}$, $\psi([) = ]$ and $\psi(\langle) = \rangle$. Choosing $w = [\langle\rangle]\langle\rangle[\ ]$, we find

$$(q_0, 1, \varepsilon) \underset{(3.1)}{\perp} (q_0, 2, [) \underset{(3.1)}{\perp} (q_0, 3, [\langle) \underset{(3.2)}{\perp} (q_1, 4, [\langle\rangle) \underset{(3.3)}{\perp} (q_0, 4, [)$$

$$\underset{(3.2)}{\perp} (q_1, 5, []) \underset{(3.3)}{\perp} (q_0, 5, \varepsilon) \underset{(3.1)}{\perp} (q_0, 6, \langle) \underset{(3.2)}{\perp} (q_1, 7, \langle\rangle)$$

$$\underset{(3.3)}{\perp} (q_0, 7, \varepsilon) \underset{(3.1)}{\perp} (q_0, 8, [) \underset{(3.2)}{\perp} (q_1, 9, []) \underset{(3.3)}{\perp} (q_0, 9, \varepsilon).$$

Hence $w \in DY_2(8)$. For $w' = [\langle]\rangle\langle\rangle[]$, we obtain

$$(q_0, 1, \varepsilon) \underset{(3.1)}{\perp} (q_0, 2, [) \underset{(3.1)}{\perp} (q_0, 3, [\langle) \underset{(3.2)}{\perp} (q_1, 4, [\langle]).$$

Thus $w' \notin DY_2(8)$.

An appropriate measure for the time $T_{DS}(w)$, $w \in DY_k(2N)$, of algorithm $DS$ is the number of moves of the input pointer during the recognition of $w$. We find immediately that $T_{DS}(w) = 2N$ for all $w \in DY_k(2N)$. Thus the maximum time is given by $T_{DS}(2N) = 2N$ for an input of length $2N$.

The space $L_{DS}(w)$, $w \in DY_k(2N)$, of the algorithm $DS$ is the length of the stack required for recognizing the Dyckword $w$. In the worst case, we have $L_{DS}(w) = N + 1$ satisfied by $w \in B_k^N \mathbf{B}_k^N$. Hence $L_{DS}(2N) = N + 1$. Using Exercise 5.10, each Dyckword $w \in DY_k(2N)$ corresponds to one of the $\dfrac{1}{N+1}\dbinom{2N}{N}$ binary trees with $(N + 1)$ leaves and vice versa. Each replacement of a pair of brackets in $w \in DY_1(2N)$ by one of the $k$ possibilities $(b, \psi(b)) \in B_k \times \mathbf{B}_k$ generates a Dyckword $w \in DY_k(2N)$. These facts imply immediately

$$d_k(2N) = k^N \frac{1}{N+1}\binom{2N}{N}.$$

Furthermore, the above one-to-one correspondence between the Dyckwords of length $2N$ and the binary trees with $(N + 1)$ leaves shows that the number $d_k(2N, p)$ of all Dyckwords $w \in DY_k(2N)$ requiring a stack length less than or equal to $k$ during the recognition of $w$ by algorithm $DS$ is equal to the product of $k^N$ and the number $t(N + 1, p)$ of ordered binary trees with $(N + 1)$ leaves which can be reduced by algorithm $S$ given in section 5.1.1 using a stack of maximum length $p$. Thus $d_k(2N, p) = k^N t(N + 1, p)$. Therefore,

$$\mathbf{L}_{DS}(2N) = d_k^{-1}(2N) \sum_{1 \leqslant p \leqslant N+1} p[d_k(2N, p) - d_k(2N, p - 1)]$$

$$= k^{-N} d_1^{-1}(2N) \sum_{1 \leqslant p \leqslant N+1} p k^N [t(N + 1, p) - t(N + 1, p - 1)]$$

$$= t^{-1}(N + 1) \sum_{1 \leqslant p \leqslant N+1} p[t(N + 1, p) - t(N + 1, p - 1)]$$

$$= m_1(N + 1),$$

where $m_1(N + 1)$ is the expected value computed in section 5.1.1. Summarizing our results, we have, with Theorem 5.3, the following theorem.

THEOREM 5.18 Assuming that all Dyckwords $w \in DY_k(2N)$ are equally likely, the average space $\mathbf{L}_{DS}(2N)$ required for the recognition of $w \in DY_k(2N)$ by algorithm $DS$ is asymptotically given by

$$\mathbf{L}_{DS}(2N) = \sqrt{\pi N} - \tfrac{1}{2} + O(\ln(N)/N^{1/2-\delta})$$

for all $\delta > 0$. The maximum space is $L_{DS}(2N) = N + 1$. The time required for recognizing $w \in DY_k(2N)$ by algorithm $DS$ is $T_{DS}(w) = \mathbf{T}_{DS}(2N) = 2N$. ∎

Note that all results derived in section 5.1.1 can directly be translated into the corresponding quantities of algorithm $DS$.

### 5.2.2 The Recognition by a Two-Way-One-Counter Automaton

In [56] there is given the following algorithm for the recognition of Dycklanguages by a two-way-one-counter automaton.

ALGORITHM $D2W1C$
Input:    $w \in (B_k \cup \mathbf{B}_k)^{2N}$, $N \geqslant 1$.
Output: $w \in DY_k$ or $w \notin DY_k$.
Method:
(1) A 5-tuple $(q, j, Z, H, t)$ will be used to denote a configuration of the algorithm.

    (a) $q$ is the state of the algorithm;
    (b) $j \in \mathbb{N}$ represents the location of the input pointer. We assume that the first 'input symbol' is the leftmost symbol in $w$. The current input symbol is denoted by $c(j)$.
    (c) $Z$ is a binary counter. The allowed operations are $Z \leftarrow Z + 1$ (addition of one) and $Z \leftarrow Z - 1$ (subtraction of one).
    (d) $H$ is an auxiliary cell; its contents is always a symbol in $B_k \cup \mathbf{B}_k$.
    (e) $t$ is a control variable. Its values are 0 or 1.

(2) The initial configuration of the algorithm is $C_0 = (q_0, 1, 1, c(1), 1)$.
(3) There are eight types of steps. These steps will be described in terms of their effect on the configurations of the algorithm. The algorithm computes successive configurations defined by a 'goes to' relation $\perp$. The notation $(q, j, Z, H, t) \perp (q', j', Z', H', t')$ means that if the current configuration is $(q, j, Z, H, t)$, then we are to go next into the configuration $(q', j', Z', H', t')$. The eight types of move are as follows:

    (3.1) Let $c(j) \in B_k$. Then

$$(q_0, j, Z, H, t) \perp (q_1, j, Z, H, 1).$$

    (3.2) Let $c(j) \in \mathbf{B}_k$. Then

$$(q_0, j, Z, H, t) \perp (q_2, j, Z, H, 0).$$

    (3.3) Let $Z \neq 0$ and $c(j + 1) \in B_k$. Then

$$(q_1, j, Z, H, t) \perp (q_1, j + 1, Z + 1, H, t).$$

    (3.4) Let $Z \neq 0$ and $c(j + 1) \in \mathbf{B}_k$. Then

$$(q_1, j, Z, H, t) \perp (q_1, j + 1, Z - 1, H, t).$$

(3.5) Let $\psi(H) = c(j)$. Then

$$(q_1, j, 0, H, t) \perp (q_{2t}, j + 1 - t, 1, c(j + 1 - t), t).$$

(3.6) Let $Z \neq 0$ and $c(j - 1) \in \mathbf{B}_k$. Then

$$(q_2, j, H, Z, t) \perp (q_2, j - 1, Z + 1, H, t).$$

(3.7) Let $Z \neq 0$ and $c(j - 1) \in B_k$. Then

$$(q_2, j, Z, H, t) \perp (q_2, j - 1, Z - 1, H, t).$$

(3.8) Let $\psi(c(j)) = H$. Then

$$(q_2, j, 0, H, t) \perp (q_{1-t}, j + t, 1, c(j + t), t).$$

The execution of the algorithm *D2W1C* is as follows:

*Step 1*  Starting in the initial configuration, compute successive configurations $C_0 \perp C_1 \perp \cdots \perp C_i \perp \cdots$ until no further configuration can be computed.

*Step 2*  If the last configuration is $(q_1, 2N, 0, \psi^{-1}(c(2N)), 0)$, then $w \in DY_k(2N)$; otherwise $w \notin DY_k(2N)$.

The algorithm *D2W1C* reads the word $w \in (B_k \cup \mathbf{B}_k)^+$ from left to right (right to left) and searches for each $b$ appearing in $w$ the corresponding bracket $\psi(b)$ to $b \in B_k$ ($\psi^{-1}(b)$ to $b \in \mathbf{B}_k$) as follows:

(a) Let $b = c(j) \in B_k$ and assume that the algorithm is in configuration $(q_0, j, 1, c(j), t)$. Since $c(j) \in B_k$, we obtain the configuration $(q_1, j, 1, c(j), 1)$ (step (3.1)). Now the input pointer moves to the right until the counter is zero the first time; in each move the counter is increased by one if the current input symbol $x$ is in $B_k$ (step (3.3)), and is decreased by one if $x$ is in $\mathbf{B}_k$ (step (3.4)). Thus we obtain a configuration $(q_1, \mu, 0, c(j), 1)$. Now the algorithm checks the condition $\psi(c(j)) = c(\mu)$ (step (3.5)). If this condition is satisfied—that is, $(c(j), c(\mu))$ is a pair of brackets—the algorithm goes into the configuration $(q_2, \mu, 1, c(\mu), 1)$. Next it has to recover the old position $j$ of the input pointer, in order to start with the next input symbol $c(j + 1)$. For this purpose, the input pointer moves to the left until the counter is zero the first time; in each move, the counter is increased by one if the current input symbol $x$ is in $\mathbf{B}_k$ (step (3.6)), and it is decreased by one if $x$ is in $B_k$ (step (3.7)). Thus we reach the configuration $(q_2, j, 0, c(\mu), 1)$. Since $(c(j), c(\mu))$ is a pair of brackets, the condition $\psi(c(j)) = H$ (step (3.8)) is satisfied and the algorithm goes into the configuration $(q_0, j + 1, 1, c(j + 1), 1)$.

(b) Let $b = c(j) \in \mathbf{B}_k$ and assume that the algorithm is in configuration $(q_0, j, 1, c(j), t)$. In this case, the algorithm goes first in state $q_2$ and the input pointer is moved to the left until the counter is zero the first time (step (3.6) and step (3.7)). Then it goes to state $q_1$ and moves the input pointer to the right until the old position $j$ is reached (step (3.3) and step (3.4)). Since $t = 0$, we finally obtain the configuration $(q_0, j + 1, 1, c(j + 1), 0)$ by step (3.5).

For example, let $N = 4$, $B_2 = \{[, \langle\}$, $\mathbf{B}_2 = \{], \rangle\}$, $\psi([) = ]$, and $\psi(\langle) = \rangle$. Choosing $w = [\langle\rangle]\langle\rangle[]$, we find the following configurations:

$$(q_0, 1, 1, [, 1) \underset{(3.1)}{\perp} (q_1, 1, 1, [, 1) \underset{(3.3)}{\perp} (q_1, 2, 2, [, 1) \underset{(3.4)}{\perp} (q_1, 3, 1, [, 1)$$

$$\underset{(3.4)}{\perp} (q_1, 4, 0, [, 1) \underset{(3.5)}{\perp} (q_2, 4, 1, ], 1) \underset{(3.6)}{\perp} (q_2, 3, 2, ], 1)$$

$$\underset{(3.7)}{\perp} (q_2, 2, 1, ], 1) \underset{(3.7)}{\perp} (q_2, 1, 0, ], 1) \underset{(3.8)}{\perp} (q_0, 2, 1, \langle, 1)$$

$$\underset{(3.1)}{\perp} (q_1, 2, 1, \langle, 1) \underset{(3.4)}{\perp} (q_1, 3, 0, \langle, 1) \underset{(3.5)}{\perp} (q_2, 3, 1, \rangle, 1)$$

$$\underset{(3.7)}{\perp} (q_2, 2, 0, \rangle, 1) \underset{(3.8)}{\perp} (q_0, 3, 1, \rangle, 1) \underset{(3.2)}{\perp} (q_2, 3, 1, \rangle, 0)$$

$$\underset{(3.7)}{\perp} (q_2, 2, 0, \rangle, 0) \underset{(3.8)}{\perp} (q_1, 2, 1, \langle, 0) \underset{(3.4)}{\perp} \ldots\ldots\ldots\ldots$$

$$\ldots\ldots\ldots\ldots \underset{(3.7)}{\perp} (q_2, 7, 0, ], 0) \underset{(3.8)}{\perp} (q_1, 7, 1, [, 0)$$

$$\underset{(3.4)}{\perp} (q_1, 8, 0, [, 0)$$

Hence $w \in DY_2(8)$. For $w' = [\langle]\rangle\langle\rangle[]$, the last configuration is $(q_1, 4, 0, [, 1)$, because $\psi([) = ] \neq c(4) = \rangle$. Therefore, $w' \notin DY_2(8)$. The space $L_{D2WIC}(w)$, $w \in DY_k(2N)$ required by algorithm $D2WIC$ is the length of the binary counter $Z$ during the recognition of $w$. In the worst case, we have $L_{D2WIC}(w) = \lfloor \mathrm{ld}(2N) \rfloor$, a fact satisfied by Dyckwords of the form $w \in B_k^N \mathbf{B}_k^N$. Therefore, the maximum space is $L_{D2WIC}(2N) = \lfloor \mathrm{ld}(2N) \rfloor$. It is well known that the algorithm $D2WIC$ is optimal, that is, each algorithm recognizing the Dycklanguage $DY_k$ requires at least $O(\mathrm{ld}(N))$ space for an input of length $2N$.

Let us now consider the average space $\mathbf{L}_{D2WIC}(2N)$ of the algorithm $D2WIC$. For this purpose, let $z_k(2N, p)$ be the number of all Dyckwords $w \in DY_k(2N)$ which can be recognized by the above algorithm, where the maximum value of $Z$ is less than or equal to $p$. It is not hard to see that $z_k(2N, p)$ is equal to the number $d_k(2N, p + 1)$ of all Dyckwords $w \in DY_k(2N)$ requiring a maximum stack length $(p + 1)$ during the recognition of $w$ by algorithm $DS$ given in section 5.2.1 (Exercise 5.11). Hence $z_k(2N, p) = k^N t(N + 1, p + 1)$, where $t(N, p)$ is the number of all ordered binary trees with $N$ leaves which can be reduced by algorithm $S$ requiring less than or equal to $p$ variables. Since $z_k(2N, p) - z_k(2N, p - 1)$ is the number of all Dyckwords $w \in DY_k(2N)$ which can be recognized by algorithm $D2WIC$, where the maximum value of $Z$ is equal to $p$—that is, $Z$ consists of exactly $\lfloor \mathrm{ld}(2p) \rfloor$ bits—we obtain

$$\mathbf{L}_{D2WIC}(2N) = d_k^{-1}(2N) \sum_{w \in DY_k(2N)} L_{D2WIC}(w)$$

$$= d_k^{-1}(2N) \sum_{1 \leqslant p \leqslant N} \lfloor \mathrm{ld}(2p) \rfloor [z_k(2N, p) - z_k(2N, p-1)]$$

$$= t^{-1}(N+1) \sum_{1 \leqslant p \leqslant N} \lfloor \mathrm{ld}(2p) \rfloor [t(N+1, p+1) - t(N+1, p)]$$

$$= t^{-1}(N+1) \left[ \sum_{1 \leqslant \lambda \leqslant \lfloor \mathrm{ld}(2N) \rfloor} \sum_{2^{\lambda-1} \leqslant j \leqslant 2^{\lambda}-1} \lambda \{ t(N+1, j+1) - t(N+1, j) \} \right.$$

$$\left. + \{ 1 + \lfloor \mathrm{ld}(N) \rfloor \} \sum_{2^{\lfloor \mathrm{ld}(n) \rfloor} \leqslant p \leqslant N} \{ t(N+1, p+1) - t(N+1, p) \} \right]$$

$$= t^{-1}(N+1) \left[ \sum_{1 \leqslant \lambda \leqslant \lfloor \mathrm{ld}(N) \rfloor} \lambda \{ t(N+1, 2^{\lambda}) - t(N+1, 2^{\lambda-1}) \} \right.$$

$$\left. + \{ 1 + \lfloor \mathrm{ld}(N) \rfloor \} \{ t(N+1, N+1) - t(N+1, 2^{\lfloor \mathrm{ld}(N) \rfloor}) \} \right]$$

$$= t^{-1}(N+1) \left[ \{ 1 + \lfloor \mathrm{ld}(N) \rfloor \} t(N+1, N+1) - \sum_{1 \leqslant \lambda \leqslant \lfloor \mathrm{ld}(N) \rfloor} t(N+1, 2^{\lambda}) \right].$$

Since $t(N+1, N+1) = t(N+1)$, we further obtain by the definition of the cumulative distribution function $V_n(x)$ defined at the end of section 5.1.1 and by an application of Exercise 5.2

$$\mathbf{L}_{D2WIC}(2N) = 1 + \lfloor \mathrm{ld}(N) \rfloor - \sum_{1 \leqslant \lambda \leqslant \lfloor \mathrm{ld}(N) \rfloor} V_{N+1}(2^{\lambda})$$

$$= 1 + \lfloor \mathrm{ld}(N) \rfloor - \sum_{1 \leqslant \lambda \leqslant \lfloor \mathrm{ld}(N) \rfloor} V_{N+1}(2^{\lambda} - 1) + O(\mathrm{ld}(N)/N^{\alpha})$$

for some $\alpha > 0$. In section 5.1.2 we have given an expression for the average number $m_1(N)$ of variables appearing in a program produced by the optimal algorithm $OP$. We have found

$$m_1(N+1) = \lfloor \mathrm{ld}(2N+2) \rfloor - t^{-1}(N+1) \sum_{1 \leqslant k \leqslant \lfloor \mathrm{ld}(2N+2) \rfloor - 1} q(N+1, k),$$

where $q(n, k)$ is the number of all ordered binary trees with $N$ leaves which can be reduced by algorithm $OP$ requiring less than or equal to $k$ variables. Using Theorem 5.8 and the definition of $V_n(x)$, we further obtain

$$m_1(N+1) = \lfloor \mathrm{ld}(2N+2) \rfloor - t^{-1}(N+1) \sum_{1 \leqslant k < \lfloor \mathrm{ld}(2N+2) \rfloor} t(N+1, 2^{\lambda} - 1)$$

$$= \lfloor \mathrm{ld}(2N+2) \rfloor - \sum_{1 \leqslant \lambda \leqslant \lfloor \mathrm{ld}(N+1) \rfloor} V_{N+1}(2^{\lambda} - 1).$$

Therefore,

$$\mathbf{L}_{D2WIC}(2N) = 1 + \lfloor \mathrm{ld}(N) \rfloor - \lfloor \mathrm{ld}(2N+2) \rfloor + m_1(N+1)$$

180.

$$+ \sum_{\lfloor \mathrm{ld}(N) \rfloor < \lambda \leqslant \lfloor \mathrm{ld}(N+1) \rfloor} V_{N+1}(2^\lambda - 1) + O(\mathrm{ld}(N)/N^\alpha)$$

$$= m_1(N+1) + O(\mathrm{ld}(N)/N^\alpha),$$

because

$$1 + \lfloor \mathrm{ld}(N) \rfloor - \lfloor \mathrm{ld}(2N+2) \rfloor + \sum_{\lfloor \mathrm{ld}(N) \rfloor < \lambda \leqslant \lfloor \mathrm{ld}(N+1) \rfloor} V_{N+1}(2^\lambda - 1)$$

$$= \begin{cases} 0 & \text{if } N \neq 2^r - 1 \\ -t^{-1}(2^r) & \text{if } N = 2^r - 1 \end{cases},$$

where

$$r \in \mathbb{N} \quad \text{and} \quad t(n) = \frac{1}{n}\binom{2n-2}{n-1}.$$

Now an application of Theorem 5.10 leads to the following result.

THEOREM 5.19  Assuming that all Dyckwords $w \in DY_k(2N)$ are equally likely, the average space $\mathbf{L}_{D2WIC}(2N)$ required for recognizing $w \in DY_k(2N)$ by algorithm $D2WIC$ is asymptotically given by

$$\mathbf{L}_{D2WIC}(2N) = \tfrac{1}{2}\mathrm{ld}(8\pi^2 N) - \frac{\gamma+2}{2\ln(2)} + F(N) + O(\mathrm{ld}(N)/N^\alpha)$$

for some $\alpha > 0$, where

$$F(N) = \frac{1}{\ln(2)} \sum_{\substack{-\infty \leqslant k \leqslant \infty \\ k \neq 0}} \left[ 2\frac{\pi i k}{\ln(2)} - 1 \right] \Gamma\left(\frac{\pi i k}{\ln(2)}\right) \zeta\left(2\frac{\pi i k}{\ln(2)}\right) \exp(\pi i k \, \mathrm{ld}(N)).$$

$F(N)$ is a bounded oscillating function with $F(N) = F(4N)$. The maximum space is $L_{D2WIC}(2N) = \lfloor \mathrm{ld}(2N) \rfloor$. ∎

This result shows that the average space required by algorithm $D2WIC$ for the recognition of $w \in DY_k(2N)$ is equal to the average number of variables appearing in a program produced by the optimal algorithm $OP$ with a $n$-node binary tree as input.

An appropriate measure for the time $T_{D2WIC}(w)$, $w \in DY_k(2N)$, of the algorithm $D2WIC$ is the number of moves of the input pointer during the recognition of $w$. We assume that in one unit of time the input pointer is moved one position to the right or left and that the counter $Z$ is increased or decreased by one. Obviously, each move of the pointer corresponds to a change of $Z$ and vice versa.

LEMMA  5.3  Let $w \in DY_k(2N)$ with $w = bu\psi(b)v$, $b \in B_k$, $\psi(b) \in \mathbf{B}_k$, $u \in DY_k(2\lambda - 2)$, and $v \in DY_k(2N - 2\lambda)$, $1 \leqslant \lambda \leqslant N$. We have

$$T_{D2WIC}(w) = T_{D2WIC}(u) + T_{D2WIC}(v) + 8\lambda - 1 - \delta_{\lambda,1} - \delta_{\lambda,N}.$$

*Proof* Evidently, each $w \in DY_k(2N)$ has a uniquely determined representation of the form $w = bu\psi(b)v$ with $u, v \in DY_k$. The number of moves $T_{D2WIC}(w)$ of the input pointer consists of:

(a) The number of moves required for recognizing $u \in DY_k(2\lambda - 2)$ (giving the contribution $T_{D2WIC}(u)$).
(b) The number of moves required for recognizing $v \in DY_k(2N - 2\lambda)$ (giving the contribution $T_{D2WIC}(v)$).
(c) The number of moves required for checking the pair of brackets $(b, \psi(b)) \in B_k \times \mathbf{B}_k$ (giving the contribution $4(2\lambda - 1)$).
(d) the moves
    (i) from $b$ to the first symbol of $u$, if $\lambda \neq 1$;
    (ii) from the last symbol of $u$ to $\psi(b)$, if $\lambda \neq 1$;
    (iii) from $\psi(b)$ to the first symbol of $v$, if $\lambda \neq N$;
    (iv) from $b$ to $\psi(b)$, if $\lambda = 1$
    (giving the contribution $3 - \delta_{\lambda,N} - \delta_{\lambda,1}$).

The sum of these contributions yields our statement.  ∎

Using Lemma 5.3, a simple induction on $N$ leads to Lemma 5.4.

**LEMMA 5.4**  Let $w_1, w_2, w \in DY_k(2N)$, $w_1 \in B_k^N \mathbf{B}_k^N$ and $w_2 \in (B_k \mathbf{B}_k)^N$. We have

$$6N - 1 = T_{D2WIC}(w_2) \leqslant T_{D2WIC}(w) \leqslant T_{D2WIC}(w_1) = 4N^2 + 2N - 1. \quad ∎$$

Hence the maximum time of algorithm *D2WIC* is $T_{D2WIC}(2N) = 4N^2 + 2N - 1$. Let us now consider the average time $\mathbf{T}_{D2WIC}(2N)$. For this purpose, let

$$M(2N) = \sum_{w \in DY_k(2N)} T_{D2WIC}(w)$$

be the sum of all moves of the input pointer required for recognizing all Dyckwords $w \in DY_k(2N)$. We shall first derive a recurrence for $M(2N)$.

**LEMMA 5.5**

$$M(0) = 0$$

$$M(2N) = k \sum_{1 \leqslant \lambda \leqslant N} [2M(2\lambda - 2) + (8\lambda - 1)d_k(2\lambda - 2)]d_k(2N - 2\lambda) - 2kd_k(2N - 2).$$

*Proof* Obviously, we have $M(0) = 0$. Now let $N \geqslant 1$. We obtain by Lemma 5.3

$$M(2N) = \sum_{w \in DY_k(2N)} T_{D2WIC}(w)$$

$$= \sum_{1 \leqslant \lambda \leqslant N} \sum_{\substack{u \in DY_k(2\lambda - 2) \\ bu\psi(b)v \in DY_k(2N)}} \sum_{v \in DY_k(2N - 2\lambda)} T_{D2WIC}(w)$$

$$= k \sum_{1 \leq \lambda \leq N} d_k(2N - 2\lambda)M(2\lambda - 2) + k \sum_{1 \leq \lambda \leq N} d_k(2\lambda - 2)M(2N - 2\lambda)$$

$$+ k \sum_{1 \leq \lambda \leq N} [8\lambda - 1 - \delta_{\lambda,1} - \delta_{\lambda,N}]d_k(2\lambda - 2)d_k(2N - 2\lambda).$$

This expression is equivalent to our statement. ∎

Since $d_k(2N) = k^N t(N + 1)$, Lemma 5.5 implies

$$M(0) = 0$$

$$M(2N) = 2k^{N+1} \sum_{1 \leq \lambda \leq N} M(2\lambda - 2)k^{-\lambda}t(N - \lambda + 1)$$

$$+ k^N \sum_{1 \leq \lambda \leq N} (8\lambda - 1)t(\lambda)t(N - \lambda + 1) - 2k^N t(N), \qquad N \geq 1.$$

Now let $M(z) = \sum_{N \geq 0} k^{-N}M(2N)z^N$ be the generating function of the numbers $k^{-N}M(2N)$. Translating the above recurrence into terms of $M(z)$, we immediately find

$$M(z) = 2zC(z)M(z) + 8z^2C(z)C'(z) + 7zC^2(z) - 2zC(z),$$

where $C(z) = \sum_{N \geq 0} t(N + 1)z^N$ is the generating function of the Catalan numbers given by $C(z) = (2z)^{-1}(1 - \sqrt{1 - 4z})$. Therefore,

$$M(z) = [8z^2C(z)C'(z) + 7zC^2(z) - 2zC(z)]/[1 - 2zC(z)]$$

$$= \left(\frac{3}{2z} - 12\right)\frac{1}{\sqrt{1 - 4z}} + \frac{1}{2z} + \frac{4}{1 - 4z} - \frac{2}{z}\sqrt{1 - 4z} + 1$$

$$= \sum_{n \geq 1} \left[4^{n+1} - \frac{6n + 5}{n + 1}\binom{2n}{n}\right]z^n.$$

Hence

$$M(2N) = k^N \langle z^N \rangle M(z) = k^N[4^{N+1} - (6N + 5)t(N + 1)].$$

Since the average time $\mathbf{T}_{D2WIC}(2N)$ is given by

$$\mathbf{T}_{D2WIC}(2N) = d_k^{-1}(2N)M(2N) = k^{-N}t(N + 1)M(2N),$$

we obtain by Stirling's formula

$$\mathbf{T}_{D2WIC}(2N) = 4^{N+1}(N + 1)\binom{2N}{N}^{-1} - 6N - 5$$

$$= 4N\sqrt{\pi N} - 6N + 4.5\sqrt{\pi N} - 5 + O(N^{-1/2}).$$

Hence we have proved the following theorem.

THEOREM 5.20 Assuming that all Dyckwords $w \in DY_k(2N)$ are equally likely, the average time $\mathbf{T}_{D2WIC}(2N)$ required for recognizing $w \in DY_k(2N)$ by algorithm *D2W1C* is asymptotically given by

$$\mathbf{T}_{D2W1C}(2N) = 4N\sqrt{\pi N} - 6N + 4.5\sqrt{\pi N} - 5 + O(N^{-1/2}).$$

The maximum time is $T_{D2W1C}(2N) = 4N^2 + 2N - 1.$ ∎

In this section we have analysed the two algorithms *DS* and *D2W1C*. In particular, we have proved for an input $w \in DY_k(2N)$, $N \geqslant 1$:

| | Time | | | Space | | |
|---|---|---|---|---|---|---|
| Algorithm | Best case | Worst case | Average case | Best case | Worst case | Average case |
| *DS* | $2N$ | $2N$ | $2N$ | 2 | $N+1$ | $\sqrt{\pi N} + O(1)$ |
| *D2W1C* | $6N-1$ | $4N^2+2N-1$ | $4N\sqrt{\pi N}+O(N)$ | 1 | $\lfloor ld(2N) \rfloor$ | $\frac{1}{2} ld(8\pi^2 N) + F(N)$ $(F(N)=F(4N))$ |

For a simulation of algorithm *D2W1C* by a two-tape Turing machine see Exercise 5.13.

### 5.3 Batcher's Algorithm

#### 5.3.1 Networks for Sorting

A *comparator module* $C(x, y)$ is a device such as that shown schematically in Figure 29; it consumes two input numbers $x$ and $y$ at a time, and produces two output numbers $MIN(x, y)$ and $MAX(x, y)$. In other words, a module exchanges its inputs, if necessary, to make the larger number appear on the lower line after passing. A *sorting network* for sequences of length $n$ is an arrangement of comparator modules such as that drawn in Figure 30; moving the $n$ input numbers $x_1, x_2, \ldots, x_n$ from left to right, the comparator modules exchange their inputs, if necessary, such that the output sequence $y_1, y_2, \ldots, y_n$ is $x_1, x_2, \ldots, x_n$ in increasing order from top to bottom. Figure 31 illustrates the transformation of a sequence of length 5 into a sorted sequence by the above network. The modules which actually perform exchanges are marked *.

A sequence $x_1, x_2, \ldots, x_{2n}$ is called *2-ordered* (see Exercise 4.4) if $x_\lambda \leqslant x_{\lambda+2}$, $1 \leqslant \lambda \leqslant 2n - 2$. An *odd–even merge* is a sorting network for 2-ordered

FIGURE 29. A comparator module $C(x, y)$.

184

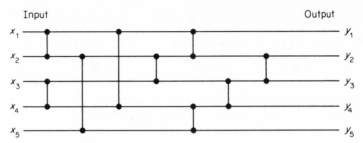

FIGURE 30. A sorting network for five elements.

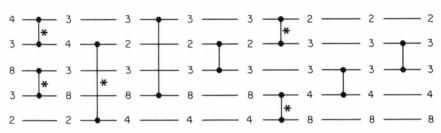

FIGURE 31. Transformation of 4, 3, 8, 3, 2 into the sorted sequence 2, 3, 3, 4, 8.

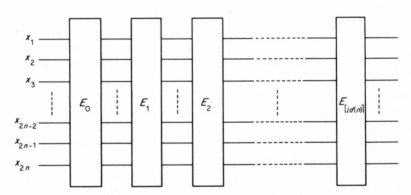

FIGURE 32. Odd–even merge $OEM(2n)$.

sequences. The odd–even merge OEM($2n$) for sequences of length $2n$ drawn in Figure 32 has been presented in [4].

The components $E_0, E_1, \ldots, E_{\lceil \mathrm{ld}(n) \rceil}$ are defined as follows:

(a) $E_0$ consists of the comparator modules $C(x_{2j-1}, x_{2j})$, $1 \leqslant j \leqslant n$.
(b) Let $m_{ji} = 2j + 2^{\lceil \mathrm{ld}(n) \rceil - i + 1} - 1$. $E_i$, $i \in [1 : \lceil \mathrm{ld}(n) \rceil]$ consists of the comparator modules $C(x_{2j}, x_{m_{ji}})$, $j = 1, 2, 3, \ldots, n - 2^{\lceil \mathrm{ld}(n) \rceil - i}$, in this order from left to right.

For example, let $n = 6$. The odd–even merge OEM(12) is illustrated in Figure 33.

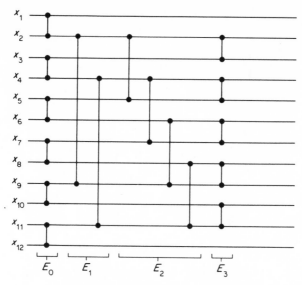

FIGURE 33. Odd–even merge $OEM(12)$.

Now let $C_{2n}$ be the number of comparator modules appearing in OEM($2n$). Obviously, the component $E_0$ consists of $n$ modules and $E_i$, $i \geqslant 1$, of $(n - 2^{\lceil \operatorname{ld}(n) \rceil - i})$ modules. Hence

$$C_{2n} = n + \sum_{1 \leqslant i \leqslant \lceil \operatorname{ld}(n) \rceil} (n - 2^{\lceil \operatorname{ld}(n) \rceil - i}) = n(\lceil \operatorname{ld}(n) \rceil + 1) - 2^{\lceil \operatorname{ld}(n) \rceil} + 1.$$

Since any merging method which can be represented as a network must use at least $\frac{1}{2}n \operatorname{ld}(n) + O(n)$ comparator modules to sort 2-ordered sequences of length $2n$ ([76]), the above odd–even merge OEM($2n$) is, in this sense, optimal. Let us turn to the number of exchanges required for a 2-ordered input sequence consisting of $2n$ distinct elements. This number does depend on the input distribution.

A representation of a 2-ordered sequence of length $2n$ as a path in a lattice diagram (illustrated in Figure 34 for $n = 6$) is given in [76]. Starting at the upper left corner $(0, 0)$, form a path whose $k$-th segment goes down (to the right) if the $k$-th smallest element of the sequence has an odd (even) position. For example, the 2-ordered sequence 2, 1, 4, 3, 7, 5, 8, 6, 9, 10, 12, 11 corresponds to the heavy line in Figure 34. The point reached after $i$ steps down and $j$ steps to the right is denoted by $(i, j)$. Thus the number of all 2-ordered sequences of length $2n$ is equal to the number of all paths from $(0, 0)$ to $(n, n)$. It is not hard to see that the sorted sequence corresponds to the 'diagonal path' whose first segment is vertical (dotted line in Figure 34). Thus the merging process consists of transformations from an arbitrary path to the diagonal path.

Now some reflection shows that the components $E_s$, $0 \leqslant s \leqslant \lceil \operatorname{ld}(n) \rceil$, of the

186

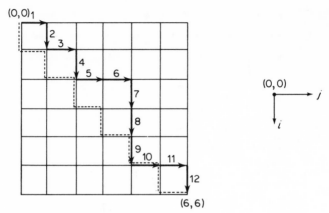

FIGURE 34. Representation of the 2-ordered sequence 2, 1, 4, 3, 7, 5, 8, 6, 9, 10, 12, 11 as a path.

odd–even merge OEM($2n$) transform the path corresponding to the input sequence as follows:

(a) $E_0$ corresponds to 'folding' the path about the main diagonal $i = j$ so that it never goes above this diagonal.

(b) $E_s$ corresponds to 'folding' the path generated by $E_0, E_1, \ldots, E_{s-1}$ about the diagonal $i = j + 2^{\lceil \operatorname{ld}(n) \rceil - s}$ so that it never goes below this diagonal, $1 \leqslant s \leqslant \lceil \operatorname{ld}(n) \rceil$.

Figure 35 illustrates this process for the sequence 2, 1, 4, 3, 7, 5, 8, 6, 9, 10, 12, 11.

This folding process yields an easy way of counting the number of exchanges used to sort any particular 2-ordered sequence consisting of $2n$ distinct elements. We assign a weight to each segment in the lattice which counts the number of exchanges in which the corresponding element will be involved, if the path includes that segment. Let $f(i, j)$ be the weight of the vertical segment from $(i, j)$ to $(i + 1, j)$. We shall derive a recursive definition of $f(i, j)$:

(a) Since the folding is done along parallel diagonals, weights along diagonals are constant. Hence

$$f(i, j) = \begin{cases} f(i - j, 0) & \text{if } i \geqslant j \\ f(0, j - i) & \text{if } i \leqslant j \end{cases}.$$

(b) The folding induced by the component $E_0$ transforms a vertical segment from $(0, j + 1)$ to $(1, j + 1)$ into the horizontal segment from $(j + 1, 0)$ to $(j + 1, 1)$ which has the same weight as the vertical segment from $(j, 0)$ to $(j + 1, 0)$. Hence $f(0, j + 1) = f(j, 0) + 1, j \geqslant 0$.

(c) The folding induced by the component $E_{\lceil \operatorname{ld}(n) \rceil - i}$ transforms a vertical segment from $(2^i + j, 0)$ to $(2^i + j + 1, 0)$, $j \in [0 : 2^i - 1]$, into the horizontal segment from $(2^i, j)$ to $(2^i, j + 1)$ which has the same weight as the

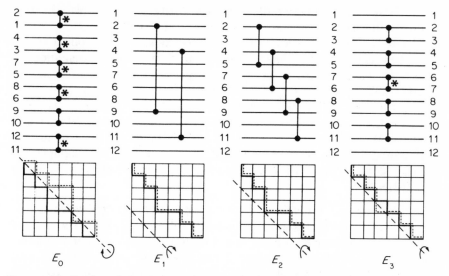

FIGURE 35. Sorting of the sequence 2, 1, 4, 3, 7, 5, 8, 6, 9, 10, 12, 11. Modules which actually perform exchanges are marked by '*'; the heavy lines in the lattice diagrams correspond to the paths after folding, the dotted lines before folding.

vertical segment from $(2^i - j - 1, 0)$ to $(2^i - j, 0)$. Thus $f(2^i + j, 0) = f(2^i - j - 1, 0) + 1$ for $0 \leqslant i < \lceil \mathrm{ld}(n) \rceil$ and $0 \leqslant j \leqslant 2^i - 1$.

(d) Since the sorted sequence requires no exchange, we have the initial condition $f(0, 0) = 0$.

This recursive definition of $f(i, j)$ shows that all weights are known if we know the values $f(j, 0), j \geqslant 0$. In other words, knowledge of the values of the function $g$ defined by

$$g(0) = 0$$

$$g(2^i + j) = g(2^i - j - 1) + 1, \qquad i \geqslant 0, 0 \leqslant j \leqslant 2^i - 1,$$

suffices to compute all values $f(i, j)$. Table 5 shows that this function has an erratic behaviour.

However, there are two suitable interpretations of $g(n)$:

(i) The binary representation of $2^i - j - 1$ $(0 \leqslant j < 2^i)$ is obtained by inverting the binary representation of $2^i + j$, that is, by changing 0 to 1, 1 to 0, and ignoring leading zeros. Thus $g(n)$ is the number of times

TABLE 5. The first few values of $g(n)$.

| $n$ | 0 | 1 | 2 | 3 | 4 | 5 | 6 | 7 | 8 | 9 | 10 | 11 | 12 |
|---|---|---|---|---|---|---|---|---|---|---|---|---|---|
| $g(n)$ | 0 | 1 | 2 | 1 | 2 | 3 | 2 | 1 | 2 | 3 | 4 | 3 | 2 |

the binary representation of $n$ changes parity. For example, $g(363) = g((101101011)_2) = 7$, because $.1.0.11.0.1.0.11$ changes parity at '.'.

(ii) The binary reflected code (standard Gray code) is an encoding of the integers as sequences of bits with the property that the representations of adjacent integers differ in exactly one binary position. For example, the Gray code representations of the integers $0, 1, 2, 3, \ldots$ are $0, 1, 11, 10, 110, 111, 101, 100, 1100, 1101, \ldots$. It is easy to see that an integer $n$ is encoded by the Gray code as the binary representation of $h(n)$, where $h(0) = 0$ and $h(2^p + \lambda) = 2^p + h(2^p - \lambda - 1)$ for $0 \leqslant \lambda < 2^p$. Hence $f(n)$ is the number of ones appearing in the Gray code representation of $n$. For example, the Gray code representation of 363 is 111011110 which implies again $g(363) = 7$.

Now, for any path through the lattice diagram, if we sum the weights of its segments and divide by two (each exchange involves two elements), we get the total number of exchanges used to sort the 2-ordered sequence corresponding to that path. Since the sum of the weights of a path's vertical segments is equal to the sum of the weights of its horizontal segments, both sums count the number of exchanges. Henceforth, we shall consider only the sum of weights of vertical segments. The number of exchanges in the worst and average case was first derived in [109]. We shall briefly discuss both cases in the subsequent sections.

### 5.3.2 The Number of Exchanges in the Worst Case

We have to find the maximal possible weight of a path in the lattice diagram, where the weight of a path is the sum of the weights of its vertical segments. The $k$-th *major diagonal* $\Delta_k$, $k = 1, 2, 3, \ldots$, is a path defined as follows: proceed right along the top line of the lattice diagram until encountering the first horizontal segment with weight $k$. Then proceed down and to the right along the diagonal segments with weight $k$. After reaching the right-hand vertical line of the lattice diagram, proceed down to $(n, n)$. Figure 36 illustrates all major diagonals together with their weights for $n = 7$.

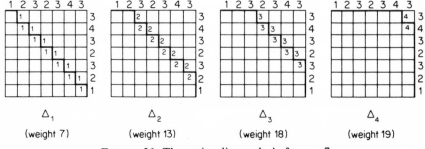

$\Delta_1$ (weight 7)    $\Delta_2$ (weight 13)    $\Delta_3$ (weight 18)    $\Delta_4$ (weight 19)

FIGURE 36. The major diagonals $\Delta_k$ for $n = 7$.

Exercise 5.14 shows that the path of highest weight through the lattice diagram is one of the major diagonals. Therefore, our problem is reduced to finding the weights of all major diagonals, and the maximum of these. For this purpose, let $w_k$ be the weight of $\Delta_{k+1}$, $k \in \mathbb{N}_0$, and $g^{-1}(k) = \text{MIN}\{j \mid g(j) = k\}$, where $g(n)$ is the arithmetical function defined in section 5.3.1. Moreover, let $G(k) = \sum_{0 \leqslant j < k} g(j)$. With these notations, $\Delta_{k+1}$ has $n - g^{-1}(k)$ vertical segments along the diagonal with weights $k + 1$, and $g^{-1}(k)$ vertical segments along the right-hand vertical line of the lattice diagram with the total weight $G(g^{-1}(k)) + g^{-1}(k)$. Thus

$$w_k = (k + 1)n + G(g^{-1}(k)) - kg^{-1}(k).$$

Using the first interpretation of $g(k)$ given in section 5.3.1, we see that the numbers whose binary representation alternate between 0 and 1, change parity most often. Thus the first numbers $j$ with $g(j) = k = 0, 1, 2, 3, 4, 5, \ldots$ are $j = 0, 1, 2, 5, 10, 21, \ldots$, whose binary representations are 0, 1, 10, 101, 1010, 10101, \ldots, respectively; it is easily shown that these numbers are given by $(2^{k+2} - (-1)^k - 3)/6$. Hence $g^{-1}(k) = (2^{k+2} - (-1)^k - 3)/6$. An application of Exercise 5.15 leads to the explicit expression

$$G(g^{-1}(k)) = \tfrac{1}{18}[(3k - 1)2^{k+1} - 9k - (-1)^k(3k - 2)].$$

Inserting these expressions for $g^{-1}(k)$ and $G(g^{-1}(k))$ into the above relation for $w_k$, we find

$$w_k = n(k + 1) - \tfrac{1}{9}[(3k + 1)2^k - (-1)^k].$$

Thus the weights of the major diagonals $\Delta_1, \Delta_2, \Delta_3, \Delta_4, \Delta_5, \ldots$ are $w_0 = n$, $w_1 = 2n - 1$, $w_2 = 3n - 3$, $w_3 = 4n - 9$, $w_4 = 5n - 23$, $\ldots$, respectively. We have now to find $E_n^{\text{MAX}} = \text{MAX}_{1 \leqslant k \leqslant k_0}(w_k)$, where $k_0$ is the index of the last major diagonal, that is, the largest integer satisfying $g(k_0) \leqslant n$. $E_n^{\text{MAX}}$ is the number of exchanges in the worst case. Since $w_k$ is increasing for small $k$ and decreasing for large $k$, the index $\mathbf{k}$ with $w_{\mathbf{k}} = E_n^{\text{MAX}}$ is the largest integer for which the difference $w_k - w_{k-1}$ is positive. Thus

$$\mathbf{k} = \text{MAX}\{j \mid \tfrac{1}{9}(3j + 4)2^{j-1} - \tfrac{2}{9}(-1)^j \leqslant n\},$$

because

$$w_k - w_{k-1} = n - \tfrac{1}{9}2^{k-1}(3k + 4) + \tfrac{2}{9}(-1)^k.$$

Since

$$n \geqslant \tfrac{1}{9}(3\mathbf{k} + 4)2^{\mathbf{k}-1} - \tfrac{2}{9}(-1)^{\mathbf{k}}$$
$$= \tfrac{1}{6}[\tfrac{2}{3}(3\mathbf{k} + 4)2^{\mathbf{k}-1} - \tfrac{4}{3}(-1)^{\mathbf{k}}] \geqslant \tfrac{1}{6}[2^{\mathbf{k}+2} - (-1)^{\mathbf{k}} - 3] = g^{-1}(\mathbf{k}),$$

the maximum at $\mathbf{k}$ is realizable. Starting with the inequalities which define $\mathbf{k}$, that is,

$$\tfrac{1}{9}(3\mathbf{k} + 4)2^{\mathbf{k}-1} - \tfrac{2}{9}(-1)^{\mathbf{k}} \leqslant n < \tfrac{1}{9}(3\mathbf{k} + 7)2^{\mathbf{k}} + \tfrac{2}{9}(-1)^{\mathbf{k}},$$

we find by taking the logarithm

$$\mathbf{k} \leqslant \mathrm{ld}(3n + \tfrac{2}{3}(-1)^k) - \mathrm{ld}(\mathbf{k} + \tfrac{4}{3}) + 1 \tag{i}$$

$$\mathbf{k} > \mathrm{ld}(3n - \tfrac{2}{3}(-1)^k) - \mathrm{ld}(\mathbf{k} + \tfrac{7}{3}). \tag{ii}$$

Iterating these inequalities leads to

$$\mathbf{k} \leqslant \mathrm{ld}(3n + \tfrac{2}{3}(-1)^k) - \mathrm{ld}(\tfrac{4}{3} + \mathrm{ld}(3n - \tfrac{2}{3}(-1)^k) - \mathrm{ld}(\mathbf{k} + \tfrac{7}{3})) + 1 \tag{i}$$

$$= \mathrm{ld}(3n) - \mathrm{ld}(\mathrm{ld}(3n)) + O(1)$$

$$\mathbf{k} > \mathrm{ld}(3n - \tfrac{2}{3}(-1)^k) - \mathrm{ld}(\tfrac{10}{3} + \mathrm{ld}(3n + \tfrac{2}{3}(-1)^k) - \mathrm{ld}(\mathbf{k} + \tfrac{4}{3})) \tag{ii}$$

$$= \mathrm{ld}(3n) - \mathrm{ld}(\mathrm{ld}(3n)) + O(1).$$

Hence

$$\mathbf{k} = \mathrm{ld}(3n) - \mathrm{ld}(\mathrm{ld}(3n)) + O(1) = \mathrm{ld}(n) - \mathrm{ld}(\mathrm{ld}(n)) + O(1).$$

Substituting this into the formula for $E_n^{\mathrm{MAX}} = w_\mathbf{k}$, we obtain

$$E_n^{\mathrm{MAX}} = n\,\mathrm{ld}(n) - n\,\mathrm{ld}(\mathrm{ld}(n)) + O(n).$$

Summarizing our results, we have proved the following theorem.

THEOREM 5.21 The maximum number $E_n^{\mathrm{MAX}}$ of exchanges required by the odd–even merge OEM$(2n)$ for sorting a 2-ordered sequence consisting of $2n$ distinct elements is

$$E_n^{\mathrm{MAX}} = (\mathbf{k} + 1)n - \tfrac{1}{9}[(3\mathbf{k} + 1)2^k - (-1)^k],$$

where $\mathbf{k} = \mathrm{MAX}\{j \mid \tfrac{1}{9}(3j + 4)2^{j-1} - \tfrac{2}{9}(-1)^j \leqslant n\}$. Asymptotically, we have

$$E_n^{\mathrm{MAX}} = n\,\mathrm{ld}(n) - n\,\mathrm{ld}(\mathrm{ld}(n)) + O(n). \qquad \blacksquare$$

The percentage of comparator modules that perform exchanges in the worst case is the ratio $E_n^{\mathrm{MAX}}/C_{2n}$, where $C_{2n}$ is explicitly computed in section 5.3.1. We find immediately that

$$E_n^{\mathrm{MAX}}/C_{2n} = 1 - \mathrm{ld}(\mathrm{ld}(n))/\mathrm{ld}(n) + O(\mathrm{ld}^{-1}(n)).$$

Thus the ratio tends to 1 very slowly for $n \to \infty$. Theorem 5.21 was first proved in [109].

### 5.3.3 The Number of Exchanges in the Average Case

The number $s(n)$ of all 2-ordered sequences consisting of $2n$ distinct elements is equal to the number of paths from $(0,0)$ to $(n,n)$ in the corresponding lattice diagram. Therefore, $s(n) = \binom{2n}{n}$ (see Example 4.3 with $n := 2n$ and $p := 0$). Now the number of paths from $(0,0)$ to $(i,j)$ is clearly $\binom{i+j}{j}$, and the number of paths from $(i + 1, j)$ to $(n, n)$ is $\binom{2n - i - j - 1}{n - j}$ (see again Example 4.3 with $n := i + j$, $p := i - j$, and $n := 2n - i - j - 1$, $p := j - i - 1$). Thus the total number of paths which pass through the vertical segment from $(i, j)$ to $(i + 1, j)$ is equal to $\binom{i + j}{j}\binom{2n - i - j - 1}{n - j}$. Since the weight of this segment is $f(i, j)$ defined in section 5.3.1, we obtain for the average number $\mathbf{E}_n$ of exchanges required by the odd–even merge OEM($2n$) for sorting a 2-ordered sequence consisting of $2n$ distinct elements

$$\mathbf{E}_n = \sum_{0 \leqslant i < n}\sum_{0 \leqslant j \leqslant n} f(i, j)\binom{i + j}{j}\binom{2n - i - j - 1}{n - j}\Big/\binom{2n}{n}.$$

Splitting the sum on $j$, we further obtain by elementary manipulations

$$\mathbf{E}_n = \sum_{0 \leqslant i < n}\sum_{0 \leqslant j \leqslant i} f(i, j)\binom{i + j}{j}\binom{2n - i - j - 1}{n - j}\Big/\binom{2n}{n}$$
$$+ \sum_{0 \leqslant i < n}\sum_{i < j \leqslant n} f(i, j)\binom{i + j}{j}\binom{2n - i - j - 1}{n - j}\Big/\binom{2n}{n}$$
$$= \sum_{0 \leqslant i < n}\sum_{0 \leqslant j \leqslant i} [f(i, i - j) + f(n - i - 1, n - i + j)]\binom{2i - j}{i - j}\binom{2n - 2i + j - 1}{n - i - 1}\Big/\binom{2n}{n}.$$

From section 5.3.1, we know that $f(i, i - j) = f(j, 0) = g(j)$ because $i \geqslant i - j$, and that $f(n - i - 1, n - i + j) = f(0, j + 1) = f(j, 0) + 1 = g(j) + 1$ because $n - i - 1 \leqslant n - i - j$. Therefore,

$$\mathbf{E}_n = \sum_{0 \leqslant j < n} [2g(j) + 1]S_{n, j}\Big/\binom{2n}{n},$$

where

$$S_{n, j} = \sum_{i \geqslant 0} \binom{2i + j}{i}\binom{2n - 2i - j - 1}{n - i - j - 1}.$$

Generally, we have the identity (see [76])

$$\sum_{k \geqslant 0} \binom{r + tk}{k}\binom{s - tk}{n - k} = \sum_{k \geqslant 0}\binom{r + s - k}{n - k}t^k.$$

Using this relation with $k := i$, $t := 2$, $r := j$, $n := n - j - 1$, and $s := 2n - j - 1$, we obtain the alternate

$$S_{n, j} = \sum_{i \geqslant 0}\binom{2n - i - 1}{n - i - j - 1}2^i.$$

A simple computation shows that $S_{n, j}$ satisfies the recurrence

$$S_{n, j} = S_{n, j - 1} - \binom{2n}{n - j},$$

192

which has the solution

$$S_{n,j} = S_{n,0} - \sum_{0 \leqslant \lambda < j} \binom{2n}{n - j + \lambda}.$$

By definition of $S_{n,j}$,

$$S_{n,0} = \sum_{i \geqslant 0} \binom{2n - i - 1}{n - i - 1} 2^i = \sum_{i \geqslant 0} \sum_{0 \leqslant j \leqslant i} \binom{i}{j} \binom{2n - i - 1}{n - i - 1}.$$

An application of Exercise 1.3 with $s := 0$, $k := i$, $u := j$, $r := 2n - 1$, and $w := n$ leads to

$$S_{n,0} = \sum_{j \geqslant 0} \binom{2n}{n + j + 1}.$$

Therefore,

$$S_{n,j} = \sum_{j \geqslant 0} \binom{2n}{n + j + 1} - \sum_{0 \leqslant \lambda < j} \binom{2n}{n - j + \lambda} = \sum_{0 \leqslant \lambda \leqslant n - j - 1} \binom{2n}{\lambda}.$$

Inserting this expression into the above formula for $E_n$, we find

$$E_n = \sum_{0 \leqslant j < n} [2g(j) + 1] \sum_{0 \leqslant \lambda \leqslant n - j - 1} \binom{2n}{\lambda} \bigg/ \binom{2n}{n}.$$

Changing $\lambda$ to $n - \lambda$ and interchanging the order of summation, we get the equivalent expression

$$\mathbf{E}_n = \sum_{k \geqslant 1} \sum_{0 \leqslant i < k} [2g(i) + 1] \binom{2n}{n - k} \bigg/ \binom{2n}{n}$$

$$= \sum_{k \geqslant 1} [2G(k) + k] \binom{2n}{n - k} \bigg/ \binom{2n}{n},$$

where $G(k) = \sum_{0 \leqslant j < k} g(j)$, defined in section 5.3.2. Since

$$\sum_{k \geqslant 1} k \binom{2n}{n - k} = \frac{n}{2} \binom{2n}{n},$$

we have proved the following theorem.

THEOREM 5.23  Assuming that all 2-ordered sequences consisting of $2n$ distinct elements are equally likely, the average number $\mathbf{E}_n$ of exchanges required by the odd–even merge OEM($2n$) for sorting such a sequence is given by

$$\mathbf{E}_n = \tfrac{1}{2}n + 2 \sum_{k \geqslant 1} G(k) \binom{2n}{n - k} \bigg/ \binom{2n}{n},$$

where $G(k)$ is the total number of ones appearing in the Gray code representations of the integers $0, 1, 2, \ldots, k - 1$.  ∎

This theorem, which was first proved in [109], shows that we have again to evaluate a sum which is similar to those presented in Theorems 5.1 and 5.9: the terms consist of a quotient of binomial coefficients times an arithmetical function.

Since

$$4^{-n}\binom{2n}{n}[\mathbf{E}_n - \tfrac{1}{2}n]$$

$$=2\cdot 4^{-n}\sum_{k\geqslant 1} G(k)\binom{2n}{n-k}$$

$$=2\cdot 4^{-n}\sum_{k\geqslant 1} G(k)\left[\binom{2n-2}{n-k}+2\binom{2n-2}{n-k-1}+\binom{2n-2}{n-k-2}\right]$$

$$=2\cdot 4^{-n}\left[\sum_{k\geqslant 0} G(k+1)\binom{2n-2}{n-k-1}\right.$$

$$\left.+2\sum_{k\geqslant 1} G(k)\binom{2n-2}{n-k-1}+\sum_{k\geqslant 2} G(k-1)\binom{2n-2}{n-k-1}\right]$$

$$=4^{-n+1}\binom{2n-2}{n-1}[\mathbf{E}_{n-1}-\tfrac{1}{2}(n-1)]+2\cdot 4^{-n}\sum_{k\geqslant 1}[g(k)-g(k-1)]\binom{2n-2}{n-k-1},$$

we obtain a simple recurrence for $4^{-n}\binom{2n}{n}[\mathbf{E}_n - n/2]$. Solving leads to the alternate

$$\mathbf{E}_n = \tfrac{1}{2}n + \tfrac{1}{2}4^n\sum_{1\leqslant j<n} 4^{-j}\binom{2j}{j}Y_{j,k}\bigg/\binom{2n}{n},$$

where

$$Y_{j,k} = \sum_{k\geqslant 1}[g(k)-g(k-1)]\binom{2j}{j-k}\bigg/\binom{2j}{j}.$$

Thus, if we are able to derive a closed expression for the Dirichlet series with coefficients $[g(k) - g(k-1)]$, the gamma function method can be applied in order to obtain an asymptotic equivalent for $Y_{j,k}$. Using Exercise 5.15, we find

$$\sum_{k\geqslant 1}[g(k)-g(k-1)]k^{-z}$$

$$=\sum_{s\geqslant 0}\sum_{j\geqslant 0}[g(2^s(2j+1))-g(2^s(2j+1)-1)][2^s(2j+1)]^{-z}$$

$$=\sum_{s\geqslant 0}\sum_{j\geqslant 0}(-1)^j 2^{-sz}(2j+1)^{-z}$$

$$=\sum_{s\geqslant 0} 2^{-sz}\sum_{j\geqslant 0}(-1)^j(2j+1)^{-z}$$

$$=2^z\beta(z)/[2^z-1],$$

where $\beta(z) = \sum_{j \geqslant 0} (-1)^j (2j+1)^{-z}$. Since

$$\beta(z) = 2 \sum_{k \geqslant 0} (4k+1)^{-z} - \sum_{k \geqslant 1} k^{-z} + \sum_{k \geqslant 1} (2k)^{-z}$$

$$= 2 \cdot 4^{-z} \zeta(z, \tfrac{1}{4}) - (2^z - 1) 2^{-z} \zeta(z),$$

where $\zeta(z, a)$ is the *Hurwitz zeta function* (Appendix B, 2.13), we finally obtain

$$\sum_{k \geqslant 1} [g(k) - g(k-1)] k^{-z} = 2^{-z+1} (2^z - 1)^{-1} \zeta(z, \tfrac{1}{4}) - \zeta(z).$$

The existence of this simple formula makes the gamma function method applicable to $Y_{j,k}$. The further computation is left to the reader (Exercise 5.16).

We will conclude this section by presenting an alternative method for the evaluation of sums of the above type. This method has first been used in [28], in order to prove Theorem 5.10 (see also [33]).

Recall that

$$\mathbf{E}_n = \tfrac{1}{2}n + 2 \sum_{k \geqslant 1} G(k) \binom{2n}{n-k} \Big/ \binom{2n}{n}$$

where $G(k) = \sum_{0 \leqslant j < k} g(j)$ is the total number of ones appearing in the Gray code representations of the integers $0, 1, 2, \ldots, k-1$. The Gray code representations of the first 16 integers together with the values of $g$ and $G$ are presented in Table 6. Note that the $k$-th column consists of an infinite

TABLE 6. The Gray code representations of $0, 1, \ldots, 15$ together with the values $g(n)$ and $G(n)$.

| n | \multicolumn{4}{c}{k} | g(n) | G(n) |
|---|---|---|---|---|---|---|
|   | 3 | 2 | 1 | 0 | | |
| 0 | | | | 0 | 0 | 0 |
| 1 | | | | 1 | 1 | 0 |
| 2 | | | 1 | 1 | 2 | 1 |
| 3 | | | 1 | 0 | 1 | 3 |
| 4 | | 1 | 1 | 0 | 2 | 4 |
| 5 | | 1 | 1 | 1 | 3 | 6 |
| 6 | | 1 | 0 | 1 | 2 | 9 |
| 7 | | 1 | 0 | 0 | 1 | 11 |
| 8 | 1 | 1 | 0 | 0 | 2 | 12 |
| 9 | 1 | 1 | 0 | 1 | 3 | 14 |
| 10 | 1 | 1 | 1 | 1 | 4 | 17 |
| 11 | 1 | 1 | 1 | 0 | 3 | 20 |
| 12 | 1 | 0 | 1 | 0 | 2 | 23 |
| 13 | 1 | 0 | 1 | 1 | 3 | 25 |
| 14 | 1 | 0 | 0 | 1 | 2 | 28 |
| 15 | 1 | 0 | 0 | 0 | 1 | 30 |

repetition of the block of bits $0^{2^k} 1^{2^{k+1}} 0^{2^k}$. In some sense, we can say that each position in the table has an expected value $\frac{1}{2}$. Let $\Delta_k(n)$ denote the difference between the number of ones actually present in the first $n$ positions of column $k$ and the numbers of ones which we would expect to find there, that is,

$$\Delta_k(n) = -\tfrac{1}{2}n + \sum_{0 \leqslant j < n} p_k(j),$$

where $p_k(j)$ denotes the $k$-th bit in the Gray code representation of $j$. As mentioned above, the $k$-th column consists of an infinite repetition of the block $0^{2^k} 1^{2^{k+1}} 0^{2^k}$. Therefore,

$$\Delta_k(\lambda 2^k) = \begin{cases} 0 & \text{if } \lambda \equiv 0 \bmod (4) \ \vee \ \lambda \equiv 2 \bmod (4) \\ -2^{k-1} & \text{if } \lambda \equiv 1 \bmod (4) \\ 2^{k-1} & \text{if } \lambda \equiv 3 \bmod (4) \end{cases} \quad ;$$

moreover, between these special values of $n$, the graph $\Delta_k(n)$ consists of linear segments. Hence $\Delta_k(n) = 2^{k+2}\Delta(n2^{-k-2})$, where $\Delta(x+1) = \Delta(x)$ for $x \geqslant 1$ and

$$\Delta(x) = \begin{cases} -\tfrac{1}{2}x & \text{if } 0 \leqslant x < \tfrac{1}{4} \\ \tfrac{1}{2}x - \tfrac{1}{4} & \text{if } \tfrac{1}{4} \leqslant x < \tfrac{3}{4}. \\ -\tfrac{1}{2}x + \tfrac{1}{2} & \text{if } \tfrac{3}{4} \leqslant x < 1 \end{cases}$$

Note that $\Delta(x) = 0$ for $x \in \mathbb{N}_0$; moreover, it is easy to verify the alternative form

$$\Delta(x) = \int_0^x (\lfloor t + \tfrac{3}{4} \rfloor - \lfloor t + \tfrac{1}{4} \rfloor - \tfrac{1}{2}) \, dt.$$

Since all the columns in Table 6 of index $k > \lfloor \mathrm{ld}(n) \rfloor$ begin with at least $n$ zeros, we further obtain

$$G(n) = \sum_{0 \leqslant j < n} g(j) = \sum_{0 \leqslant j < n} \sum_{k \geqslant 0} p_k(j)$$

$$= \sum_{0 \leqslant k \leqslant \lfloor \mathrm{ld}(n) \rfloor} [\Delta_k(n) + \tfrac{1}{2}n]$$

$$= \tfrac{1}{2}n(\lfloor \mathrm{ld}(n) \rfloor + 1) + \sum_{0 \leqslant k \leqslant \lfloor \mathrm{ld}(n) \rfloor} 2^{k+2}\Delta(n2^{-k-2})$$

$$= \tfrac{1}{2}n(\lfloor \mathrm{ld}(n) \rfloor + 1) + \sum_{k \geqslant 0} 2^{\lfloor \mathrm{ld}(n) \rfloor - k + 2}\Delta(n2^{-\lfloor \mathrm{ld}(n) \rfloor + k - 2})$$

$$= \tfrac{1}{2}n(\lfloor \mathrm{ld}(n) \rfloor + 1) + 2^{\lfloor \mathrm{ld}(n) \rfloor + 2}h(n2^{-\lfloor \mathrm{ld}(n) \rfloor - 2}),$$

where $h(x) = \sum_{j \geqslant 0} 2^{-j}\Delta(2^j x)$. Since this series converges uniformly on $\mathbb{R}$, the function $h(x)$ is continuous. Denoting the fractional part $x - \lfloor x \rfloor$ of $x$ by $\{x\}$, this expression for $G(n)$ can be easily transformed into

$$G(n) = \tfrac{1}{2}n \, \mathrm{ld}(n) + nF(\mathrm{ld}(n)),$$

where

$$F(x) = \tfrac{1}{2}(1 - \{x\}) + 2^{2-\{x\}}h(2^{\{x\}-2}).$$

Obviously, $F(x)$ is periodic and continuous on $[0,1\rangle$ by continuity of $h$. Moreover,

$$F(0) = \tfrac{1}{2} + 4h(\tfrac{1}{4}) = \tfrac{1}{2} + 4 \sum_{j \geqslant 0} 2^{-j}\Delta(2^{j-2}) = \tfrac{1}{2} + 4(-\tfrac{1}{8} + 0) = 0.$$

Since $F(x)$ approaches 0 as $x$ approaches 1 from below, $F$ is continuous on $\mathbb{R}$. Let us now compute the Fourier series of $F$ given by

$$F(x) = \sum_{-\infty \leqslant k \leqslant \infty} f_k \exp(2k\pi ix),$$

where

$$f_k = \int_0^1 F(u) \exp(-2k\pi iu) \, du.$$

By definition of $F(u)$, we find $f_k = a_k + b_k$, where

$$a_k = \frac{1}{2} \int_0^1 (1 - u) \exp(-2k\pi iu) \, du$$

$$= \begin{cases} \tfrac{1}{2}u(1 - \tfrac{1}{2}u)|_0^1 & \text{if } k = 0 \\ \dfrac{1}{4k\pi i}\left(\dfrac{1}{2k\pi i} - 1 + u\right)\exp(-2k\pi i)|_0^1 & \text{if } k \neq 0 \end{cases}$$

$$= \begin{cases} \tfrac{1}{4} & \text{if } k = 0 \\ \dfrac{1}{4k\pi i} & \text{if } k \neq 0 \end{cases}$$

and

$$b_k = \int_0^1 2^{2-u}h(2^{u-2}) \exp(-2k\pi iu) \, du.$$

Since $h(x) = \sum_{j \geqslant 0} 2^{-j}\Delta(2^j x)$, $b_k$ can be transformed into

$$b_k = \sum_{j \geqslant 0} \int_0^1 2^{2-u-j}\Delta(2^{u+j-2}) \exp(-2k\pi iu) \, du.$$

The interchange of summation and integration is justified because $h(x)$ is a uniformly convergent series. Substituting $u = 2 - j + \mathrm{ld}(v)$, we further obtain

$$b_k = \frac{1}{\ln(2)} \sum_{j \geqslant 0} \int_{2^{j-2}}^{2^{j-1}} \frac{\Delta(v)}{v^2 + 2k\pi i/\ln(2)} \, dv$$

$$= \frac{1}{\ln(2)} M(1 + 2\pi ik/\ln(2)),$$

where

$$M(z) = \int_{1/4}^{\infty} \Delta(v)/v^{z+1} \, dv.$$

Using the above integral representation of $\Delta(v)$ and integrating $M(z)$ by parts, we find

$$M(z) = \int_{1/4}^{\infty} \left[ \int_0^v (\lfloor t + \tfrac{3}{4} \rfloor - \lfloor t + \tfrac{1}{4} \rfloor - \tfrac{1}{2}) \, dt \right] \Big/ v^{z+1} \, dv$$

$$= -z^{-1} v^{-z} \Delta(v)|_{1/4}^{\infty} + z^{-1} \int_{1/4}^{\infty} (\lfloor v + \tfrac{3}{4} \rfloor - \lfloor v + \tfrac{1}{4} \rfloor - \tfrac{1}{2})/v^z \, dz$$

$$= -\tfrac{1}{2} z^{-1} 4^{z-1} + z^{-1} \int_{1/4}^{\infty} (\lfloor v + \tfrac{3}{4} \rfloor - \lfloor v + \tfrac{1}{4} \rfloor - \tfrac{1}{2})/v^z \, dz.$$

Thus we have to evaluate this integral. Since for $\mathrm{Re}(z) > 2$, $a \in \langle 0, 1]$,

$$\frac{1}{2} \int_{1/4}^{\infty} \frac{dv}{v^z} = \tfrac{1}{2} 4^{z-1}/(z-1)$$

and

$$(z-1) \int_a^{\infty} \lfloor v + 1 - a \rfloor v^{-z} \, dv = \lim_{n \to \infty} (z-1) \int_a^{n+a} \lfloor v + 1 - a \rfloor v^{-z} \, dv$$

$$= \lim_{n \to \infty} \sum_{1 \leqslant \lambda \leqslant n} \lambda \int_{a+\lambda-1}^{a+\lambda} (z-1) v^{-z} \, dv$$

$$= \sum_{\lambda \geqslant 1} \lambda [(a + \lambda - 1)^{-z+1} - (a + \lambda)^{-z+1}]$$

$$= \sum_{\lambda \geqslant 1} (\lambda + a)^{-z+1}$$

$$= \zeta(z - 1, a),$$

where $\zeta(z, a)$ is the Hurwitz zeta function, we further obtain

$$M(z) = -\frac{1}{2(z-1)} 4^{z-1} + \frac{1}{z(z-1)} [\zeta(z - 1, \tfrac{1}{4}) - \zeta(z - 1, \tfrac{3}{4})]$$

for $\mathrm{Re}(z) > 2$. By analytic continuation, this equation also holds for $\mathrm{Re}(z) > 0$ with $z \neq 1$. Finally, an application of (B132) with $l = 2$ and $l = 4$ leads to $\zeta(z, \tfrac{3}{4}) = (4^z - 2^z)\zeta(z) - \zeta(z, \tfrac{1}{4})$; hence

$$M(z) = -\frac{1}{2(z-1)} 4^{z-1} + \frac{1}{z(z-1)} [2\zeta(z - 1, \tfrac{1}{4}) - (4^{z-1} - 2^{z-1})\zeta(z - 1)].$$

Therefore, $b_0 = M(1)/\ln(2)$, and for $k \neq 0$

$$b_k = \frac{1}{\ln(2)} M(1 + 2\pi i k/\ln(2))$$

$$= -\frac{1}{4\pi i k} + \frac{\ln(2)}{\pi i k[2\pi i k + \ln(2)]} \zeta\left(2, \frac{\pi i k}{\ln(2)}, \frac{1}{4}\right).$$

An application of (B126), (B127), and (B73) yields immediately

$$M(z) = 2\ln(\Gamma(\tfrac{1}{4})) - \tfrac{3}{2}\ln(2) - \ln(\pi) - \tfrac{1}{2} + O(z-1);$$

hence

$$b_0 = 2\,\mathrm{ld}(\Gamma(\tfrac{1}{4})) - \tfrac{3}{2} - \mathrm{ld}(\pi) - \frac{1}{2\ln(2)}.$$

Summarizing our results, we obtain the following theorem ([33]).

THEOREM 5.24   Let $G(n)$ be the total number of ones appearing in the Gray code representation of the integers $0, 1, 2, 3, \ldots, n-1$. There exists a continuous function $F: \mathbb{R} \to \mathbb{R}$, periodic with period 1, such that

$$G(n) = \tfrac{1}{2}n\,\mathrm{ld}(n) + nF(\mathrm{ld}(n)).$$

The Fourier series $F(x) = \sum_{-\infty \leqslant k \leqslant \infty} f_k \exp(2k\pi i x)$ of $F$ converges absolutely, and its coefficients are given by

$$f_0 = 2\,\mathrm{ld}(\Gamma(\tfrac{1}{4})) - \mathrm{ld}(\pi) - \frac{1}{2\ln(2)} - \frac{5}{4},$$

$$f_k = \frac{\ln(2)}{k\pi i[2k\pi i + \ln(2)]} \zeta\left(2, \frac{\pi i k}{\ln(2)}, \frac{1}{4}\right), \qquad k \neq 0$$

where $\zeta(z, a)$ is the Hurwitz zeta function. ∎

For similar results concerning such sums, see [22], [33], [84].

We will now use Theorem 5.24 in order to compute the asymptotic behaviour of the average number $\mathbf{E}_n$ of exchanges required by the odd–even merge OEM($2n$) for sorting 2-ordered sequences consisting of $2n$ distinct elements. Applying the approximation (F4) (section 5.1.1) to the result given in Theorem 5.23, we find

$$\mathbf{E}_n = \tfrac{1}{2}n + 2 \sum_{1 \leqslant k \leqslant n^{1/2+\varepsilon}} G(k)\exp(-k^2/n)[1 + O(n^{-1+\delta})],$$

because the terms for $k > n^{1/2+\varepsilon}$ are exponentially small. Taking advantage of the information on the structure of $G(k)$ presented in Theorem 5.24, we further obtain

$$\mathbf{E}_n = \tfrac{1}{2}n + 2 \sum_{1 \leqslant k \leqslant n^{1/2+\varepsilon}} [\tfrac{1}{2}k\,\mathrm{ld}(k) + kF(\mathrm{ld}(k))]\exp(-k^2/n)[1 + O(n^{-1+\delta})].$$

Splitting this sum into two parts, we find

$$E_n = \tfrac{1}{2}n + [S_1(n) + 2S_2(n)][1 + O(n^{-1+\delta})],$$

where

$$S_1(n) = \sum_{1 \leqslant k \leqslant n^{1/2+\varepsilon}} k \, \mathrm{ld}(k) \exp(-k^2/n)$$

and

$$S_2(n) = \sum_{1 \leqslant k \leqslant n^{1/2+\varepsilon}} k F(\mathrm{ld}(k)) \exp(-k^2/n).$$

For $S_1(n)$, we can use *Euler's summation formula* (Appendix A, 7) and obtain by an elementary computation

$$S_1(n) = \int_1^{n^{1/2+\varepsilon}} x \, \mathrm{ld}(x) \exp(-x^2/n) + O(n^{1/2+\varepsilon})$$

$$= \int_1^{\infty} x \, \mathrm{ld}(x) \exp(-x^2/n) + O(1) + O(n^{1/2+\varepsilon})$$

$$= \tfrac{1}{2}n \, \mathrm{ld}(n) \int_0^{\infty} t \exp(-t^2) \, dt + \frac{n}{\ln(2)} \int_0^{\infty} t \ln(t) \exp(-t^2) \, dt + O(n^{1/2+\varepsilon})$$

$$= \tfrac{1}{4}n \, \mathrm{ld}(n) - \frac{\gamma n}{4 \ln(2)} + O(n^{1/2+\varepsilon}),$$

because the first integral is equal to $\tfrac{1}{2}$ and the second integral is equal to $-\gamma/4$.

Let us now consider the sum $S_2(n)$. Since the function $F(x)$ is not differentiable, Euler's summation formula is not applicable. However, the sum $S_2(n)$ can be handled as follows:

Recall that

$$F(x) = \tfrac{1}{2}(1 - \{x\}) + 2^{2-\{x\}}h(2^{\{x\}-2}),$$

where

$$h(x) = \sum_{j \geqslant 0} 2^{-j}\Delta(2^j x).$$

The definition of $\Delta(x)$ implies that this function has maximum slope $\tfrac{1}{2}$; hence $\Delta(x)$ satisfies the Lipschitz condition $|\Delta(b) - \Delta(a)| \leqslant \tfrac{1}{2}|b - a|$. Now let $I_k$ be an interval of length $1/k$. Splitting up the sum for $h(x)$ at the $\lfloor \mathrm{ld}(k) \rfloor$-term, we find that

$$h(x) = \sum_{0 \leqslant j < \lfloor \mathrm{ld}(k) \rfloor} 2^{-j}\Delta(2^j x) + 2^{-\lfloor \mathrm{ld}(k) \rfloor}h(2^{\lfloor \mathrm{ld}(k) \rfloor}x).$$

Since $2^{-\lfloor \mathrm{ld}(k) \rfloor}h(2^{\lfloor \mathrm{ld}(k) \rfloor}x) = O(1/k)$ and the summation involves $\lfloor \mathrm{ld}(k) \rfloor$ terms, each of which satisfies the above Lipschitz condition, we get $\mathrm{osc}(h(x), I_k) = O(k^{-1} \mathrm{ld}(k))$, where $\mathrm{osc}(f(x), I)$ denotes the oscillation of the function $f$ on the interval $I$ defined by $\mathrm{osc}(f(x), I) = \sup_{x \in I} f(x) - \inf_{x \in I} f(x)$. Returning to $F(x)$, we may conclude that $\mathrm{osc}(F(x), [\mathrm{ld}(k), \mathrm{ld}(k+1)]) = O(k^{-1} \mathrm{ld}(k))$, because the length of $[\mathrm{ld}(k), \mathrm{ld}(k+1)]$ is essentially $1/k$. Thus

$$\text{osc}(xF(\text{ld}(x))\exp(-x^2/n),[k,k+1]) = O(\text{ld}(k))$$

and

$$\left| S_2(n) - \int_1^{n^{1/2+\varepsilon}} xF(\text{ld}(x))\exp(-x^2/n)\,dx \right| \leqslant \sum_{1 \leqslant k < n^{1/2+\varepsilon}} O(\text{ld}(k)) = O(n^{1/2+\varepsilon}\text{ld}(n)).$$

This relation follows from the well-known result that

$$\left| \int_a^b f(x)\,dx - \sum_{0 < i \leqslant n} (x_i - x_{i-1})f(x_i) \right| \leqslant (b-a) \sup_{0 < i \leqslant n} \text{osc}(f,[x_i,x_{i+1}]),$$

where $f$ is continuous on $[a,b]$ and $x_i$, $0 \leqslant i \leqslant n$, is an increasing sequence of points of $[a,b]$ with $a = x_0 < x_1 < x_2 < \cdots < x_n = b$. Changing the limits of integration to 0 and $\infty$, only an additional $0(1)$ term is introduced. Therefore,

$$S_2(n) = \int_0^\infty xF(\text{ld}(x))\exp(-x^2/n)\,dx + O(n^{1/2+\varepsilon}\text{ld}(n)).$$

Substituting the Fourier series of $F$ (which converges absolutely), we may interchange summation and integration and obtain with Theorem 5.24 and (B106)

$$S_2(n) = \sum_{-\infty \leqslant k \leqslant \infty} f_k \int_0^\infty x^{1+2\pi i k/\ln(2)}\exp(-x^2/n)\,dx + O(n^{1/2+\varepsilon}\text{ld}(n))$$

$$= \tfrac{1}{2}n \sum_{-\infty \leqslant k \leqslant \infty} f_k \exp(k\pi i\,\text{ld}(n)) \int_0^\infty t^{k\pi i/\ln(2)}\exp(-t)\,dt + O(n^{1/2+\varepsilon}\text{ld}(n))$$

$$= \tfrac{1}{2}n \sum_{-\infty \leqslant k \leqslant \infty} f_k \exp(k\pi i\,\text{ld}(n))\Gamma\!\left(1 + \frac{\pi i k}{\ln(2)}\right) + O(n^{1/2+\varepsilon}\text{ld}(n)).$$

Summarizing our results, we have proved the following theorem.

THEOREM 5.25  Assuming that all 2-ordered sequences consisting of $2n$ distinct elements are equally likely, the average number $\mathbf{E}_n$ of exchanges required by the odd–even merge OEM($2n$) for sorting such a sequence is asymptotically given by

$$\mathbf{E}_n = \tfrac{1}{4}n\,\text{ld}(n) + n\left[\text{ld}(\Gamma^2(\tfrac{1}{4})/\pi) - \frac{\gamma+2}{4\ln(2)} - \frac{3}{4} + H(n)\right] + O(n^{1/2+\varepsilon}\text{ld}(n))$$

for all $\varepsilon > 0$, where

$$H(n) = \sum_{\substack{-\infty \leqslant k \leqslant \infty \\ k \neq 0}} [2k\pi i + \ln(2)]^{-1}\Gamma\!\left(\frac{\pi i k}{\ln(2)}\right)\zeta\!\left(2\frac{\pi i k}{\ln(2)},\frac{1}{4}\right)\exp(\pi ki\,\text{ld}(n))$$

is an oscillating function with $H(n) = H(4n)$. ∎

Theorem 5.25 has first been proved in [109] by an application of the gamma function method; there is shown that the error term can be reduced to

$O(\sqrt{n}\,\mathrm{ld}(n))$. On the other hand, the method that we have just described seems somewhat more straightforward and direct than the gamma function method.

## Exercises

**5.1** Use the functional equation $\Gamma(z+1) = z\Gamma(z)$ in order to show that $\operatorname{Res}_{z=-r}(\Gamma(z)) = (-1)^r/r!$, $r \in \mathbb{N}_0$.

**5.2** Let $V_n(x)$ be the cumulative distribution function given in Theorem 5.5.

(a) Show that $V_n(x)$ is strictly increasing for $x \geqslant 0$.

(b) Show that $V_n(x) - V_n(x-1) = O(n^{-\alpha})$ for some $\alpha > 0$.

**5.3** Show that complete ordered binary trees with $n$ leaves can always be reduced by a $\lfloor\mathrm{ld}(2n)\rfloor$-program.

**5.4** (Open) Give an explicit one-to-one correspondence between the classes of trees defined in Theorem 5.8.

**5.5** (a) Compute the higher moments defined in Theorem 5.9.

(b) Let $V_n(x)$ be the probability that an ordered binary tree with $n$ leaves can be reduced by algorithm $OP$ using less than or equal to $k$ variables. Derive an expression for $V_n(x)$.

**5.6** Prove Lemma 5.1.

**5.7** (Open) Give an explicit one-to-one correspondence between the classes of trees defined in Theorem 5.13.

**5.8** Prove Theorem 5.16.

**5.9** Prove Lemma 5.2.

**5.10** Let $\mathbf{B}_1 = \{b\}$, $\mathbf{B}_1 = \{\bar{b}\}$, and $PO(T)$ be the post-order of the nodes of an ordered binary tree $T$ with a set of leaves $L$ and a set of interior $I$; moreover, define the monoidhomomorphism $\varphi: (I \cup L)^* \to (B_1 \cup \mathbf{B}_1)^*$ by $\varphi(x) := if \ x \in L \ then \ b \ else \ \bar{b};$.

(a) Show that $\varphi(PO(T))\bar{b} \in DY_1$, where $DY_1$ is the Dycklanguage with one type of bracket.

(b) Give a one-to-one correspondence between the set of Dyckwords of length $2n$ and the set of ordered binary trees with $(n+1)$ leaves.

**5.11** Show that the number $z_k(2N, p)$ of all Dyckwords $w \in DY_k(2N)$ which can be recognized by algorithm $D2W1C$ using a maximum value $p$ of $Z$ is equal to the number $d_k(2N, p+1)$ of all $w \in DY_k(2N)$ requiring a maximum stack length $(p+1)$ during the recognition of $w$ by algorithm $DS$.

**5.12** Prove Lemma 5.4.

**5.13** Consider the following implementation of algorithm $D2W1C$ on a two-tape off-line Turing machine $T$: the moves on the input tape are identical to the moves of the input pointer in the description of $D2W1C$; the binary counter $Z$ is simulated by the second tape of $T$ as follows: performing the operation $Z \leftarrow Z + 1$ $(Z \leftarrow Z - 1)$, the head moves from the rightmost position in $(Z)_2$ to the left and replaces all ones by zeros (all zeros by ones) until it has found the rightmost zero (one) in $(Z)_2$; after replacing this symbol by one (zero), it starts back until the rightmost position in the new inscription is reached. Thus the average number $\tau(2n)$ of moves required by $T$ for recognizing $w \in DY_k(2n)$ is given by $\tau(2n) = \mathbf{T}_{D2W1C}(2n) + \mathbf{T}_Z(2n)$, where $\mathbf{T}_Z(2n)$ is the average number of moves on the second tape.

(a) Show that for all $\delta > 0$

$$\mathbf{T}_Z(2n) = (8n+9)\sqrt{\pi n} - 8(n+1)\,\mathrm{ld}(4\pi\sqrt{n}) + n\left[\frac{4\gamma}{\ln(2)} + 12 + \frac{8}{\ln(2)}F_0(n)\right]$$

$$+ 12 + \frac{12\gamma - 4}{3\ln(2)} + \frac{4}{\ln(2)}F_1(n) - \frac{4}{3\ln(2)}F_2(n) + \frac{8}{\ln(2)}F_0(n) + O(n^{-\delta}),$$

where

$$F_s(n) = \sum_{\substack{-\infty \leqslant k \leqslant \infty \\ k \neq 0}} \Gamma\left(s + \frac{\pi i k}{\ln(2)}\right) \zeta\left(2\frac{\pi i k}{\ln(2)}\right) \exp(\pi i k \, \mathrm{ld}(n))$$

is an oscillating function with $F_s(n) = F_s(4n)$.

(b) Show that, for large $n$, one move on the input tape corresponds to two moves on the second tape, on average.

**5.14** Consider the lattice diagram introduced in section 5.3.2. Show that the path from $(0, 0)$ to $(n, n)$ of highest weight must be one of the major diagonals.

**5.15** Let $g(k)$ be the number of ones in the Gray code representation of $k \in \mathbb{N}_0$, $g^{-1}(k) = \mathrm{MIN}\{j \mid g(j) = k\}$, and $G(n) = \sum_{0 \leqslant k < n} g(k)$.

(a) Show that

$$g(2^s(2j + 1)) = (-1)^j + g(2^s(2j + 1) - 1) \quad \text{for } s, j \in \mathbb{N}_0.$$

(b) Show that

$$G(2^n) = n2^{n-1}.$$

(c) Let $n \geqslant 0$ and $2^{n-1} < k \leqslant 2^n$. Show that

$$G(k) = (n - 2)2^{n-1} + k - G(2^n - k).$$

(d) Show that

$$g^{-1}(k) = 2^k - 1 - g^{-1}(k - 1) \quad \text{for } k \geqslant 1.$$

(e) Show that

$$G(g^{-1}(k)) = g^{-1}(k) + (k - 2)2^{k-1} - (k - 1) - G(g^{-1}(k - 1)), \qquad k \geqslant 1.$$

(f) Deduce from (b), (c), (d), and (e)

$$G(g^{-1}(k)) = \tfrac{1}{18}[(3k - 1)2^{k+1} - 9k - (3k - 2)(-1)^k].$$

**5.16** Prove Theorem 5.25 by the gamma function method.

**5.17** Prove Theorem 5.10 by the method presented at the end of section 5.3.3. (*Hint:* Show the following result ([22]) which is quite similar to that given in Theorem 5.24:

Let $S_2(k)$ be the number of ones appearing in the binary representation of $k \in \mathbb{N}_0$ and let $F(n) = \sum_{0 \leqslant k < n} S_2(k)$. There exists a continuous function $M: \mathbb{R} \to \mathbb{R}$, periodic with period 1, such that for $n \geqslant 1$: $F(n) = \frac{1}{2}n\,\mathrm{ld}(n) + nM(\mathrm{ld}(n))$. The Fourier series $M(x) = \sum_{-\infty \leqslant k \leqslant \infty} f_k \exp(2k\pi i x)$ of $M$ converges absolutely, and its coefficients are given by

$$f_0 = \tfrac{1}{2}\,\mathrm{ld}(\pi) - \frac{1}{2\ln(2)} - \frac{1}{4}$$

$$f_k = -\frac{\ln(2)}{2k\pi i[\ln(2) + 2k\pi i]}\,\zeta\left(2\frac{k\pi i}{\ln(2)}\right), k \neq 0.)$$

**5.18** (Open) Give a detailed average case analysis of the time required by algorithm $D_k$ for reducing ordered binary trees with $n$ leaves.

**5.19** Reducing an ordered binary tree $T$ with $n$ leaves by algorithm $S$, in one unit of time, zero or two nodes are removed from the top of the stack and one node is stored in the stack.

(a) Assume that all ordered binary trees with $n$ leaves are equally likely and show that the average number $R(n, t)$ of nodes stored in the stack after $t$ units of time is given by

$$R_1(n, 2t + b) = 2\frac{2n - 1}{(2t + b)(2n - 2t - b)} \sum_{k \geqslant 0} (2k + b)^3 \binom{2t + b}{t - k}\binom{2n - 2t - b}{n - t + k} \Big/ \binom{2n}{n},$$

where $b \in \{0, 1\}$.

(b) Prove the identities

(i) $\displaystyle\sum_{k \geqslant 0} (2k)^3 \binom{2n}{n-k}\binom{2m}{m+k} = 4 \frac{m^2 n^2}{(m+n)(m+n-1)} \binom{2m}{m}\binom{2n}{n}$

(ii) $\displaystyle\sum_{k \geqslant 0} (2k+1)^3 \binom{2n+1}{n-k}\binom{2m-1}{m+k} = w(n, m) \binom{2m-2}{m-1}\binom{2n}{n}$,

where

$$w(n, m) = \frac{(2n+1)(2m-1)}{(n+m)(n+m-1)} [(2n+1)(2m-1) - (n+m)].$$

(c) Deduce from (a) and (b)

$$R_1(n, t) = 4\sqrt{n\rho(1 - \rho)/\pi} + O(n^{-1/2})$$

where $\rho = t/(2n)$ is a constant.

(d) Find an approximation for $\dbinom{2t+b}{t-b}\dbinom{2n-2t-b}{n-t+k} \Big/ \dbinom{2n}{n}$ and deduce from (a) by the gamma function method

$$R_1(n, t) = 4\sqrt{n\rho(1 - \rho)/\pi} - [5\rho^2 - 5\rho + 1]/[2\sqrt{n\rho(1 - \rho)\pi}] + O(n^{-1+\delta})$$

for all $\delta > 0$, where $\rho = t/(2n)$ is a constant.

(e) Show that the variance is for all $\varepsilon > 0$ given by

$$\sigma^2(n, t) = \left(6 - \frac{16}{\pi}\right)\rho(1 - \rho)n + \left(9 - \frac{20}{\pi}\right)\rho(1 - \rho) - \left(2 - \frac{4}{\pi}\right) + O(n^{-1/2+\delta}).$$

**5.20** Let $DY_1$ be the Dycklanguage with one type of bracket. The level of a bracket appearing in $w \in DY_1$ is the number of preceding opening brackets minus the number of preceding closing brackets. Assuming that all Dyckwords $w \in DY_1(2n)$ are equally likely, compute the average maximum level of a bracket appearing in $w$.

**5.21** Assume that all $n$-node ordered trees with $m$ leaves are equally likely and show that the average height $\mathbf{h}(n, m)$ is asymptotically given for all $\delta > 0$ and fixed $\rho = m/n$, $0 < \rho < 1$, by

$$\mathbf{h}(n, m) = \sqrt{1/\rho - 1}\,\sqrt{\pi n} + \tfrac{3}{2} - 1/\rho + O(\ln(n)/n^{1/2-\delta}).$$

# Appendix A

## 1. Basic Definitions of Probability Theory

### 1.1 Real Valued Function

A real valued function $F(x)$ is called a (univariate) *cumulative distribution function* if (i) $F(x_1) \leqslant F(x_2)$ for $x_1 \leqslant x_2$, (ii) $F(x) = \lim_{\varepsilon \to 0+} F(x + \varepsilon)$, and (iii) $\lim_{x \to -\infty} F(x) = 0$, $\lim_{x \to \infty} F(x) = 1$.

The function $F(x)$ signifies the probability $Pr(X \leqslant x)$ of the event '$X \leqslant x$', where $X$ is a *random variable*, i.e. $Pr(X \leqslant x) = F(x)$. *Discrete distribution* is characterized by the random variable $X$ taking on an enumerable number of values $\ldots, x_{-1}, x_0, x_1, \ldots$ with point probabilities $p_n = Pr(X = x_n) \geqslant 0$, where $\sum_{-\infty \leqslant k \leqslant \infty} p_k = 1$.

### 1.2 Characteristics

$$\mathbb{E}(X^n) = \sum_k x_k^n p_k \qquad \text{($n$-th moment about the origin of $X$)} \qquad \text{(A1)}$$

$$\mathbb{E}(X) = \sum_k x_k p_k \qquad \text{(mean or expected value of $X$)} \qquad \text{(A2)}$$

$$\sigma^2 = \mathbb{E}((X - \mathbb{E}(X))^2)$$

$$= \mathbb{E}(X^2) - \mathbb{E}(X)^2 \qquad \text{(variance)} \qquad \text{(A3)}$$

$$\sigma = [\mathbb{E}(X^2) - \mathbb{E}(X)^2]^{1/2} \qquad \text{(standard deviation)} \qquad \text{(A4)}$$

### 1.3 Relations

Let $X$ be a random variable which takes on non-negative integer values. The function $P(z) = \sum_{n \geqslant 0} p_n z^n$ is called the *probability generating function*.

$$\mathbb{E}(X) = P'(1) \qquad \text{(A5)}$$

$$\mathbb{E}(X^2) = P'(1) + P''(1) \qquad \text{(A6)}$$

$$\sigma^2(X) = P'(1) + P''(1) - [P'(1)]^2 \qquad \text{(A7)}$$

$$\mathbb{E}(X^n) = \left(z\frac{\mathrm{d}}{\mathrm{d}z}\right)^n P(z)\big|_{z=1} \tag{A8}$$

$$Pr(|X - \mathbb{E}(X)| \geqslant k\sigma) \leqslant k^{-2} \quad \text{(Chebyshev inequality)} \tag{A9}$$

## 2. Grammars—Formal Power Series

### 2.1 Context-free Substitution Scheme

A *context-free substitution scheme* is a 4-tuple $G = (V_N, V_T, P, S)$, where (i) $V_N$ is a countable set of *non-terminals*, (ii) $V_T$ is a countable set of *terminals*, (iii) $P \subseteq V_N \times (V_N \cup V_T)^*$ is a countable set of *rules* or *productions* and $S \in V_N$ is the *start symbol*. A context-free substitution scheme is called a *context-free grammar* if the sets $V_N$, $V_T$, and $P$ are finite. Here, $G$ is said to be *linear* if $P \subseteq V_N \times (V_N V_T \cup V_T V_N \cup V_T \cup \{\varepsilon\})$, where '$\varepsilon$' is the *empty word* (unit element) in the *free monoid* $(V_N \cup V_T)^*$ generated by $V_N \cup V_T$, that is, the set of all *strings* (*words*) obtained by juxtaposition of the elements of $V_N \cup V_T$. Here, $G$ is *proper* if there is no production in $(A, w) \in P$ with $w = \varepsilon$ or $w \in V_N$.

The relation $\rightarrow_r \subseteq (V_N \cup V_T)^* \times (V_N \cup V_T)^*$ is defined as follows: for any $\alpha, \beta \in (V_N \cup V_T)^*$, $\alpha \rightarrow_r \beta$ if and only if $\alpha = \alpha_1 A \alpha_2$, $\beta = \alpha_1 \gamma \alpha_2$, $\alpha_2 \in V_T^*$ and $(A, \gamma) \in P$ for some $A \in V_N$ and $\alpha_1, \alpha_2 \in (V_N \cup V_T)^*$. The string $\beta$ is *derivable* from $\alpha$ by $G$ if $\alpha \xrightarrow{*}_r \beta$, where $\xrightarrow{*}_r$ is the reflexive–transitive closure of $\rightarrow_r$. The set $\mathscr{L}_A(G) = \{w \in V_T^* \mid A \xrightarrow{*}_r w\}$ consists of all derivable words from the non-terminal $A$; $\mathscr{L}_S(G)$ is called the *language generated by* $G$. A context-free substitution scheme is *unambiguous* if there is exactly one derivation $S \xrightarrow{*}_r w$ for all $w \in \mathscr{L}_S(G)$.

### 2.2 Formal Power Series

A *formal power series* over the free monoid $X^*$ is a mapping $r: X^* \rightarrow \mathbb{N}_0$, written symbolically as $r = \sum_{w \in X^*} r(w)w$, where $r(w)$ is called the coefficient of $w$. Defining $r_1 + r_2$ and $r_1 \cdot r_2$ as the formal power series having the coefficients

$$(r_1 + r_2)(w) = r_1(w) + r_2(w) \quad \text{and} \quad (r_1 \cdot r_2)(w) = \sum_{w_1, w_2 \in X^*, w = w_1 w_2} r_1(w_1)r_2(w_2),$$

respectively, the set of formal power series forms a semi-ring. This semi-ring also has an operation of scalar multiplication by elements of $\mathbb{N}_0$.

### 2.3 Relations

Let $G = (V_N, V_T, P, S)$ be a context-free proper substitution scheme. The formal power series $\mathrm{car}(\mathscr{L}_A(G)) = \sum_{w \in V_T^*} \mathrm{car}(\mathscr{L}_A(G))(w)w$, $A \in V_N$, where $\mathrm{car}(\mathscr{L}_A(G))(w) = 1$ if $w \in \mathscr{L}_A(G)$, and $\mathrm{car}(\mathscr{L}_A(G))(w) = 0$ if $w \notin \mathscr{L}_A(G)$, is the *characteristic power series* of $\mathscr{L}_A(G)$.

The set of formal equations

$$\left\{ A = \sum_{w \in \{u \mid (A,u) \in P\}} w \mid A \in V_N \right\}$$

is the *set of equations induced by G.*

Fact: Let $G$ be a context-free, proper, unambiguous substitution scheme. If we substitute $\mathrm{car}(\mathscr{L}_A(G))$ for each occurrence of $A \in V_N$ in the set of equations induced by $G$ we get a true set of identities in the corresponding semi-ring of formal power series.

This relation does not hold for ambiguous schemes.

## 3. Generating Functions

### 3.1 Ordinary Generating Function

The *ordinary generating function* for a sequence $a_0, a_1, a_2, \ldots$ of numbers is the power series $A(z) = \sum_{i \geq 0} a_i z^i$. The *exponential generating function* for $a_0, a_1, a_2, \ldots$ is given by $\mathbf{A}(z) = \sum_{i \geq 0} a_i z^i / i!$.

$$a_n = \frac{1}{n!} \frac{\mathrm{d}^n}{\mathrm{d}z^n} A(z) \bigg|_{z=0}, \qquad a_n = \frac{\mathrm{d}^n}{\mathrm{d}z^n} \mathbf{A}(z) \bigg|_{z=0} \tag{A10}$$

$$a_n = (2\pi i)^{-1} \int_C z^{-n-1} A(z) \, \mathrm{d}z \tag{A11}$$

($A(z)$ is analytic for $|z| < r$ and continuous for $|z| \leq r$, $r > 0$; $C$ is the contour $|z| = r$ and the integration is counterclockwise.)

### 3.2 Principal Generating Functions

$$(1 - z)^{-n-1} = \sum_{k \geq 0} \binom{n+k}{k} z^k \tag{A12}$$

$$\exp(z) = \sum_{k \geq 0} z^k / k! \tag{A13}$$

$$\ln(1 + z) = \sum_{k \geq 1} (-1)^{k+1} z^k / k \tag{A14}$$

$$\ln(1 - z) = -\sum_{k \geq 1} z^k / k \tag{A15}$$

$$(1 - z)^{-1/2} = \sum_{k \geq 0} \binom{2k}{k} 4^{-k} z^k \tag{A16}$$

$$(1 - \sqrt{1 - 4z})/(2z) = \sum_{k \geq 0} \frac{1}{k+1} \binom{2k}{k} z^k. \tag{A17}$$

For further generating functions see (B1), (B8), (B11), (B12), (B33), (B38), (B42), (B47), (B50), (B54), (B61), (B69), (B76), (B83), (B88), (B94), (B99), (B102).

## 4. Linear Recurrences

A *homogeneous linear recurrence with constant coefficients* has the form $\sum_{0 \leq i \leq k} a_i x_{n-i} = 0$, where each $a_i$ is a constant. The *characteristic equation* of the recurrence is given by $\sum_{0 \leq i \leq k} a_i r^{n-i} = 0$.

Fact: Let the roots of the characteristic equation be $r_i, i = 1, 2, \ldots, m$, and let their respective multiplicities be $w_i, i = 1, 2, \ldots, m$. Any solution $x_n$ of the linear recurrence is of the form

$$x_n = \sum_{1 \leq i \leq m} r_i^n \sum_{0 \leq j < w_i} C_{ij} n^j,$$

where the $C_{ij}$ are constants determined by the initial conditions of the recurrence.

## 5. Dirichlet Series

The series $\sum_{n \geq 1} a_n n^{-z}$ is called the *Dirichlet series with coefficients $a_n$*.

Fact: Assuming that the Dirichlet series $\sum_{n \geq 1} a_n n^{-z}$ does not converge for all $z$ or diverge for all $z$, then there is a real number $\sigma_a$ such that the series $\sum_{n \geq 1} a_n n^{-z}$ converges absolutely if $\text{Re}(z) > \sigma_a$ but does not converge absolutely if $\text{Re}(z) < \sigma_a$.

### 5.1 Convolution Theorem

Given two functions $F(z)$ and $G(z)$ represented by the Dirichlet series, $F(z) = \sum_{n \geq 1} f_n n^{-z}$, $\text{Re}(z) > a$, and $G(z) = \sum_{n \geq 1} g_n n^{-z}$, $\text{Re}(z) > b$. Then in the half-plane where both series converge absolutely we have $F(z)G(z) = \sum_{n \geq 1} h_n n^{-z}$, where $h_n$ is the Dirichlet convolution of $f_n$ and $g_n$ defined by $h_n = \sum_{d \mid n} f_d g_{n/d}$.

## 6. Laurent Series—Residues—Cauchy Integral Formula

Let $z_0$ be a complex number, let $0 \leq \alpha < \beta \leq \infty$, and let $f$ be analytic in the annulus $A = \{z \mid \alpha < |z - z_0| < \beta\}$. Here, $f$ can be uniquely represented by $f(z) = \sum_{-\infty \leq n \leq \infty} a_n (z - z_0)^n$ for all $z \in A$ (*Laurent series*), where

$$a_n = \frac{1}{2\pi i} \int_{C_p} \frac{f(t)}{(t - z_0)^{n+1}} \, dt;$$

$C_p$ denotes the circle $z = z_0 + p \cdot \exp(i\alpha)$, $0 \leq \alpha \leq 2\pi$. The coefficient $a_{-1}$ is called the *residue of $f$ at $z_0$* and is denoted by $\text{Res}_{z = z_0} f(z)$.

### 6.1 Residue Theorem

Let $f$ be analytic up to isolated singularities at the points $z_i$, $1 \leqslant i \leqslant m$, in the simply connected domain $R$ and let $C$ be a positively oriented Jordan curve, where the points $z_i$, $1 \leqslant i \leqslant m$, lie in the interior of $C$. Then

$$\frac{1}{2\pi i} \int_C f(z)\, dz = \sum_{1 \leqslant k \leqslant m} \operatorname*{Res}_{z = z_k} f(z).$$

### 6.2 Cauchy Integral Formula

Let $R$ be a simply connected domain, let $f$ be analytic everywhere in $R$, and let $z_0$ be a point of $R$. If $C$ is a positively oriented Jordan curve that contains the point $z_0$ in its interior, then

$$f(z_0) = \frac{1}{2\pi i} \int_C \frac{f(z)}{z - z_0}\, dz.$$

### 7. Euler's Summation Formula

$$\sum_{1 \leqslant k < m} f(k) = \int_1^m f(x)\, dx - \tfrac{1}{2}[f(m) - f(1)] + \tfrac{1}{12}[f'(m) - f'(1)] + O\left(\int_1^m |f''(x)|\, dx\right).$$

# Appendix B

## 1. Numbers in Combinatorial Analysis

*1.1 q-Nomial Coefficients* $\begin{pmatrix} x, q \\ n \end{pmatrix}$

$$\sum_{n \geqslant 0} \binom{x, q}{n} z^n = \left[ \sum_{0 \leqslant i < q} z^i \right]^x, \qquad q \in \mathbb{N}_0. \tag{B1}$$

$$\sum_{n \geqslant 0} \binom{x, 2}{n} z^n = (1 + z)^x \qquad \text{(binomial coefficients, } \binom{x, 2}{n} = \binom{x}{n}\text{).} \tag{B2}$$

$$\sum_{n \geqslant 0} \binom{x, 3}{n} z^n = (1 + z + z^2)^x \qquad \text{(trinomial coefficients).} \tag{B3}$$

$$\binom{n, q}{k} = \frac{2}{\pi} \int_0^{\pi/2} \left( \frac{\sin(q\varphi)}{\sin(\varphi)} \right)^n \cos((n(q - 1) - 2k)\varphi) \, d\varphi \tag{B4}$$

$$\sup_k \binom{n, q}{k} \sim q^n \sqrt{6/[(q^2 - 1)\pi n]}, \qquad n \to \infty. \tag{B5}$$

$$\binom{n}{k} = \binom{n - 1}{k} + \binom{n - 1}{k - 1}. \tag{B6}$$

$$\binom{n, 3}{k} = \binom{n - 1, 3}{k - 2} + \binom{n - 1, 3}{k - 1} + \binom{n - 1, 3}{k}. \tag{B7}$$

|   |   |   |   | k |   |   |   |
|---|---|---|---|---|---|---|---|
| n | 0 | 1 | 2 | 3 | 4 | 5 | 6 |
| 1 | 1 | | | | | | |
| 2 | 1 | 2 | 1 | | | | |
| 3 | 1 | 3 | 3 | 1 | | | |
| 4 | 1 | 4 | 6 | 4 | 1 | | | (binomial coefficients) |
| 5 | 1 | 5 | 10 | 10 | 5 | 1 | |
| 6 | 1 | 6 | 15 | 20 | 15 | 6 | 1 |

$$k$$

| n | 0 | 1 | 2 | 3 | 4 | 5 | 6 | 7 | 8 | 9 | 10 | 11 | 12 |
|---|---|---|---|---|---|---|---|---|---|---|----|----|----|
| 1 | 1 | 1 | 1 |   |   |   |   |   |   |   |    |    |    |
| 2 | 1 | 2 | 3 | 2 | 1 |   |   |   |   |   |    |    |    |
| 3 | 1 | 3 | 6 | 7 | 6 | 3 | 1 |   |   |   |    |    |    |
| 4 | 1 | 4 | 10 | 16 | 19 | 16 | 10 | 4 | 1 |   |    |    |    |
| 5 | 1 | 5 | 15 | 30 | 45 | 51 | 45 | 30 | 15 | 5 | 1 |    |    |
| 6 | 1 | 6 | 21 | 50 | 90 | 126 | 141 | 126 | 90 | 50 | 21 | 6 | 1 |

(trinomial coefficients)

## 1.2 Stirling Numbers $S_n^{(m)}$ of the First Kind

$$\binom{x}{r} = \frac{1}{r!} \sum_{0 \leq i \leq r} S_r^{(i)} x^i. \tag{B8}$$

$$S_n^{(0)} = \delta_{n,0}, \qquad S_0^{(m)} = \delta_{m,0}$$
$$S_{n+1}^{(m)} = S_n^{(m-1)} - n S_n^{(m)}, \qquad n \geq m \geq 1. \tag{B9}$$

$$S_n^{(1)} = (-1)^{n-1}(n-1)!, \qquad S_n^{(n)} = 1, \qquad S_n^{(n-1)} = -\binom{n}{2},$$
$$S_n^{(n-2)} = \tfrac{1}{24} n(n-1)(n-2)(3n-1). \tag{B10}$$

$$1 + \sum_{n \geq 1} \sum_{1 \leq k \leq n} u^n t^k S_n^{(k)}/n! = (1+u)^t. \tag{B11}$$

$$\sum_{n \geq 0} z^n S_n^{(k)}/n! = \ln^k(1+z)/k!, \qquad |z| < 1. \tag{B12}$$

$$S_n^{(m)} = (-1)^{n+m} \sum_{0 < k_1 < \cdots < k_{n-m} < n} k_1 k_2 \ldots k_{n-m}. \tag{B13}$$

$$S_{n+1}^{(k+1)} \sim (-1)^{k+n} n! \ln^k(n)/k!, \qquad k \text{ fixed}, n \to \infty. \tag{B14}$$

$$S_{n+1}^{(k+1)} \sim (-1)^{k+n} n! [\gamma + \ln(n+1)]^k/k!, \qquad k = o(\ln(n)), n \to \infty. \tag{B15}$$

$$k$$

| n | 1 | 2 | 3 | 4 | 5 | 6 |
|---|---|---|---|---|---|---|
| 1 | 1 |   |   |   |   |   |
| 2 | −1 | 1 |   |   |   |   |
| 3 | 2 | −3 | 1 |   |   |   |
| 4 | −6 | 11 | −6 | 1 |   |   |
| 5 | 24 | −50 | 35 | −10 | 1 |   |
| 6 | −120 | 274 | −225 | 85 | −15 | 1 |

(B16)

## 1.3 Stirling Numbers $\mathscr{S}_n^{(m)}$ of the Second Kind

$$x^n = m! \sum_{0 \leqslant m \leqslant n} \mathscr{S}_n^{(m)} \binom{x}{m}. \tag{B17}$$

$$\mathscr{S}_n^{(0)} = \delta_{n,0}, \qquad \mathscr{S}_0^{(m)} = \delta_{m,0}$$
$$\mathscr{S}_{n+1}^{(m)} = m\mathscr{S}_n^{(m)} + \mathscr{S}_n^{(m-1)}, \qquad n \geqslant m \geqslant 1. \tag{B18}$$

$$\mathscr{S}_n^{(1)} = 1, \qquad \mathscr{S}_n^{(n)} = 1, \qquad \mathscr{S}_n^{(n-1)} = \binom{n}{2}$$
$$\mathscr{S}_n^{(n-2)} = \tfrac{1}{24}n(n-1)(n-2)(3n-5). \tag{B19}$$

$$\sum_{n \geqslant 0} z^n \mathscr{S}_n^{(m)}/n! = (\exp(z) - 1)^m/m!. \tag{B20}$$

$$\sum_{k \geqslant 1} k^m z^k/k! = \exp(z) \sum_{1 \leqslant k \leqslant m} z^k \mathscr{S}_m^{(k)}, \qquad m \geqslant 1. \tag{B21}$$

$$\mathscr{S}_n^{(k)} = \sum_{0 \leqslant k_1 \leqslant \cdots \leqslant k_{n-m} \leqslant m} k_1 k_2 \ldots k_{n-m}. \tag{B22}$$

$$\mathscr{S}_n^{(k)} \sim k^n/k!, \qquad k \text{ fixed}, n \to \infty. \tag{B23}$$

$$\mathscr{S}_{n+k}^{(k)} \sim k^{2n}2^{-n}/n!, \qquad n = o(\sqrt{k}), n \to \infty. \tag{B24}$$

$$u_n = \sum_{0 \leqslant k \leqslant n} \mathscr{S}_n^{(k)} v_k \Leftrightarrow v_n = \sum_{0 \leqslant k \leqslant n} S_n^{(k)} u_k \quad \text{(Stirling inversion)}. \tag{B25}$$

|       |   | $k$ |    |    |    |   |
|-------|---|----|----|----|----|---|
| $n$   | 1 | 2  | 3  | 4  | 5  | 6 |
| 1     | 1 |    |    |    |    |   |
| 2     | 1 | 1  |    |    |    |   |
| 3     | 1 | 3  | 1  |    |    |   |
| 4     | 1 | 7  | 6  | 1  |    |   |
| 5     | 1 | 15 | 25 | 10 | 1  |   |
| 6     | 1 | 31 | 90 | 65 | 15 | 1 |

(B26)

## 1.4 Generalized Harmonic Numbers $H_n^{(r)}$

$$H_n^{(r)} = \sum_{1 \leqslant k \leqslant n} k^{-r}. \tag{B27}$$

$$H_n^{(1)} = (-1)^{n+1} S_{n+1}^{(2)}/n! \quad \text{(harmonic number)}. \tag{B28}$$

$$H_n^{(1)} = \ln(n) + \gamma + \frac{1}{2n} - \frac{1}{12n^2} + O\left(\frac{1}{n^4}\right). \tag{B29}$$

$$H_n^{(2r)} \sim \frac{(2\pi)^{2r}}{2(2r)!} |B_{2r}|, \qquad r \geqslant 1, r \text{ fixed}, n \to \infty. \tag{B30}$$

$$H_n^{(2r+1)} \sim \frac{(-1)^{r+1}(2\pi)^{2r+1}}{2(2r+1)!} \int_0^1 B_{2r+1}(t) \tan^{-1}(\pi t)\, dt,$$
$$r \geqslant 1, r \text{ fixed}, n \to \infty. \tag{B31}$$

| $n$ | 0 | 1 | 2 | 3 | 4 | 5 | 6 | 7 | 8 | 9 | 10 |
|---|---|---|---|---|---|---|---|---|---|---|---|
| $H_n^{(1)}$ | 0 | 1 | $\frac{3}{2}$ | $\frac{11}{6}$ | $\frac{25}{12}$ | $\frac{137}{60}$ | $\frac{49}{20}$ | $\frac{363}{140}$ | $\frac{761}{280}$ | $\frac{7129}{2520}$ | $\frac{7381}{2520}$ |

$$\tag{B32}$$

## 1.5 Eulerian Numbers $A(n,k)$

$$1 + \sum_{n \geqslant 1} \sum_{1 \leqslant k \leqslant n} A(n,k) z^k t^n / n! = \frac{(1-z)}{1 - z \exp(t(1-z))}. \tag{B33}$$

$$A(n,0) = \delta_{0,n}, \qquad A(0,k) = \delta_{0,k}$$
$$A(n,k) = (n-k+1)A(n-1,k-1) + kA(n-1,k). \tag{B34}$$

$$A(n,k) = \sum_{0 \leqslant j \leqslant k} (-1)^j \binom{n+1}{j} (k-j)^n, \qquad n, k \geqslant 0. \tag{B35}$$

$$x^n = \sum_{1 \leqslant k \leqslant n} A(n,k) \binom{x+k-1}{n}, \qquad n \geqslant 1. \tag{B36}$$

| $n$ | $k$ | | | | | |
|---|---|---|---|---|---|---|
| | 1 | 2 | 3 | 4 | 5 | 6 |
| 1 | 1 | | | | | |
| 2 | 1 | 1 | | | | |
| 3 | 1 | 4 | 1 | | | |
| 4 | 1 | 11 | 11 | 1 | | |
| 5 | 1 | 26 | 66 | 26 | 1 | |
| 6 | 1 | 57 | 302 | 302 | 57 | 1 |

$$\tag{B37}$$

## 1.6 Euler Numbers $E_n$

$$\frac{1}{\cos(ix)} = \frac{2}{\exp(x) - \exp(-x)} = \sum_{n \geqslant 0} E_n x^n / n!, \qquad |x| < \pi/2. \tag{B38}$$

$$E_n = 2^n E_n(\tfrac{1}{2}). \tag{B39}$$

$$E_{2n+1} = 0, \qquad n \geqslant 0 \tag{B40}$$

$$E_{2n} = (-1)^n(2n)!\,\pi^{-2n-1}4^{n+1}\sum_{k\geqslant 0}(-1)^k(2k+1)^{-2n-1}, \qquad n \geqslant 0.$$

| $n$ | 0 | 1 | 2 | 3 | 4 | 5 | 6 | 7 | 8 | 9 | 10 |
|---|---|---|---|---|---|---|---|---|---|---|---|
| $E_n$ | 1 | 0 | $-1$ | 0 | 5 | 0 | $-61$ | 0 | 1385 | 0 | $-50521$ |

$$(B41)$$

## 1.7 Bernoulli Numbers $B_n$

$$\frac{x}{\exp(x)-1} = \sum_{n\geqslant 0} B_n x^n/n!, \qquad |x| < 2\pi. \tag{B42}$$

$$B_n = B_n(0) = (-1)^n B_n(1). \tag{B43}$$

$$B_{2n+1} = 0, \qquad n \geqslant 1 \tag{B44}$$

$$B_{2n} = 2(-1)^{n-1}(2n)!\,\pi^{-2n}4^{-n}\sum_{k\geqslant 1}k^{-2n}, \qquad n \geqslant 1.$$

$$B_n = \sum_{0\leqslant k\leqslant n}(-1)^k k!\,\mathscr{S}_n^{(k)}/(k+1). \tag{B45}$$

| $n$ | 0 | 1 | 2 | 3 | 4 | 5 | 6 | 7 | 8 | 9 | 10 |
|---|---|---|---|---|---|---|---|---|---|---|---|
| $B_n$ | 1 | $-\frac{1}{2}$ | $\frac{1}{6}$ | 0 | $-\frac{1}{30}$ | 0 | $\frac{1}{42}$ | 0 | $-\frac{1}{30}$ | 0 | $\frac{5}{66}$ |

$$(B46)$$

## 1.8 Bell Numbers $\omega_n$

$$\exp(\exp(t)-1) = \sum_{n\geqslant 0}\omega_n t^n/n!. \tag{B47}$$

$$\omega_n = \sum_{0\leqslant k\leqslant n}\mathscr{S}_n^{(k)}. \tag{B48}$$

$$\omega_n = e^{-1}\sum_{\lambda\geqslant 0}\lambda^n/\lambda!, \qquad n \geqslant 1. \tag{B49}$$

| $n$ | 1 | 2 | 3 | 4 | 5 | 6 | 7 | 8 | 9 | 10 |
|---|---|---|---|---|---|---|---|---|---|---|
| $\omega_n$ | 1 | 2 | 5 | 15 | 52 | 203 | 877 | 4140 | 21147 | 115975 |

## 2. Special Functions

### 2.1 Bell Polynomials $\mathscr{B}_n(x)$

$$\mathscr{B}_n(x) = \sum_{0 \leqslant k \leqslant n} \mathscr{S}_n^{(k)} x^k. \tag{B50}$$

$$\mathscr{B}_{n+1}(x) = x\mathscr{B}_n(x) + x\mathscr{B}_n'(x). \tag{B51}$$

$$\begin{aligned}
\mathscr{B}_0(x) &= 1 \\
\mathscr{B}_1(x) &= x \\
\mathscr{B}_2(x) &= x^2 + x \\
\mathscr{B}_3(x) &= x^3 + 3x^2 + x \\
\mathscr{B}_4(x) &= x^4 + 6x^3 + 7x^2 + x.
\end{aligned} \tag{B52}$$

$$\mathscr{B}_n(x) = x^n + O(x^{n-1}), \qquad x > 1. \tag{B53}$$

### 2.2 Eulerian Polynomials $A_n(x)$

$$A_0(x) = 1; \qquad A_n(x) = \sum_{1 \leqslant k \leqslant n} A(n, k)x^k. \tag{B54}$$

$$A_n(x) = x \sum_{1 \leqslant k \leqslant n} k! \, \mathscr{S}_n^{(k)}(x - 1)^{n-k}, \qquad n \geqslant 1. \tag{B55}$$

$$\sum_{\lambda \geqslant 0} \lambda^s x^\lambda = A_s(x)/(1 - x)^{s+1}, \qquad s \geqslant 0. \tag{B56}$$

$$\frac{\mathrm{d}^\lambda}{\mathrm{d}x^\lambda} A_n(x) \bigg|_{x=1} = \lambda! \, (n - \lambda)! \, \mathscr{S}_{n+1}^{(n-\lambda+1)}. \tag{B57}$$

$$A_n(x) = (1 - x)^{n+1} \sum_{\lambda \geqslant 1} \frac{x^\lambda}{1 - x^\lambda} \lambda^n \prod_{\substack{p | \lambda \\ p \, \text{prime}}} (1 - p^{-n}). \tag{B58}$$

$$A_{2n+1}(-1) = (-1)^n 4^n (4^n - 1) B_{2n+2}/(2n). \tag{B59}$$

$$\begin{aligned}
A_1(x) &= x \\
A_2(x) &= x + x^2 \\
A_3(x) &= x + 4x^2 + x^3 \\
A_4(x) &= x + 11x^2 + 11x^3 + x^4.
\end{aligned} \tag{B60}$$

### 2.3 Euler Polynomials $E_n(x)$

$$\frac{2 \exp(xt)}{\exp(t) + 1} = \sum_{n \geqslant 0} E_n(x)t^n/n!, \qquad |t| < \pi. \tag{B61}$$

$$E'_n(x) = nE_{n-1}(x), \qquad n \geqslant 1. \tag{B62}$$

$$E_n(x+1) + E_n(x) = 2x^n, \qquad n \geqslant 0. \tag{B63}$$

$$E_n(x) = \sum_{0 \leqslant k \leqslant n} \binom{n}{k} 2^{-k} E_k (x - \tfrac{1}{2})^{n-k}, \qquad n \geqslant 0. \tag{B64}$$

$$E_n(\tfrac{1}{2}) = 2^{-n} E_n, \qquad n \geqslant 0$$
$$E_n(0) = -E_n(1) = -2(2^{n+1} - 1)B_{n+1}/(n+1), \qquad n \geqslant 1. \tag{B65}$$

$$B_n(x) = 2^{-n} \sum_{0 \leqslant k \leqslant n} \binom{n}{k} B_{n-k} E_k(2x), \qquad n \geqslant 0. \tag{B66}$$

$$\sum_{0 \leqslant k \leqslant m} (-1)^{m-k} k^n = \tfrac{1}{2}[E_n(m+1) + (-1)^m E_n(0)]. \tag{B67}$$

$$E_0(x) = 1$$
$$E_1(x) = x - \tfrac{1}{2}$$
$$E_2(x) = x^2 - x \tag{B68}$$
$$E_3(x) = x^3 - \tfrac{3}{2}x^2 + \tfrac{1}{4}$$
$$E_4(x) = x^4 - 2x^3 + x.$$

## 2.4 Bernoulli Polynomials $B_n(x)$

$$\frac{t \exp(xt)}{\exp(t) - 1} = \sum_{n \geqslant 0} B_n(x) t^n / n!, \qquad |t| < 2\pi. \tag{B69}$$

$$B'_n(x) = nB_{n-1}(x), \qquad n \geqslant 1$$
$$B_n(x+1) - B_n(x) = nx^{n-1}, \qquad n \geqslant 0. \tag{B70}$$

$$B_n(\tfrac{1}{2}) = -(1 - 2^{1-n})B_n, \qquad n \geqslant 0$$
$$B_n(0) = (-1)^n B_n(1) = B_n. \tag{B71}$$

$$\sum_{0 \leqslant k \leqslant m} k^n = [B_{n+1}(m+1) - B_{n+1}]/(n+1). \tag{B72}$$

$$B_0(x) = 1$$
$$B_1(x) = x - \tfrac{1}{2}$$
$$B_2(x) = x^2 - x + \tfrac{1}{6} \tag{B73}$$
$$B_3(x) = x^3 - \tfrac{3}{2}x^2 + \tfrac{1}{2}x$$
$$B_4(x) = x^4 - 2x^3 + x^2 - \tfrac{1}{30}.$$

## 2.5 Chebyshev Polynomials $U_n(x)$ of the Second Kind

$$U_n(x) = \frac{\sin[(n+1)\arccos(x)]}{\sin[\arccos(x)]}$$

$$= \frac{1}{2i}(1-x^2)^{-1/2}[(x+i\sqrt{1-x^2})^{n+1} - (x-i\sqrt{1-x^2})^{n+1}]. \tag{B74}$$

$$U_n(x) = \sum_{0\leqslant m\leqslant\lfloor n/2\rfloor}(-1)^m \frac{(n-m)!}{m!(n-2m)!}(2x)^{n-2m}. \tag{B75}$$

$$\frac{1}{1-2tx+t^2} = \sum_{n\geqslant 0}U_n(x)t^n. \tag{B76}$$

$$U_{n+1}(x) = 2xU_n(x) - U_{n-1}(x), \qquad n\geqslant 1. \tag{B77}$$

$$U_{2n+1}(0) = 0, \qquad n\geqslant 0$$
$$U_{2n}(0) = (-1)^n, \qquad n\geqslant 0. \tag{B78}$$

$$U_n(\cos(\alpha)) = \frac{\sin((n+1)\alpha)}{\sin(\alpha)}$$

$$U_n(-x) = (-1)^n U_n(x). \tag{B79}$$

$$U_n\left(\cos\left(\frac{\pi m}{n+1}\right)\right) = 0, \qquad 1\leqslant m\leqslant n. \tag{B80}$$

$$U_0(x) = 1$$
$$U_1(x) = 2x$$
$$U_2(x) = 4x^2 - 1$$
$$U_3(x) = 8x^3 - 4x \tag{B81}$$
$$U_4(x) = 16x^4 - 12x^2 + 1.$$

## 2.6 Hermite Polynomials $H_n(x)$

$$H_n(x) = \sum_{0\leqslant m\leqslant\lfloor n/2\rfloor}(-1)^m \frac{n!}{m!(n-2m)!}(2x)^{n-2m}. \tag{B82}$$

$$\exp(2tx-t^2) = \sum_{n\geqslant 0}H_n(x)t^n/n!. \tag{B83}$$

$$H_{n+1}(x) = 2xH_n(x) - 2nH_{n-1}(x), \qquad n\geqslant 1. \tag{B84}$$

$$H_{2n+1}(0) = 0, \qquad H_{2n}(0) = (-1)^n(2n)!/n!, \qquad n\geqslant 0$$
$$H_n(-x) = (-1)^n H_n(x). \tag{B85}$$

$$H_0(x) = 1$$
$$H_1(x) = 2x$$
$$H_2(x) = 4x^2 - 2 \tag{B86}$$
$$H_3(x) = 8x^3 - 12x$$
$$H_4(x) = 16x^4 - 48x^2 + 12.$$

## 2.7 Generalized Laguerre Polynomial $L_n^{(\alpha)}(x)$

$$L_n^{(\alpha)}(x) = \sum_{0 \le m \le n} (-1)^m \binom{n+\alpha}{n-m} x^m/m!. \tag{B87}$$

$$(1-z)^{-\alpha-1} \exp\left(\frac{xz}{z-1}\right) = \sum_{n \ge 0} L_n^{(\alpha)}(x) z^n, \qquad |z| < 1. \tag{B88}$$

$$L_0^{(\alpha)}(x) = 1, \qquad L_1^{(\alpha)}(x) = \alpha + 1 - x \tag{B89}$$

$$L_{n+1}^{(\alpha)}(x) = \frac{2n+\alpha+1-x}{n+1} L_n^{(\alpha)}(x) - \frac{n+\alpha}{n+1} L_{n-1}^{(\alpha)}(x), \qquad n \ge 1.$$

$$L_n^{(\alpha)}(0) = \binom{n+\alpha}{n}. \tag{B90}$$

$$L_0^{(0)}(x) = 1$$
$$L_1^{(0)}(x) = 1 - x$$
$$L_2^{(0)}(x) = 1 - 2x + \tfrac{1}{2}x^2 \tag{B91}$$
$$L_3^{(0)}(x) = 1 - 3x + \tfrac{3}{2}x^2 - \tfrac{1}{6}x^3$$
$$L_4^{(0)}(x) = 1 - 4x + 3x^2 - \tfrac{2}{3}x^3 + \tfrac{1}{24}x^4.$$

## 2.8 Legendre Polynomials $P_n(x)$

$$P_n(x) = 2^{-n} \sum_{0 \le m \le \lfloor n/2 \rfloor} (-1)^m \binom{n}{m}\binom{2n-2m}{n} x^{n-2m}$$

$$P_n(x) = \sum_{0 \le m \le n} \binom{n}{m}\binom{n+m}{m} 2^{-m}(x-1)^m \quad \text{(Murphy's formula).} \tag{B92}$$

$$P_n(x) = \frac{1}{\pi} \int_0^\pi [x + \sqrt{x^2-1}\,\cos(\alpha)]^n \, d\alpha, \qquad z \in \mathbb{R}, z \ge 1. \tag{B93}$$

$$\frac{1}{\sqrt{1-2tx+t^2}} = \sum_{n \ge 0} P_n(x) t^n, \qquad |t| < \text{MIN}|x \pm \sqrt{x^2-1}|. \tag{B94}$$

$$P_{n+1}(x) = \frac{2n+1}{n+1} x P_n(x) - \frac{n}{n+1} P_{n-1}(x), \qquad n \ge 1. \tag{B95}$$

$$(x^2 - 1)P_n'(x) = nxP_n(x) - nP_{n-1}(x), \qquad n \geqslant 1. \tag{B96}$$

$$P_{2n+1}(0) = 0, \qquad P_{2n}(0) = (-1)^n 4^{-n} \binom{2n}{n}, \qquad n \geqslant 0$$

$$P_n(-x) = (-1)^n P_n(x), \qquad n \geqslant 0. \tag{B97}$$

$$P_0(x) = 1$$
$$P_1(x) = x$$
$$P_2(x) = \tfrac{3}{2}x^2 - \tfrac{1}{2}$$
$$P_3(x) = \tfrac{5}{2}x^2 - \tfrac{3}{2}x$$
$$P_4(x) = \tfrac{35}{8}x^4 - \tfrac{15}{4}x^2 + \tfrac{3}{8}. \tag{B98}$$

## 2.9 Meixner Polynomials $M_n(x)$

$$\frac{1}{\sqrt{1+t^2}} \exp(x \arctan(t)) = \sum_{n \geqslant 0} M_n(x)t^k/k!. \tag{B99}$$

$$M_{n+1}(x) = xM_n(x) - n^2 M_{n-1}(x), \qquad n \geqslant 1. \tag{B100}$$

$$M_0(x) = 1$$
$$M_1(x) = x$$
$$M_2(x) = x^2 - 1$$
$$M_3(x) = x^3 - 5x$$
$$M_4(x) = x^4 - 14x^2 + 9. \tag{B101}$$

## 2.10 Poisson–Charlier Polynomials $C_n(x)$

$$C_n(x) = \sum_{0 \leqslant m \leqslant n} (-1)^{n-m} \binom{n}{m}\binom{x}{m}m!. \tag{B102}$$

$$(1+t)^z \exp(-t) = \sum_{n \geqslant 0} C_n(z)t^n/n!. \tag{B103}$$

$$C_{n+1}(x) = [x - n - 1]C_n(x) - nC_{n-1}(x), \qquad n \geqslant 1. \tag{B104}$$

$$C_0(x) = 1$$
$$C_1(x) = x - 1$$
$$C_2(x) = x^2 - 3x + 1$$
$$C_3(x) = x^3 - 6x^2 + 8x - 1$$
$$C_4(x) = x^4 - 10x^3 + 29x^2 - 24x + 1. \tag{B105}$$

*2.11 Gamma Function* $\Gamma(z)$

$$\Gamma(z) = \int_0^\infty t^{z-1} \exp(-t)\, dt, \qquad \text{Re}(z) > 0. \tag{B106}$$

$$\Gamma(z) = \int_0^\infty (t-z)t^{z-1} \ln(t) \exp(-t)\, dt, \qquad \text{Re}(z) > 0. \tag{B107}$$

$$\Gamma(z+1) = z\Gamma(z). \tag{B108}$$

$$\Gamma(z+1) = z!, \qquad z \in \mathbb{N}_0. \tag{B109}$$

$$\Gamma(z) = z^{z-1/2} \exp(-z)\sqrt{2\pi}\left[ 1 + \frac{1}{12z} + \frac{1}{288z^2} - \frac{139}{51480z^3} - \frac{571}{2488320z^4}\right.$$

$$\left. + O(z^{-5})\right], \qquad z \to \infty, |\arg(z)| < \pi$$

$$\text{(Stirling's formula).} \tag{B110}$$

(For $z$ real and positive, the remainder of this series is less than the last term that is retained.)

$$\ln(\Gamma(z)) \sim (z - \tfrac{1}{2})\ln(z) - z + \tfrac{1}{2}\ln(2\pi) + \sum_{m \geqslant 1} \frac{B_{2m}}{2m(2m-1)z^{2m-1}},$$

$$z \to \infty \text{ in } |\arg(z)| < \pi. \tag{B111}$$

$$\Gamma(n + \tfrac{1}{2}) = (2n)!\, 4^{-n}\sqrt{\pi}/n!, \qquad \Gamma(n - \tfrac{1}{2}) = (-1)^n n!\, 4^n \sqrt{\pi}/(2n)!,$$

$$n \in \mathbb{N}_0. \tag{B112}$$

$$\Gamma'(1) = -\gamma = 0.577\,215\,664\,9\ldots \quad \text{(Euler's constant).} \tag{B113}$$

$$\lim_{|y| \to \infty} |\Gamma(x + iy)|\, |y|^{1/2 - x} \exp(\pi|y|/2) = \sqrt{2\pi}, \qquad x, y \in \mathbb{R}. \tag{B114}$$

$\Gamma(z)$ is a fractional analytic function with simple poles at the points $z = -k$, $k \in \mathbb{N}_0$, to which correspond the residues $(-1)^k/k!$. $\tag{B115}$

*2.12 Psi Function* $\psi(z)$

$$\psi(z) = \frac{d}{dz}\ln(\Gamma(z)). \tag{B116}$$

$$\psi(z+1) = \psi(z) + z^{-1}. \tag{B117}$$

$$\psi(n) = -\gamma + H^{(1)}_{n-1}, \qquad n \in \mathbb{N}. \tag{B118}$$

$$\psi(n \pm \tfrac{1}{2}) = -\gamma - 2\ln(2) + 2\sum_{0 \leqslant k < n} (2k+1)^{-1}, \qquad n \in \mathbb{N}. \tag{B119}$$

$$\psi'(1) = \frac{\pi^2}{6}, \qquad \psi'(\tfrac{1}{2}) = \frac{\pi^2}{2}. \tag{B120}$$

$$\psi(z) \sim \ln(z) - \frac{1}{2z} - \sum_{n \geqslant 1} \frac{1}{2n} B_{2n} z^{-2n}, \qquad z \to \infty \text{ in } |\arg(z)| < \pi. \tag{B121}$$

### 2.13 Hurwitz (Riemann) Zeta Function $\zeta(z, a)$ $(\zeta(z))$

$$\zeta(z, q) = \frac{1}{2\pi i} \Gamma(1 - z) \int_C t^{z-1} \exp(qt)/(1 - \exp(t)) \, dt$$

(Hurwitz zeta function). (B122)

(The contour $C$ starts at infinity on the negative real axis, circles the origin once in a positive direction excluding the points $\pm 2n\pi i$, $n \in \mathbb{N}$, and returns to the starting-point.)

$$\zeta(z, 1) = \zeta(z) \quad \text{(Riemann zeta function)}. \tag{B123}$$

$$\zeta(z, q) = \sum_{n \geqslant 0} (q + n)^{-z}, \qquad \mathrm{Re}(z) > 1. \tag{B124}$$

$$\zeta(z)(1 - 2^{-z}) = \sum_{n \geqslant 0} (2n + 1)^{-z}. \tag{B125}$$

$$\zeta(-n, q) = -\frac{1}{n + 1} B_{n+1}(q), \qquad q \in \mathbb{N}_0. \tag{B126}$$

$$\zeta'(0, q) = \ln(\Gamma(q)) - \tfrac{1}{2} \ln(2\pi). \tag{B127}$$

$$\zeta(z, q) = \frac{1}{z - 1} - \psi(q) + O(z - 1). \tag{B128}$$

$\zeta(z, q)$ is regular for all values of $z$ except for the simple pole at $z = 1$ with residue 1. (B129)

$$|\zeta(z)| = O(|z|^{q+1}), \qquad \mathrm{Re}(z) \geqslant -q. \tag{B130}$$

$$|\zeta(x + iy, q)| = O(|y|^{1-x}), \qquad x \geqslant -1. \tag{B131}$$

$$\sum_{1 \leqslant i \leqslant l} \zeta\left(z, \frac{i}{l}\right) = l^z \zeta(z). \tag{B132}$$

# References

[1] Abramowitz, M., and Stegun, I. A.    *Handbook of Mathematical Functions.* Dover, 1970.

[2] André, D.    Sur les permutations alternées. *J. Math. Pur. Appl.,* **7** (1881) 167–184.

[3] Apostol, T. M.    *Introduction to Analytic Number Theory.* Springer, 1976.

[4] Batcher, K. E.    Sorting networks and their applications. In: *Proc. AFIPS Spring Joint Comp. Conf.* (1968), pp. 307–314.

[5] Bender, E. A.    An asymptotic expansion for coefficients of some formal power series. *J. London Math. Soc.,* **1975**, 451–458.

[6] Bender, E. A.    Asymptotic methods in enumeration. *SIAM Rev.,* **16**, (4) (1974), 485–514.

[7] Bender, E. A.    Central and local limit theorems applied to asymptotic enumeration. *J. Comb. Theory,* (A) **15** (1973) 91–111.

[8] Berstel, J.    Sur la densité asymptotique des langages formels. In: *Automata, Languages and Programming* (Nivat, M. ed.), 1973, pp. 345–358. North Holland Publishing Co.

[9] Brillhart, J.    Note on the single variable Bell polynomials. *Amer. Math. Monthly,* **1967**, 695–696.

[10] Carlitz, L., Roselle, D. P., and Scoville, R. A.    Some remarks on ballot-type sequences of positive integers. *J. Comb. Theory,* (A) **11** (1971), 258–271.

[11] Carlitz, L.    Permutations with a prescribed pattern. *Math. Nachr.,* **58** (1973), 31–53.

[12] Cayley, A.    A theorem on trees. *Quart. J. of Pure and Applied Math.,* **23** (1889), 376–378.

[13] Chandrasekharan, K.    *Arithmetical Functions.* Springer, 1970.

[14] Chomsky, N., and Schützenberger, M. P.    The algebraic theory of context-free languages. In: *Computer Programming and Formal Systems* (Braffort, P., and Hirschberg, D. eds.), 1963, pp. 118–161. North Holland Publishing Co.

[15] Comtet, L.    *Advanced Combinatorics.* Reidel, 1974.

221

222

[16] de Bruijn, N. G.    On MAHLER'S partition problem. *Koninklijke Nederlandsche Akademie van Wetenschappen, Proc. Vol.*, **LI** (6) (1948), 659–669.

[17] de Bruijn, N. G.    *Asymptotic Methods in Analysis.* North-Holland, 1961.

[18] de Bruijn, N. G.    Polya's theory of computing. In: *Applied Combinatorial Mathematics* (Beckenbach, E. F. ed.), 1964, pp. 144–184. Wiley, New York.

[19] de Bruijn, N. G.    Color patterns that are invariant under a given permutation of the colors. *J. Comb. Theory*, **2** (1967) 418–421.

[20] de Bruijn, N. G., and Morselt, B. J. M.    A note on plane trees. *J. Comb. Theory*, **2** (1967), 27–34.

[21] de Bruijn, N. G., Knuth, D. E., and Rice, S. O.    The average height of planted plane trees. In: *Graph Theory and Computing* (Read, R. C. ed.), 1972, pp. 15–22.

[22] Delange, H.    Sur la fonction sommatoire de la fonction „somme des chiffres". *L'Enseignement Math.*, **1975**, 31–47.

[23] Erdélyi, A. et al.    *Higher Transcendental Functions*, Vols. I, II and III. McGraw-Hill, 1953.

[24] Erdélyi, A. et al.    *Tables of Integral Transforms*, Vols. I and II. McGraw Hill, 1954

[25] Entringer, R. C.    A combinatorial interpretation of the Euler and Bernoulli numbers. *Nieuw. Arch Wisk.*, **14** (1966), 241–246.

[26] Everett, C. J., and Stein, P. R.    The asymptotic number of integer stochastic matrices. *Discrete Math.*, **1** (1971), 55–72.

[27] Feller, W.    *An Introduction to Probability Theory and its Applications*, Vols. I and II. Wiley, 1968.

[28] Flajolet, Ph., Raoult, J. C., and Vuillemin, J.    *The Number of Registers Required for Evaluating Arithmetic Expressions.* Techn. Rep. 228, IRIA, 1977.

[29] Flajolet, Ph.    *Analyse d'Algorithmes de Manipulation de Fichiers.* Techn. Rep. 321, IRIA, 1978.

[30] Flajolet, Ph.    Analyse en moyenne de la détection des arbres partiels. In: *Les Arbres en Algèbre et en Programmation.* (3eme Colloq.), Lille, 1979.

[31] Flajolet, Ph., Raoult, J. C., and Vuillemin, J.    The number of registers required for evaluating arithmetic expressions. *Theoret. Comp. Sc.*, **9** (1979), 99–125.

[32] Flajolet, Ph.    Analyse d'algorithmes de manipulation d'arbres et de fichiers. Thèse, Université de Paris-Sud, Centre d'Orsay, 1979.

[33] Flajolet, Ph., and Ramshaw, L.    A note on gray-code and odd–even merge. *SIAM Journal on Comp.*, **9** (1979), 142–158.

[34] Flajolet, Ph., Françon, J., and Vuillemin, J.    Sequence of operations analysis for dynamic data structures. *J. of Algorithms*, **1** (1980), 111–141.

[35] Flajolet, Ph., and Odlyzko, A.    Exploring binary trees and other simple trees. In: *Proc. of the 21st Ann. Symp. on Found. of Comp. Sc.* (1980), pp. 207–216.

[36] Flajolet, Ph., and Steyaert, J. M. On the analysis of tree matching algorithms. In: *Automata, Languages and Programming (ICALP)*, (de Bakker, J. W. and van Leeuwen, J. eds.), 1980, pp. 208–219. Springer Verlag.

[37] Flajolet, Ph., and Odlyzko, A. *The average Height of Binary Trees and Other Simple Trees. JCSS*, **25** (1982), 171–213

[38] Foata, D., and Strehl, V. Rearrangements of the symmetric group and enumerative properties of the tangent and secant numbers. *Math. Z.*, **137** (1974), 257–264.

[39] Foster, F. G., and Stuart, A. Distribution-free tests in time-series based on the breaking of records. *J. Roy. Stat. Soc.*, **B16** (1954), 1–22.

[40] Foulkes, H. O. Enumeration of permutations with prescribed up–down and inversion sequences. *Disc. Math.*, **15** (1976), 235–252.

[41] Foulkes, H. O. Eulerian numbers, Newcomb's problem and representations of symmetric groups. *Disc. Math.*, **30** (1980), 3–49.

[42] Françon, J. Sur le théorème de Flajolet–Raoult–Vuillemin. Private communication to the author, 1977.

[43] Françon, J. Histoires de fichiers. *RAIRO Inform. Theor.*, **12** (1978), 49–67.

[44] Françon, J., and Viennot, G. Permutations selon les pics, creux, doubles montées, doubles descentes, nombre d'Euler et nombres de Genocchi. *Disc. Math.*, **28** (1979), 21–35.

[45] Françon, J. Combinatoire des structures de données. Thèse, Université Louis Pasteur, Strasbourg, 1979.

[46] Frobenius, F. G. Über die Bernoullischen Zahlen und die Eulerschen Polynome. *Sitz. Ber. Preuss, Akad. Wiss.*, **1910**, 808–847.

[47] Gassner, B. J. Sorting by replacement selecting. *CACM*, **10** (1967), 89–93.

[48] Gradshteyn, I. S. and Ryzhik, I. M. *Table of Integrals, Series and Products*. Academic Press, 1980.

[49] Greene, D. H., and Knuth, D. E. *Mathematics for the Analysis of Algorithms*. Birkhäuser, 1981.

[50] Harary, F., Prins, G., and Tutte, W. R. The number of plane trees. *Indag. Math.*, **26** (1964), 319–329.

[51] Harary, F. *Graph Theory*. Addison-Wesley, 1969.

[52] Harary, F., and Palmer, E. *Graphical Enumeration*. Academic Press, 1973.

[53] Harrison, M. A. *Introduction to Formal Language Theory*. Addison-Wesley, 1978.

[54] Henrici, P. *Applied and Computational Complex Analysis*, Vols. I and II. Wiley, 1974, 1977.

[55] Hooker, W. W. On the expected lengths of sequences generated in sorting by replacement selecting. *CACM*, **12** (1969), 411–413.

[56] Hotz, G., and Messerschmidt, F. *Dycksprachen sind in Bandkomplexität log(n) analysierbar*. Techn. Rep. A75/1, Universität des Saarlandes, 1975.

[57] Kementy, J. G., and Snell, J. L. *Finite Markov Chains*. Van Nostrand, 1963.

224

[58] Kemp, R.     *The Average Number of Registers Needed to Evaluate a Binary Tree Optimally.* Techn. Rep. A77/04, Universität des Saarlandes, 1977.

[59] Kemp, R.     *The Average Height of a Derivation Tree Generated by a Linear Grammar in a Special Chomsky-normalform.* Techn. Rep. A78/01, Universität des Saarlandes, 1978.

[60] Kemp, R.     The average number of registers needed to evaluate a binary tree optimally. *Acta Informatica*, **11** (1979), 363–372.

[61] Kemp, R.     On the average stack size of regularly distributed binary trees. In: *Automata, Languages and Programming (ICALP)* (Maurer, H. A. ed.), 1979, pp. 340–355. Springer Verlag.

[62] Kemp, R.     The average depth of a prefix of the Dyck-language $D_1$. In: *Fundamentals of Computation Theory (FCT)* (Budach, L. ed.), 1979, pp. 230–236. Akademic Verlag, Berlin.

[63] Kemp, R.     The average stack size of a derivation tree generated by a linear context-free grammar. *Inf. & Contr.*, **42** (1979), 354–365.

[64] Kemp, R.     The average height of $r$-tuply rooted planted plane trees. *Computing*, **25** (1980), 209–232.

[65] Kemp, R.     A note on the stack size of regularly distributed binary trees. *BIT*, **20** (1980), 157–163.

[66] Kemp, R.     On the average depth of a prefix of the Dyck-language $D_1$. *Disc. Math.*, **36** (1981), 155–170.

[67] Kemp, R.     On the average oscillation of a stack. *Combinatorica* **2** (1982), 157–176.

[68] Kemp, R.     *The Average Height of Planted Plane Trees with M leaves.* J. Comb. Theory (B), **34** (1983), 191–208.

[69] Kemp, R.     *The Reduction of Binary Trees by Means of an Input-Restricted Deque.* RAIRO Inform. Theor., **17** (1983), 249–284

[70] Kemp, R.     On the number of words in the language $\{w \in \sum^* \mid w = w^R\}^2$. *Disc. Math.*, **40** (1982), 225–234.

[71] Kemp, R.     *On the Number of Deepest Nodes in Ordered Trees.* Preprint, Johann Wolfgang Goethe-Universität Frankfurt a.M., 1982.

[72] Kemp, R.     The expected number of nodes and leaves at level k in ordered trees. *Lect. Notes in Comp. Sc.*, **145** (1983) 153–163.

[73] Kirschenhofer, P., and Prodinger, H.     *On the Average Height of Monotonically Labelled Binary Trees.* Presented at: 6th Hungarian Colloquium on Combinatorics, Eger, 1981.

[74] Kirschenhofer, P., and Prodinger, H.     *On the Average Oscillation of the Contour of Monotonically Labelled Ordered Trees.* Preprint, TU Wien, 1981.

[75] Kirschenhofer, P., and Prodinger, H.     On the Average Hyperoscillations of Planted Plane Trees. *Combinatorica* **2** (1982), 177–186.

[76] Knuth, D. E.     *The Art of Computer Programming.* Vols. I, II, and III. Addison-Wesley, 1973, 1969, 1973.

225

[77] Kreweras, G.    Sur les éventails de segments. *Cahier du B.U.R.O.*, **15** (1970), 1–41.

[78] Kuich, W., Prodinger, H., and Urbanek, F. J.    On the height of derivation trees. In: *Automata, Languages and Programming (ICALP)* (Maurer, H. A. ed.), 1979, pp. 370–384. Springer Verlag.

[79] Kuich, W.    Quantitative Aspekte bei Ableitungsbäumen. *Wiss. Z. Tech. Univ. Dresden*, **29** (1980), 370–375.

[80] Kuich, W.    Generating functions for derivation trees. *Inf. & Control*, **45** (1980), 199–216.

[81] Lifschitz, V.    The efficiency of an algorithm of integer programming: a probabilistic analysis. *Proc. Amer. Math. Soc.*, **79** (1980), 72–76.

[82] Lifschitz, V., and Pittel, B.    The number of increasing subsequences of the random permutation. *J. Comb. Theory* (A), **31** (1981), 1–20.

[83] MacMahon, P. A.    *Combinatory Analysis*, Vols. I and II. Chelsea, 1960.

[84] McIlroy, M. D.    The number of 1's in binary integers: bounds and extremal properties. *SIAM J. on Comp.*, **3** (1974), 255–261.

[85] Meir, A., and Moon, J. W.    Packing and covering constants for certain families of trees, I. *J. Graph Theory*, **1** (1977), 157–174.

[86] Meir, A., and Moon, J. W.    On the altitude of nodes in random trees. *Can. J. Math.*, **30** (1978), 997–1015.

[87] Meir, A., Moon, J. W., and Pounder, J. R.    On the order of random channel networks. *SIAM J. Alg. Disc. Meth.*, **1** (1980), 25–32.

[88] Mohanty, S. G.    Some properties of compositions and their application of the ballot problem. *Can. Math. Bull.*, **8** (1965), 359–372.

[89] Moser, L., and Wyman, M.    On the solutions of $x^d = 1$ in symmetric groups. *Can. J. Math.*, **7** (1955), 159–168.

[90] Nakata, I.    On compiling algorithms for arithmetic expressions. *CACM*, **10** (1967), 492–494.

[91] Narumi, S.    On a power series having only a finite number of algebraic–logarithmic singularities on its circle of convergence. *Tohoku. Math. J.*, **30** (1929). 185–201.

[92] Odlyzko, A. M.    *Periodic Oscillations of Coefficients of Power Series that Satisfy Functional Equations.* Preprint, Bell. Lab., Murray Hill, 1979.

[93] Polya, G.    Kombinatorische Anzahlbestimmungen für Gruppen, Graphen und chemische Verbindungen. *Acta Math.*, **68** (1937), 145–254.

[94] Perron, O.    *Die Lehre von den Kettenbrüchen*, Vols. I and II. Teubner, 1977.

[95] Prodinger, H.    *The Average Maximal Lead Position of a Ballot Sequence.* Preprint, TU Wien, 1979.

[96] Prodinger, H.    The average height of a stack where three operations are allowed and some related problems. *J. Comb. Inf. Syst. Sc.*, **5** (1980), 287–304.

[97] Prodinger, H.    *On two Combinatorial Identities of R. Kemp.* Preprint, TU Wien, 1980.

226

[98] Prodinger, H., and Panny, W. *The Expected Height of Paths for Several Notions of Height.* Preprint, TU Wien, 1981.

[99] Prodinger, H., and Urbanek, F. J. On monotone functions of tree structures. *Disc. Appl. Math.*, **5** 1983, 223–239.

[100] Prodinger, H., and Urbanek, F. J. *On Monotone Bijections of Tree Structures.* Preprint, TU Wien, 1981.

[101] Ramshaw, L. H. *Formalizing the Analysis of Algorithms.* Techn. Rep. STAN-CS-79-741, Stanford University, 1979.

[102] Rényi, A., and Szekeres, G. On the height of trees. *Aust. Math. Soc.*, **17** (1967), 497–507.

[103] Riordan, J. *An Introduction to Combinatorial Analysis.* Wiley, 1958.

[104] Riordan, J. *Combinatorial Identities.* Wiley, 1968.

[105] Roselle, D. P. Permutations by number of rises and successions. *Proc. Amer. Math. Soc.*, **19** (1968), 8–16.

[106] Ruskey, F. On the average shape of binary trees. *SIAM J. Alg. Disc. Math.* **1** (1980), 43–50.

[107] Salomaa, A., and Soittola, M. *Automata-Theoretic Aspects of Formal Power Series.* Springer, 1978.

[108] Schützenberger, M. P. Some remarks on Chomsky's context-free languages. *Quat. Prog. Rep.*, **58**, MIT (1961).

[109] Sedgewick, R. Data movement in odd–even merging. *SIAM J. on Comp.*, **7** (1978), 239–273.

[110] Sethi, R., and Ullman, J. D. The generation of optimal code for arithmetic expressions. *JACM*, **17** (1970), 715–728.

[111] Shreve, R. L. Statistical law of stream numbers. *J. Geology*, **74** (1966), 17–37.

[112] Spitzer, F. *Principles of Random Walks.* Springer, 1976.

[113] Tanny, M. S. Permutations and successions. *J. Comb. Theory (A)*, **21** (1976), 196–202.

[114] Touchard, J. Sur certaines équations fonctionelles. In: *Proc. Int. Math. Congress*, Toronto, 1928, p. 465.

[115] Wall, H. S. *Analytic Theory of Continued Fractions.* Chelsea, 1967.

[116] Whittaker, E. T., and Watson, G. N. *A Course of Modern Analysis.* Cambridge Univ. Press, 1952.

# Index of Notation

| | |
|---|---|
| $\varnothing$ | empty set |
| $\mathbb{N}$ | positive integers |
| $\mathbb{N}_0$ | $\mathbb{N} \cup \{0\}$ |
| $\mathbb{N}_n$ | $\{i \in \mathbb{N} \mid 1 \leqslant i \leqslant n\}$ |
| $\mathbb{Z}$ | integers |
| $\mathbb{Q}$ | rational numbers |
| $\mathbb{R}$ | real numbers |
| $\mathbb{C}$ | complex numbers |
| $\{a \mid R(a)\}$ | set of all $a$ for which the relation $R(a)$ is true |
| $A \times B$ | cartesian product of the sets $A$ and $B$ |
| $A \cup B$ | union of the sets $A$ and $B$ |
| $A \cap B$ | intersection of the sets $A$ and $B$ |
| $A \backslash B$ | complement of the set $B$ with respect to the set $A$ |
| $A \subseteq B$ | $A$ is a subset of $B$ |
| $\mathfrak{P}(A)$ | powerset (set of all subsets) of $A$ |
| $x \in A$ | $x$ is an element of $A$ |
| $x \notin A$ | $x$ is not an element of $A$ |
| $[a:b]$ | $\{x \in \mathbb{Z} \mid a \leqslant x \leqslant b\}$ |
| $[a, b]$ | $\{x \in \mathbb{R} \mid a \leqslant x \leqslant b\}$ |
| $[a, b\rangle$ | $\{x \in \mathbb{R} \mid a \leqslant x < b\}$ |
| $\langle a, b]$ | $\{x \in \mathbb{R} \mid a < x \leqslant b\}$ |
| $\langle a, b\rangle$ | $\{x \in \mathbb{R} \mid a < x < b\}$ |
| card($A$) | cardinality of $A$ (number of elements in $A$) |
| MAX$\{x_1, \ldots, x_k\}$ | maximum value of all $x_i$, $1 \leqslant i \leqslant k$ |
| MIN$\{x_1, \ldots, x_k\}$ | minimum value of all $x_i$, $1 \leqslant i \leqslant k$ |
| $x \mid y$ | $x$ divides $y$ |
| $x \bmod (y)$ | mod function (*if* $y = 0$ *then* 0 *else* $x - y \lfloor x/y \rfloor$) |
| $a \equiv x \bmod (y)$ | relation of congruence ($a = x + yt$, $t \in \mathbb{N}_0$) |
| $x = y$ | $x$ is equal to $y$ |

| | |
|---|---|
| $x := y$ | $y$ defines $x$ |
| $x \leqslant y$ | $x$ is less than or equal to $y$ |
| $x < y$ | $x$ is less than $y$ |
| $x \geqslant y$ | $x$ is greater than or equal to $y$ |
| $x > y$ | $x$ is greater than $y$ |
| $\delta_{n,m}$ | Kronecker delta (*if* $n = m$ *then* 1 *else* 0) |
| $\gcd(x, y)$ | greatest common divisor of $x$ and $y$ |
| $\|x\|$ | absolute value of $x$ (*if* $x < 0$ *then* $-x$ *else* $x$) |
| $\lfloor x \rfloor$ | greatest integer function ($\mathrm{MAX}\{K \in \mathbb{N} \mid K \leqslant x\}$) |
| $\lceil x \rceil$ | least integer function ($\mathrm{MIN}\{K \in \mathbb{N} \mid K \geqslant x\}$) |
| $\mathrm{Re}(z)$ | real part of $z = x + iy \in \mathbb{C}(x)$ |
| $\mathrm{Im}(z)$ | imaginary part of $z = x + iy \in \mathbb{C}(y)$ |
| $n!$ | $n$ factorial |
| $\exp(z)$ | exponential of $z$ |
| $\sin(z)$ | sine-function |
| $\cos(z)$ | cosine-function |
| $\tan(z)$ | tangent-function |
| $\arctan(z)$ | inverse hyperbolic function of $\tan(z)$ |
| $\arg(z)$ | argument of $z = x + iy \in \mathbb{C}(\arctan(y/x))$ |
| $\mathrm{ch}(z)$ | $\cos ix$, where $i^2 = -1$ |
| $\Gamma(z)$ | gamma function |
| $\Psi(z)$ | psi function |
| $\zeta(z, q)$ | Hurwitz zeta function |
| $\zeta(z)$ | Riemann zeta function ($\zeta(z, 1)$) |
| $\mathscr{B}_n(x)$ | Bell polynomial |
| $A_n(x)$ | Eulerian polynomial |
| $E_n(x)$ | Euler polynomial |
| $B_n(x)$ | Bernoulli polynomial |
| $U_n(x)$ | Chebyshev polynomial of the second kind |
| $H_n(x)$ | Hermite polynomial |
| $L_n^{(\alpha)}(x)$ | generalized Laguerre polynomial |
| $P_n(x)$ | Legendre polynomial |
| $M_n(x)$ | Meixner polynomial |
| $C_n(x)$ | Poisson–Charlier polynomial |
| $\ln(x)$ | natural logarithm (base e) |
| $\mathrm{ld}(x)$ | binary logarithms (base 2) |
| $\langle z^n \rangle f(z)$ | coefficient of $z^n$ in the expansion of $f(z)$ |
| $\sup\limits_{x \in A} f(x), \inf\limits_{x \in A} f(x)$ | supremum and infinum of $f$ in $A$ |
| $f^{(n)}(z), \dfrac{\mathrm{d}^n}{\mathrm{d}z^n} f(z)$ | $n$-th derivative of $f(z)$ |
| $f_{x_i}(x_1, \ldots, x_n), \dfrac{\partial}{\partial x_i} f(x_1, \ldots, x_n)$ | partial derivative of $f(z)$ with respect to $x_i$ |

| | |
|---|---|
| $\int_C f(t)\,dt$ | line integral along the curve $C$ |
| $\int_a^b f(t)\,dt$ | integral from $a$ to $b$ |
| $\lim_{n\to\infty} x_n$ | limit of $x_n$ for $n\to\infty$ |
| $f(n) = O(g(n))$ | large $O$ notation ($f(n)/g(n)$ is bounded as $n\to\infty$) |
| $f(n) = o(g(n))$ | small $o$ notation ($f(n)/g(n)$ tends to zero as $n\to\infty$) |
| $f(n) \sim g(n)$ | asymptotic equality ($f(n) = g(n)[1 + o(1)]$) |
| $\mathop{\mathrm{Res}}\limits_{z=z_k} f(z)$ | residue of $f$ at $z_k$ |
| $\begin{pmatrix} x,q \\ n \end{pmatrix}$ | $q$-nomial coefficient |
| $\begin{pmatrix} x \\ n \end{pmatrix}$ | binomial coefficient |
| $(z)_n$ | Pochhammer's symbol ($(z)_0 = 1$, $(z)_n = \Gamma(z+n)/\Gamma(z)$) |
| $S_n^{(m)}$ | Stirling numbers of the first kind |
| $\mathscr{S}_n^{(m)}$ | Stirling numbers of the second kind |
| $H_n^{(r)}$ | generalized harmonic number |
| $A(n,k)$ | Eulerian number |
| $E_n$ | Euler number |
| $B_n$ | Bernoulli number |
| $\omega_n$ | Bell number |
| $\pi$ | Ludolph's number ($3.141\,592\,6\ldots$) |
| $e$ | Euler's number base of natural logarithms ($\sum_{k\geqslant 0} 1/k! = 2.718\,281\,8\ldots$) |
| $\gamma$ | Euler's constant ($0.577\,215\,7\ldots$) |
| $\infty$ | infinity (larger than any number) |
| $\vec{x}$ | vector |
| $\det(A)$ | determinant of square matrix $A$ |
| $(A)_{i,j}$ | the element at position $(i,j)$ in the matrix $A$ |
| $I$ | identity matrix |
| $\forall$ | for all |
| $\exists$ | there exists at least |
| $\wedge$ | conjunction |
| $\vee$ | disjunction |
| $\sum_{R(k)} x_k$ | sum of all $x_k$ such that $k$ is an integer and the relation $R(k)$ is true (zero if $R = \varnothing$) |
| $\prod_{R(k)} x_k$ | product of all $x_k$ such that $k$ is an integer and the relation $R(k)$ is true (one if $R = \varnothing$) |
| $\left.\dfrac{a_1}{\vphantom{b}}\right|_{b_1} + \left.\dfrac{a_2}{\vphantom{b}}\right|_{b_2} + \ldots\,.$ | continued fraction $\cfrac{a_1}{b_1 + \cfrac{a_2}{b_2 + \cfrac{a_3}{\ddots}}}$ |

# *Index*

(The letter A indicates a reference to an appendix)